Aging and Mental Health

UNDERSTANDING AGING
The Psychology of Adult Development

General Editor
James E. Birren

Editorial Advisory Board
Stig Berg, Dennis Bromely, Denise Park, Timothy A. Salthouse,
K. Warner Schaie, and Diana S. Woodruff-Pak

During this century, life expectancy at birth has increased more for the average person than it did from Roman times to 1900: there are a greater number of old people today and they live longer than ever before. Within universities there is pressure to educate younger students about the scientific facts of adult development and aging as well as to train professionals to serve an aging society. The past twenty years have seen an exponential growth in material published.

This new series of modular texts has been designed to meet the need to integrate, interpret, and make this new knowledge available in an efficient and flexible format for instructors, students, and professionals worldwide. Each book will present a concise, authoritative, integrated, and readable summary of research and theory in a clearly defined area. Bridging the gap between introductory texts and research literature, these books will provide balanced coverage and convey the excitement and challenge of new research and developments. The modular format allows the series to be used as a complete sequence in primary courses in other fields.

Published
The Social Psychology of Aging
Michael W. Pratt and Joan E. Norris

The Neuropsychology of Aging
Diana S. Woodruff-Pak

Aging and Mental Health
Michael A. Smyer and Sara H. Qualls

In preparation

The Psychology of Aging: An Overview
James E. Birren and Timothy A. Salthouse

Cognitive Psychology of Aging
Denise C. Park

Gender and Aging
Nathan Kogan and Kathryn N. Black

Aging and Mental Health

Michael A. Smyer

and

Sara H. Qualls

BLACKWELL
Publishers

First published 1999

2 4 6 8 10 9 7 5 3 1

Blackwell Publishers Inc.
350 Main Street
Malden, Massachusetts 02148
USA

Blackwell Publishers Ltd
108 Cowley Road
Oxford OX4 1JF
UK

Library of Congress Cataloging-in-Publication Data

Smyer, Michael A.
Aging and mental health / Michael A. Smyer and Sara H. Qualls.
p.   cm. – (Understanding aging)
Includes bibliographical references and index.
ISBN   1-55786-556-6 (hc. : alk. paper). – ISBN   1-55786-557-4 (pbk.
: alk. paper)
1. Aged–Mental health.   2. Geriatric psychiary.   I. Qualls,
Sara H.   II. Title.   III. Series.
RC451.4.A5S66   1998   98-20919
618.97'689—dc21   CIP

British Library Cataloguing in Publication Data

A CIP catalogue record for this book is available from the British Library.

Typeset in $10\frac{1}{2}$ on $12\frac{1}{2}$ pt Bembo by Best-set Typesetter Ltd., Hong Kong
Printed in Great Britain by MPG Books, Bodmin, Cornwall

DEDICATION

To all who have taught us that there are many ways to age well, and many lenses for viewing the process; and to those who have made our learning meaningful, especially Patsy, Brendan, and Kyle, and Mark and Morgan.

Contents

Figures

Tables

Boxes

Preface

What is important in knowledge is not quantity, but quality. It is important to know what knowledge is significant, what is less so, and what is trivial.

Leo Tolstoy

In this book we have tried to take Tolstoy's maxim to heart, sorting out the significant from the trivial in the domain of aging and mental health. As we did so, we had two audiences in mind: today's clinicians and the clinicians of the future. The first group includes clinicians who are already in practice settings but who want to know more about working with older adults. The second group encompasses students in the professions that work with older adults (e.g., psychology, social work, nursing, psychiatry).

Both groups must face the issues of aging summarized by Michel Philibert, a French philosopher: "Of aging, what can we know? With aging, what must we do?" (Philibert, 1979, p. 384). These are also issues that older adults and their family members must face. In a way, they are variations on the questions that often arise in clinical settings. Consider the following example:

> Betty was worried about Alex. His memory seemed to be failing him more often. He'd get to the store and forget half of the things she'd sent him there for. He seemed more tired than usual, with less energy for his hobbies at the end of the day or on week-ends. He didn't want to go out with friends to the movies or to dinner. Alex didn't notice anything different in his behavior. Betty called to ask your advice: "Should I get him tested at the local Alzheimer's Center?"

How would you answer Betty? What would you need to know? Which portion of her story is significant in forming your answer? Which less so?

In answering these questions, you are implicitly answering Philibert's queries as well. You are implicitly making a differential diagnosis of Alex's situation: Is this a part of normal aging? Is this a pathological pattern? Is it a combination of the two? (Of aging, what can we know?)

You may also be linking your answer to an implicit action plan. Betty certainly is: Diagnose the problem and then decide what kind of treatment is most appropriate. (With aging, what must we do?)

To answer Betty's question fully requires much more information about aging in general, about patterns of mental health and mental illness in particular, and about Alex's distinctive history and pattern of functioning. This book is designed to provide you with frameworks for considering each element.

The first section is an overview of basic gerontology, the study of the aging process. This background information forms a context for answering the simple question often posed by clients and their relatives: Should I be worried about this pattern of behavior (e.g., Alex's apparent memory problems)? To answer this deceptively simple question requires that we sort out the influences of illness, basic processes of aging, and the intersection of historical and social trends as they affect older adults' functioning. In the first section we outline the basic parameters of mental health in later life.

In the second section we consider basic models of mental illness. Each model provides a set of assumptions about mental health and the development of mental health problems, their assessment, and their treatment. These assumptions direct the clinician's attention to specific aspects of older adults and their functioning. For example, assume for the moment that Alex's memory problems are not organically caused. The behavioral perspective might highlight the context of the older adult's behavior. Several important models of mental health and mental illness are outlined in the chapters of Section 2. In each chapter we focus on an important question for older adults and those who work with them: How is this approach relevant to older adults and the problems they encounter in later life?

The third section focuses attention on the most commonly occurring mental illnesses in later life: depression, cognitive impairment, serious mental illness, and other common disorders. In each chapter we outline the prevalence of the condition, the most appropriate assessment approaches for older adults, and the most effective treatment strategies for the elderly. We were fortunate to be able to call upon Steven Bartels and Kim Mueser for their expertise in the diagnosis and treatment of chronic mental illness.

The fourth section highlights the contexts of geriatric mental health practice. One physical setting is particularly important in geriatric mental health care: nursing homes. Although they were not designed for it, they are a major treatment setting for mentally ill elderly. Of course, other contexts affect how, where, and why mentally ill elderly are diagnosed and treated. We discuss these contexts (e.g., public policy, insurance mechanisms, professions' self-definitions) in this section.

Colleagues and friends in several settings have helped us write this book:

the faculty, students, and staff in the Department of Human Development and Family Studies at Penn State University, colleagues in the Department of Psychology of the University of Colorado at Colorado Springs, and friends and colleagues in the Graduate School of Arts and Sciences at Boston College. We have also benefited from the guidance and advice of Jim Birren and two anonymous reviewers. Nicole Simi and Maureen Wilson of Boston College provided valuable help in finalizing the references and citations. Finally, Stephanie Autenrieth of Boston College helped us translate across word-processing systems, across miles, and across drafts. We eagerly acknowledge our debt to each, while also admitting that any remaining flaws are ours.

Our goal throughout this book is to provide information and a set of frameworks that will be useful in working with older adults and their families. In the end, we hope that you will conclude that there is much to hope for in aging, and much that we can do about mental health and mental illness in later life.

Acknowledgments

The authors and publishers gratefully acknowledge permission from the sources listed below to reproduce copyright matter:

Fig. 1.1: from P. V. Rabins, Prevention of mental disorder in the elderly. *Journal of the American Geriatrics Society*, 40, pp. 727–33.

Fig. 1.2: from *Journal of the American Medical Association*, 262/7, pp. 907–13. Copyright 1989, American Medical Association.

Figs. 1.3, 1.4: from *Aging, health behaviors, and health outcomes* (pp. 24, 26), by House, J. S., Kessler, R. C., Herzog, A. R., Mero, R. P., Kinney, A. M., & Breslow, M. J., 1992, Hillsdale, NJ: Lawrence Erlbaum Associates. Copyright 1992 by Lawrence Erlbaum. Reprinted with permission.

Fig. 1.5: from Y. Conwell, Suicide in elderly patients, in *Diagnosis and treatment of depression in late life*, ed. L. S. Schneider, C. F. Reynolds, B. D. Lebowitz, and A. J. Friedhoff. American Psychiatric Press, 1994.

Box. 2.1: reprinted with permission from *Dimensions*, 4/3, pp. 3–5, 1997. Copyright © The American Society on Aging, San Francisco, California.

Fig. 2.1: from R. Malmgren, Epidemiology of aging, in *Textbook of geriatric neuropsychiatry*, ed. C. E. Coffey and J. L. Cummings. American Psychiatric Press, 1994.

Fig. 2.2: from K. W. Schaie and S. L. Willis, *Adult development and aging*, 3rd edn, 1991. Reprinted by permission of Addison-Wesley Educational Publishers, Inc.

Fig. 2.3: from E. Murphy, J. Lindesay, and E. Grundy, 60 years of suicide in England and Wales, *Archives of General Psychiatry*, 43, pp. 969–76, 1986. Copyright 1986, American Medical Association.

Fig. 2.4: from M. Gatz, J. E. Kasl-Godley, and M. Karel, Aging and mental disorders, in *Handbook of psychology of aging*, 4th edn, ed. J. E. Birren and K. W. Schaie. Academic Press, Inc., 1996.

Fig. 3.1: reprinted by permission of the publisher from *The wisdom of the ego* by George E. Vaillant, Cambridge, MA: Harvard University Press, Copyright © 1993 by the President and Fellows of Harvard College.

Fig. 3.2: from B. D. Starr, M. B. Weiner, and M. Rabetz, *The projective assessment of aging method (PAAM)*, 1979, © Springer Publishing Company, Inc. Used by permission of Springer Publishing Company, Inc., New York 10012.

Table 3.1: R. C. Carson and J. N. Butcher, *Abnormal psychology and modern life*, 9th edn, 1992. Reprinted by permission of Addison-Wesley Educational Publishers, Inc.

Table 3.2: from R. A. Nemiroff and C. A. Colarusso, Frontiers of adult development in theory and practice, in *New dimensions in adult development*, ed. R. A. Nemiroff and C. A. Colarusso. Basic Books, 1990.

Table 3.3: from *Vital involvement in old age: the experience of old age in our time* by Erik H. Erikson, Joan M. Erikson, and Helen Q. Kivnick. Copyright © 1986 by Joan M. Erikson, Erik H. Erikson, and Helen Q. Kivnick. Reprinted by permission of W. W. Norton & Company, Inc.

Table 4.1: reprinted from J. A. Yesavage, T. L. Brink T. L. Rose O. Lum, V. Huang, M. Adey, and V. O. Leirer, Development and validation of a geriatric depression screening scale, *Journal of Psychiatric Research*, 17, 1983, with permission from Elsevier Science.

Table 4.4: from A. T. Beck, A. J. Rush, B. F. Shaw, and G. Emery, *Cognitive therapy of depression*, 1979. Reprinted with permission of Guilford Publications, Inc.

Figs. 5.1, 5.4: from M. L. Wykle, E. Kahana, and J. Kowal, eds, *Stress and health among the elderly*, copyright © Springer Publishing Company, Inc. Used by permission of Springer Publishing Company, Inc., New York 10012.

Fig. 5.2: reproduced, with permission, from the *Annual Review of Psychology*, vol. 31, © 1980, by Annual Reviews Inc.

Fig. 5.3: from L. A. Bond, S. J. Cutler, and A. Grams, eds, Promoting successful and productive aging, pp. 153–70, copyright © 1995 by Sage Publications, Inc. Reprinted by permission of Sage Publications, Inc.

Table 5.1: from S. Cohen and G. Williamson, Perceived stress in a probability sample of the United States, in *The social psychology of health*, ed. S. Spacapan and S. Oskamp, pp. 31–67, copyright © 1988 by Sage Publications, Inc. Reprinted by permission of Sage Publications, Inc.

Fig. 6.2: from P. G. Boss, W. J. Doherty, R. LaRossa, W. R. Schumm, and S. K. Steinmetz, eds, *Sourcebook of family theories and methods*, Plenum Publishing Corporation, 1993.

Fig. I1: Reprinted with permission from *Reducing risks for mental disorders*. Copyright 1994 by the National Academy of Sciences. Courtesy of the National Academy Press, Washington, DC.

Fig. 7.1: from K. W. Schaie, The course of adult intellectual development, *American Psychologist*, 49, pp. 304–13. Copyright © 1994 by the American Psychological Association. Reprinted with permission.

Fig. 7.2: from S. H. Qualls, Transitions in autonomy, *Family Relations*, 46, pp. 41–5. Copyrighted 1997 by the National Council on Family Relations, 3989 Central Ave. NE, Suite 550, Minneapolis, MN 55421. Reprinted by permission.

Fig. 7.3: from M. P. Lawton and L. Nahemow, Ecology and the aging process, in *The psychology of adult development and aging*, ed. C. Eisdorfer and M. P. Lawton. Copyright © 1973 by the American Psychological Association. Reprinted with permission.

Tables 7.1, 7.2: Reprinted with permission from the *Diagnostic and statistical manual of mental disorders*, 4th edn. Copyright 1994 American Psychiatric Association.

Table 7.3: from L. L. Carstensen, B. A. Edelstein, and L. Dornbrand, eds, *The practical handbook of clinical gerontology*, pp. 239–54, copyright © 1996 by Sage Publications, Inc. Reprinted by permission of Sage Publications, Inc.

Table 7.4: adapted from S. H. Zarit, N. K. Orr, and J. M. Zarit, *The hidden victims of Alzheimer's disease*, New York University Press, 1985.

Table 7.6: from M. A. Butters, D. P. Salmon, and N. Butters, Neuropsychological assessment of dementia, in *Neuropsychological assessment of dementia and depression in older adults*, ed. M. Storandt and G. R. VandenBos. Copyright © 1994 by the American Psychological Association. Reprinted with permission.

Table 7.7: from A. LaRue, J. Yang, and S. Osato, Neuropsychological Assessment, in *Handbook of Mental Health and Aging*, Academic Press, Inc., 1992.

Fig. 8.1: from M. M. Weissman, M. L. Bruce, P. J. Leaf, L. P. Florio, and C. Holzer, Affective disorders, in *Psychiatric disorders in America*, ed. L. N. Robins and D. A. Regier. Free Press, 1991, pp. 53–81.

Fig. 8.2: from D. G. Blazer, Epidemiology of late-life depresseion, in *Diagnosis and treatment of depression in late life*, ed. L. S. Schneider, C. F. Reynolds, B. D. Lebowitz, and A. J. Friedhoff, American Psychiatric Press, 1994.

Fig. 8.3: from Philadelphia College of Pharmacy and Science, Tailoring the AHCPR clinical practice guildelines on depression in primary care for use in long-term care facilities, copyright 1995.

Table 8.1: Reprinted with permission from the *Diagnostic and statistical manual of mental disorders*, 4th edn. Copyright 1994 American Psychiatric Association.

Table 8.2: from L. K. George, Social factors and depression in late life, in *Diagnosis and treatment of depression in late life*, ed. L. S. Schneider, C. F. Reynolds, B. D. Lebowitz, and A. J. Friedhoff, American Psychiatric Press, 1994.

Figs. 10.1, 10.3: from C. S. Aneshensel, L. I. Pearlin, J. T. Mullan, S. H. Zarit, and C. J. Whitlach, *Profiles in caregiving*, Academic Press, Inc., 1995.

Fig. 10.2: from M. Gatz, V. L. Bengtson, and M. J. Blum, Caregiving families, in *Handbook of psychology and aging*, 3rd edn, ed. J. E. Birren and K. W. Schaie, Academic Press Inc., 1990.

Table 11.1: from J. M. Wiener, L. H. Illston, and R. J. Hanley, *Sharing the burden*, Brookings Institution, 1994.

Table 11.2: from D. G. Shea, Nursing homes and the costs of mental disorders, copyright 1994.

Tables 11.3, 11.4: from P. A. Lichtenberg, *A guide to psychological practice in geriatric long-term care*. Copyright 1994, Haworth Press, Binghamton, New York.

Table 11.5: adapted from M. D. Cohn, M. A. Smyer, and A. L. Horgas, *The ABCs of behavior change*. State College, PA, Venture Publishing, 1994. Reprinted with permission of the publisher.

Box 11.1: from M. A. Smyer and C. T. Walls, Design and evaluation of interventions in nursing homes, in *Applied Developmental Psychology*, ed. C. B. Fisher and R. M. Lerner. Cambridge, MA: McGraw-Hill Publishing Company, 1994.

Fig. 12.1: adapted from M. Smyer, K. W. Schaie, and M. B. Kapp, eds, *Older adults' decision-making and the law*, 1996, © Springer Publishing Company,

Inc. Used by permission of Springer Publishing Company, Inc., New York 10012.

Fig. 12.2: from the Kaiser Medicare Policy Project, Medicare managed care enrollment, Medicare chart book: historical data from the Health Care Financing Administration, Office of Managed Care, 1995. Projections from the Congressional Budget Office, 1997. Henry J. Kaiser Family Foundation.

Table 12.1: from a draft report of the APA Interdivisional Task Force on Qualifications for Practice in Clinical and Applied Geropsychology, 1996. Unpublished manuscript, American Psychological Association, Division 12, Section II, and Division 20.

Tables 12.3a, 12.3b: from *Psychologists in Long Term Care Newsletter*, 11/1, 1997.

Table 12.4 (was Table 12.3): reprinted with permission from *Managing Managed Care*. Copyright 1997 by the National Academy of Sciences. Courtesy of the National Academy Press, Washington, DC.

Quotations

p. 42: "Warning," from *Selected Poems* published by Bloodaxe Books Ltd., copyright © Jenny Joseph 1992.

p. 89: from C. J. Johnson and F. A. Johnson, Psychological distress among inner-city American elderly, *Journal of Cross-Cultural Gerontology*, 7/3, pp. 221–36, Kluwer Academic Publishers. Reprinted with kind permission from Kluwer Academic Publishers.

p. 138: from M. A. Smyer, *Counseling Psychologist*, 12/2, pp. 17–28, copyright © 1984 by Sage Publications, Inc. Reprinted by permission of Sage Publications, Inc.

p. 244: reprinted from *Growing up* © 1985 by Russell Baker. Used with permission by NTC/Contemporary Publishing Group.

p. 248: from R. R. Shield: *Uneasy endings*, Cornell University Press, 1988.

pp. 261–4: from P. A. Lichtenberg, *A guide to psychological practice in geriatric long-term care*, Copyright 1994, Haworth Press, Binghamton, New York.

The publishers apologize for any errors or omissions in the above list and would be grateful to be notified of any corrections that should be incorporated in the next edition or reprint of this book.

Part I

Introduction

1

Mental Health and Aging:
An Introduction

Consider the following case description:

Grace, director of a senior center in your area, calls you about Mr T. Although Mr T used to come to the center three or four times a week, he hasn't come at all since the death of his friend Mr W four months ago. Grace had called Mr T at home to say how much he'd been missed. When she asked if he wasn't coming because he was still upset over Mr W's death, he denied it. Instead, Mr T said that he wanted to return to the center, but he was in terrible pain. In fact, he was in so much pain that he really couldn't talk on the phone; and he hung up. Grace was worried that Mr T might not be getting the medical attention that he really needed. She asked you to make a home visit, which you agreed to do. You call Mr T and set up an appointment.

As you prepare to visit Mr T, what are the basic questions you might ask about him and his situation? Which factors do you think are important to explore with Mr T? How would you assess Mr T's functioning?

Your answer to these simple inquiries reflects your implicit model of mental health and aging. In this book, especially in Section 2, we will illustrate several different conceptual models of mental illness and aging. In doing so, we will emphasize the links between starting assumptions and subsequent strategies for assessment and intervention. You will come to see that your philosophical assumptions about mental health, mental illness, and aging shape the interpretive process of working with older adults and their families (Philibert, 1979).

Mr T's current functioning raises a basic question: Is his behavior just a part of normal aging or is this a problem that requires professional attention? Our answer represents implicit and explicit assumptions regarding the continuum of functioning that runs from outstanding functioning through usual aging to pathological patterns of behavior.

What Is Normal Aging?

The starting point for mental health and aging must be a general understanding of *gerontology*, the study of normal aging, and *geriatrics*, the study of the medical aspects of old age and the prevention and treatment of the diseases of aging. In Mr T's case, we want to know if his reaction is a part of a normal grieving process or an indication of a disease process (e.g., a depressive disorder). To answer this requires a starting definition of normal aging.

A conceptual definition

Recent discussions have focused attention on three different patterns of aging: normal or usual aging; optimal or successful aging; and pathological aging (e.g., Rowe & Kahn, 1987). Baltes and Baltes (1990a) provide definitions of normal and optimal aging:

> Normal aging refers to aging without biological or mental pathology. It thus concerns the aging process that is dominant within a society for persons who are not suffering from a manifest illness. Optimal aging refers to a kind of utopia, namely, aging under development-enhancing and age-friendly environmental conditions. Finally, sick or pathological aging characterizes an aging process determined by medical etiology and syndromes of illness. A classical example is dementia of the Alzheimer type. (pp. 7–8)

A statistical definition

Distinguishing between normal aging and optimal aging requires us to sort out statistical fact from theoretically desirable conditions. For example, the Baltes and Baltes definition suggests that normal aging does not include "manifest illness." However, in the United States today, chronic disease is typical of the experience of aging: More than 80 percent of those 65 and older have one or more chronic medical diseases (US Senate Special Committee on Aging, 1987–8).

For example, almost half of those over age 65 report having arthritis (Cassel, Rudberg, & Olshansky, 1992). Moreover, among the oldest old groups (75+ or 85+) there are substantially higher rates. Thus, from a statistical perspective arthritis is certainly modal, and may be considered a part of normal aging. We will return to this in Chapter 2.

A functional definition

Another approach to defining normal aging arises from defining "manifest illness." By focusing not on presence or absence of a chronic disease, such as arthritis, but on the *impact* of that disease, we may get another depiction of "normal aging." Here again, though, the definition of terms can affect our conclusion regarding normal aging.

Consider the prevalence of disability among older adults. Functional disability could be considered one indicator of manifest illness among older adults. So far, so good. However, how shall we define functional disability? The answer may determine our conclusion about what is or is not normal for later life. Again, Mr T's situation may help us clarify the issues:

> When you get to Mr T's house, you find an apathetic, listless, very thin man of 81. He seems to be fairly isolated socially, having few friends and even fewer family members in the area. (He never married and he has no living siblings.) Although he seems physically able to cook, he says that he hasn't been eating (or sleeping) regularly for quite a while – and he doesn't care if he never does again.

Is Mr T functionally disabled? If so, is this normal for someone of his age? According to the US Department of Commerce (1994), most persons aged 75 or above have a disability: 64 percent of those between 75 and 84 had a disability, with 42 percent having a "severe disability." In contrast, Manton and his colleagues (1993) reported that 67 percent of the 75–84 age group was "non-disabled." How could such differing pictures of the elderly emerge?

The answer lies in the definition of disability. The Department of Commerce focuses on difficulty with functional activity for its definition of disability. The range of functional activities is somewhat broader than in traditional definitions: lifting and carrying a weight as heavy as 10 pounds; walking three city blocks; seeing the words and letters in ordinary newsprint; hearing what is said in normal conversation with another person; having one's speech understood; and climbing a flight of stairs. In contrast, Manton and his colleagues focused on activities of daily living (ADL) and instrumental activities of daily living (IADL) items: eating; getting in or out of bed; getting around inside; bathing; dressing; getting to the bathroom or using a toilet; light housework; doing the laundry; meal preparation; grocery shopping; etc.

Not surprisingly, these different definitions of disability produce different depictions of functioning and normal aging. The metric we use in assessing functional ability is important for two reasons: the specific activities may be important in and of themselves; and the ability to complete activities (such as ADL and IADL activities) acts as a proxy for underlying physical, cognitive, and social skills (Kemp & Mitchell, 1992). Thus, depending upon the range of functioning we wish to assess, we may conclude that Mr T is either disabled or not and that such a pattern of functioning is either normal or unusual aging!

What Is Abnormal or Unusual Aging?

Thus far, we have considered merely one side of the dilemma: what is normal aging? We have also limited ourselves to *physical* and *functional* definitions, steering clear of similar issues focusing on *mental* health or illness.

> *You notice that Mr T doesn't mention being in any terrible pain – that is until you mention his friend Mr W. When you do, Mr T grabs his side and says how much it hurts to talk. You suggest that he lie down and rest for a minute, which he does.*

> *From the couch, Mr T begins to talk about Mr W. It turns out that the two men were not just "friends," as Grace had implied. They were like brothers (if not closer) and had been since they were boys. "I'm good for two things," Mr T said, "no good and good for nothing. But Ed (Mr W) was my buddy anyway. Don't know why he bothered with me. I never made much of my life. But I do know that it won't be hunting season without him. Just can't do it alone and nobody in their right mind would want to hunt with an old fool like me."*

Again, Mr T challenges us. Is he mentally ill? The answer depends upon resolving other issues: How will we define mental health among older adults? Conversely, how will we define mental illness among older adults? In the third section of this book we will discuss assessment and treatment approaches for several specific mental disorders. Here, however, we start at the beginning: definitions of mental health and mental illness.

Mental Health and Mental Illness

Mental health among older adults is a multifaceted concept that reflects a range of clinical and research activity, rather than a unified theoretical entity (Lebowitz & Niederehe, 1992). Definitions of mental health in later life combine several complex elements: statistical normality; the link between individual functioning and group norms; the extent to which specific disorders can be effectively treated or controlled; and ideals of positive functioning (Butler, Lewis, & Sunderland, 1991; Lebowitz & Neiderehe, 1992).

In contrast, there is greater agreement on definitions of mental illness among older adults. For both clinical and research purposes, operational definitions of mental illness usually follow the guidelines of the American Psychiatric Association (APA) (American Psychiatric Association, 1994). Thus, mental illness in older adults is operationally defined by patterns of disorders as outlined in the APA manual.

The Epidemiologic Catchment Area (ECA) study provides the most comprehensive description of older adults' patterns of mental disorders (Rabins, 1992; Regier et al., 1988). Two important themes emerge from the ECA data. First, mental illness is *not* a part of normal aging. Approximately 12 percent of community-dwelling elderly have a diagnosable mental disorder. Equally important, older adults' rates of mental illness are the lowest prevalence rates of any age group (see figure 1.1). Secondly, the ECA data also reflect the difficulty of discerning "normal aging" from pathological aging. Consider the case of depression: depression in later life appears in several guises. When diagnostic criteria are applied, older adults have low rates of major depression (0.7 percent) and dysthymic disorder (1.85 percent) over a six-month period (Regier et al., 1988). However, the prevalence of

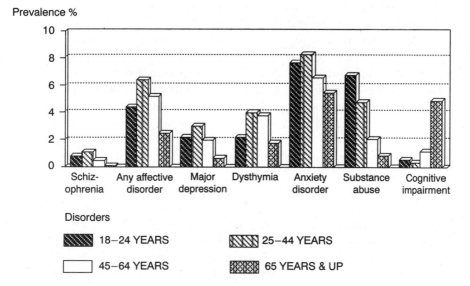

Figure 1.1 Prevalence of mental disorders by age
Source: Rabins, 1992.

depressive *symptoms* among older adults is much higher: at least 8 percent of community-dwelling elderly have serious symptoms of depression and approximately 19 percent have less severe dysphoric symptomatology (Blazer, 1993).

Again, the challenge is distinguishing between normal and pathological aging: Are Mr T's sleep and appetite disturbances a sign of depression, a part of the normal aging process, or a combination of the two?

Finally, the ECA data also indicate that rates of disorders vary by setting. For example, older adults in institutional settings present a very different picture: 40 to 50 percent of older adults hospitalized for medical conditions also have psychiatric conditions (Rapp, Parisi, & Walsh, 1988); between 65 and 90 percent of nursing-home residents have a diagnosable mental disorder, depending upon the methods used to assess and diagnose residents (Burns, Wagner, Taube, et al., 1993; Lair & Lefkowitz, 1990).

Linking the Physical and Mental in Later Life: Comorbidity

Mr T's pattern of symptoms – his lethargy, his social withdrawal, and his reported physical pain – remind us of the importance of comorbidity: combinations of more than one mental or physical illness or a combination of both (Cohen, 1992; Lebowitz & Neiderehe, 1992).

For example, Stewart and her colleagues (Stewart et al., 1989) assessed the relationship between chronic physical conditions and six areas of functioning: physical functioning (comparable to ADLs and IADLs); role performance; social functioning; mental health; health perceptions; and bodily pain. Using data from the Medical Outcomes Study, they found interesting patterns of interrelationships among these domains, varying by specific chronic condition (see figure 1.2). Their conclusion underscores the interrelationships of domains: "The impact of chronic conditions on health is substantial, varies according to condition, and, for most conditions, involves all aspects of functioning and well-being" (Stewart et al., 1989, p. 911).

Cohen (1985, 1992) provides a context for these findings by outlining four useful paradigms for the interaction of physical and mental well-being among older adults. Cohen notes that our initial concern may be raised by either a physical or a mental health problem.

Psychogenic stress may lead to physical health problems. In Mr T's case, abdominal pain may be a reaction to his grief over Mr W's death. For example, the physical symptom may be a more socially acceptable way for Mr T to express pain.

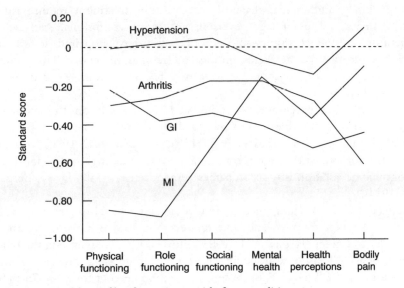

Figure 1.2   Health profiles for patients with four conditions
Notes: Dotted line indicates patients with no chronic conditions.
GI = gastrointestinal disorder; MI = myocardial infarction.
Source: Stewart et al., 1989.

The direction of causality may be reversed, however, with a physical disorder leading to psychiatric disturbance. Consider the following sentence:

The five senses tend to decline with senescence.

Remove the f's, s's, and th's. Now try to make sense of what's left:

e ive en tend to decline wi ene e.

This example mimics high frequency hearing loss among older adults (Butler, Lewis, & Sunderland, 1991) and gives you a sense of how easily such a hearing loss might lead to delusions and confusion among older adults.

A third possibility is that coexisting physical and mental disorders may interact. The ECA data highlight a category of mental disorders among older adults that underscores this interplay: cognitive impairment, including the dementias.

Cognitive impairment among older adults is a challenge for interdisciplinary diagnosis and treatment. Approximately 20 percent of what appear to be dementias are reversible if promptly diagnosed and treated (McKhann et al., 1984). Differential diagnosis and prompt treatment require ruling out a myriad of potentially reversible causes of confusional states: drug reactions; emotional disorders; metabolic disorders; impaired vision and hearing; nutritional deficiencies; tumors and traumas; infections. This requires an interdisciplinary collaboration designed to assess complex patterns of comorbidity.

Currently, resources are being invested in research on the biological bases of Alzheimer's disease and related disorders (e.g., Banner, 1992), the social impact of these diseases (e.g., Light & Lebowitz, 1990), and the potential for preventive interventions aimed at avoiding the personal and economic devastation that accompanies dementia (e.g., Gatz, Lowe, Berg, et al., 1994).

Again, the ECA data reflect the individual and societal importance of this work: a 4.9 percent prevalence rate for severe cognitive impairment among those 65 and older (Regier et al., 1988). However, the rate among the oldest age groups follows a now-familiar pattern of increasing prevalence with increasing age: 2.9 percent for those 65 to 74; 6.8 percent for those 75 to 84; and 15.8 percent for those 85 and over. Estimates are that as many as 4 million Americans currently have Alzheimer's disease and related dementias (ADRD), with 2.5 to 3 million of these patients suffering from Alzheimer's disease (AD). Conservative estimates suggest that the number of AD patients will increase to more than 6 million by the year 2040 (Advisory Panel on Alzheimer's Disease, 1993).

A different estimate of the prevalence of dementia comes from a representative sample of 85-year-olds living in Gothenburg, Sweden (Skoog et al., 1993). This study differed from the ECA study in several ways: a different sample (urban older adults over the age of 85); a different method of questioning (a psychiatric examination and an informant interview); and explicit criteria for dementia and sub-groups of dementia (e.g., Alzheimer's disease; vascular dementia; and other types).

Not surprisingly, how you ask the question affects the answer. Skoog and colleagues (1993) reported a much higher prevalence of dementia: 29.8 percent. Of these, 8.3 percent were categorized as having mild dementia, 10.3 percent were deemed as having moderate dementia, and 11.1 percent were considered to have severe dementia (Skoog et al., 1993).

Finally, even with dementing disorders, social and psychosocial resources can affect their course. As Cohen (1993) has noted: biography can be as important as biology. The social environment can affect the concomitants of the degeneration caused by dementia – for example, the agitation that often accompanies a dementing illness.

Individual Differences and Assessment of Risk

Thus far we have sketched general patterns of mental health and mental illness among older adults as a context for working with Mr T. One question has been implicit in this discussion: How is Mr T like other older adults of his age? In this section the emphasis shifts to another question: How is Mr T different from other individuals his age?

What do we know about Mr T that would differentiate him from other 81-year-olds? What are the categories of information we would use in sorting older adults? Socioeconomic status (SES) dramatically affects the experience of aging. Consider the relationships among age, number of chronic conditions, and SES (see figure 1.3). House and his colleagues (1992) noted that those in the lowest SES category have the highest rates of chronic conditions throughout adulthood. Moreover, by mid-life (ages 55 to 64) those in the lower SES group already have a number of chronic conditions comparable to the number experienced by the highest SES group at age 75. A similar pattern emerged when assessing the relationships among age, activity limita-

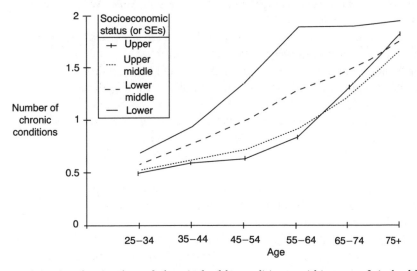

Figure 1.3 Age by number of chronic health conditions, within one of six health domains and within levels of socioeconomic status
Source: House et al., 1992.

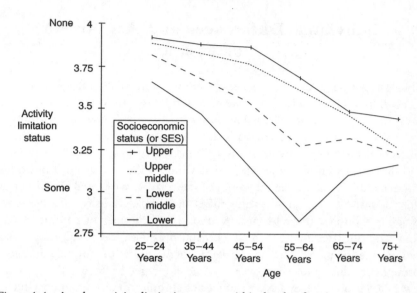

Figure 1.4 Age by activity limitation status within levels of socioeconomic status
Source: House et al., 1992.

tions, and SES (see figure 1.4). Again, the lowest SES group had the highest
rates of impairment, peaking in mid-life. (Perhaps those who are sickest do
not survive into later life.)

Variability in risk among older adults is not limited to the physical or
functional domains, however. There are similar patterns of variability in risk
of mental disorders. Consider the risk for suicide.

We resume our conversation with Mr T:

> . . . *"I never made much of my life. But I do know that it won't be hunting
> season without him (Mr W). Just can't do it alone, and nobody in their right
> mind would want to hunt with an old fool like me."*

These words have a haunting finality to them. As you hear them, you begin
to wonder about Mr T's will to live, his plans for the future. Should you ask
him about these elements, about his potential for suicide?

Psychiatric epidemiological data can be helpful in tracing overall patterns
of suicide risk among older adults, as well as differential patterns of risk: the
threat of suicide is substantial in later life, with the highest rates appearing
among those 80 to 84 years old (28.0/100,000 vs. 12.4/100,000 for the
general population). Older adults are more "successful" in completing suicide
than any other age group, and depression in older adults is closely linked to

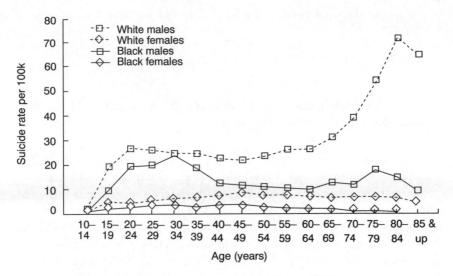

Figure 1.5 Suicide by age, race, and sex: United States, 1988
Source: Conwell, 1994.

suicide among the elderly. Suicide among the elderly is associated with diagnosable psychopathology (most often affective disorders) in approximately 90 percent of cases (Conwell, 1994).

The group at highest risk consists of white males aged 80 to 84, with a rate of suicide six times the nation's age-adjusted rate (see figure 1.5). Sadly, the majority of suicide victims had seen their primary care physician within the month before suicide. Thus there is a serious need for better preparation of physicians for screening and treatment of geriatric depression, and for screening and prevention of older adults at risk for suicide (Conwell, 1994; NIH Consensus Panel, 1992).

Armed with this knowledge of differential risk – particularly for white males over 80 – you ask Mr T about his current plans and perspectives:

"It sounds like you're feeling pretty blue. Have you ever thought about ending things?"

"I may be down, but I'm not crazy!"

Mr T quickly gives you a sense of his own perspective on his problems, allowing you to follow up with specific questions regarding intent. The conversation could have gone in a different direction:

"It sounds like you're feeling pretty blue. Have you ever thought about ending things?"

"Every now and then I get that feeling."

"How would you do it?"

"I'd use that shotgun that I keep loaded next to the door – just head out to the barn, clear out the cows and have at her . . ."

This conversation confirms your fears – he has motivation, a way to achieve that purpose, and seemingly very little concern about the consequences.

These two resolutions to the inquiry highlight the theme of variability among and between older adults. This variability is a hallmark of aging: as we get older we get more distinct from our age-mates. This diversity among older adults (often called inter-individual differences) is the result of the complex patterns of both biological and biographical functioning across the life-span.

The biographical elements may play a key role in two different ways: the history of the disorder and the history of the individual. In the case of Mr T's suicide potential, for example, we will want to know something about his previous experience with suicidal ideation: Has he been suicidal for many years, and now grown older? Has he grown older and now become suicidal? These two divergent paths both arrive at suicide in later life, but they offer very different suggestions for treatment attempts, the availability of social and emotional resources, and the likelihood of successful intervention (Kahn, 1975).

In summary, we will want to know more about several key elements of Mr T's history: his social and economic resources, his current and past physical health, his current and past mental health, and his functional abilities (NIH Consensus Statement, 1988). Approaches to these issues will be presented in Section 2 of this book.

The Context of Clinicians and Clients: Now What Do We Do?

Thus far we have had one conversation with Mr T and we have gathered information about his current functioning, his previous history, and his future ability to continue to cope on his own. What will we do next?

Our approach to Mr T is a function of several interrelated elements: our sense of his strengths and weaknesses (e.g., how acute is his crisis; is he a threat to himself or others; how has he handled personal challenges in the past; etc.); our assessment of his capacity to be involved in health-care decision-making as an active participant in developing the treatment plan; and the service setting and context within which we work. These issues are discussed in sections 3 and 4 of this book.

The context of mental health services for older adults has changed substantially during the last two decades. As part of a larger public policy of deinstitutionalization there were increases in *both* institutional and outpatient services. In the institutional sector, inpatient services were shifted from state mental hospitals to private psychiatric hospitals, psychiatric units in general hospitals, and "swing beds" in general hospitals. One other setting became increasingly important as a receiving site for mental ill elderly: nursing homes (Gatz & Smyer, 1992).

In outpatient settings, older adults continue to be under-served by community mental health centers (CMHCs). They comprise 6 percent of the caseload of CMHCs and under 8 percent of the population receiving outpatient or partial care. Only 56 percent of older adults' service use for mental disorders is provided through the mental health specialty sector; the balance (44 percent) is provided through the general health sector, mainly primary care physicians (Burns & Taube, 1990).

In inpatient settings, older adults represent 11 percent of the population receiving care in specialty institutions and general hospitals (Rosenstein et al., 1990). However, they represent 90 percent of the mentally ill population in nursing homes (Lair & Lefkowitz, 1990). This pattern reflects an overreliance on nursing homes as a treatment setting for mentally ill elderly.

These patterns of care – with a substantial bias toward inpatient, medically oriented services – form only one of two major elements that shape the availability of and access to mental health care for older adults. The second consists of the combined priorities of major funding sources for geriatric mental health: Medicare, Medicaid, and private insurance plans (Smyer & Shea, 1996).

In 1985 (the last year for which complete economic data are available) the core costs of health care for mentally ill elderly were $17.3 billion dollars (Rice, Kelman, & Miller, 1992). These costs included the direct costs of care, plus the indirect costs of associated morbidity and mortality. Thus, from an economic perspective, geriatric mental health care is worthy of attention – if only to foster cost-containment efforts.

Medicare is a federal health insurance program for older adults. Its eligibility criteria and scope of covered services are standardized throughout the United States. Unfortunately, Medicare coverage, although improved in recent years, is still somewhat restrictive. For example, it covers only 50 percent of outpatient services provided by a psychiatrist, psychologist, or other mental health professional, while it includes 80 percent of comparable services provided in an inpatient setting (Smyer & Shea, 1996).

Medicaid is the US national health insurance program for the indigent. It is funded through a combination of state and federal funds, and coverage varies from state to state. Medicaid has emerged as the payer of last resort in nursing-home care for older adults, accounting for just over half of the more than $60 billion spent on this care in the United States each year. Medicaid pays approximately 51 percent of the costs for nursing-home care for mentally ill older adults.

Private insurance plans also provide some assistance for mentally ill older adults. Two private options are available for the elderly: "Medigap" policies, that cover the co-payment portions of Medicare part B; and insurance provided to retirees by their former employers. Medigap policies are now standardized into ten plans; all have limited outpatient mental health coverage and none provides extra coverage for inpatient mental health services (Rice & Thomas, 1992). Plans provided by former employers generally offer more coverage than the Medigap policies (Jensen & Morrisey, 1992).

These contextual factors – institutional patterns of service provision, insurance coverage, fee structures – affect the choices for services for Mr T. To work effectively with him, you will need to understand the coverage of mental health services that he has, the availability of services in your local community, and the range of services for which you can be reimbursed. These issues will be discussed in Section 3.

Summary and Conclusion

In this chapter we have introduced several themes that will re-emerge throughout the book. First, we have highlighted the importance of philosophical assumptions regarding normal and abnormal functioning in shaping our assessment strategies, targets for intervention, and definitions of therapeutic success. Next, we have emphasized the importance of individual differences in shaping our understanding of the etiology and presentation of mental illness in later life. Finally, we have discussed briefly the fiscal and political context that shapes the availability of mental health services for older adults. These themes – ranging from individual functioning to social policy – illustrate the complexity of the task of providing mental health services to older adults. We hope that these themes also reflect the excitement inherent in trying to bring order out of the chaos of needs and services, of trying both to understand older clients and to match their needs with the services available.

2

Basic Gerontology for Working with Older Adults

Introduction

Imagine that you have been hired as a consultant by a local nursing home. To prepare you for your first visit, the facility staff have developed two case descriptions:

> *Max won't move. He used to be a successful accountant, but he hasn't worked in several years when he began to forget things. Now he barely allows himself to be nagged out of the bed or dressed . . . He seems physically able to do things for himself but just mumbles "I can't" when the nurses' aides encourage him to do anything. He looks very sad. When his photo album is brought to him he does spend some time mumbling and paging through it, but generally spends his time alone. He has been this way day in and day out, for as long as anyone can remember . . . (Cohn et al., 1994, p. 152)*

> *Molly collects spoons, both clean and dirty, from the dining room and trays and stores them very carefully in her dresser drawer. She argues violently when the nurse tries to remove them. The nurse gives long explanations of why they need to go back to the kitchen, but Molly insists that the staff are stealing her things. (Cohn et al., 1994, p. 179)*

Imagine that your consulting company has just landed a contract with a continuing care retirement community, or life-care community. The head of social services calls with the following referral:

> *Mrs G has moved to the assisted living portion of the community, following hip replacement surgery. She had lived in her own apartment for four years before the surgery. During that time she had been an active participant in the read-aloud program at a local school, a member of the "galloping gourmet" club (featuring dinners in each other's apartment every month), and an avid bridge player. Now*

Mrs G is demanding to move back to her apartment. She complains that she wants more scheduling freedom, that she wants to cook her own meals again, and that she doesn't need any more "help." The social worker is concerned about Mrs G's physical abilities and her capacity to make decisions on her own. Is Mrs G's demand for "freedom" a sign of good mental health or a denial of her changed physical and mental abilities?

As a good consultant, you're immediately faced with a simple challenge: Do my knowledge and skills allow me to respond effectively? For those who work with older adults, there is often a variation on this theme: What do I need to know to work effectively with older adults?

This chapter is designed to provide an initial answer to that simple question. We begin with a brief depiction of the basic developmental issues necessary for a full understanding of aging and mental health. We end the chapter with a two-part question: How is working with mentally ill elderly similar to working with the mentally ill of other ages? How is it different?

Developmental Issues in Mental Health and Aging

Schaie (1995) has identified several key developmental issues that provide a useful foundation for clinical work with older adults. His suggested topics form an outline of mental health and aging: normal and pathological aging; individual differences in aging; age differences and age changes; changing person/environment interactions; and reversibility of age-related behavior changes.

Normal and pathological aging

As noted in Chapter 1, gerontology is the study of the process of aging; geriatrics is the study and treatment of the diseases associated with aging. The boundaries between these two fields have become more and more blurred as researchers and clinicians question our basic assumptions about the course of development.

How can we differentiate normal from pathological aging? As noted in Chapter 1, if we take a statistical view, we might assume that chronic illness is part of normal aging. Consider arthritis, for example. More than 50 percent of women over age 65 have arthritis, and almost 50 percent of men over age 75 are similarly afflicted. However, the condition is not a *universal* part of aging and therefore is not part of the normal process of senescence.

Similarly, consider the epidemiological data on the prevalence of mental illnesses at different ages presented in Chapter 1 (see figure 1.1). Several trends in the Epidemiological Catchment Area (ECA) data are important: first, with one exception (cognitive impairment), older adults have the lowest rate of mental illness of any age group; second, at any age, and especially in later life, it is a minority of adults who have a mental illness. Thus, mental illness is definitely *not* a part of normal aging. Approximately 22 percent of adults over 65 meet the criteria for a mental disorder, either emotional dysfunction or cognitive impairment or both (Gatz & Smyer, 1992). Even with cognitive impairment – presumably a marker for Alzheimer's disease and other dementias – it is a minority of elderly who are afflicted.

In sum, it is important to recall the distinctions among normal, optimal, and pathological aging. Equating age with disease is mistaking gerontology for geriatrics – a mistake in either research or clinical work.

Individual differences

Throughout life, three systems of influence work to assure that differences among people increase with age: age-graded, history-graded, and non-normative influences (Baltes, Reese, & Lipsitt, 1980; Marsiske et al., 1995).

Age-graded influences are universal, normative time-ordered biological or environmental processes that affect development. Age–norms or developmental tasks that are age-linked illustrate this type of influence. For example, in the United States most children enter first grade at age six or seven.

History-graded influences are biological and environmental aspects that vary over a particular historical time. For example, the great depression (Elder, 1974) and school desegregation (Coles, 1967) were major social developments anchored in particular historical conditions that affected the development of children and adults (see box 2.1).

The aging of our global society is another example of a history-graded influence on development (see figure 2.1). Demographic data portray two simple facts: over the coming decades we will witness increasing numbers and proportions of older adults throughout the world. At the same time the oldest old (those aged 85 and over) represent the fasting growing portion of the elderly. In 1994 in the United States, for example, the oldest old formed 10 percent of the elderly and 1 percent of the population as a whole; by 2050 it is estimated that those over 85 will be 24 percent of the elderly and 5 percent of the US population (US Department of Commerce, 1995). These demographic patterns influence the experience of aging across the life-span.

Non-normative influences are biological or environmental aspects that are not age- or history graded and that are more idiosyncratic. These include the

Box 2.1 Aging Holocaust survivors and PTSD

Every evening in nursing homes across the country, the staff assist wheelchair-bound residents to bed. One night, as Mrs S was sitting in her wheelchair in the community room and the aide came over to take her to her room, she began to thrash her arms and legs. She refused to be moved, screaming what seemed like nonsense, that she wasn't going to allow the staff to take her away and kill her. For her, this nightly ritual of taking residents out of the room one at a time triggered memories of her experience during the Holocaust when those who were taken away never returned.

Mr M was in the hospital for minor surgery. As it was anticipated that he would be weak during the first few days following the operation, an aide was assigned to assist him with bathing and grooming. The first morning the aide helped him into the bathroom and turned on the shower. Mr M's face turned white and he refused to step into the shower. Although the aide did not know it, Mr M never took showers. He took baths and used a hand-held shower head because for him the stand-up shower triggered memories of the showers of poison gas used in the concentration camps.

Mrs F joined a bereavement group following the death of her husband. At the first meeting the members of the group introduced themselves and shared a bit about their recent losses. Mrs F, however, did not speak at all of her husband. Instead she spoke at great length, and very emotionally, about her parents and her siblings who were killed by the Nazis. This was the first time she had ever spoken of this and once she started, she could not stop.

Although it has been more than 50 years, and the atrocities committed by the Nazis and their supporters during World War II continue to affect many of those who survived, Mrs S, Mr M, and Mrs F are among the Holocaust survivors who suffer from post-traumatic stress disorder as it is defined in the DSM-IV: they were exposed to a traumatic event(s); they persistently re-experience the trauma; they persistently avoid stimuli associated with the trauma and experience numbing of general responsiveness; and they experience persistent symptoms of increased arousal. While this may not be such a surprise due to the magnitude of the trauma they survived, what is perhaps surprising is that Mrs S, Mr M, and Mrs F were not diagnosed with PTSD until their later years. It seems that the experience of growing older, their normative aging superimposed upon their Holocaust experiences, triggered the start of these symptoms.

Retirement, physical deterioration and loss are a part of the aging process, yet each of these can force flashbacks to the war years, bringing unresolved issues from those traumas to the surface. Many survivors busied themselves in their careers not only to make enough money to support their post-war families, but also to distract themselves from the painful memories of what they had lost and what they had experienced. Retirement frees the older adult from the busy work schedule, yet the free time may allow the deeply buried memories to resurface.

For many, acknowledging illness during the war meant sudden death. Concentration camp inmates were taken directly to the gas chambers or tortured in medical experiments instead of receiving treatment. Illness or physical deterioration even 50 years later can bring back fears of what happened during the war. For this reason, some survivors may, perhaps subconsciously, downplay poor health or their medical needs. They, and their families, may also disregard the seriousness of illness in old age, unwilling to believe that having survived in hiding, in the ghettos or in the concentration camps a survivor could succumb to "normal" diseases such as pneumonia, cancer or a heart attack. Alzheimer's disease, or other dementing illnesses, can be particularly difficult for survivors. As they lose their short-term memories and the ability to differentiate past and present, the pain of their long-term memories can be almost overwhelming. For those old enough at the time of the war to remember pre-war experiences, focusing them back to those very early days can actually be a blessing, but for others, the pain of the war years is their earliest memory.

The seemingly everyday sights, sounds and smells found in hospitals, retirement facilities and nursing homes can also bring back memories of ghettos and concentration camps. The antiseptic smells, white lab coats of doctors or uniforms of security guards, and sounds of people crying or screaming from loneliness, sickness or fear may trigger reactions ranging from withdrawal to aggressive behavior. Other triggers include bright lights, sirens, dogs and people with heavy accents. . . . Some concrete interventions can reduce the trauma that is triggered. For example, in the case of Mrs S, the nursing home staff was able to calm her fears by bringing back one of the residents who had previously been taken to her room. This reassured Mrs S that the residents were not being taken away to be killed, and she consented to be wheeled to her room in the company of this other resident. In another case, a resident was hoarding food, bringing something back to her room after every meal. Staff tried to reinforce the policy against food in the rooms, reminding her that three meals per day were served and there was always plenty of food. As this resident was responding to hunger pains from years ago at a time when sufficient food was not available, she did not respond to the staff's request to leave the food in the dining room. The facility feared spoiled food and bugs, while the resident needed the security of food in various hiding places in her room. To meet the needs of both, the resident was allowed as much canned foods and canned beverages as she wanted, instead of perishables like fresh fruit and milk. In both these examples, the flexibility on the part of the staff, and the awareness of the issues at play, enabled them to address the situations in a way that met the needs of the clients, even if it was not following standard policy.

 ... the author certainly does not mean to suggest that all Holocaust survivors suffer from PTSD or react to the stimuli described above. However, for those who do, the awareness and sensitivity of clinicians can ease the pain of the return of the trauma.

 Ann Hartman, MAJCS, MSW LCSW, is coordinator of Hineinu, a program addressing the unique aspects of aging for survivors of Nazi persecution and their families, at Council for Jewish Elderly in Chicago.

Source: Hartman, 1997.

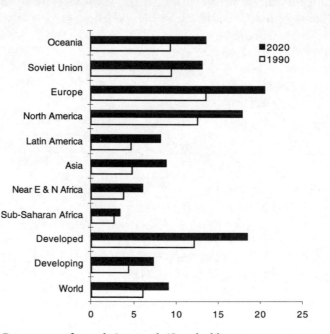

Figure 2.1   Percentage of population aged 65 and older
Source: adapted from Malmgren, 1994.

impact of genetic predispositions, family configurations, and individual life events, such as winning the lottery, being adopted, or surviving a plane crash (Martin & Smyer, 1990).

It is important to note that all three types of influence interact continually across the life-span. In addition, the same influence may affect individuals differently depending upon their age at the time (e.g., Elder's work on the differential effects of the great depression) or the interaction of influences. For example, Grundmann (1996) studied the impact of father absence on different cohorts of German men. Those who experienced father absence either before or after World War II, when such absence was socially non-normative, delayed their own transition to fatherhood. In contrast, those who experienced father absence linked to World War II, when such absences were socially normative, accelerated their own transition to fatherhood.

Another aspect of individual differences is inter- and intra-individual variability. For example, variability is a hallmark of older adults with mental illness. We must differentiate among three patterns of geriatric mental illness: those who had a mental disorder early in life and grew old; those who grew old and experienced mental illness for the first time in later life; and those who came to later life with a liability (e.g., genetic influence, life stress, etc.) that was exacerbated by the conditions of later life, producing mental illness (Kahn, 1977; Gatz, Kasl-Godley, & Karel, 1996).

In sum, our clinical work must place older adults in a variety of contexts that produce individual differences: social, historical, and individual. We must understand the various influences that shape development across the life-span producing the variability that accompanies aging.

Age differences and age changes

Understanding aging and its effects requires assessing several influences at once. Consider some of the basic questions of gerontology and geriatrics: Does intelligence decline with age? Is the risk of suicide greater in later life than in young adulthood? How would you investigate these questions?

One approach compares adults from different ages at one point in time. This *cross-sectional* approach confuses several elements at once, though: age differences, age changes, cohort effects, and time of measurement effects. A cross-sectional approach assumes that age *differences* reflect underlying age *changes*. This does not take into account the differences across the cohorts represented at any one point in time. It also does not consider the possible effect of when the study was done.

A second approach would follow the same people over a long period of time, measuring the group at several different ages. This *longitudinal approach* allows you to observe actual age changes in the individuals' functioning. This approach, however, has the limitation of following only one cohort of individuals. In doing so, you might mistake the characteristics of that particular cohort's experience for general patterns of aging.

Data on intellectual functioning across the life-span offer a compelling demonstration of the difference between cross-sectional and longitudinal views (see figure 2.2). These data represent performance on a verbal meaning

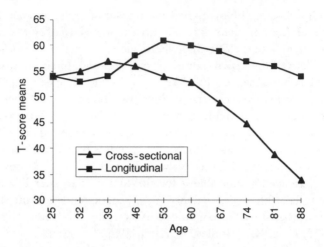

Figure 2.2 Comparable cross-sectional and longitudinal age gradients for the verbal meaning test
Source: adapted from Schaie & Willis, 1991.

test. The cross-sectional results represent age differences. If interpreted as age changes, we might think that verbal meaning performance declines steeply starting around age 46. In contrast, when individuals are followed longitudinally, we see that their performance in fact increases until age 53. The decline that follows is less steep than the cross-sectional view suggested. Thus the age changes reflected in the longitudinal perspective are less dramatic and severe than the cross-sectional results suggested.

Comparing cross-sectional and longitudinal perspectives can also be helpful when considering other domains, for example, rates of suicide. Recent data compiled by Murphy and her colleagues suggest several interesting patterns (see figure 2.3): first, there are consistent age differences in prevalence rates of suicide, with the oldest groups (65+) having the highest risk since the 1920s; second, the rates for the oldest group have declined over the 50 years reported on, while those for youngest groups (below 40) have remained relatively stable. Thus, although there are still striking age differences in risk for suicide, there are also striking cohort differences.

The distinction between age differences and age changes is important for the clinician for several reasons. First, it is an important reminder to assess the client's current functioning in comparison to his or her own baseline, not solely in comparison to age-mates or to those in different age groups. Second, it is another reminder of the importance of placing the person in context – in this case, in a cohort context of historical, educational, and

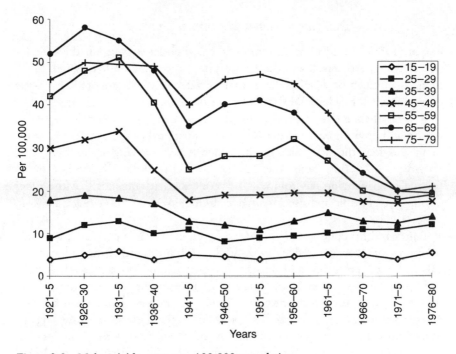

Figure 2.3 Male suicide rates per 100,000 population
Source: adapted from Murphy et al., 1986.

social expectations, opportunities, and challenges. Consider the following example:

> *The interview took place on a rural farm, a sharecropper's homestead. Mrs Smith, now in her late 80s, was surrounded by her children (in their late 50s and early 60s) and grandchildren. The multidimensional assessment began with a mental status test. Mrs Smith did well until asked to perform "serial 7s": Please start at 100 and subtract 7, then 7 from that number, etc. She faltered and then explained: "I never was all that good at counting. I left school after third grade."*

In Mrs Smith's case, school was not one of the opportunities available to her rural cohort. It was clear that Mrs Smith was educationally impaired. As it turns out, she was not also cognitively impaired. Her self-report reflected a comparison to her former functioning ("I never was all that good at counting"), a self-report confirmed by her children. In short, to equate her current inability with an age-related decline would have been off the mark.

Changing person/environment interactions

Lewin (1935) alerted us to the importance of concentrating on the interaction between the person and the environment more than 60 years ago. Since then, a number of scholars have concentrated on the importance of the environment for older adults' continuing functioning.

Several themes are important in conceptualizing the interplay between person and environment in later life. Some suggest that the optimal environment provides the best "fit" to the older person's changing abilities (e.g., Kahana, 1982). For some, the concept of fit includes the notion of an optimally challenging environment – a context that demands that the older person stretch a bit and use his or her abilities to the utmost (e.g., Lawton, 1980, 1982).

Baltes and his colleagues (e.g., Marsiske et al., 1995) suggest that the basic dynamics of later life reflect two subtle and profound shifts: a changing balance between gains and losses, with increasing social, psychological, and physical losses; and an increasing investment of the individual's reserve capacity toward maintenance functions, rather than toward growth. These generalizations, of course, provide a framework for assessing an older individual's unique combination of gains and losses, his or her idiosyncratic combination of physical, psychological, and social growth and maintenance.

Gatz et al. (1996) describe the mental health impact of the changing dynamics between the environment and older adults' vulnerabilities. They expand upon the diathesis–stress model of Zubin and Spring (1977) to emphasize three interrelated elements: biological vulnerability (including genetic influences); stressful life events (including physical and social losses or challenges), and psychological diathesis or stress. Gatz and her colleagues suggest that the changing interplay among these elements produce the curvilinear pattern of depressive symptoms and age often reported in the literature (see figure 2.4). For our purposes, the lesson is simple: understanding the interaction between an older person and the social, physical, and psychological environment is essential for successful assessment and treatment of mental disorders in later life. Viewing the individual out of context will lead to ineffective treatment.

Reversibility of age-related behavior change

How inevitable are the losses associated with aging? Can you teach an old dog new tricks? Is there anything we can do about the most common mental disorders in later life? A generation ago, much of the research and clinical

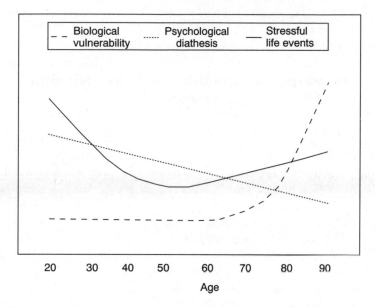

Figure 2.4 Depiction of developmental changes in the magnitude of influence on depressive symptomatology exerted by biological vulnerability, psychological diathesis, and stressful life events
Source: Gatz et al., 1996.

lore focused on depicting the expectable losses of old age, with an emphasis on prompt treatment of excess disability.

More recently, however, attention has shifted to preventive interventions and effective strategies for coping with the most usual problems of later life. A common theme has emerged: the "plasticity" of behavior in later life (Baltes & Baltes, 1990b). In short, results from a number of areas confirm that there are a variety of strategies and approaches that can be effective in reducing some of the deficits of later life.

Consider the area of intellectual decline with age. Several studies have documented the impact of training interventions designed to improve the functioning of older adults. In either small group or individual sessions, Schaie and Willis have documented the impact of five-hour training programs on older adults' cognitive functioning on laboratory tests. Moreover, they have documented the lasting impact of such interventions with follow-ups seven years later. (See Schaie, 1996, for a summary of this work.)

There are a variety of approaches that can mitigate some of the losses of later life. The challenge for both the clinician and the older adult is to assess realistically the rewards of improvement likely to come from an investment of time and personal attention. These issues will be considered in more detail throughout the third section of the book.

Working with Older Adults: Similar or Different?

Most mental health practitioners who work with older adults are not geriatrics or gerontology experts. Many have come to the issues of later life after working with other populations. Even those who have specialty training in gerontological psychology must focus on a simple question when working with older adults: Are the basic approaches to assessment and treatment different when working with the elderly or are they the same as when working with other adult populations? Our answer is similar to the advice attributed to Yogi Berra: When you come to a fork in the road, take it. Working with older adults is both different from and similar to working with other age groups. In this section, we will briefly review both aspects. (For a more detailed discussion, see Knight, 1996.)

Differences

The differences in therapeutic approach to working with older adults stem from changes over time in older adults themselves, differences between the contexts of older people and younger people, and potential differences in the therapeutic alliance.

Physical comorbidities Older adults come to late life with a variety of physical challenges and comorbidities. Apart from a modest developmental change of central nervous system slowing, the major physical challenges for the mental health professional and the older client involve the interrelationship of physical and mental health. As noted in Chapter 1, Cohen (1992) suggested four paradigms for examining the links between physical and mental health, reflecting the complexity of physical and mental interactions for older adults: psychogenic stress may lead to physical health problems; a physical disorder may lead to a psychiatric disturbance; coexisting physical and mental disorders may interact; and social and psychological resources can affect the course of a physical disorder.

These complex interactions of physical and mental health for older adults require that the clinician monitor closely the older client's physical well-being. This situation also requires close collaboration with a range of people who interact with the older client: family members, friends, other health-care and social service providers. (We will return to this collaborative theme shortly.)

Interpersonal qualities Two aspects of older adults' functioning may differentiate them from younger adults: an increasing cognitive maturation and a changing sense of time.

Knight (1993; Knight & Qualls, 1995) has suggested that older adults develop increasing expertise in family, work, and social relationships across the life-span. In addition, older adults may show increasing emotional complexity, with a greater understanding and control of their affective states. From a therapeutic perspective, this may offer an opportunity to collaborate with the older client in reflecting on the current problem within a perspective of past problem-solving successes: "How have you handled similar challenges in the past?"

Another frequently differentiating aspect of working with older adults is their sense of time. First, there is the obvious difference that more time has passed for older adults – giving them both more experience and the opportunity for greater perspective, an opportunity unfortunately missed by some.

> *A frequent benchmark used by one of our older friends reflects this greater perspective. When faced with a problem, he routinely asked: "Will it matter a year from now?" If the answer was no, he would not worry too much about that particular problem.*

A second aspect of time reflects a subtle change in older adults' temporal calculus: oftentimes there is a shift from focusing on time lived to concentrating on the time left to live. For some, shuttling between these two represents one of the therapeutic challenges – how to keep focused on the present and the future, without either denying or being consumed by the past.

Contextual complexity Working effectively with older adults requires recognizing the complexity of their lives and the impact of their contexts. We discussed the potential impact of the physical environment earlier. Here, we focus on the complexity of two aspects of the social, interpersonal environment: family members and those who provide care and support to the older client.

Knowing a person's age can tell you some information about the historical time and cohort experiences to which they have been exposed. Knowing their generational position can also tell us much about the resources and demands presented by family members, about the give and take of family members and friends (Bengtson, Rosenthal, & Burton, 1996). Consider two men:

> *Bryce is the 67-year-old CEO of a billion-dollar-a-year company. He is a middle-generation adult, with care-giving concerns for his 89-year-old mother and his two children in their 20s. Charles is a 38-year-old professional. He also is a middle-generation adult who divides his time and resources among his 80-year-old mother and his children who are in elementary school.*

While these men differ in age and life stage, they share a generational position that affects their psychological well-being. Focusing solely on their ages would overlook the psychological and social complexity of their generational positions.

Family members provide the majority of assistance to older adults who need help because of physical or mental health problems. Oftentimes, however, the family caregivers are complemented by formal and informal services provided by physicians, social agency staff members, and friends. Again, to understand effectively the life context of the older client, the therapist must assess the availability of two types of support: emotional support in the give and take of daily interactions; and support that would be available in a time of crisis. In addition, the mental health professional must understand the affection and support that the older client provides to other family members.

In many cases, the task of the therapist is one of trying to exterd the influence of gerontological expertise. This requires sharing problem-solving approaches with those who have the most frequent contact with the older client: family members, friends, and other service providers, especially primary care physicians. Collaboration is a keystone in effective assessment and treatment of mentally ill elderly.

Cohort differences Each of us carries with us the imprint of the culture and time in which we live. Think of today's oldest old: born 80 or more years ago; witnesses to almost unimaginable technological changes; participants in world war and cold war; survivors of economic upheavals; among the earliest beneficiaries of Medicare and Medicaid. These experiences affect the ways in which older adults encounter the challenges of later life.

Members of different cohorts, for example, may use different language to describe similar reactions.

> *Hazel reported that she was "frustrated" when the hospital social worker reported that Medicare would not pay for her medications.*

The mental health professional probed Hazel's frustration. It became clear that younger clients might have used another word: angry.

Cohorts may also differ in their patterns of help-seeking and problem definition. When faced with a mental health problem, today's elderly might first seek out a primary care physician, a minister, or a neighbor – but not a mental health professional. Tomorrow's elderly, in contrast, may be more comfortable with mental health treatment, perhaps changing the profile of where mental health treatment is provided for older adults. At the very least, mental health professionals should reflect on the role that the older adult's cohort experience might play in problem identification, patterns of help-seeking, and expectations for change.

Countertransference issues Encountering older adults as clients is likely to elicit a range of responses from the therapist, including stereotypical assumptions, fantasies, and projections about aging and older adults (Knight, 1996). At times, the countertransference issues raised may be either current issues in the therapist's own relationship with his or her parents or grandparents, or future issues on the horizon in the therapist's own family. Similarly, working with older adults may raise concerns about one's own aging, dying, and death. In each instance, the therapist must first be aware of the potential for countertransference processes and then depend upon supervision or collegial support to help differentiate the therapist's projections from the client's reality.

Similarities

Working with older clients is not entirely different from working with other groups, however. Throughout this book we will be discussing approaches to assessment and treatment that build upon techniques developed and used with other age groups. In some cases there have been modifications to accommodate age-related changes (e.g., large-print versions of assessment instruments). In other cases there has been a relatively straightforward application of previously developed approaches to the problems of later life (e.g., cognitive-behavioral therapy). Our working assumption is that the essential skills that contribute to an effective clinician are also necessary for working effectively with older adults – necessary but not sufficient. In addition, the therapist must also call upon an appreciation of the developmental influences at work in later life.

Throughout the life-span, theoretical perspectives of the etiology, assessment, and treatment of disorders mold the therapist's approaches. In the next section we will introduce several models, emphasizing those aspects that are most salient in each. Our working assumption is that the therapist's implicit and explicit models shape problem identification and treatment, regardless of the age of the client. The challenge, therefore, is to identify the strengths and shortcomings of each model. We turn to this challenge in the next section.

Part II

Models of Mental Health in Later Life

Introduction

Discussions about the mental health of any population often begin with disclaimers about the ambiguity of the construct of mental health or mental illness. A serious conversation with your peers focused on the task of defining mental health would generate quite diverse ideas and not just a small amount of controversy. Conceptions of health and illness are varied, at least in part, because of the variety of assumptions made concerning the nature of human beings and their interactions with the environment.

Introductory chapters in abnormal psychology textbooks (e.g., Davison & Neale, 1994) typically summarize the major strategies for defining normal or abnormal behavior using a core set of definitions of abnormal that includes statistical definitions of abnormality (i.e., what is non-normative), moral definitions (i.e., what is inappropriate), definitions of disability or dysfunction (what impairs social or occupational functioning), and definitions based on what is personally distressing. The fourth edition of the *Diagnostic and statistical manual of mental disorders* (*DSM4*) defines mental disorder as:

> a clinically significant behavioral or psychological syndrome or pattern that occurs in an individual and that is associated with present distress (e.g., a painful symptom) or disability (i.e., impairment in one or more important areas of functioning) or with a significantly increased risk of suffering death, pain, disability, or an important loss of freedom. In addition, this syndrome or pattern must not be merely an expectable and culturally sanctioned response to a particular event, for example, the death of a loved one. (American Psychiatric Association, 1994, p. xxi)

These definition alternatives can be used to examine the absence of mental health of older persons. Each provides some insights, but each also runs into conceptual conundrums. If an illness process or organ deterioration is normative among 85-year-olds, does that mean it is normal? Can we talk meaningfully about what might be normal for 85-year-olds that would not be normal in 25-year-olds (i.e., is age per se a moderator of our definition of normal)? Perhaps we might acknowledge differences based on age in the area of memory or attention, but what about depression? Based on the moral definition of normal, the old woman in the famous poem "When I am an old woman I shall wear purple" might be considered abnormal, although biological definitions might find her extraordinarily capable.

Warning

When I am an old woman I shall wear purple
With a red hat which doesn't go, and doesn't suit me.
And I shall spend my pension on brandy and summer gloves
And satin sandals, and say we've no money for butter.
I shall sit down on the pavement when I'm tired
And gobble up samples in shops and press alarm bells
And run my stick along the public railings
And make up for the sobriety of my youth.
I shall go out in my slippers in the rain
And pick the flowers in other people's gardens
And learn to spit.

You can wear terrible shirts and grow more fat
And eat three pounds of sausages at a go
Or only bread and pickle for a week
And hoard pens and pencils and beermats and things in boxes.

But now we must have clothes that keep us dry
And pay out rent and not swear in the street
And set a good example for the children.
We must have friends to dinner and read the papers.

But maybe I ought to practise a little now?
So people who know me are not too shocked and surprised
When suddenly I am old, and start to wear purple.

(Joseph, 1991)

Mental health or well-being is no easier to define than abnormality. Definitions may focus on competence, maturity, responsibility for actions, or freedom to love and work. Jahoda (1958) provided six highly cited criteria of positive mental health: positive self-attitudes, growth and self-actualization, integration of the personality, autonomy, reality perception, and environmental mastery. We appreciate the qualitative richness of the definition offered by Birren and Renner (1980) that, at any age, mentally healthy people "have the ability to respond to other individuals, to love, to be loved, and to cope with others in give-and-take relationships" (p. 29).

Clinical work with older persons is sometimes challenging simply because it forces us to articulate our conception of normal mental health, and then adjust it (as needed) for older persons. As Birren and Renner (1980) acknowledge, the conceptual dichotomies implicit in most distinctions of mental health and illness become even more complicated when applied to older adults. "The conceptual dichotomies . . . – health and illness, competence and incompetence, and intrapsychic and interpersonal processes – seem, in the minds of the present authors, to have rather different implications for older adults in which there can be many coexisting features" (p. 7). The person described in the following case study pushes the clarity of our definitions of normality.

Case Example

Joan Rankin is a 74-year-old woman who lives in her home in a small rural community. Her husband, Jim, died two years ago, following a five-year bout with cancer. Now that she is alone, Joan is tempted to move closer to her children, but cannot quite make up her mind. Her house is paid for, and she is not sure she could buy a comparable house in a city with the proceeds from a sale of this house. She has a modest pension that will be sufficient unless she needs major medical care. Sometimes she worries about not having enough money to carry her through. She chooses to live frugally with an occasional indulgence.

Joan belongs to the local garden club, but is not a particularly active member. She does enjoy working in her own small flower garden during the nice weather seasons. She also attends church almost weekly. Joan has a few close friends, but many of those friendships were strained by the period of Jim's illness. Even two years after his death, she is not sure how to fill her days. Her nights are usually tolerable, although sometimes she lies awake for long periods in the middle of the night. At those times she feels overwhelmingly alone and scared.

Joan is generally healthy, although she has high blood pressure and some difficulties with thyroid and arthritis. She takes Tylenol for the arthritis, propanolol for blood pressure, and synthroid to regulate her thyroid.

Joan's two children live 300 miles away in major cities. Her daughter, Jeannie, is married, has three children (ages 4, 7, and 10), and teaches school. Her son, John, a very successful realtor, is currently engaged to be remarried. He was divorced four years ago from his wife of 18 years, who has custody of their two children, ages 8 and 13. Jeannie and John have never been very close. Nor was John close to his father, although he confided his troubles and joys to his mother privately.

Joan has two younger sisters still living, and two older brothers who died more than five years ago. Her sister Betty lives only two blocks away from Joan, and calls her daily. Sometimes Joan even resents the call because Betty is so perky and enthusiastic about life. Betty insists that Joan get out to social events regardless of how tired or sick Joan is feeling. Betty has always been the cheerful one, encouraging all around her to enjoy life. Recently she has hinted that she might like to move in with Joan to share expenses.

Her other sister Vivian lives with her husband 30 miles away on a farm. They stay busy with farm responsibilities, and with their children and grandchildren. Joan sees them only at family gatherings on holidays. Vivian has always been the quiet, solid one in the family. Joan would like to spend more time with her, but can see that she is too busy with daily responsibilities to socialize.

Her brothers, Elwood and Milt, were in business together in a city 150 miles from Joan's home. They died of heart attacks exactly one year apart. They left their families quite well off financially, and their children and grandchildren have continued their business. Joan only visits with her sisters-in-law or their offspring at the annual family reunion each summer.

Is Joan mentally healthy? Clinicians would readily recognize several symptoms in this brief description of Joan that might be clinically meaningful. For example, she has difficulty with decision-making, worries, has mild insomnia, and is socially withdrawn. Could she be diagnosed with a mental disorder? Is her current distress caused by her recent widowhood, her health, her struggle to create meaning, the family and social systems conflicts, or some inadequacy in her personality that inhibits her coping? Given her circumstances, what would mentally healthy look like? Where would you begin to look for additional information to help you understand Joan's well-being?

A systematic examination of conceptualizations of the mental health of older persons leads us to examine the broader paradigms of psychology. A paradigm is a framework used to construct our understanding of the world. Such frameworks make basic assumptions about the nature of human beings, including assumptions about motivation, cognition, emotion, personality, and behavior. Built on those assumptions are postulates or theories that attempt to explain particular behavior patterns, including patterns defined as mental health and illness.

In the section that follows, a series of chapters describes four basic paradigms used often by psychologists: the psychodynamic, behavioral, stress, and systems paradigms. Each chapter will review the basic assumptions and core theoretical contributions of one paradigm. Specifically, descriptions are offered of the assumptions about what well-being looks like and how disorders are defined and conceptualized. Because approaches to assessment and intervention are rooted in the assumptions about mental health and mental illness or disorder, each chapter also includes a description of the major approaches to assessment and intervention that have arisen from each paradigm.

Gerontology has not produced totally new paradigms for defining and examining human lives. It has instead applied existing frameworks to the unique and common problems of older persons. There is no single way to answer the questions raised at the beginning of this introduction regarding Joan Rankin. As will become evident, each paradigm produces a different (although perhaps related) explanation of Joan's mental health.

Regardless of paradigm or theory, gerontologists have developed a profound respect for the influence of culture and cohort experience on well-being. Subcultures offer specific definitions and mechanisms for demonstrating mental health and illness. These definitions and mechanisms for experiencing well-being also vary by the historical period into which individuals are born and live (birth cohort). If Joan Rankin were Chinese, German, or Cherokee, how would that influence your understanding of her behavior and/or your analysis of her well-being? How would her experience be different and what different meanings would be embedded in her behavior if she lived in the seventeenth, twentieth, or twenty-first century?

As you study the chapters in this section, engage yourself in the challenge of creating meaningful models for mental health and disorder in older adults. What paradigms explain behavior most adequately and parsimoniously? What tenets from each paradigm seem most credible? As you read, you may find it useful to write an analysis of Joan Rankin's story from each paradigm. When you have completed all four chapters, consider writing an integration essay that articulates your personal model of mental health and disorder in older adults.

3

Psychodynamic Model

The psychodynamic model of psychological functioning is one of the earliest comprehensive models of psychological well-being and disorder. The progenitor of this line of theory was Sigmund Freud's psychoanalytic model (Freud, 1940). Later contributors (e.g., Jung, 1933; Erikson, 1963; Horney, 1945; Sullivan, 1953; and Kohut, 1977) developed varied approaches to the inner dynamics of personality but stayed true to core assumptions about the importance of intrapsychic functioning, the balance of genetic and environmental influence on personality, and the key role of relationships in normal and abnormal development. Thus, although the theories covered in this chapter offer a range of constructs and explanations, they share a common focus on the motivational and personality aspects of human beings. Consider the following case and ask yourself what explains the client's distress.

Maria Jiminez is increasingly isolated because she often just does not feel like getting out. Up until a few years ago her home was the constant gathering place of the extended family. After her husband's death, the nieces and nephews quit coming around. Her children and grandchildren visit, but seem to resent it. The entire family continues to mourn the death of Juan, the warm, generous and fun-loving patriarch of the family. Although Maria had always cooked for the family, she was not known for a generous spirit. In family gatherings she usually kept to herself, portraying a rather quiet person who waited for others to notice what she needed or wanted. Her daughters feel obligated to care for their mother, but it is a fairly joyless relationship on both sides. The "girls" can never quite get it right. If they make apple pie, she wanted peach. If they clean the kitchen, she laments about the dirt in the bathroom. The doctors don't pay enough attention to her, the home health aide "is just working for money" and doesn't have any feelings. Everyone recognizes Maria's depression, and is encouraging her to seek help from a mental health professional. She resists professional help, claiming "any woman would feel depressed if she had a life like mine." Somehow she has made it to your office to tell you her sad story.

She obviously likes having you listen to her, but tells you that she is sure you can't help her.

How does the psychodynamic model describe and explain Maria's distress? As with any model, basic assumptions about human beings are embedded in core constructs that are used to explain behavior. Within psychodynamic theory, the core constructs focus on the dynamics among personality structures and between people. These dynamics are viewed as the primary determinants of behavior. In the following sections the psychodynamic approaches to personality structure, the processes by which personality develops, and the mechanisms by which mental disorders are created will be described. Adaptations of the theory for psychological functioning in later life are specifically addressed, followed by a discussion of approaches to assessment and treatment of older adults.

Personality: A Dynamic Interplay

The psychodynamic view of human beings emphasizes the complex inter-relationships among cognition, emotion, motivation, and external reality in the formation of personality. The complexity into which our highly evolved cognitive and affective structures are organized gives humans a tremendous advantage over other species of animals in the task of managing their basic needs (e.g., food, shelter, procreation). However, these capacities are also postulated to generate anxiety. For example, the struggle to survive, along with the knowledge that survival is tenuous, generates anxiety (Becker, 1973).

Conflicts among parts of the personality, and between the individual and the external world, also generate conflict. This model postulates that the personality is comprised of core desires (e.g., drives, motives, emotion, Freud's "id"), a conscience (e.g., cultural taboos, family rules, moral codes, Freud's "superego"), and a rational organizing function (the ego) that helps the individual meet needs while managing the inevitable conflict between the desires and conscience. The ego also has the significant task of negotiating the individual's real needs in a real world. The well developed ego plays a key role as a modulator of emotion because it is able to evaluate situations rationally and determine the most useful way to proceed to meet the individual's needs. Vaillant (1993) summarized the multiple sources of conflict in figure 3.1. As is evident in the figure, the ego, or the executive function, sits at the center of the four sources of conflict that derive from internal and external sources.

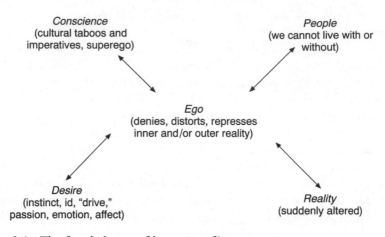

Figure 3.1   The four lodestars of human conflict
Source: Vaillant, 1993, p. 29.

Unfortunately, in the real world, anxiety often undermines the ego's functioning, rendering it less than fully capable. Conditions of threat (e.g., external dangers or internal dangers such as those that occur when the ego cannot be trusted to manage drives) are what generate a sense of anxiety powerful enough to disrupt ego functioning.

> Thus the ego, driven by the id, confined by the superego, repulsed by reality, struggles to master its economic task of bringing about harmony among the forces and influences working in and upon it; and we can understand how it is that so often we cannot suppress a cry: "Life is not easy!" If the ego is obliged to admit its weakness, it breaks out in anxiety – realistic anxiety regarding the external world, moral anxiety regarding the superego, and neurotic anxiety regarding the strength of the passions in the id. (Freud, 1933)

When anxious, the ego reverts to automatic processes called defense mechanisms (Freud, 1937). These mechanisms serve to reduce anxiety by avoiding the cause of the anxiety rather than by solving the problem directly. A list of several defense mechanisms, their strategy for managing anxiety, and their level of maturity is presented in table 3.1. For example, repression simply prevents intolerable thoughts, impulses, and feelings from reaching consciousness, but does nothing to address the concerns behind the thoughts directly. The defense mechanisms vary in their usefulness for managing both the immediate threat and the overall well-being of the individual. Although the least mature mechanisms provide little benefit in either the short or long

Table 3.1 Schematic table of adaptive mechanisms

Level of maturity	Defense mechanisms	Description
Psychotic mechanisms	Denial	Protecting self from unpleasant reality by obliterating it
	Distortion	Insisting that external imaginary figures are available to comfort or that internal desires are both virtuous and instantly gratifiable
	Delusional projection	Externalizing inner conflicts by attributing unacceptable motives to others whose bizarre actions are fantastical
Immature mechanisms	Fantasy	Fulfilling desires by imagining acting them out
	Projection	Externalizing inner conflicts by attributing unacceptable motives to others whose actions are realistically possible
	Hypochondriasis	Transforming reproach toward others into self-reproach and then into complaints of physical pain or illness
	Passive–aggressive behavior	Converting inner desires into behavior that punishes the self and the other simultaneously
	Acting out	Expressing directly an unconscious desire without regard to consequences, in order to avoid being conscious of the emotions behind the desire
Neurotic mechanisms	Intellectualization	Cutting off feelings or separating incompatible motives by isolating them from cognition and relying on contrived explanations for motives
	Repression	Maintaining awareness of motives and emotions outside of consciousness while acting on them directly or indirectly

Table 3.1   continued

Level of maturity	Defense mechanisms	Description
	Reaction formation	Preventing awareness of thought and emotion by valuing intensively the opposite of the unacceptable desire
	Displacement	Redirecting thoughts and emotions from an unacceptable object to one deemed less dangerous
Mature mechanisms	Sublimation	Channeling the energy from desires and emotions into more acceptable activities that still bring pleasure without adverse consequences
	Altruism	Joyfully giving to another in order to feel gratification despite self-denial of desires
	Suppression	Choosing semiconsciously to postpone a conscious impulse or conflict
Anticipation		Planning realistically for future discomfort based on conscious awareness of feelings and thoughts
Humor		Keeping idea, emotion, and object in mind while playing like it is a game, giving pleasure to subject and object

Source: adapted from Vaillant, 1993; Carson & Butcher, 1992.

term, the more mature mechanisms can enhance individuals' well-being despite limited direct addressing of basic anxiety.

Personality Development

Psychodynamic theories emphasize the interpersonal contexts in which the developing capability of the ego or Self emerges and forms a distinctive style (e.g., Sullivan, 1953). Basic personality structures are established very early in life as the infant and very young child experience their basic needs and the external world's response to them. The primary relationships on which infants depend are known as their attachment relationships (Bowlby, 1969). Attachment figures are the persons who teach infants and toddlers about the external world (e.g., its safety, trustworthiness, and availability of nurturance).

Attachment figures are particularly important because all humans begin as helpless, dependent creatures whose experience of helplessness generates very basic survival anxiety. According to this model, strong nurturant caretakers who teach the child that Others will reliably and competently care for their needs are doing much more than caring for basic needs. These caretakers are providing a framework for basic trust in the world that forms the basis for all subsequent development (Erikson, 1963). Conversely, Others whose behavior increases anxiety or rage will not only teach the child about an unreliable, unsafe external world, but also their behavior patterns are captured in internal representations of the world as an unsafe, unreliable Self (Bowlby, 1969). Thus, the child will define his or her understanding of both the internal and external worlds based on experience with primary caretakers.

Throughout much of the twentieth century the development and evolution of personality structures was the purview solely of child psychologists interested in the initial structuring of personality during the first five years of life. Certainly, the experiences of childhood continue to be recognized as particularly profound because the early experiences establish lifelong styles or strategies for managing internal conflicts and adapting to external changes. For example, empirical links have been demonstrated between childhood attachment styles and subsequent patterns of adult sexuality and care-giving across the life span (Shaver and Hazan, 1988). Secure attachment styles in childhood are expressed in adulthood as mutuality in the processes of care-giving, intimacy, and sexuality. Avoidant attachment styles, in contrast, constrain the individual's subsequent ability or willingness to give or receive care, or to connect emotionally within a sexual relationship (leading to distancing or promiscuity). Although childhood styles are correlated with subsequent relationship styles, much of the variability in adult relationships is not explained by childhood personality.

Adult Development: The Context for Aging

Recently, the developmental processes of adulthood have also become a focus of investigation among psychodynamic theorists. Adult responses to the many tasks and crises encountered in the course of normal adulthood can produce development as well as pathology. Colarusso and Nemiroff (1979) offered seven hypotheses regarding the nature of development in adulthood that can be viewed as basic postulates of psychodynamic views of adult development (see table 3.2). These statements claim that the commonalties between child and adult developmental processes are more striking than their differences, which occur primarily in form and content. In other words, the basic structures through which development is evoked and expressed remain the same throughout the life-span.

What shapes personality in the course of adulthood? Within the psychodynamic frameworks, adult developmental processes have been outlined in terms of the tasks that provoke change (e.g., marriage, entry of children; Erikson, 1963), the effects of adult experiences on development of the personality (e.g., Jung, 1933), or the development of internal structures such as defense mechanisms (e.g., Vaillant, 1977; 1993).

Developmental tasks and stages

A popular framework for conceptualizing development is to divide the life-span into stages that are characterized by common life tasks, especially those

Table 3.2 Psychodynamic model of adult development

Hypothesis I	The nature of the developmental process is basically the same in the adult as in the child.
Hypothesis II	Development in adulthood is an ongoing, dynamic process.
Hypothesis III	While childhood development is focused primarily on the "formation" of psychic structure, adult development is concerned with the continuing "evolution" of existing psychic structure and with its "use."
Hypothesis IV	The fundamental developmental issues of childhood continue as central aspects of adult life but in altered form.
Hypothesis V	The developmental processes in adulthood are influenced by the "adult" past as well as the childhood past.
Hypothesis VI	Development in adulthood, as in childhood, is deeply influenced by the body and physical change.
Hypothesis VII	A central, phase-specific theme of adult development is the normative crisis precipitated by the recognition and acceptance of the finiteness of time and the inevitability of personal death.

Source: adapted from Colarusso & Nemiroff, 1979.

related to family development and work roles (Gould, 1978; Levinson et al., 1978). Erik Erikson's (1963) early model of development across the life-span is one of the most important stage or task models that emphasizes the opportunities for adults to mature by restructuring internally in response to the major tasks of the life course. In their more recent formulation of the model, Erikson et al. (1986) describe specific life themes that, although present throughout the life-span, are most salient at the point in the life cycle when internal and external pressures highlight one particular theme (table 3.3). These themes are experienced within the dynamics of the personality as children and adults struggle with the use of their personality strengths and weaknesses to address life tasks. For example, the theme of autonomy that emerges so powerfully in toddlerhood when the child first experiences the power and frustration of the will is again significantly addressed in adolescence, and yet again in old age. The substantive issues that generate the struggle vary, but the thematic focus on autonomy is similar. According to Erikson (1963), the struggle with the opposing alternative responses to life challenges is what produces the potential for growth of character or virtues. Learning to balance the alternatives generates maturity.

Erikson (1963) argued for a distinct aspect of development in later life: the unique potential for wisdom. As the individual makes peace with his or her life as it was lived, he or she must integrate satisfactions and regrets into an acceptable life story. If regrets dominate the life review, the person is at risk for despair as he or she realizes that the life cannot be relived. Of course, life review does not happen for the first time in later life. Like other Eriksonian themes, the life review task and the struggle between the polarity of ego integrity versus despair is present in all stages of life, but is believed to have particular developmental salience in later life.

> Throughout life, the individual has, on some level, anticipated the finality of old age, experiencing an existential dread of "not-being" alongside an ever-present process of integrating those behaviors and restraints, those choices and rejections, those essential strengths and weaknesses over time that constitute what we have called the sense of "I" in the world. In old age, this tension reaches its ascendancy. The elder is challenged to draw on a life cycle that is far more nearly completed than yet to be lived, to consolidate a sense of wisdom with which to live out the future, to place him- or herself in perspective among those generations now living, and to accept his or her place in an infinite historical progression. (Erikson et al., 1986, p. 56)

Reflections on one's personal past require effort to maintain a coherent narrative, despite the disruptive effects of past events that challenged

Table 3.3 Psychosocial themes and stages of life

Older adulthood	57	58	59	60	61	62	63	64 — Integrity & despair. WISDOM
Middle adulthood	49	50	51	52	53	54	55 — Generativity & self-absorption. CARE	56
Young adulthood	41	42	43	44	45	46 — Intimacy & isolation. LOVE	47	48
Adolescence	33	34	35	36	37 — Identity & confusion. FIDELITY	38	39	40
	25	26	27	28	29	30	31	32

School age	17	18	19	20 — Industry & inferiority. COMPETENCE	21	22	23 (24)
Play age	9	10	11 — Initiative & guilt. PURPOSE	12	13	14	15 (16)
Toddlerhood	2 / 10 — Autonomy & shame/doubt. WILL	3	4	5	6	7	8
Infancy	1 — Basic trust & basic mistrust. HOPE	2	3	4	5	6	7 (8)

Source: adapted from Erikson et al., 1986.

coherence and future events that include one's own death. Both types of events can be viewed by the wise elder as "problems to be studied rather than outcomes to be assumed" (Cohler, 1993, pp. 119–20) (see table 3.3).

The basic principles of Erikson's model are shared by most psychodynamic theorists: People use the styles and strategies embedded in their personality structure to address the psychosocial tasks of their life stage. Although the psychological work of each stage is not unique to that stage (i.e., major psychological tasks require work across the entire life-span), the salience of the work increases because of the social demands of that period of life. The socially structured tasks or crises of adulthood challenge familiar personality styles and strategies, creating anxiety that sets the stage for either growth within the personality or a breakdown in functioning (regression).

Internal developmental processes

Other models of adult development focus on internally driven changes. Jung (1933) postulated that awareness of a finite life-span dawns in mid-life, bringing with it an interest in pursuing development in the underdeveloped aspects of personality. Neugarten (1979) hypothesized that, sometime in the middle of their life, people begin to count time in terms of time-until-death rather than in terms of time-since-birth. Having achieved a stable life struc-ture, and given increased awareness of the limits of their life-span, humans are prompted to re-examine their life for unused opportunities and unknown aspects of the self. Jung (1933) observed a tendency for men and women to become androgynous by exploring characteristics of the other gender during the second half of their life. He argued that men explore their feminine side while women are drawn to explore their underdeveloped masculine charac-teristics. For example, high-powered business executives may choose to paint, garden, and build close ties to family after mid-life. Extroverts may explore their introverted side through keeping a journal, meditation, or interests that draw upon the inner resources of creativity.

Gutmann (1987; 1992) has expanded on this theme by offering another reason why personality shifts in the second half of life. He argues that parenting is such a demanding task that it organizes life structures during early adulthood into patterns we refer to as gender roles. He suggests that it is efficient for couples to organize their work into roles, traditionally along gender-based lines. Once the "chronic parental emergency" ends, individuals are free to resume the full range of their development, both masculine and feminine aspects.

Development of defensive styles

A third adult development process that has been offered by psychodynamic theorists is Vaillant's idea that defense mechanisms mature across the life-span. One study that attempted to examine the idea of maturation across the life-span was a study of Harvard sophomores that was launched in the early 1940s (Vaillant, 1977). Although the study contained an obviously limited sample (e.g., bright, well-to-do white males who were in an elite college during World War II and were selected by the deans at Harvard for being academically and emotionally strong), its longitudinal nature has offered an opportunity to observe change in personality structures over time through in-depth clinical interviews. One question guiding the research was whether these men who had society's most ideal developmental conditions in young adulthood (financial and educational resources, social status, and personality strength) would continue to mature throughout adulthood. Under what conditions would they mature, and what would stunt the maturational process? Specifically, would the men mature through a hierarchy of defense mechanisms as they experienced the challenges of adulthood (note that table 3.1 listed the defenses according to their level of maturity). Results of the clinical interviews when the men were 25, 30, 47, and 57 showed that, indeed, there was a tendency for them to use increasingly mature defense mechanisms with increased age. One life story that depicts this kind of transition is described in box 3.1.

Mental Health in Later Life

With rare exceptions, psychodynamic theorists have focused on pathology or maintenance of function in the face of loss and deterioration far more than on positive potentials. However, a developmental approach to personality dynamics implies that positive mental health requires a richer definition than merely the absence of pathology. Development implies a progression toward some completed, mature state. What is the direction toward which personality development is oriented? Emotional integration or deepening of personality is described by some developmentalists as a positive developmental potential in old age (Butler, Lewis, & Sunderland, 1991; Ryff, 1982). Vaillant (1993) argues that the ego gains wisdom over the experience of a lifetime, as is evident in the maturing of defense mechanisms. Kivnick (1993) suggests that positive development can be observed in the vitality with which meaning is inserted into daily activities.

Box 3.1   The maturity of defenses across the life-span

Vaillant (1977) described Godfrey Minot DeMille, MD, one of the grant study participants, as an illustration of the maturity of defenses across the life-span. Following one of the initial interviews conducted while Godfrey was in college, the staff of the study consensually rated him as very unstable in personality and fully unsuited for his chosen profession of medicine. Godfrey frequented the campus health services with more than 20 outpatient visits (in which no illness was diagnosed) and five hospitalizations. Hypochondriasis was his primary defensive strategy. Following medical training he shifted his focus from physical illnesses to psychiatric illnesses, culminating in a suicide attempt and psychiatric hospitalization after his graduation from medical school. Although it took him several years to complete a much-feared internship in which he actually would have to begin to care for patients, he ultimately was able to maintain a private practice. He matured into using conversion reactions (physical symptoms that were accurately recognized as consequences of significant emotional stress) and displacement (e.g., giving to others what he wanted for himself) as his primary defenses. When he became ill in his mid-30s, Dr DeMille was finally able to receive the full caring attention of a medical staff for an entire year, a degree of caring he had never experienced in his entire life. As his illness improved, he began serious psychoanalytic work, a continuation of caring that was needed for him to progress in his psychological functioning. Ultimately, he was able to engage in the full care of patients, functioning as internist and psychiatrist for allergy patients. He was increasingly able to use altruism as a defense against anxiety, and to engage in a fuller range of human functioning (e.g., he was married, and was able to engage in play).

Throughout the life cycle, everyday mental health may be described as an attempt to live meaningfully, in a particular set of social and environmental circumstances, relying on a particular collection of resources and supports. Simply said, we all try to do the best we can with what we have. Part of this effort involves developing internal strengths and capacities; part involves identifying and using external resources; part involves compensating for weaknesses and deficits. (Kivnick, 1993, p. 24)

Meaning also must be worked out for the entire life cycle in the form of a coherent narrative that explains the continuity of an individual life in the face of interruptions and adverse events (Cohler, 1993). Other psychodynamic theorists have noted that mental well-being is evidenced when functioning is maintained despite substantial anxiety and loss (Horney, 1945; Sullivan, 1953). In other words, maintenance of personality integrity in the face of serious decline in physical capacity is an indication of maturity.

Development of Psychopathology

Theorists who focus on developmental tasks unique to each life stage typically link later life to themes of loss, such as grief over loved ones within one's intimate circle, loss of roles, loss of physical capacity and resulting dependency, and loss of opportunity to alter one's life course (Busse & Pfeiffer, 1969). The belief that the loss theme dominates the aging experience often leads newcomers to the field of aging to assume that depression rates are particularly high in older adults. Surprisingly, however, older adults report lower rates of clinical depression than most adult populations (see Chapter 8). Clearly, the tasks of later life alone do not explain the emergence of psychopathology.

Psychodynamic theory points to internal rather than external causes of psychopathology because the external events or challenges associated with aging are experienced by far more older adults than those who develop psychiatric symptoms (Gutmann, 1992). Explanations of the etiology of psychopathology presume one or more of the following causal factors: 1) losses of later life re-enact significant childhood losses (Gutmann, 1992); 2) an underdeveloped self or immature defense mechanisms provide insufficient strength for handling the psychological challenges of later life (Vaillant, 1993); 3) loss of physical, cognitive, and emotional strengths with advanced old age undermine the functioning of the ego (Gutmann, 1992); and/or 4) the personal narrative cannot integrate meaningfully the events and transitions of later life (Cohler, 1993).

Losses

Classic psychoanalytic theory proposes that loss is particularly threatening to older adults if it evokes strong unresolved grief over a childhood loss (Bowlby, 1980). The model emphasizes the critical negative impact of childhood loss on formation of intrapsychic structures. Specifically, loss of an attachment figure evokes extremely powerful grief that overwhelms the young child's adaptive capacity. The resulting anxiety about living in a profoundly unstable, unprotected world is a significant wound that may never heal, or may produce significant emotional scar tissue. Defense mechanisms may protect an individual from severe depression until such time as the

defense mechanisms themselves are taxed by a life event or task too momen-
tous for adaptation by the current psychological structures.

Psychoanalytic theory postulates that the significant losses of later life leave
a person particularly vulnerable to re-experiencing the almost unmanage-
able feelings evoked during the childhood grief experience (Gutmann, 1986).
When the grief over significant attachment figures re-enacts the childhood
loss, this model predicts a regression in functioning into some form of
psychopathology. This loss model is relevant primarily in the latest phase of
the life-span when social and physical losses are pervasive, but does not
address the issues of the young-old (Gutmann, 1986).

Within the loss model, it is postulated that early childhood trauma inflicts
permanent personality scars that become points of vulnerability in old age.
Gutmann (1986) uses an immune system analogy to describe the relationship
between loss and personality defenses. The pathogen (loss) is powerful only
to the extent that the immune system (personality structure) is vulnerable to
that pathogen. Later life losses are particularly lethal to persons whose personality structures adapted to early losses in immature ways. Thus an underdeveloped self exacerbates the power of loss to evoke psychopathology in late
life.

> *The fact that Maria Jiminez was unable to give much nurturance during her
> adult life would lead a psychodynamic clinician to suspect that she failed to
> receive sufficient nurturance in her own childhood to have a fully functioning ego.
> It turns out that Maria was the sixth of nine children in a very poor and busy
> household. Her mother was very ill for several months after her birth, leaving her
> in the care of her eight-year-old sister. This type of chronic, pervasive loss of
> parenting at a critical period limited her potential to engage in rich attachment
> relationships. Always seeking a caregiver, Maria had limited care to give.*

Underdeveloped self or immature defenses

Throughout the life-span, developmental tasks are most challenging to those
who lack internal structures sufficient to support adaptation. In his model of
successive tasks, Erikson (1963) noted that those who have not mastered
previous developmental challenges are considerably handicapped in their
efforts to adapt when faced with subsequent tasks. Indeed, as described above,
Vaillant (1977; Vaillant & Vaillant, 1990) demonstrated that men whose
defense strategies in young adulthood were more primitive had worse outcomes in later adulthood. Similar data are now available on women, showing
also that, for both genders, maturation of defensive styles across the life-span
improves outcomes (Vaillant, 1993).

Gutmann's (1987) theory regarding the inhibiting effects of parenting on development uses a normative developmental process to explain limitations on growth. The consequences of stunted growth, even due to this "normal" cause, are often deleterious to mental health. As wishes and urges to develop the underdeveloped self surface, the young-old find their personal myths (or stories that describe self-identity to themselves) threatened by parts of the self that have not previously been integrated into the myth (e.g., weaknesses). Anxiety over the need to learn about new parts of the self and integrate them into the myth can spawn pathological reactions such as anxiety, depression, or more primitive psychotic reactions.

Maria used primitive defense mechanisms to protect her from the terror of being unnurtured in a dangerous world. She commonly projected her feelings onto other family members and neighbors, was a noted hypochondriac, and dealt with her anger consistently in passive-aggressive ways. The children knew not to ever confront her version of reality directly, or she would withdraw for days at a time, after which she always had a new illness "because of the stress of this family." Prior to her husband's death she had fared considerably better because she had managed to marry a nurturer who doted on her with tremendous amounts of warmth and affection. As the children perceived it, he was the "giver" and she was the "receiver" throughout their lives. Juan never complained, but the children could see his frustration at her constant manipulation of circumstances to ensure that her desires were met. After his death, Maria obviously was bereft of her primary caretaker and often behaved like a lost child.

Compensation for lost ego strength

Psychodynamic psychologists describe the devastating impact on the self of the many age-correlated experiences such as loss of physical strength, cognitive abilities, and energy (Gutmann, 1992). Diminished capacity and energy are postulated to undermine self-esteem, forcing the person to find restitution for the loss. If the environment is insufficient to maintain the ego functions, a frail older adult may use compensatory mechanisms that appear pathological, such as recounting past glories or blaming others for lost items. A supportive environment, however, can make it possible for even very frail, depleted older persons to maintain a coherent, strong sense of self. Indeed, one purpose of supportive therapy and paraprofessional interventions (e.g., friendly visitors) could be conceptualized as providing external support for a fragile ego.

After her husband's death, Maria's environment clearly lacked sufficient structure and care-taking to maintain her highest possible level of functioning. Her constant blaming of the daughters for not doing enough was insufficient to make her feel better, but protected her from the reality that a perfect caretaker was simply unavailable. If she could just keep at them, the daughters could take care of her well enough, she was sure.

Inability to preserve or build coherent narrative

Later life is the period in which each individual is particularly challenged to integrate a meaningful ending to his or her life narrative that is also internally consistent with the entire story (Cohler, 1993). Erikson (1963) theorized that the awareness of the pending ending of one's own life prompts a life review in which past choices are examined. Cohler suggests that awareness of one's own death prompts the need to write an ending to one's life story that is coherent with the previous chapters.

> . . . the so-called wisdom achieved in later life consists of the ability to maintain a coherent narrative of the course of life in which the presently remembered past, experienced present, and anticipated future are understood as problems to be studied rather than outcomes to be assumed. The question is not whether older adults are able to realize wisdom but rather how these older adults are able to continue to experience a sense of coherence while confronting factors associated with the loss of personal integrity, as well as feelings of fragmentation and disruption of the life story across the course of their lives. (Cohler, 1993, pp. 119–20)

Cohler further postulates that the life constructs from earlier adulthood may not be adequate to integrate the experiences and expectations of later life into the personal narrative, necessitating a true developmental shift. For example, when an ambitious, demanding woman whose retirement propelled her into volunteer leadership chose to back out of those responsibilities in order to care for her infirm husband, she slipped into a depression. Claiming that she was perfectly satisfied with a life centered around providing her care, she struggled to integrate the loss of meaning that was previously gleaned from her leadership experiences. When asked to consider the sources of meaning in her life, she readily acknowledged that her relationship with her husband was of utmost importance, but that her community service was also a core part of her identity. Her psychotherapist encouraged her to choose one or two community roles that could keep her active in the outside world but with minimal interference with her care-taking commitment. She observed that her advancing age was inevitably going to limit her community activities, but that it felt better to ease out rather than terminating abruptly. In this way, the meaning she gained from service was retained in her life, both in the familiar mechanism of community service and the less familiar role of personal caretaker for her husband. The developmental shift that occurred for her was observed in her openness to a new role within the agencies she served in the communities. Although previously presuming she had to be a leader, she was able to embrace the idea of "passing the mantle" of primary responsibility to the next generation while retaining a meaningful role of service.

If a developmental shift cannot be made in a way that maintains coherence within the narrative, the individual is vulnerable to psychopathology characteristic of personal fragmentation that may become evident in psychotic thought styles, depression, or debilitating anxiety. Such fragmentation occurs when the ego cannot maintain coherence of self and of story. In Erikson's terms, the ego lacks integrity when faced with the termination of life that one considers inadequately lived.

Maria's adolescence and young adulthood were a Cinderella story. Raised doing the hard labor of women in a poor family, Maria was rescued by Prince Charming, who was the only person who truly recognized her for the princess that she really was. Unfortunately, he took her to a blue-collar subsistence in a small town rather than a true castle, a failing for which she never quite forgave him. The world could never know just what she could have become if the circumstances had been right, and now it never would. Not only is it hard to be an aging princess, but her prince is gone. No one else treats her like she deserves; if she doesn't demand good work, they will all do just the minimum. Maria sees herself as stuck in a bad fairytale that won't force the wicked stepsisters to recognize the true beauty of a princess. The narratives of old age that describe contentment from a life lived well and making peace with lost opportunities and the limited accomplishments of a human life are a foreign language to Maria.

Assessment

Psychodynamic theorists and clinicians focus assessment on internal personality structures: beliefs, narratives, emotional responses, values, meanings, and the expressions of internal structures in behavior patterns. The personality constructs are inferred primarily from the client's ways of talking about his or her life, and the interaction with the therapist that projects the client's assumptions about how the world works (and should work) onto the therapist.

A developmental history of the individual life cycle is a key starting point, including developmental stages, tasks, and themes (Nemiroff & Colarusso, 1990). Early childhood experiences hold obvious importance within this model, which presumes that early development constrains later developmental styles. Of particular importance are the critical early events or traumas, and the attachment relationships within which all early experiences were processed. The process of obtaining a developmental history may, itself, stimulate a life review process that focuses a client on missed opportunities, poor choices, and unfulfilled meaning. Thus the process of gathering information about the client's background also offers insight into the client's capacity to construct a life review with appropriately complex emotions and reflections into a coherent life story or narrative.

The assessment process also focuses on the reasons for which treatment was sought. King (1980) suggests the following list of common reasons for older adults to seek treatment: 1) fear of loss of sexual potency, 2) fear of loss of effectiveness in work, 3) worries about retirement, 4) anxieties regarding marriage relationship following the launching of children, 5) awareness of aging, illness, and dependency, 6) a growing awareness of the inevitability of death. To date, no evidence exists to claim that reasons for seeking treatment are different for young and old. However, the different life contexts make it likely that the salience of life themes will vary across the life–span.

Projective testing techniques are often used by psychodynamic therapists as a method of assessing unconscious processes. Projective techniques present ambiguous stimuli (e.g., pictures, inkblots) to which respondents must structure their responses according to the basic organizing characteristics of their personalities: defense, distortions, ego strengths, etc. Often, the stimuli are standardized so responses can be compared against normative data once response styles have been collected. Complex scoring systems have been developed for some projective devices (e.g., the Exner system for scoring the Rorschach; Exner, 1974,1978), although other tests such as the "Draw-a-Person Test" are evaluated solely intuitively, making use of clinical guidelines (e.g. Groth-Marnat, 1984). The projective assessment of aging method (Starr et al., 1979) is one test that is available specifically to elicit responses regarding aging. Picture cards show older adults engaged in activities and interactions typical of everyday life (an example is shown in figure 3.2). No norms or structured scoring system are available for this test, however. Projective tests continue to be used for a variety of clinical and research purposes, although their use is controversial (Hayslip & Lowman, 1986).

Another focus of assessment is the capacity for insight. Psychodynamic treatments rely upon the patient's insight into his or her own personality in order to make conscious the structures and processes that influence behaviors

Figure 3.2 A sample projective picture stimulus
Source: Starr et al., 1979.

and self-perception. Thus capacity for insight is a key determinant of the focus and style of therapeutic intervention. Clients with limited capacity for insight are more likely to be engaged in supportive therapy than insight-oriented therapy that is targeted at personality change. Essentially, capacity for insight is inversely related to the maturity of defenses, such that the least mature defenses afford the least capacity for insight and indicate that therapy will require more support and, likely, longer therapy to achieve development.

In addition to identifying pathology and personality weaknesses, psychodynamic therapists want to evaluate strengths. Kivnick (1993) developed an interview schedule for eliciting information specifically about life strengths. Drawing on her interview experience with elderly participants in the longitudinal study reported by Erikson et al. (1986), she designed this instrument to reflect the language and themes relevant to the psychological work typical of old age. The interview is devised to solicit primarily positive aspects of development that are presumed to have emerged within the Eriksonian stages of development. Excerpts from the instrument are presented in table 3.4. Information about positive aspects of the personality are used to

Table 3.4 Excerpts from the life strengths interview guide

Introduction
What is it about your life:
　. . . that is most worth living for?
　. . . that makes you feel most alive?

Hope and faith (trust & mistrust)
What is it in your life that gives you hope?
How do moral beliefs and values fit into your life?

Willfulness, independence, and control (autonomy & shame/doubt)
What parts of your life is it most important that *you* stay in charge of?
What kinds of control are easier to give up, as long as you remain in charge of
　what's really important?

Care and productivity (generativity & self-absorption)
Whom or what do you especially care about?
How do you show your caring?
Who is there that you lean on, these days? Who leans on you?

Source: Kivnick, 1993.

affirm ego strength and as resources for developmental work on less well developed aspects of personality.

Treatment

The goal of psychodynamic treatment with older adults is either 1) to achieve insight, 2) to modify personality structure, or 3) to develop more mature defense mechanisms (Newton et al., 1986). An alternative psychodynamic treatment, supportive psychotherapy, is considered appropriate when the capacity for insight that is necessary to produce personality change is limited due to personality disorder or cognitive impairment. Generally, older adults are engaged in therapeutic processes very similar to those used in psychoanalytic and psychodynamic work with younger adults.

Supportive therapy

As described above, the compensatory structures that may have defended the adult against primary anxiety throughout most of adulthood may not provide adequate protection against the intense vulnerabilities of later life. Two interventions can help reinstate some protection. The therapist can provide support to the ego by offering reassurance, comfort, and affirmation. Also, the environment can be structured to provide more external supports for daily functioning, thus reducing visible evidence of the ego's weakened state. For example, memory aids or simplified environmental demands such as single-floor living reduce the constant awareness that the individual is impaired. For example, supportive therapy might be used with personality disordered older adults or those with more primitive defense mechanisms that are too well defended for insight, but whose defenses are insufficient to compensate for the internal or external assault on the ego. Specifically, supportive therapy would be used when a person with early stage cognitive impairment or a broken hip renders him or her unable to maintain a sense of self as competent and independent. In essence, when environmental enrichment is not possible, or is insufficient to rebuild the ego functions, supportive psychotherapy may be all that is appropriate.

Given the intensity with which ego functioning can be undermined by the losses of later life, there are occasions when it is most appropriate to begin with supportive therapy and progress to insight-oriented therapy only when it is evident that the ego has regained sufficient strength to tolerate depth work (Gutmann, 1992). Once the ego is shored up sufficiently to reinstate the compensatory structures or the environment is enriched to provide more external support for basic ego functioning, the therapy can either terminate or transition from a focus on support to a focus on work on development.

Maria Jiminez would likely be considered an appropriate candidate for supportive psychotherapy. Presumably, her capacity for insight is quite limited. She has used immature defense mechanisms her entire life, and is only now in exceptional distress because the environment no longer supports her sufficiently. As she becomes more physically dependent on others, she will probably become more depressed unless given sufficient support. Supportive therapy may focus on helping her adjust to being an unrecognized princess in a foreign land. Given enough nurturance from the therapist, Maria's ego strength may be sufficient to engage in less destructive interpersonal relationships. For example, although the therapist's nurturance may be perceived as her due, Maria may be sufficiently gratified that she reduces her verbal abuse to her daughters.

Psychotherapy process

As with younger adults, the patient–therapist relationship is a primary tool for treatment. In the traditional psychoanalytic model, therapy consists of *working through* resistance to improving. The resistance is believed to protect the individual from conscious awareness of the powerful unconscious processes that are so anxiety provoking. The process of working through the resistance is believed to require a long-term commitment to talk therapy in which the client gains awareness of how he or she is repeating earlier conflicts in the relationship with the therapist. *Transference* is the term applied to the projected internal conflicts that the client puts onto the therapist.

Psychodynamic therapists conceptualize *transference* as the process by which a client projects onto the therapist characteristics of significant persons (e.g., parents) whose interactions with the client shaped his or her basic beliefs about human beings and interactions (Butler & Strupp, 1991). These projections are based not on the real interactions of client and therapist, but on projected assumptions about how the relationship functions. Interpersonal therapists also emphasize that transference projections significantly shape the interaction because of their profound impact on the therapist. In other words, therapists respond to transference projections in ways that further maintain the client's framework because the client's projections pull for specific, familiar responses from others. Thus the interpersonal school puts more emphasis on the circular, interactional nature of the exchange between therapist and client than the traditional psychoanalytic model, which presumes that the client's behaviors are responding almost solely to internal events (Butler & Strupp, 1991).

Application of these models to therapy with older adults focuses on work with the inner dynamics as well as the interpersonal components. By late life, most adults are presumed to have created ways to adapt to the scars, limitations, and strengths of their personality structures. Crises of later life, however, can disrupt those familiar and more or less effective modes of functioning. For example, positively distorted views of the self's capacity may protect the ego from its terror of helplessness until the losses of advanced old age strip away the defenses, leaving the ego vulnerable to terrifying levels of anxiety.

In particular, Newton et al. (1986) acknowledge the potency of the therapeutic relationship for persons who live isolated, lonely lives. Such persons experience tremendous validation of the self merely from interaction with an empathic, caring figure. For most older clients, however, the relationship is experienced through the transference and the therapy process. Transference processes can be particularly complex, because a lifetime of powerful relationship experiences is available for projection onto the therapist of an older client. The therapist may be responded to as if he or she were a lover of 40 years ago, a parent, a child, a grandchild, or a significant mentor. The therapist is encouraged to identify the patient's "secret inner age" that holds the key to the transference projection (Berezin, 1972). This age is inferred from the subtler aspects of the interaction between therapist and client that demonstrate the projection.

Countertransference refers to the therapist's process of projecting onto the client his or her own perceptions that are not based on the real interaction or person, but on the therapist's own conceptual and emotional framework that derives from past experience with significant persons. Counter-transferences are particularly complex in work with older adults because therapists are generally younger than their elderly patients and thus have not personally experienced either the clients' historical period or the developmental stages (Knight, 1996). Previous developmental experiences may also be acted out in the therapy relationship (Grotjahn, 1955), as the therapist must deal with his or her own anxieties about aging, death, or limits to narcissistic power over one's own body (Newton et al., 1986).

The psychotherapy process uses a variety of techniques to prompt insight into the developmental processes described above. Life review or reminiscence is commonly used to assist the patient's integration of life experiences into a coherent narrative. By engaging in multiple life review processes over a period of many years, the client may rewrite his or her story several times during the course of psychological work. Traditional strategies such as interpretation of dreams and exploration of ambivalence are also used with older adults.

Confirmation of the patient's strengths in the face of mounting deficits is an important role for therapists working with frail older persons within the psychodynamic framework (Newton et al., 1986; Gutmann, 1986). The battered ego may need to be supported by a therapist who can hold up a mirror to the patient's life so it is easier to see the full array of strengths and resources that have sustained the person throughout the life-span. The therapist helps regain perspective on the entire life as it was lived, a process that gives courage to a fragile ego whose capacities have diminished. At times, therapists need to encourage particularly depleted clients to engage in self-enhancing behaviors (e.g., telling stories to their family about past accomplishments) just to regain some semblance of experienced strength.

Critique and Summary

Psychodynamic theories of personality have been examined primarily in the context of qualitative research and clinical case studies. Two major criticisms of the psychodynamic approach to personality continue to be raised: 1) the theory does not lend itself readily to empirical test, and 2) the distinctions among the many psychodynamic theories are often unclear. Many of the core constructs of psychodynamic theories have been difficult to test empirically because they relate to unconscious processes. Recent efforts to demonstrate that cognitive processes operate outside of conscious awareness to manage anxiety lend increasing support to key aspects of the theory, however (e.g., Greenberg et al., 1994). The fact that the theory has evolved over the decades adds to its complexity and to the difficulty of nailing down testable hypotheses.

Despite the paucity of empirical research regarding the basic propositions in the theory, a growing body of therapy outcome studies show its effectiveness, including effectiveness with older adults. Controlled outcome studies demonstrate similar efficacy rates for brief psychodynamic psychotherapy with older adults, as have been shown for cognitive-behavioral therapies (Gallagher-Thompson, Hanley-Peterson, & Thompson, 1990; Thompson, Gallagher, & Breckenridge, 1987) or pharmacotherapy (Sloane et al., 1985). Older adults respond as well as mid-life adults to brief psychodynamic treatment (Reynolds, Frank, Kupfer et al., 1996). Traditional psychoanalytic methods have not been tested in rigorous clinical trials of this type, although clinical reports are provided in the literature of successful treatment of older adults (see review of early psychoanalytic work by Rechtschaffen, 1959).

In summary, the psychodynamic model can have useful applications across the life-span. By alerting the therapist to the continuing impact of early events, current losses, and the therapeutic relationship, the framework provides a rich foundation for conceptualizing human behavior. The model is weak in testability, although developmental, social, and personality psychologists have begun to derive testable hypotheses. Given the emphasis on unconscious processes, psychodynamic therapists tend not to rely on self-report assessment tools. Rather, the therapist's assessment of the patient is ongoing as behavior within the therapeutic context is interpreted within the framework (e.g., transference and resistance). Treatment studies demonstrate efficacy for short-term psychodynamic psychotherapies, but no controlled outcome studies have been done on traditional psychoanalysis. This model attempts to explain the variability in response to aging among older adults by examining personality characteristics and strategies for handling loss. Short-term psychodynamic psychotherapies show similar rates of effectiveness with older adults as other therapies.

4

Behavioral Model

The nursing home staff are very annoyed at Anna Tweed because she constantly stands at the nurses' station asking them questions. Even if they answer the questions, she won't go away. When the staff try to involve her in something else, she returns to the nurses' station within a few minutes. Nurses and CNAs complain that they get headaches from trying to write their notes or answer phones while she is constantly talking. Staff understand that she has a severe memory problem but they don't know how to get her to stop asking the repeated questions.

Joanna Jenkins came to the mental health clinic because her daughter insisted that she do so. Her daughter is worried and frustrated that her mother is so lethargic and uninterested in life. Joanna doesn't believe you can do anything for her because nothing in particular is wrong with her. She is just old, and she is waiting to die.

Introduction to the Model

As its title suggests, the behavioral model focuses attention on *behavior* rather than unconscious motives or biological factors (Kazdin, 1975). Behaviors are believed to be under the direct control of environmental events and cues, which influence the acquisition, performance rate, and termination of specific behaviors according to principles of learning theory. The focus is primarily on observable behaviors, although some private events (e.g., thoughts and feelings) are considered to be equally under the influence of learning principles and thus modifiable by behavioral techniques.

The behavioral model emphasizes the benefits of empirical scientific research, and organizes its assessments and interventions accordingly. Behavioral mental health providers draw heavily from the empirical literature that reports on the efficacy of interventions whose impact has been evaluated according to rigorous scientific criteria (i.e., with research designs that control for alternative explanations). Training in single-subject (Hersen & Barlow, 1976) as well as group designs is considered imperative for effective design and evaluation of behavioral interventions.

The literature on behavioral interventions with elderly persons covers a wide range of behaviors, including self-care, social interaction and participation, memory and language, health care, disruptive behaviors, depression, anxiety, and sexual disorders (Gallagher-Thompson & Thompson, 1996; Wisocki, 1991; Zeiss & Steffen, 1996). Much of the published literature consists of single case designs of various degrees of methodological rigor, although an increasing number of rigorous single-subject and group comparison designs have been used. The empirical results are clear: many behaviors previously believed to be a normal product of aging have been demonstrated to be modifiable by changes in the environmental context. Perhaps most dramatic are the effects of behavior modification programs in institutional settings with particularly low functioning ill elderly persons. Unfortunately, generalization across time and setting often has not been evaluated or could not be demonstrated, thus limiting the practical utility of the interventions in many facilities with limited staffing to maintain the time intensive programs. Furthermore, the challenges of integrating behavioral interventions into real world settings is daunting because of the intensity of time required to assess and respond to behavior, and to evaluate outcomes.

Assessment and intervention generally focus on observable variables – what people do. Most behaviorists refer to themselves as cognitive-behaviorists because they recognize the important role of cognition in mediating the relationship between environment and behavior. The behavioral focus on observable characteristics can be contrasted with other models whose domain of work is motives, drives, traits, or unconscious processes that are inferred from patient behavior but cannot be observed directly.

Behaviorists observe human behavior in context because behavior is believed to be an adaptive response to help the organism meet its needs in a particular environment. The principles used by behaviorists to describe human behavior link the behavior to the information available to the organism in the environment, especially information contiguous in time with the behavior. Antecedents refer to the information available to the organism immediately prior to the target behavior, and consequences refer to the information available immediately following the behavior.

Traditional learning theory offers two theories to explain the acquisition and maintenance of human behavior: classical and operant conditioning. Classical conditioning occurs when a previously neutral stimulus elicits a response that is reflexive or automatic in the presence of a natural stimulus. Drawing from his famous experiments in which dogs learned to salivate to the sound of a bell that immediately preceded the presentation of their food, Pavlov created labels for the natural and conditioned stimuli. The reflexive or automatic response to a natural (Unconditioned) stimulus was called an Unconditioned Response. Classical conditioning occurs when the Unconditioned Stimulus (UCS) is paired with a previously neutral stimulus (now the Conditioned Stimulus; CS) to produce the target response (e.g., salivating) without the UCS ever being presented. When Pavlov's dogs salivated to the sound of the bell (CS) alone, the target response was called a Conditioned Response (CR). Classical conditioning theory explains behavior that occurs in the presence of an apparently neutral stimulus by demonstrating that the behavior is under the control of the antecedent conditions.

Operant learning theory maintains that the acquisition and performance of behavior is controlled by the consequences of behaviors (Skinner, 1953). The principle of reinforcement states that behaviors will increase in frequency if they are followed closely in time by positive events. The positively experienced event is called a reinforcer if it increases the rate of behavior. Negatively experienced events that decrease the rate of behavior are called punishers. Elderly nursing-home residents have learned to increase the rate of self-care behaviors when staff attention or other positive consequences are contingent on the performance of the targeted behaviors (see review by Wisocki, 1991).

As the behavioral theories evolved, it became clear that the complexity of the brain/behavior relationships required more explanatory variables than were provided by classical and operant learning theories. Several different cognitive-behavioral approaches emerged to describe how various cognitive processes influenced the acquisition and performance of behaviors (e.g., expectancies, internalized rules, performance standards, self-instruction, and imagery) (Bandura, 1977; Mahoney, 1974).

Direct application of cognitive-behavioral principles to mental health problems has been made by cognitive therapy theorists, including Aaron Beck and his colleagues, who focus on the role of thought distortion in the production of affective disorders such as depression and anxiety (Beck, Emery, & Greenberg, 1985; Beck, Rush et al., 1979). These theorists and clinicians identified a specific set of inaccurate core world-view assumptions and related thought distortions that produce and maintain mental disorders. Beck and others developed interventions that restructure cognition patterns to produce more adaptive and realistic appraisals of self, the world, and the future than is typical of depressed persons' ways of thinking.

Mental Health

How does this model define "mental health"? Technically, it does not offer a definition. Behaviorists focus on adaptation, the capacity to meet one's own needs effectively within the environment, a preferred alternative to the term "mentally healthy." Behaviors that meet an individual's physical, social, and emotional needs within the particular relevant environment are considered adaptive. Persons who cannot meet their needs effectively are viewed as having problems in living that occur because of one of the following:

1 they have learned maladaptive behavior or frameworks;
2 they failed to learn effective or appropriate behavior or frameworks because of a poor learning environment;
3 they are responding to the wrong environmental contingencies or are self-regulating poorly.

Cognitive-behaviorists must balance the individual's subjective sense of distress with some objective judgment about adaptability to the immediate environment. Distress is experienced when an individual is unable to meet his or her own goals, including internalized goals in the form of standards or expectations. For example, a common problem for depressed persons is negative self-evaluation that occurs when a perfectionistic standard cannot be met. Some goals exist only at a cognitive level. In summary, cognitive-behaviorists use adaptation and subjective distress to measure well-being.

The two cases presented at the beginning of this chapter show the value of using multiple criteria for defining disorder. Anna Tweed is not particularly distressed, but her behavior is not adaptive in that environment. Or is it? Her constant questioning may gain her additional staff attention, interpersonal interaction, and cognitive stimulation that may be lacking elsewhere in the nursing home. Her behavior is disruptive for staff more than for her. Of course, the ethics of intervening with an individual's behavior for the good of the institution must be examined carefully. Joanna Jenkins is distressed but does not seek help because she does not believe there is help. Her behavior is also not adaptive because she is no longer attempting to meet her own social needs due to lethargy.

Mental Health in Older Adults

The definition of mental health for older persons would be the same as for any other population – adaptation to the environment such that needs can be

met. However, changes with age may occur in the array of available antecedents and consequences, the contingent relationships among antecedents-
behaviors-consequences, and the needs of the individual. In the young-old
years (60s and early 70s), adults are likely to live within environments and
contingency patterns similar to those of middle adulthood. With advanced
age, physical impairments may limit mobility, dull sensation, and force
changes in the environments within which older adults live and meet their
needs.

Changes in the living environment may simply alter which antecedents
and consequences are available, or they may increase or decrease the number
or frequency of availability of the contingencies. For example, moving from
one's suburban home to a senior high-rise apartment complex may significantly enrich the array of social stimuli, or may simply change which social
relationships are available while holding steady the amount and reinforcement value of the relationships. On the other hand, the presence of 100 other
residents of a high rise may not compensate for the loss of access to close
friends in the former neighborhood.

Physical illnesses characteristic of old age are likely to restrict the range of
activities in which frail old persons can engage. Limited mobility, restricted
vision and hearing, or cognitive impairment may alter the older adult's ability
to respond to environmental contingencies. Later life also brings freedom
from some demanding roles characteristic of young and mid-life adulthood.
That freedom may enhance elderly persons' responsiveness to environmental
stimuli might be the case for a recent retiree whose freedom from work
structures allows him or her to be much more socially responsive to neighbors and friends.

Changes in the contingency patterns can also occur. Reinforcement contingencies may be changed such that a different set of behaviors is required
to obtain the same environmental response. For example, attention reinforcers that were readily available to a highly attractive young woman may
continue to be available after her aging appearance fails to meet cultural
standards only *if* she learns other behaviors that are deemed attractive.

Baltes and Baltes (1990a) suggest that older adults show high rates of
adaptability or *behavioral plasticity*. Recall that early behavioral research demonstrated that behaviors commonly thought to be typical of old age were
actually under the control of environmental contingencies. Baltes and Baltes
go a step further to argue that older adults naturally modify their behavior in
predictable ways to adapt to changing capabilities and changing environments, a process reflecting the role of adaptability in mental health. Specifically, they suggest that older adults draw upon their areas of competence to
compensate for areas in which they have lost function or in which the

environment is more impoverished. The process of adaptation involves "selective optimization with compensation." However, one special instance of behavior that requires a close examination of our assumptions about the value of adaptability is the case of dependent behavior, especially that found in long-term care institutions.

Nursing-home life presents a serious challenge to the adaptability and well-being of some older adults (Smyer, Cohn, & Brannon, 1988). Institutions such as nursing homes provide very few natural reinforcers because the organization regiments so many aspects of daily life, including bathing, dressing, sleep schedules, and food schedules and selection; it may even structure social interaction (Goffman, 1961). Residents of nursing homes are physically very frail and often cognitively impaired, which limits further the sources of pleasure available to them and their capacity to respond to environmental contingencies. The rates of mental disorders such as depression are particularly high in nursing homes, as might be predicted. In addition to the frailty produced by illnesses, however, many nursing-home residents show high rates of what has been deemed *excess disability*, or dependency.

In a series of studies in the past two decades, Margret Baltes and her colleagues in the United States and Germany have demonstrated that many dependent behaviors, even in nursing homes, are under the control of environmental contingencies. Thus behaviors that appear to be dysfunctional (e.g., need for assistance with basic self-care when physical capacity is intact) may actually be responsive to the environment, even though they fail to bring personal pleasure or satisfaction to the individual. Initially, Baltes and her colleagues showed that operant conditioning could increase independent behaviors such as self-feeding, self-dressing, and other self-care activities (Baltes & Barton, 1979). In an ambitious research program, they then demonstrated that dependent behavior was consistently reinforced with social interaction with staff (Baltes, 1988). In contrast, independent behaviors initiated little or no social interaction. From these patterns they infer that dependency behavior can bring gains as well as losses (Horgas et al., 1996).

So, is dependent behavior adaptive? Under what conditions would one attempt to increase independence if an individual is accruing social gains with dependent behavior? Horgas et al. (1996) recommend examining whether the dependent behavior is a problem (and if so, for whom), in addition to investigating its antecedents and consequences. Dependency that is self-selected for a specific goal may be considered adaptive, whereas dependency that exists primarily because of the power of what they refer to as the *dependency-script* of staff selectively reinforcing dependent behavior will be less likely to be seen as adaptive. Dependent behavior has been used as an illustration of the application of behavior theory to adaptation because it is behavior that appears to be maladaptive to an extent that might in another theoretical model be labeled mental disorder. Yet it has been demonstrated to be functionally adaptive in the impoverished environments of a nursing home, and to be reversible if the environmental contingencies have shifted.

Assessment

Look back at the case scenarios presented at the beginning of the chapter. Consider yourself a consultant to these two women. What kind of assessment needs to be done in order to design the best intervention to help Anna Tweed and Joanna Jenkins? Take a moment to review the principles we have presented and develop a conceptualization and hypothesis for the two cases. Your framework for the problem will, of course, determine where you begin with assessment. In both cases you will obviously need considerably more information than was given initially. What do you need to know, and how will you gather the information (e.g., from whom, in what format)?

Purposes of assessment

Behavioral assessment is used exclusively to assist with the design and evaluation of interventions. Assessment for the purpose of a richer understanding of the client, or even to formulate an accurate diagnosis, is considered frivolous unless it directly benefits the intervention. Although behaviorists do not necessarily ascribe to the medical model of diagnosis on which the DSM-IV is based, they support the use of diagnostic categories if they are used for scientific purposes of producing homogeneous client groups in which to test interventions.

The primary focus of assessment is on behavior patterns, identifying the cognitive and environmental variables that mediate behavior. Assessment data serve as the basis for identifying the appropriate strategies for intervention (e.g., whether cognitive techniques would be useful) as the baseline against which progress will be measured and the rate and locus of progress. Assessments are used as feedback for the therapist and the client regarding the impact of particular interventions.

Principles of behavioral assessment

Behaviorally oriented mental health providers follow general practice guidelines for older adults by initially examining the medical data available to see if the problem could be caused by disease or medication. For example, a behavioral therapist would recognize that Joanna Jenkins's scenario matches the general profile of a depressed person. However, the description is also consistent with a treatable physical illness (including medication-induced delirium) or dementia. If Joanna Jenkins has not had a thorough medical physical examination to rule out potentially reversible medical causes of the symptom profile, that is the first order of business. Only after physical causes of the symptoms have been ruled out would a strictly behavioral approach to assessment and intervention be appropriate. If Joanna has a chronic medical condition that is not reversible and it is unclear whether the symptoms are due to her illness or her response to the illness, behavioral interventions may be the primary focus of intervention. However, for the sake of simplicity, let us presume that an appropriate medical evaluation has been completed, and Ms Jenkins is physically healthy and on no medications that could produce this behavior profile.

With the strong commitment to gathering empirical data regarding behavior, a behaviorally oriented mental health provider would focus assessment on specific problem behaviors. If staff or family members have framed the problem as "she's manipulative" or "her life has no purpose," the behaviorist would ask questions about specific behaviors until the exact behaviors that are problematic are defined in terms that render them directly observable. Exactly what does Joanna do all day? How is this different from one or five years ago? How much distress does she experience? What self-care behaviors does she do for herself? In the Anna Tweed scenario, exactly when and for how long does Anna Tweed stand at the nurses' station? How many questions does she ask? What is the content of her questions? Careful questioning of the exact behavior patterns observed by staff will give a mental health consultant enough information to form hypotheses about the reinforcement contingencies.

Behavioral assessment also focuses on the context of the problem behavior. Exactly when and under what conditions does she leave the desk? What is the exact context when she asks questions (e.g., who is present; are others also talking or does she wait for a break in conversation)? What time of day does the questioning intensify and reduce? The behavioral assessment will show the contextual variables that serve as reinforcers and punishers (increasing or decreasing the frequency of specific behaviors).

Behaviorists also want to know when the problem behavior is not present. When does Anna Tweed leave the nurses' station? Are there ever occasions when she maintains attention focused on something other than the nurses' station? It is important to know if alternative behaviors exist within the client's behavioral repertoire but are not being used, or if the client has no alternative behaviors. How sensitive is she to social cues? She may have appropriate behaviors, but they are not being controlled by appropriate cues and contingencies. In the case of Joanna Jenkins, one might ask when she shows the most animation and energy. Are there days or hours when she feels better than other times?

The process of obtaining a behavioral assessment often requires several methods of data collection. Self-reports of distress may be obtained from the clients and the involved care providers. For example, Anna Tweed may be asked about the goal of her questioning behavior. Likely, Anna is experiencing a dementia that has severely impaired her memory so she is unaware of the frequency of her questions. However, it is important to check with the client because her behavior may be explicitly goal directed. In this case, Anna Tweed is experiencing a dementia, and her questioning behavior appears to be a consequence of severe memory impairment.

In an effort to measure the client's distress as well as her adaptability, Joanna Jenkins may complete a self-report depression scale. This scale may help with the diagnostic evaluation, and can serve as a baseline against which treatment progress can be evaluated. Several self-report inventories on depression are described in chapter 8. Ms Jenkins's responses to a popular one, the Geriatric Depression Scale (GDS; Yesavage et al., 1983), are shown in table 4.1.

Take a moment to look at the specific symptom description you get from this instrument. Now look back at the initial description of Ms Jenkins's problem in the first lines of this chapter. Based on the GDS data, you know that she is experiencing boredom and a sense of emptiness. She reports having trouble with concentration and worries that disturb her. She also reports feeling worthless. Clinical interview would be needed to elicit further details about each symptom. For example, what kind of worry? How much difficulty with concentration? The brief self-report symptom inventories are used by behaviorists throughout the intervention to track progress in the patient's level of distress. A graph like that shown in figure 4.1 would provide evidence of the effectiveness of an intervention. More objective data may be requested to clarify the actual frequency and context of the problem behavior. Joanna Jenkins may report her activities and mood in a mood and behavior log.

The staff at the nursing home may be asked to keep a record of the frequency of Anna Tweed's questions asked in order to identify variations in the frequency pattern. A behavioral observer may collect descriptive data regarding the frequency, content, and context of the questions over the course of a day. A typical behavior recording chart of a scenario like Anna Tweed's is shown in table 4.2.

Table 4.1 Geriatric depression scale for Joanna Jenkins

		Yes	No
1. Are you basically satisfied with your life?	N	0	1
2. Have you dropped many of your activities and interests?	Y	1	0
3. Do you feel your life is empty?	Y	1	0
4. Do you get bored often?	Y	1	0
5. Are you hopeful about the future?	N	0	1
6. Are you bothered by thoughts you can't get out of your head?	N	1	0
7. Are you in good spirits most of the time?	N	0	1
8. Are you afraid that something bad is going to happen to you?	N	1	0
9. Do you feel happy most of the time?	N	0	1
10. Do you often feel helpless?	N	1	0
11. Do you often get restless and fidgety?	Y	1	0
12. Do you prefer to stay at home, rather than going out and doing new things?	Y	1	0
13. Do you frequently worry about the future?	Y	1	0
14. Do you feel you have more problems with memory than most?	N	1	0
15. Do you think it is wonderful to be alive now?	N	0	1
16. Do you often feel downhearted and blue?	N	1	0
17. Do you feel pretty worthless the way you are now?	Y	1	0
18. Do you worry a lot about the past?	N	1	0
19. Do you find life very exciting?	N	0	1
20. Is it hard for you to get started on new projects?	Y	1	0
21. Do you feel full of energy?	N	0	1
22. Do you feel that your situation is hopeless?	N	1	0
23. Do you think that most people are better off than you are now?	N	1	0
24. Do you frequently get upset about little things?	Y	1	0
25. Do you frequently feel like crying?	N	1	0
26. Do you have trouble concentrating?	Y	1	0
27. Do you enjoy getting up in the morning?	N	0	1
28. Do you prefer to avoid social gatherings?	Y	1	0
29. Is it easy for you to make decisions?	N	0	1
30. Is your mind as clear as it used to be?	N	0	1
		21	

Source: Yesavage et al., 1983.

You will note that there is a pattern evident in this record of behavior. Ms Tweed's question-asking is more intense when more persons are present. When the staff leave the nursing station, so does Ms Tweed. What hypothesis might you form about the reinforcement contingencies for Ms Tweed's

Table 4.2 Record of questioning behavior by Anna Tweed

Date	Time start	Time end	Who present?	Content of questions	How questioning ended?	Staff init.
3/16	0830	0840	Nurse CNA Activ. Dir.	When is lunch	Activ. Dir. took to room	
	0915	0930	Nurse CNA	What to do next	Nurse took to day room	
	1110	1145	Nurse, QA Staff	When is lunch	CNA took to lunch	
	1430	1450	Nurse, SW, CNA	Where is her daughter	Activ. Dir. took to activity	
	1500	1530	2 Nurses	Where is her daughter	CNA took to activity	
	1600	1620	Nurse, family member	When is dinner	CNA took to dinner	
	1730	1740	CNA	Where is daughter	Volunteer took to day room	
	1820	1845	Nurse, family	What happened to sweater?	Nurse took to room	
3/17	0840	0850	Nurse CNA	When is lunch	CNA took to bath	
	0955	1005	Nurse Activ. Dir.	What to do next	Activ. Dir. took to Activity	
	1050	1100	Nurse, Activ. Aide	When is lunch	CNA took to lunch	
	1320	1330	Nurse CNA	What to do next	CNA took to room–TV	
	1610	1625	Nurse	Where is daughter	Activ. Aid took to hairdresser	
	1730	1745	Nurse, Family Member	Where is daughter	CNA – TV in Day room	
	1930	1950	Nurse	Needs Pill	Nurse took to room	

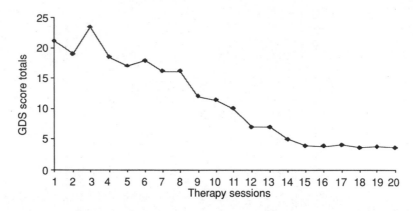

Figure 4.1   Geriatric depression scale scores for Joanna Jenkins

question-asking behavior? As noted above, the recording of specific details is what made a pattern evident. Staff might have stated, "she's there all of the time," a fact that matches their experience while they are at the nurses' station, but was not the whole picture.

The role of assessment in designing an intervention also is illustrated in the treatment of Joanna Jenkins. As described in more detail in Chapter 8, the behavioral model for treating depression postulates that depression is caused and maintained by a deficiency in the amount of response-contingent positive reinforcement. The deficiency may be caused by several factors, the most common of which are a low rate of engagement in pleasant activities, high levels of anxiety that interfere with actually experiencing the pleasantness, and high rates of unpleasant activities. Therapists begin detailed assessment with daily mood monitoring. Depressed clients tend to believe that they always feel bad, and that nothing ever happens to make them feel good. They do not believe the depression is under their control, or even the control of environmental factors (e.g., pleasant events). Daily mood monitoring demonstrates to the client that, although their mood may never be great, it does indeed fluctuate in ways that reflect that some days are better than others, or, as the depressed client would report, some days are worse than others. Figure 4.2 shows Ms Jenkins's first week of mood monitoring. Typical of persons who are depressed, she reports that her mood fluctuates along the lower end of the mood scale. Can you see any pattern in the days that are better vs. those with the lowest scores?

Joanna Jenkins would also be asked to complete a "pleasant events" schedule, on which she would indicate the frequency with which she engages in a set of different activities that many older persons find pleasant. The Older

Daily Mood Rating Form

1. Please rate your mood for this day, i.e., how good or bad you felt, using the nine-point scale shown below. If your felt good put a high number on the chart below. If your felt "so-so" mark five, and if you felt low or depressed mark a number lower than five.

```
   |     |     |     |     |     |     |     |     |
   1     2     3     4     5     6     7     8     9
  very              so-so                    very
depressed                                    happy
```

2. On the two lines next to your mood rating for each day, please briefly give two major reasons why you think you felt that way. Try to be as specific as possible.

Date	Mood score	Why I think I felt this way
Mon. 5/10	*1*	1. *Bored. Watched TV* 2.
Tues. 5/11	*1*	1. *Worried about daughter* 2.
Wed. 5/12	*3*	1. *Son & children stopped by* 2.
Thurs. 5/13	*2*	1. *Neighbor took a walk with me* 2.
Fri. 5/14	*1*	1. *Worried about checkbook balance* 2.
Sat. 5/15	*4*	1. *Grandchildren brought new puppy to* 2. *visit.*
Sun. 5/16	*4*	1.*Church and lunch with friends* 2.
		1. 2.
		1. 2.
		1. 2.

Figure 4.2 Daily mood rating form for Joanna Jenkins

Person's Pleasant Events Scale (Teri & Lewinsohn, 1982) contains activities commonly enjoyed by older adults. On this scale Ms Jenkins would also rate each activity as to its subjective pleasantness for her. A few items from Ms Jenkins's scale are recorded in table 4.3. Specific items that she rated low in frequency but high in pleasantness would then be selected for daily monitoring. She would be asked to indicate whether she engaged in that activity each day. The therapist would begin graphing her mood and the rate at which she engaged in pleasant activities. This is both an assessment and an intervention

Table 4.3   Older Adult Pleasant Events Schedule completed by Joanna Jenkins

	Frequency rating			Pleasantness rating		
	Often	Sometimes	Never	Very pleasant	Somewhat pleasant	Not at all pleasant
Listening to music	3	2	1	3	2	1
Shopping	3	2	1	3	2	1
Smiling at people	3	2	1	3	2	1
Arranging flowers	3	2	1	3	2	1
Solving a problem, puzzle, or crossword	3	2	1	3	2	1
Baking a new recipe	3	2	1	3	2	1
Going to church	3	2	1	3	2	1
Thinking about people I like	3	2	1	3	2	1
Listening to birds sing	3	2	1	3	2	1
Having a clean house	3	2	1	3	2	1
Looking at stars or moon	3	2	1	3	2	1

tool, because in a short time Ms Jenkins would be able to see quite clearly the relationship between mood and pleasantness.

Cognitive aspects of Ms Jenkins's depression may become the focus of therapy as well. Interviews are often used to identify thought patterns, assumptions, and world-views with a specific focus on those cognitive patterns that produce negative affect (e.g., depression or anxiety). One tool often used to identify the pattern related to the thought is the Dysfunctional Thought Record (DTR). A sample DTR for Joanna Jenkins is shown in table 4.4.

Many other specific tools can be created to assist behaviorists in measuring and recording subjective experiences, thoughts, and behaviors. The cognitive-behavioral model provides primarily a framework within which a behavior problem can be analyzed. Individualized assessment tools are frequently developed to facilitate tracking of specific targeted thoughts, feelings, and behaviors for a particular client.

Table 4.4 Dysfunctional Thought Record for Joanna Jenkins

Situation	Daily record of dysfunctional thoughts		Rational response	Outcome
	Emotions(s)	Automatic thought(s)		
Describe:				
1. Actual event leading to unpleasant emotion, or	1. Specify sad/anxious, angry, etc.	1. Write automatic thought(s) that preceded emotion(s)	1. Write rational response to automatic thought(s)	1. Rerate belief in automatic thought(s)
2. Stream of thoughts, daydreams or recollection, leading to unpleasant emotion	2. Rate degree of emotion 0–100%	2. Rate belief in automatic thought(s) 0–100%	2. Rate belief in rational response 0–100%	2. Specify and rate subsequent emotions 0–100%
Date				
5/11 *Worry about daughter*	*anxious and sad 70%*	*She is going to be an unhappy lonely old woman now that she is divorced 95%*	*Divorce doesn't have to mean she is lonely. She might not be unhappy forever 20%*	*80% – still anxious but I can't worry forever and worrying won't do her any good*

Explanation: When you experience an unpleasant emotion, note the situation that seemed to stimulate the emotion (if the emotion occurred while you were thinking, daydreaming, etc., please note this). Then note the automatic thought associated with the emotion. Record the degree to which you believe this thought 0% = not at all, 100% = completely. In rating degree of emotion 1 = a trace 100 = the most intense possible.
Source: Beck et al., 1979.

Treatment

The goal of behavior therapy is indeed to modify behavior, whether overt or thought-behaviors. The principles by which behavior can be changed are really quite simple and straightforward (see Kazdin, 1975). Behavior therapy, or (its synonymous term) behavior modification, has been applied in numerous settings with a wide variety of populations, including the elderly (Burgio, 1996; Hussian & Davis, 1985; Pinkston & Linsk, 1984; Wisocki, 1991), with whom it is highly acceptable (Burgio & Sinnott, 1989). Many of the behaviors targeted for intervention are among the most difficult behaviors produced by persons with dementias. For example, urinary incontinence (Burgio & Locher, 1996), wandering and aggression (Cohen-Mansfield et al., 1996), sleep disturbances (Bootzin et al., 1996), and depression (Teri, Logsdon, Uomoto, & McCurry, 1997) are all responsive to behavioral interventions. In the sections that follow, the basic principles of behavior therapy are described and illustrated with research and clinical descriptions of effectiveness with older adults.

Alter reinforcement contingencies

Altering the contingencies for behavior involves changing or adding reinforcers in order to produce the desired behavior more often, or adding punishers to decrease the frequency of undesirable behavior. In order to change the reinforcement contingencies, a true reinforcer must be identified. Pleasant events or rewards for good behavior may be experienced as positive, but are not considered to be a reinforcer unless they actually change the rate of the targeted behavior. Similarly, an aversive consequence to a behavior is only a true punishment contingency if it decreases the rate of behavior.

A reinforcement intervention might be appropriate for Anna Tweed. The first step would be to identify the desired behavior. The goal in this case is to decrease the frequency of a behavior that is noxious to staff (asking questions at the nurses' station), so a desirable behavior that is incompatible with the undesirable behavior must be identified. The goal behavior might be engaging in pleasant activity in the day room. The next step would then be to identify a reinforcer for her – i.e., some event or item that is so valuable to her that she increases the frequency of the desired behavior in order to obtain or experience it. Nursing staff may have noticed that when one of them talks with her in her room she does not engage in the constant questioning behavior, nor does she seek to return to the nurses' station. Staff attention is likely to be a reinforcer for her that could be administered contingent on the targeted behavior. A behavioral program might be designed in which staff talk with her in the day room contingent on her engaging in a certain period of appropriate behavior that does not include questioning. Staff attention is being used to reinforce her for engaging in activities away from the nurses' station. Punishments are unlikely to be used to decrease this particular behavior because it is generally considered unethical to use punitive strategies in an institutional setting to control behavior that is not harmful to self or others.

Differential reinforcement

Often, the desired behaviors are occurring, but in an inappropriate context. Perhaps the behavior occurs where it is annoying to others, or perhaps the behavior is simply not reaping the desired effects for the older person. For example, a perfectly appropriate question asked to a person with severe hearing impairment may yield no effect. The questioning behavior was appropriate, but the context was not appropriate to yield the desired effects.

Interventions can be established to differentially reinforce the behavior in one context but not another. For example, Anna Tweed might be given attention for asking questions of staff if the behavior occurs in her room, but not at the nurses' station.

Generalization (of stimuli and of responses)

While new behavior patterns are being established, reinforcement contingencies and eliciting stimuli are tightly controlled to maximize the efficiency with which the behavior is learned. Typically, however, the desired outcome is for the client to be able to perform that behavior in a variety of appropriate settings. Stimulus generalization refers to the process by which a person learns to perform the desired behavior in the presence of a wider variety of stimuli. If a reinforcement training program were established for Anna Tweed, it might be implemented by one or two staff initially. Eventually, however, the goal would be for Anna to be able to distinguish between a broader category of "busy staff" and "staff available to talk." This latter discrimination requires her to generalize her initial learning about talking with staff only in the day room, and never at the nurses' station, to a much broader set of cues that staff are busy.

Response generalization refers to the fact that reinforcement of one response may increase the probability of other responses that are similar (Skinner, 1953). Reinforcing Anna Tweed's conversations with staff who enter the day room may not only increase her rate of interaction with staff, but may lead her to increase her interaction with other people. Combined with stimulus generalization, the effects of response generalization would create for Ms Tweed a more appropriate, active social life away from the nurses' station.

Extinction

Behaviors decrease if the positive reinforcement contingencies are removed. The gradual elimination of behavior following the removal of reinforcement contingencies is called extinction. Many behaviors are maintained by positive social consequences such as attention or praise. Removal of attention in response to the performance of the targeted behavior will result in a lower frequency of that behavior. This principle is particularly useful when working with behaviors that are either self-defeating or aversive to others. For example, Anna Tweed's behavior at the nurses' station may be reinforced by social interaction from nurses during the time she stands at the station and asks questions. An extinction intervention would require all staff to ignore consistently Anna's presence and her verbalizations while she is standing at the nurses' station. Unfortunately, nursing-home residents are often unintentionally on an extinction paradigm for behavior the staff actually desires.

Shaping/chaining

Desired behaviors do not always occur spontaneously in the environment in which we want to reinforce them. The procedure of shaping involves reinforcing tiny steps toward the desired behavior. In the classic animal paradigms, pigeons were initially reinforced for turning toward the stimulus with which they were to interact. Once they were consistently turning toward the stimulus, they were reinforced only if they took steps toward the stimulus. Eventually, they had to complete the full behavior of turning, walking, and pecking the stimulus (the desired behavior) in order to be reinforced. The pecking behavior was shaped through reinforcement of small successive approximations of the desired behavior. As long as Joanna Jenkins is depressed, she may never spontaneously behave in a way that would elicit positive social reinforcement for her in a natural environment. A therapist or family member might establish a shaping procedure in which she is initially reinforced for behaving in a slightly less negative way than is typical for her. Increasing standards of positiveness would be required in her behavior in order to elicit the stimulus over time, until she is behaving in ways that will more naturally elicit positive social reinforcement from her natural social network.

Chaining refers to the process by which a person learns to emit a series of behaviors in a particular sequence. Reinforcement is initially given for a single behavior. Later, another behavior is required before the reinforcer is given. Finally, the full series of behaviors must be accomplished prior to reinforcement. Older adults who have experienced a stroke may need to relearn how to dress. Dressing is a long series of discrete behaviors that must be accomplished in sequence. A chaining procedure might be created to teach the steps of dressing oneself.

A Practical Concern

Behavioral interventions are time intensive for the persons responsible for designing and implementing the altered contingency patterns. Procedures such as shaping and chaining require significant investments of time to achieve the desired new behavior. In institutional or home settings, this usually means that staff or family members must add to their other responsibilities the tasks of monitoring behavior, measuring outcomes, administering reinforcers, and altering environmental cues. Self-administered behavioral interventions (e.g., for depression) use self-monitoring and self-reinforcement, and thus are less vulnerable to being discontinued when someone tires of maintaining the reinforcement schedule. Interventions in institutions, however, are often not successful in the long term because staff fail to carry on the reinforcement contingencies. Some efforts to alter staff behavior so behavioral interventions can be more successful have shown modest success (Hawkins et al., 1992), but the challenges involved in maintaining behavioral gains will require considerably more research.

Ethical Considerations

Interventions to alter behavior always require careful examination of ethics. When designing interventions for frail persons either who cannot collaborate in the establishment of treatment goals (e.g., cognitively impaired persons) or whose power to refuse the intervention is compromised (e.g., in a nursing home), behaviorists must be particularly careful to examine the ethical implications of their decision to intervene (Carstensen & Fisher, 1991). For example, when is family or staff displeasure a sufficient reason to intervene? How much understanding must be present for informed consent to be truly informed? Behaviorists must respect the burden of ethical consideration that is placed on them by the very power of their tools.

Conclusion

The behavioral model is rooted in the scientific approach to investigating efficiency and effectiveness of interventions. As such, the amount of evidence supporting the utility of this model to explain behavior problems and to design interventions is impressive. Behaviorists working with cognitively intact persons have demonstrated significant impact with challenging problems such as depression, health behaviors, and insomnia. Many interventions have been successful even with cognitively impaired individuals (e.g., incontinence programs and self-care programs). The difficulties of achieving generalization and maintenance noted briefly above provide substantial challenges to those working within the model. In addition, the ethical concerns about manipulating environmental cues and contingencies to achieve changes in behavior, regardless of the older person's desire to change the behavior, raise important ethical considerations. What is unique about this model, however, is that it has spawned interventions that address behavior problems for which other models provide little assistance.

5

Stress and Coping

Introduction

Consider the following example:

Mrs C is an 80-year-old African-American woman whose adaptation in late life is plagued by disruptive relocation and very poor health. Not surprisingly, she exhibits severe psychological distress, and her medical chart includes a diagnosis of clinical depression. She is currently surviving on the barest social, economic, and health resources. She is also socially isolated. "My family – they're all dead, my mama, my papa, everyone." She had been married in her late teens and widowed before thirty – "so long ago I can hardly remember it." Her son and a grandson died many years previously, and she subsequently lost contact with a second grandson.

Before retiring because of illness, she worked as a domestic for forty years. Currently she subsists on SSI. Compounding her many losses, she was recently evicted from an apartment where she had resided for 30 years. This event was especially traumatic because it removed her from a familiar neighborhood, proximity to her church, and friends of long standing. Following her eviction she rented a room from an "odd" landlady. "I won't say nothing. I might get kicked out." The waiting list for senior housing is long, and she has resisted moving to general public housing. "That's where all the bad folks are." She has one male friend whom she sees every Saturday, when they go out for breakfast and then to his place to watch ball games on television. She has no friends living near her current residence and spends her days by herself reading the Bible and singing hymns. She complains of loneliness and feels her doctor is her only confidante. Her declining physical health is a serious factor in her current distress. According to her medical charts, she was recently diagnosed as having cervical cancer and nodular shadows were seen on her chest X-ray. She and her doctors were most troubled about the possibility of a serious systemic disease. (Johnson & Johnson, 1992, p. 233)

Mrs C's situation challenges her and those who are working with her. How do we conceptualize her problems? What can we do for her and with her? Not surprisingly, Mrs C has multiple problems with which she is struggling: cancer, a disrupted living situation, limited economic resources, dwindling social resources, and a personal wariness that may keep her from seeking help.

This chapter outlines a stress and coping perspective that may be useful for working with older adults like Mrs C. We draw upon research and clinical work from several different disciplines to help sketch an understanding of the stress and coping process and its implications for assessment and treatment.

Theoretical Framework

Well-being

Have you ever been "stressed out"?

How do you know? In developing your answer, you had an implicit model of what stress is and how it works. For some, stress is a physical reaction: sweating, chills, quickened heartbeats. For some, stress is a combination of feelings: tension and anxiety. For others, stress is identified with external problems: problems in paying bills, with too much work and too little time.

Consider a softball player. Her team is tied in the bottom of the last inning. She is at bat with two strikes called against her. Is this situation stressful? Is it unhealthy for her? Your answer depends upon your implicit model of the stress process and its implications for well-being.

Is Mrs C stressed out?

Again, your answer depends on your implicit model of stress and differences between "normal" stress and abnormal or unhealthy levels of stress. Gatz (1992) provided a framework for considering the different interacting elements that affect the relationship between stress and well-being (see figure 5.1). For Gatz, as for Aldwin (1994), stress refers to that quality of experience, produced through a person–environment transaction, that, through either over-arousal or under-arousal, results in psychological or physiological distress. Notice that this is a comprehensive definition that encompasses different levels of individual functioning (physiological, cognitive, affective, social) and focuses our attention on both excesses and deficits (over- and under-arousal). Gatz's scheme allows us to focus on several key elements in the stress process. Here, we will highlight three: stressful life events, chronic strains, and vulnerabilities and resources.

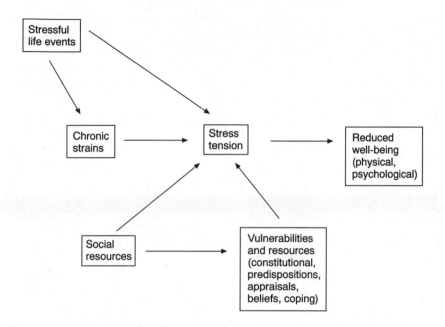

Figure 5.1 Stress, control, and psychological processes
Source: adapted from Gatz, 1992, p. 214.

Stressful life events The concept of stressful life events shifts our attention to the social, historical, and physical context that surrounds older adults. As noted in Chapter 2, Baltes and his colleagues (1980) suggested that three types of influences shape the individual's life course: age-graded, history-graded, and non-normative events. Age-graded influences are associated with a specific chronological age; for example, entering school or graduating from high school are usually linked to a narrow age band. An example of an age-graded influence for older adults is access to social security benefits. History-graded influences are linked to the particular historical period in which the individual has lived (e.g., the great depression, the Vietnam War, the Oklahoma City bombing). Non-normative events are influences that occur at any time in the life-span but are not part of the "expected" life pattern (e.g., death of one's parents at an early age, winning the lottery). Baltes and his colleagues (1980) hypothesized that these influences varied across the life-span (see figure 5.2).

In the case of Mrs C, we might use these frameworks to consider the history-graded, age-graded, and non-normative influences that have shaped her development. An 80-year-old, she was born in 1915. She experienced

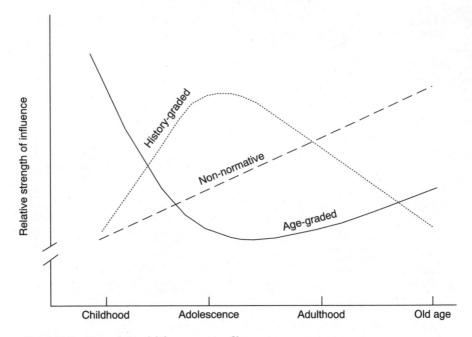

Figure 5.2   Hypothetical life-course profiles
Source: Baltes et al., 1980.

the great depression as an adolescent, married during the depression, and was widowed during World War II. She has had several other non-normative events befall her: death of a grandson and eviction.

The deaths of her family members remind us that Mrs C's life events are interwoven with the events of her family members and friends. This is also a reminder that Gatz's categories of stressful life events and social resources are interrelated. Pruchno and her colleagues (Pruchno, Blow, & Smyer, 1984) described "life event webs" as a way of reminding us of interdependent lives. A life event for a family member (e.g., her son's death) not only affects that member but also has ripple effects for other family members. In Mrs C's case, potential sources of support are denied her through the deaths of her husband, son, and grandson.

Chronic strains Mrs C has also coped with two chronic strains: physical illness and financial strain. From the brief case description, we know that Mrs C is currently coping with cervical cancer and the possibility of other health problems. It will be important to assess her history of coping with chronic illness, since this chronic strain has been found to be the single strongest predictor of mental well-being in later life (Krause, 1991).

The concept of strain encompasses both physiological and emotional reactions (Aldwin, 1994). Recently, the links between stress and immune system functioning have received a great deal of research and clinical attention (e.g., Stone & Porter, 1995; Weisse, 1992). Herbert and Cohen (1993a) have reviewed the literature and highlighted several important themes: first, both objective stressful events and subjective reports of stress are related to immune changes; second, objective events have a greater impact than subjective reports; and, third, the nature of the events (e.g., interpersonal stress vs. non-social events) affects the type of immune response.

How does this help us understand Mrs C's situation? To begin with, we might attend to the objective stressful events that have occurred for her and their likely impact on her physiological functioning. For example, consider only two aspects of her situation: depression and cancer. There is a substantial link between clinical depression and immune system functioning (Herbert and Cohen, 1993b). In addition, the effects are greatest among older and hospitalized patients. In short, Mrs C is at risk for immune system alterations.

Similarly, there is a clearly established link among the stress of cancer diagnosis and treatment, other life stresses, and subsequent health or illness (Andersen et al., 1994). In short, there is good reason to suspect that the stresses of clinical depression and a cancer diagnosis and treatment regimen – apart from any of the other objective stressors or subjective perceptions – put Mrs C at risk for suppressed immune functioning and poor disease prognosis.

In the financial area, Mrs C's career as a domestic suggests that she has not been highly paid, and her current subsistence on SSI confirms this suspicion. Krause (1991; 1995a) recently summarized the impact of chronic financial strain on older adults' social and mental well-being. He noted that financial strain has a significant impact on depressive symptoms – second only to the impact of a physical illness (Krause, 1991). In Mrs C's case, we might ask what the impact of this chronic stressor has been for her depressive symptoms (Belle, 1990; Krause, 1995a): Has it caused depression to occur for the first time in later life? Has it prolonged an already existing episode? Has it caused a relapse of a previously diagnosed disorder? These are leads that we may want to pursue in our history-taking with Mrs C.

Lazarus (1990) highlighted another type of chronic strain: daily hassles which he equated with chronic role strain. Some have argued that everyday stress or hassles have a larger impact on health and well-being than life events that occur relatively infrequently (Lazarus & Folkman, 1984). For example, DeLongis et al. (1988) developed a hassles scale that includes interpersonal problems at work (with the boss or with co-workers), not getting enough sleep, not enough time for entertainment and recreation, troublesome neighbors, and other areas. Again, in working with Mrs C we might focus attention on the daily irritants that arise in the give-and-take of her life.

Vulnerabilities and resources The third element of Gatz's scheme reminds us of the interaction between the person and the environment. The basic assumption is that the person's perception of the stressor affects his or her coping response. For example, imagine that you are taking a course. An exam is coming up. You might view this impending stressor in at least two different ways: a threat to your mental health and educational well-being or a challenge to your intellectual skills. How you view it may very well affect what you do about it.

Lazarus and his colleagues have highlighted two basic approaches to coping that are linked to the perception of stress: problem-focused coping and emotion-focused coping (Folkman, Lazarus, Gruen, & Delongis, 1986; Folkman, Lazarus, Pimley, & Novacek, 1987). Problem-focused coping seeks to alter the distressing person–environment interaction. Emotion-focused coping seeks to regulate distressing emotions. The type of coping that is used in response to a particular stress is a function of the individual's perceptions, the specific types of stress, and the context for coping.

A central element of perception is the individual's sense of control over the event. Zautra et al. (1995) have focused on the links among older adults' sense of control, loss of autonomy, and mental health. They found that it is important to assess the individual's sense of control that derives from experience with the possibility of shaping the events of life – both positive and negative. They focused on mental health and adaptation in the face of a loss of autonomy because of either physical disability or conjugal bereavement. Their results were impressive: a sense of personal control over events was associated with mental health and adaptation in the face of increased disability or decreased autonomy (see figure 5.3).

What about Mrs C? How does she view the stresses in her life? How much control does she feel she has? Her comments about her landlady ("I won't say nothing. I might get kicked out.") suggest that she feels little sense of control over her living situation.

Another potential resource for Mrs C and many others in later life is religion (Pargament et al., 1995). For example, we know that Mrs C "spends her days by herself reading the Bible and singing hymns." We also know that her recent move was traumatic, in part, because it separated her from her church. In this regard, Mrs C is like many older adults. For example, Koenig et al. (1988) surveyed 100 older adults, asking them what specific coping behaviors they found especially useful in getting through the worst experi-

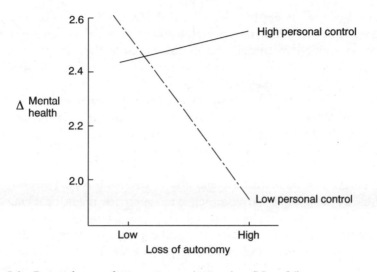

Figure 5.3 Personal control × autonomy interaction (N = 96)
Source: Zautra et al., 1995.

ence in their whole lives, in the last ten years, and in the present. Religion was spontaneously mentioned as the most frequent coping strategy. Not surprisingly, religious coping encompassed a wide range of behaviors, including prayer, turning to church friends, and reading the Bible.

Pargament and his colleagues (1995) summarized the literature on religion and coping:

> . . . religion works in different ways for different people. For some, it may operate as a "stress buffer," becoming increasingly effective as stress increases. For others, it may be a "distress-deterrent," proving equally helpful to people regardless of their levels of stress. And for others, religion may be a "stress suppressor," with stress leading to increases in religious involvement which, in turn, bolsters the individual in coping. (p. 56)

Stress and Coping: Normal and Abnormal Adaptation

Is Mrs C's profile of strain, stressors, and transactions normal for older adults? A recent review summarized our state of ignorance:

Although a great deal has been learned about stress and its effect in recent decades, little of the research has been oriented to learning about the distribution of stressors across the ranks of the old. Particularly lacking are studies that identify the onset and effects of chronic stressors that may be intertwined with aging . . .

. . . [W]e know less than we should about the stressors that distinctively impinge on older populations and, indeed, whether old age is a particularly difficult time of life in comparison to other segments of the life course. (Pearlin & Skaff, 1995, p. 19)

We cannot chart the normal ebb and flow of stress and coping across the lifespan for all older adults. A more pragmatic approach might be asking about the individual's own development and deviations from their own baseline of functioning. For each individual, successful coping with stress is a function of three elements: their level of vulnerability, the stress that they encounter, and protective factors (Gatz, Kasl-Godley, & Karel, 1996). Individual vulnerability includes genetic influences, acquired biological vulnerabilities, and psychological factors that affect the individual's adaptation. Stress incorporates psychosocial elements, environmental elements, and the individual's perception of these. Protective factors include biological, psychological, or social elements that can either buffer the older adult from stress or moderate its impact.

With Mrs C, we might begin by asking how her current adaptation compares to her earlier situation. We know that many of her social supports are no longer available – her son, grandsons, previous neighbors. We also know that the familiar physical environment has changed (after she was evicted). Her medical status is threatened (with the cancer diagnosis), and her current psychological adjustment is poor (with a diagnosis of depression).

As we review her history and consider her current adjustment, we have an implicit view of the interaction between Mrs C and her interpersonal, social, and physical environment. This perspective is consistent with Lewin's (1935) emphasis on the interaction between person and environment and recent work in geropsychology focusing on the interaction between the individual's capacity and environmental characteristics that may affect the development and course of disorders (e.g., Lawton, 1980, 1982). As described in chapter 2, Gatz and her colleagues, for example, used this framework to depict the factors that affect the probability of developing a depressive disorder in later life (see figure 2.4). The important element is the interaction among the individual's biological vulnerability or predisposition, the situational stressors of life events or life circumstances, and the individual's psychological coping mechanisms. This conceptualization provides a framework for assessment and subsequent intervention.

Assessment Strategies

Assessment within the stress and coping framework focuses on the individual's vulnerabilities, the stresses to which they are exposed, and the protective factors that may mitigate the stress process.

Assessing individual vulnerabilities

One of the key elements for assessment is Mrs C's biological vulnerability. Two aspects are particularly important when getting Mrs C's history: her experience of chronic illness, and previous episodes of mental illness – in this case depression.

The interaction of physical and mental well-being in later life is a complex, interdependent process (Cohen, 1985, 1990). Thus we need to understand where in the coping process we encounter Mrs C as she faces the chronic illness of cancer and its treatment. Is she just finding out how to cope with cancer? Has she been managing a cancer treatment regimen for some time? Mrs C's experience in the "trajectory of the illness" may affect both her own physical resources and the social and economic resources upon which she can call.

Another focus of history-taking should be the history of the mental disorder itself: Is this Mrs C's first bout of depression? Is it a recurrent pattern? Did Mrs C have significant depression earlier in life, only to have it vanish until recently? Each of these patterns would have different implications for treatment and the likely course of the disorder (Coyne & Downey, 1991).

Assessing life stresses

It is important to assess two aspects of life stresses: the individual's subjective perception of the stress; and the "objective" indicators of stress. Emphasizing both the subjective and objective aspects is consistent with an interactionist perspective on stress and coping (Aldwin, 1994).

Assessing Mrs C's subjective perception of stress focuses us on a simple question: What is Mrs C's assessment of how stressful, upsetting, or overwhelming her situation is? Cohen and his colleagues developed a set of 14 questions for this purpose, the Perceived Stress Scale (PSS) (Cohen, Kamarck, & Mermelstein, 1983; Cohen & Williamson, 1988) (see table 5.1). They

Table 5.1   Perceived stress scale

---

1. In the last month, how often have you been upset because of something that happened unexpectedly?
2. In the last month, how often have you felt that you were unable to control the important things in your life?
3. In the last month, how often have you felt nervous and "stressed"?
4. In the last month, how often have you dealt successfully with day to day problems and annoyances?
5. In the last month, how often have you felt that you were effectively coping with important changes that were occurring in your life?
6. In the last month, how often have you felt confident about your ability to handle your personal problems?
7. In the last month, how often have you felt that things were going your way?
8. In the last month, how often have you found that you could not cope with all the things that you had to do?
9. In the last month, how often have you been able to control irritations in your life?
10. In the last month, how often have you felt that you were on top of things?
11. In the last month, how often have you been angered because of things that happened that were outside of your control?
12. In the last month, how often have you found yourself thinking about things that you have to accomplish?
13. In the last month, how often have you been able to control the way you spend your time?
14. In the last month, how often have you felt difficulties were piling up so high that you could not overcome them?

Source: Cohen, Kamarck, & Mermelstein, 1983.

found that perceived stress was associated with illness, illness symptoms, and a range of health behaviors. The PSS illustrates the usefulness of a structured inquiry into the individual's perceptions.

Objective assessments of stress have typically focused on checklists of life events such as the Social Readjustment Rating Scale (Holmes and Rahe, 1967) or the Psychiatric Epidemiology Research Interview (Dohrenwend et al., 1978). However, there has been a growing dissatisfaction with checklists. If Mrs C merely endorses an item (e.g., indicating the death of a spouse or a son) it tells us little about the impact of that event on her subsequent adjustment. Coyne and Downey (1991) summarize the concerns well:

... we doubt that various checklists adequately capture the patterns in the particulars of people's lives. The limitations of such instruments may be fundamental, and their objectivity illusory, particularly when it comes to substantive interpretation of their correlates. (p. 420)

Instead of checklists, Coyne and Downey suggest using semi-structured interviews to assess current stresses. For example, some researchers have listed life stresses under the major roles that older adults play, such as spouse, parent, grandparent, etc. (e.g., Krause, 1995b). In addition to having a standardized list, it is also helpful to ask an open-ended question at the end of each section. For example, under the section on the parental role, it is useful to ask whether anything else had happened with their children (Krause, 1995b). Another follow-up inquiry may focus on whether the life stress was desirable or undesirable.

In short, by using an interview format, the clinician can gauge three elements of the older adult's life stresses: their frequency, their perceived saliency, and their desirability. In Mrs C's case, the semi-structured interview might reveal the importance of her role as a church volunteer, and the impact that losing this role has had on her well-being.

Assessing protective factors

Two types of protective factors will be important to assess: the individual's own coping capacity and the environment, which can either help or hinder coping.

Individual coping There are two basic approaches to assessing an individual's coping: a trait approach or a state approach (see Aldwin, 1994, for a thorough review). The trait approach assumes that the individual's coping style is fairly stable, regardless of the particular type of stress that they encounter. In contrast, the state approach assumes that the process of coping may vary across time and depending upon the particular stressor encountered. These different assumptions have different implications for assessment strategies.

Those who focus on coping styles as traits use standardized questionnaires to assess the individual's general pattern of coping. For example, McCrae (1989) used a coping questionnaire to assess the stability of 28 different coping mechanisms (e.g., seeking help; perseverance; escapist fantasy; etc.). Similarly, Diehl et al. (1996) used structured questionnaires that are consistent with a dynamic perspective on coping and defense mechanisms: the Defense Mechanism Inventory (Gleser & Ihilevich, 1969; Ihilevich & Gleser, 1986) and the California Psychological Inventory (CPI) (Gough, 1987). They arrayed the CPI items into ten coping (e.g., empathy, sublimation) and ten defense scales (e.g., rationalization, denial).

Trait approaches have also been prominent in discussions of personality change and stability in aging. Costa and McCrae (1988,1992a) have defined personality traits as "dimensions of individual differences in tendencies to show consistent patterns of thoughts, feelings, and actions" (McCrae & Costa, 1990, p. 23). They have argued that basic tendencies can be categorized into five broad domains: Neuroticism (N), Extraversion (E), Openness to Experience (O), Agreeableness (A), and Conscientiousness (C). Costa and McCrae have used the NEO personality inventory (Costa & McCrae, 1985; 1992b) to assess stability and change in personality across adulthood. They conclude: "the data are overwhelmingly consistent in showing that personality is highly predictable over long periods of time. We can make excellent guesses about what we and our friends will be like many years from now: we will all be very much as we are" (Costa, Metter, & McCrae, 1994, p. 48). Trait theorists such as Costa and McCrae would argue that it is important to assess Mrs C's basic tendencies and style of encountering the world, using a structured assessment instrument like the NEO personality inventory.

In contrast, the process-oriented measures focus on the individual's reaction to a specific stressor or type of stressor. For example, specific measures have been developed to assess how a person has coped with depression (Burns, Shaw, & Crocker, 1987), myocardial infarction (Coyne & Smith, 1991), and arthritis (Manne & Zautra, 1990; Regan et al., 1988). In Mrs C's case, we might focus on how she has coped with depression in the past (Burns and Nolen-Hoeksema, 1991), perhaps using the Self-Help Inventory (Burns, Shaw, & Crocker, 1987): 45 items that include behavioral strategies (e.g., "get busy"), cognitive strategies (e.g., "remind myself that my upset will pass and I will feel good again"), and interpersonal strategies (e.g., "talk to a friend or relative that I like").

The most widely used process measure of coping is the Ways of Coping Scale (WOCS) (Folkman & Lazarus, 1980; Folkman, Lazarus, Dunkel-Schetter et al., 1986) and its revision (e.g., Vitaliano et al., 1985). Early work in factor-analyzing the WOCS identified seven factors: instrumental action; escapism; exercising caution; growth-oriented coping; self-blame; minimizing threat; and seeking social support (Aldwin et al., 1980, cited in Aldwin, 1994). Despite this last factor, however, some have suggested that the WOCS underemphasizes the interpersonal, interactive nature of coping (Aldwin, 1994). In addition, Aldwin (1994) pointed out that the original items for the WOCS did not include prayer; her own subsequent scale development included a factor with three items focusing on prayer.

The context for coping It is also important to assess the individual's context for coping: Does it present additional challenges in the face of impairment? Does is facilitate their adaptation? Consider Mrs C's situation: she has recently moved from a familiar physical environment (her home of 30 years), and she reports a dwindling social environment (only one friend whom she regularly sees).

We shouldn't focus solely on her friends and family, however. It is also important to gauge the range of institutional and organizational resources upon which Mrs C can call (Smyer, 1995a). For example, we know that she receives Supplemental Security Income (SSI). Is she also linked to the "aging network" in her community? Does she receive meals on wheels? Does she attend the programs at her local senior citizens center?

Most impaired elderly do not receive formal services from agencies or organizations (Short & Leon, 1990). Roughly one-third use either formal services or a combination of formal and informal help. Another third receive help solely from friends and family members. Thus, when assessing the coping environment, both informal and formal elements must be gauged. Assessing these resources often leads directly to the development and implementation of a treatment plan.

Treatment Strategies

Five major treatment strategies are consistent with a stress and coping theoretical framework: eliminating stressors; modifying the physical and social environment; teaching coping skills; providing social support; and improving health practices (Gatz, 1992) (see figure 5.4). As this list suggests, often the therapist must pursue several simultaneous intervention strategies, depending upon the client's life history and life circumstances.

Eliminating stressors

If life stress is a major contributing factor to mental disorders, then one effective intervention may be to eliminate as many stressors as possible. The clinician can use the assessment information regarding the client's perceptions of stressors to target specific stresses for elimination. In Mrs C's case, for example, a major stressor seems to be her recent relocation from her familiar neighborhood, with its links to friends and the church. One intervention strategy, therefore, might be to explore the possibility of relocating Mrs C back into her old neighborhood, in a setting that she can afford.

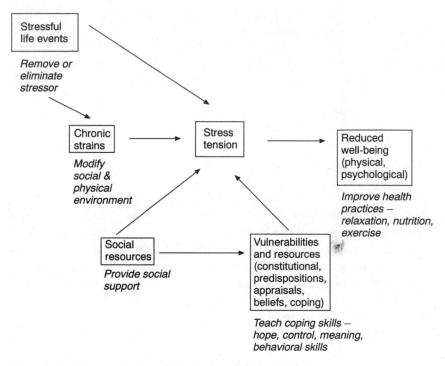

Figure 5.4 Stress, control, and psychological interventions
Source: Gatz, 1992, p. 214.

Modifying the environment

Within the interactionist perspective on stress and coping, the context directly affects the individual's well-being. Therefore, intervention strategies can target aspects of the physical or social environment that work against the client. For example, the physical environment may act as a barrier to the older client's active social involvement (see box 5.1).

Consider the case of an older woman with deteriorating arthritis in her knees. She lives on the second floor of a duplex, with steep stairs. She enjoyed gardening for many years, but she can no longer bend or stoop in the garden. She refuses to change apartments to the ground floor: "It's too dangerous. You never know who's going to break in and knock you in the head." Yet she complains that there's nothing left for her to do. The solution? Consider a window garden, or involving her in a 4-H urban gardening program that can bring gardening enthusiasm and aid to her apartment. The specifics will vary by location and the resources available.

Box 5.1 Prevention starts at home: eliminating potential problems in the physical environment

The physical environment may present additional stresses for an older adult. Several areas are important as potential sources of trouble:

1. Medications: Are they stored and labeled in easy-to-read letters?
2. Stairways: Are they free from clutter? Are there gates to prevent falls?
3. Water temperature: Is the water heater set to 120 or lower? Are hot water pipes insulated or exposed?
4. Is the kitchen safe? Is there clutter near the stove? Are the knobs on the stove or the setting clearly indicated?
5. Is the bathroom safe? Are there grab bars near the toilet and the shower or tub? Is there a bath mat that might slip? (Could it be replaced with bathroom carpeting?) Is there a skid-resistant mat in the shower or tub?

Source: adapted from Mace & Rabins, 1981.

The universal element, however, is that the therapist broadens the therapeutic role to consider the ecology of the coping that the client brings with her, the fit between the client's capacities and the demands of the physical and social environment (Lawton, 1980, 1982).

Teaching coping skills

A third strategy focuses on improving the client's skills for coping with current and future stressors. Consider the case of mild to moderate depression. A skill-based approach has been developed focusing on the client's skills in identifying the proximal causes of negative and positive mood changes, the link between daily events and mood, and the client's control over these elements (Lewinsohn et al., 1986). This approach has been extended to older adults with impressive results (Gallagher & Thompson, 1983).

Similarly, interventions have been designed to increase older clients' sense of control over positive events and mastery of negative events (e.g., Reich & Zautra, 1989, 1990). In this case, the focus was not solely depressed elderly. The target audiences were recently bereaved or disabled people. The common element, however, was a skill-building emphasis on increasing self-initiated positive events and responding effectively to negative events.

In Mrs C's case, we might try to increase her skill at controlling her depressed mood by helping her identify what she can do to give herself some pleasure in her day, as well as what she can do to avoid its negative stresses. By giving her skills to manage moods, we may improve her adaptation, even in the face of chronic, challenging stresses.

Providing social support

A common strategy for those encountering life stresses is to find others who are coping with similar problems. For many older adults, however, this is easier said than done. Consider the case of a 90-year-old widow who has outlived her older friends, her age-mates, and even many of her younger friends. Her children are in their late sixties, coping with the challenges of their own aging. Mrs C, our 80-year-old, reflects this situation in her lament: "My family – they're all dead, my mama, my papa, everyone." Perhaps one tack for the therapist is to engage others as social supports for Mrs C.

Two challenges quickly arise, however: what type of support and how? There are two major types of support: emotional support and instrumental support. The timing of these, however, may vary depending upon when we encounter the client:

> . . . the needs of clients may vary depending upon where clients are located temporally in the natural history of an event. Early in the history of a stressor, emotional support may be most useful, but later on tangible assistance may be more helpful as the client becomes more willing to take concrete steps to reconstruct his or her life. (Krause, 1995a, p. 213)

In Mrs C's case, for example, she may need emotional support in coping with the recently discovered cancer diagnosis. A support group that can provide a shared sense of experience and understanding may be an important first step of linking her to outside help. Later on, she may call upon group members for their advice on how to handle the details of chemotherapy and its accompanying illness. Another source of support may be the members of her former church. All social support is not the same, however. Some peers may encourage you to "lean on me" – let me share your burden. Others might encourage you to "pull yourself up by your bootstraps." This advice is fairly common from relatives and friends of clients with depression. Which type of support is best?

Recent evidence suggests that the effectiveness of each strategy depends upon the timing of the support in relation to the impairment:

> It comes as no surprise that healthy individuals gain in mental health with a social network that encourages self-reliance. For those with an established impairment, these types of messages may also ease feelings of helplessness. It is during the time of loss that the social network messages of self-reliance are incongruent with the person's experience and his or her needs. During this period of crisis, receiving messages that you can rely on others, the "lean on me" message, appears to play a valuable part in limiting the damage caused by the crisis events, perhaps by providing ways of maintaining a sense of control. (Zautra et al., 1995, pp. 167–8)

In Mrs C's case, she may be in need of emotional support that allows her to rely on others as she copes with the recent diagnosis of cancer. Thus the nature of the support group that she joins may be very important.

Improving health practices

The interaction of physical and mental well-being in later life makes working with older adults a challenge (Cohen, 1985; 1990). Chronic stress can affect the client's immune system functioning and health status (Herbert & Cohen, 1993a, 1993b). For example, the chronic stress of care-giving for a demented relative adversely affects immune system functioning and rates of infectious illness, as well as depressive symptoms (Kiecolt-Glaser et al., 1991). In contrast, a variety of strategies (e.g., relaxation, hypnosis, exercise, etc.) can positively affect immune system functioning (Kiecolt-Glaser & Glaser, 1992) and, perhaps, health. In short, the interaction of physical and mental well-being requires the therapist to work closely with the client's medical team.

In Mrs C's case, for example, we may want to assess her current nutritional status, assure that the cancer treatments are undertaken, and coordinate with her doctor, upon whom she relies.

General Treatment Considerations

As in the other frameworks, treatment within the stress and coping paradigm follows from the assessment approaches. A comprehensive assessment should highlight those areas needing prompt intervention and those that form longer-term objectives. A comprehensive treatment plan should include social, physical, and mental well-being. Throughout, realistic goals should be established, focusing on those elements that are controllable. Finally, the initial assessments should be viewed as a baseline against which to judge the impact of treatment at follow-up. (See Chapter 12 for a fuller discussion.)

Caution is also necessary, however, since our understanding of life stresses and aging is in its infancy:

> . . . there is a tremendous amount we do not know about the genesis or origins of stressors, the natural history or course of these events through time, the interface between stressful life events and coping resources, and the way that the effects of stress manifest. (Krause, 1995a, pp. 217–18)

Despite these limitations, however, the stress and coping framework can be a useful way of thinking about older clients and their challenges.

6

Family Systems Model

Why consider a family model of mental health and aging? Aren't older adults often abandoned by family members and left to live isolated, lonely lives in an institutional setting? We have chosen to include a family systems model for conceptualizing mental health of older persons precisely because the myth of the isolated, abandoned elder is just that – a myth. Indeed, older adults nearly always are in frequent, close contact with their families (Shanas, 1979). Because of the close interrelatedness of later life families, we believe it is important both to consider ways in which to support positive mental health of older persons by supporting family functioning, and to explore the possibility that family dysfunction might deleteriously affect the mental health of older members. The systems model for examining family relationships is a useful guide in those two endeavors, and will be described below. Before examining the conceptual model, however, a brief description of later life families may help dispel a few other myths regarding relationships between older adults and their families. The following two family situations will be used to illustrate points throughout the discussion.

Jason Martinez, age 21, lives with Ruth and James Jones, his grandmother and her husband, in the San Francisco Bay area. Jason's parents live by a rule that all of their children must move out on their own at age 18. Jason found it difficult to earn enough money to maintain an apartment and a car, and have a social life. After two failed roommate arrangements, he asked Ruth and James if he could live in their basement for a few months until he could get back on his feet. They agreed readily, hoping to be of some help to a grandson they viewed as floundering. Ruth and James have a long-standing conflict with Jason's parents, Nancy and Reuben, over what Ruth views as "mean rules that don't help the kids grow up." Although the entire family typically gathers for the major holidays, no one has initiated a gathering since Jason moved in with Ruth and James, a loss that Ruth mourns but accepts because she believes they are just doing "what they have to do, and if Nancy can't understand that then it's her loss."

Jillian Jarvis insists vehemently that she will never leave the family farm in rural Nebraska. Last month when her daughter Jean came to visit from Chicago she was appalled to see the unkempt house, the lack of food in the refrigerator, and Jillian's obvious dishevelment. Jean immediately drove her mother to a major medical center in a nearby city for a full evaluation. The initial evaluation showed that Jillian was malnourished and had significant bruising on several parts of her body, and that her vision and hearing were significantly impaired. Despite Jillian's protests, Jean made arrangements to place her mother in a nursing home in the city. Before the hospital social worker could accomplish the placement, John and JoAnn, Jean's brother and sister, arrived on the scene and insisted on taking Jillian back home "where she wants to be and where she belongs." They angrily demanded that the social worker produce evidence of their mother's incompetence "before she just goes and puts her away for all time." Jillian kept wringing her hands and saying she was sure that if Ed were only alive he would know what to do to keep the kids from fighting. The physician and social worker decided to hold Jillian in the hospital two more days to try to resolve the family disagreement, despite the fact that insurance was no longer paying for the hospital care.

Aging Families

When you think of family, what do you picture? Do you picture children with parents whose task it is to rear them? Do you picture aunts, uncles, grandparents, and cousins? Family theorists traditionally have referred to the first kind of family as a nuclear family and the second set of relationships as extended family (Parsons, 1949). The implication is that the nuclear family is more important to individual development than is the extended family. Recent theory and data, however, suggest that the extended family is intimately involved with daily life functions of persons of all ages (Antonucci & Akiyama, 1995). Grandparents rear grandchildren with increasing frequency. Sibling relationships are powerful relationships in adulthood just as they are in childhood. Parenting does not end when children go off to college or even when they create their own nuclear families. In essence, a model of family development, like models of individual development, cannot presume that development ends when children enter adulthood. Family development is truly a life cycle phenomenon. Thus the primacy of nuclear family relationships should not be presumed.

Marriage is an obvious form of daily family contact experienced by most older men (75 percent) and some older women (41 percent) over the age of 65 (Taeuber, 1993). Due to widowhood, the rates decrease with advanced age, resulting in much lower rates of marriage for older women in particular (7 to 10 percent over age 85 are married). Generally, older persons report high rates of satisfaction with their later life marriages (Levenson et al., 1993; Gilford & Bengtson, 1979), a phenomenon that appears to be at least partially a function of the tendency of the current elderly cohort to prize marital longevity, commitment, and contentment.

Contact with children occurs regularly for the vast majority of older persons. In contrast to the myth that our mobile society has limited face-to-face contact between adults and their aging parents, several studies report that even among very old (85+) adults, the vast majority maintained weekly face-to-face contact with at least one child and very high rates of telephone/letter/gift contact with children (Troll & Bengtson, 1993). Even those living far away are involved in elderly person's lives through contacts, photographs, and memories.

Sibling relationships are also highly valued by older adults, despite the fact that they generally involve weaker ties of obligation than do other nuclear family relationships (Bedford, 1995). The sibling relationship evolves across the life-span, with lower rates of contact and investment in early adulthood that increase into old age. Siblings are not often the primary care providers, but maintain ties of mutual assistance and emotional connection that gain in meaning and salience across the life-span.

Most older adults are grandparents (over 75 percent) and many are great-grandparents (50 percent) (Shanas, 1980). Grandparents are known to be involved in the socialization of younger family members and the exchange of goods and services within families, and to assist their children in times of crisis (e.g., divorce, illness) (Robertson, 1995). The meaning of the grandparent role varies, however. Kivnick (1985) describes five dimensions of meaning that mid-life and older adults may derive from the role: role centrality, valued eldership, immortality through clan, reinvolvement with personal past, and indulgence. As with other family relationships, the timing and sequencing of grandparenting within the life course of the specific elderly person will shape the role definition and meaning.

Other family ties certainly exist as well, but much less is known about them. Nieces and nephews, cousins, in-laws, and the variety of blended relationships that occur as a consequence of divorce and remarriage also are part of the relationship network of older adults.

What do people do in these relationships? A popular image is that of a frail older person being cared for by children and grandchildren. And this image is accurate – care-giving and care receiving is an important function of later life families (Aneshensel et al., 1995). However, family members of all ages are engaged in giving and receiving services (Cohler & Grunebaum, 1981).

Aging increases the probability that care recipients will be parents rather than children, but does not guarantee it. Older adults provide a significant amount of child-care services to their children, grandchildren, and great-grandchildren. They also give care to adult children who need assistance because of disability, injury, or illness (e.g., Cook, 1988). Typically, only in the very last years of the life-span do aging individuals need assistance from family members.

Families serve a variety of functions other than providing care for frail or disabled persons. As is true at any age, family relationships support the development of family members in a myriad of ways. Families often celebrate individual developmental milestones, provide mutual support in periods of stress, and share decision-making. Families are also the context in which values are socialized, a sense of personal lineage is created, and the most powerful individual developmental tasks are accomplished (Hagestad, 1986). For example, family relationships are the context within which individuals struggle with the dialectics between autonomy and dependency, connected-ness and separateness, and continuity and change (Bengtson & Kuypers, 1984).

Individual developmental tasks and the events of later life often affect other family members. Three later life transitions usually force a restructuring of family relationships: 1) the emptying and re-emptying of the "nest"; 2) retirement; and 3) onset of chronic physical illness. Several key aspects of family relationships are affected by individual life transitions: time structure, roles, communication, power balance, and nurturance (Qualls, 1995b). Fami-lies are primary components of the "life event web" in which the ripple effects of major life changes are felt (Pruchno, Blow, & Smyer, 1984).

Despite the familiar normative patterns of family contact among genera-tions across the life-span, families often find themselves organized in complex new structures. Recent decades have witnessed profound changes in the structure of Western populations that also affect family functioning. Among the demographic changes that alter family life are increased life expectancy, declining fertility, increased participation of women in the workforce, in-creased rates of divorce, and ethnic diversification (Kinsella, 1995). The separate and cumulative effects of these shifts alter the structure and function-ing of families. For example, families are far more likely to contain three or more generations. Family members tend to spend far more years in each relationship (e.g., perhaps 80 to 90 years as a sister and 60 to 70 years as a mother), but have fewer sisters or aunts or cousins from which to choose models or special relationships (Hagestad, 1988).

In summary, families are an active, powerful interpersonal context for older adults. Family contact is frequent and meaningful. Like younger persons, older adults meet many basic social needs within the family context and thus are vulnerable to the rippling effects of major life events in the lives of many family members. Deaths, divorces, marriages, births, retirement, illness, injury, misfortune – all occur in the families of older persons and alter the ways in which older persons' needs are met.

Family Dynamics: A Systems Model

How do families interact to accomplish their tasks? What causes conflict? Distress? What family interactions might create mental disorder in older persons? What impact does mental disorder have on the families of older persons and on their efforts to provide care?

As applied to behavioral sciences, the systems model emphasizes the social context in which human beings live (Whitchurch and Constantine, 1993). Problems are conceptualized as residing in the social unit rather than in the individual. Systems theory acknowledges that there are indeed organically based problems (e.g., Alzheimer's disease) but the problems are experienced as particularly distressing or problematic when the social unit cannot manage them effectively.

As a primary social unit, families are usually the focus of systems theorists' conceptualizations of mental health (Whitchurch & Constantine, 1993). The family of an older adult is highly likely to be an idiosyncratically defined extended family constellation. In other words, it is not perfectly obvious who is "the family" that is relevant to a systems analysis. Spouses, adult children, nieces and nephews, siblings, and neighbors may be among those who are involved in significant ways in the life of the older person seeking assistance. The systems model would suggest beginning with those whose regular contact is important to the daily functioning of the older person. Other key persons may be included later if their interaction patterns are demonstrated to be significant to the functioning of the unit (e.g., in Jillian Jarvis's family, the hospital social worker found that she was not dealing with all of the relevant members of the system). In the case of institutionalized older adults, the social unit might include key staff (e.g., the nurse aides who tend to the resident regularly, the charge nurse, the social worker, and perhaps a dietitian or administrator, depending on the nature of the problem) plus relevant members of the family (Smyer, Cohn, & Brannon, 1988).

The system is considered to be a complex interactive unit whose members are directly and indirectly affected by each other continually. Each member of the unit is both actor and reactor. In traditional social science frameworks, cause and effect relationships are conceptualized as if they occur in linear sequences (e.g., A causes B; his remark made me angry). Systems theory argues that complex systems such as families are better conceptualized in terms of circular causality. Events are related through multiple interacting cycles in which it is arbitrary to identify one event as the cause and one as the consequence, because if one interrupted the cycle at another moment those same events might be conceptualized differently. For example, a common scenario in which one person's angry remark provokes an angry response might be interpreted by those using linear causality as a two-point sequence in which the first angry remark caused the second. Systems theorists would point out that there was some preceding event that provoked the first angry remark that is just as relevant to understanding the sequence as either of the two recorded remarks. So Person A's perception that Person B put him down might be another point in the chain that warrants attention. Person B's quiet leering look that preceded Person A's perception of the put down might add further information. In other words, human interactions tend to consist of complex cycles of ongoing communication via behavior, expectations and beliefs about behavior, and reactions to behavior. Thus, in families, every person's behavior is believed to be related directly or indirectly to every other person in the system.

Given the importance of understanding the circular causal sequences in human interactions, behaviors are observed carefully for their communication function (Watzlawick, Beavin & Jackson, 1967). The vast majority of communication is accomplished non-verbally. In familiar social settings, an even greater percentage of communication occurs at the non-verbal level. Words are certainly used to communicate, but the context of the words creates the meaning of the communication. Actors make their living by learning the subtleties of communicating very different messages with the same text by altering tone of voice or body language. Relationships form an even more powerful context within which communication occurs.

Relationships are structured with specific power dimensions and hierarchical linkages. A faculty member's casual inquiry to a student, "So, did you go partying last night?" may elicit a defensive response simply because the student hears the question within the context of his or her salient awareness of the power differential in their relationship. A peer asking the same question may elicit a long excited description of the events of the previous evening. In the first family described above, Jason Martinez's parents may be withdrawing from contact with Ruth and James because Nancy and Reuben perceive the invitation for Jason to live with his grandparents as a direct insult. The previous relationship between Nancy and her mother and stepfather is the context in which Jason's living arrangement will be interpreted by all parties involved.

Family relationship structures are similarly powerful factors influencing family interactions. Generational hierarchies are among the most prominent structures, but gender roles, favorite son designations, or family scapegoat roles will also set the context for interpreting all interactions. The term "rules" is used to articulate the typically unspoken observations of behavior patterns that not only describe but usually prescribe behavior. For example, "One must never show anger" is a family rule that will constrain behavior of family members. The very presence of this rule prescribes masking attempts, and establishes a family member as a rebel or a problem if he or she expresses overtly his or her anger. A family with such a rule may very well label a child as behaviorally disturbed if he acts out anger, even if the behavior would be considered appropriate by society at large or even by mental health professionals. This example suggests that the child's "problem" may actually be a family system problem. In Jason Martinez's family, the unspoken rule may be "If you believe someone has insulted you, don't talk to that person."

Ironically, elderly family members who are identified as problems within a family may have invested considerable effort earlier in life enforcing family rules that they find unacceptable later in life. For example, an older person who decides to co-reside with a partner without marrying may find him- or herself experiencing outrage from adult children who were taught by this elderly parent that such behavior was immoral. Even behavior that is caused by a dementing illness can be particularly upsetting to family members if it goes against the family rules (e.g., angry, combative behavior; sexual behavior). Any elderly person whose behavior changes from previously established family norms is particularly likely to elicit strong emotional responses from other family members because the elder him- or herself had participated in generating or maintaining the very rules he or she is now breaking.

Boundaries are the rules that define who participates in what roles and which forms of participation are acceptable (Minuchin, 1974). The purpose of boundaries is to differentiate members within a family. For example, there are boundaries that define who makes financial decisions, who provides emotional support, and who disciplines children. Many systems theorists believe that the clearer the boundaries, the greater the probability that the family is healthy. However, family dysfunction may occur with boundaries that are too rigid as well as too diffuse. Therapists refer to families with extremely rigid boundaries as disengaged (the boundaries keep them from being flexible in roles when adaptation is needed) and to families with diffuse boundaries as enmeshed (everyone engages in all possible roles). Most families are believed to fall somewhere between these polarities.

Later life families seldom share the same immediate household as is characteristic of child-rearing nuclear families, but can nonetheless be conceptualized as functioning systems whose interaction patterns are governed by rules. Interactions consist of verbal and non-verbal behaviors that occur in repeating cycles. For example, when a decision must be made about the housing and medical care of Grandma, her oldest daughter and son-in-law typically decide what they believe is best and then call her other two children to get their approval. The rule in this case could be stated, "oldest daughter and son-in-law decide what is best, and inform other siblings, who are expected to approve." If a brother were to disapprove, he might be labeled a troublemaker. Or, if the oldest daughter and son-in-law were to be away on vacation when a crisis in care occurred, the family might be confused about how to proceed because the familiar rule could not be enacted. Think back to the conflict among Jillian Jarvis's children over how to decide about her care. The siblings probably have not ever had to negotiate explicitly their rules about how to make decisions about their mother. Neither has Jillian had experience letting her children decide, so her fantasy is to go back to the original nuclear structure in which her husband ruled over all of them.

Each member of the system carries a set of beliefs about what the rules are, why they are structured in that way, and what would be the consequences of breaking them. Attributions for the rules may be based on the personality of the persons involved (e.g., "she has to keep control over Grandma," or "he won't help so I don't bother asking"). Such personality-based attributions are focused on traits that appear to be unalterable and are likely not to generate task-focused problem-solving efforts. Indeed, many family difficulties arise from failed attempts to solve problems (Herr & Weakland, 1979). Personality-based attributions for family rules may generate attempts to change the personality of a person, an effort that is likely to be resisted by the target of the change efforts. Jillian Jarvis's children appear locked in a personality-attribution model that undermines their ability to cooperate to address the task at hand effectively.

Members of systems can generate many more solution alternatives when they work from behavioral descriptions of the behavior sequences (e.g., "when a problem arises in Grandma's care I decide what to do, arrange for it, and then place telephone calls to my three siblings in which I describe what has been done; I do not expect or solicit any input and am surprised and insulted if my siblings want to participate in the decision with any communication except statements of approval"). Behavior descriptions offer multiple points for intervention and usually make it evident that a variety of interventions initiated by any one person in the sequence would alter its pattern and outcome.

The hospital social worker in the Jarvis case will need to help the adult children define the task at hand behaviorally. Rather than framing the question as, "Does Jean have a right to place her mother in a nursing home?", the family needs to work to meet Jillian's needs. Instead of focusing on the differences between the personalities of Jean, whose style is to "get the job done," and John, whose style is to "consider every option before acting," the siblings need to focus on the task. First they need information. Exactly which of Jillian's capabilities are compromised? Which housing options are congruent with her level of functioning? The children's values and preferences about their mother's housing can be examined in the context of which options best serve her needs. Likely, all of the children want her to be safe and well cared for, yet as autonomous as possible. The task they need to accomplish is to identify the set of options that meet those values.

Family members are often bound to one another in particular kinds of ties that shape the dynamics of the family. Three kinds of relational ties that are often tracked in family systems are alliances, triangles, and coalitions. Alliances involve two persons who share a common interest not shared by a third person. In other words, two persons ally together "against" another. Triangles describe the relationship that occurs when two persons manage conflict by funneling it through a third person. The classic paradigm for triangles in child-rearing families shows a child with behavior problems (the "identified patient") who is triangulated between parents experiencing serious marital unhappiness or conflict. In aging families the structure of the triangle is more variable (i.e., it is less likely to involve a married couple triangulating a child in their conflict). A prototypical scenario might involve two siblings with a long-standing conflicted relationship who enact their conflict by taking incompatible approaches to caring for a parent. The parent's care becomes a huge problem that deflects focus from the underlying sibling conflict, as appears to be the case in the Jarvis family. Many other family structures also can triangulate. A mother and daughter conflict can be deflected by their mutual concern over the father. In other words, the triangles cross generational lines and sibling, parent, cousin, aunt/uncle, grandparent structures in diverse ways. Nancy and Reuben Martinez may feel that Jason and Nancy's mother are allying against them in a way that undermines Jason's development. Ruth Jones may believe Jason's struggle to launch into adulthood is a result of his parents' marital dysfunctional, and thus Ruth is willing to offer him room and board.

Mental Health within a Systems Model

Systems that meet members' needs are considered functional and those that inhibit one or some members from meeting needs are considered problematic. Mental health, therefore, is not conceptualized as an individual-level construct. An older adult whose self-care capacity, social needs, or self-esteem needs are not met would not be labeled "mentally ill." Rather, the systems model would argue it is more appropriate to examine the interpersonal context that elicits or supports this behavior. The specific interpersonal system relevant to an individual older person's problem would be examined to identify the circular causal loops that maintain the problematic behavior.

The current interpersonal interactions that are maintaining the problem behavior are the most important behavior sequences to track. Finding the historical cause of the behavior may help the members of the system understand how the circular loop evolved, but the immediate interpersonal interactions are far more important. Herr and Weakland (1979) point out that a family system's first attempts to solve a problem are often unsuccessful, yet the same strategy may be maintained over time because the family cannot identify an alternative approach. The failed solution is likely to create another behavior problem (often the one for which help is sought) as a consequence of the ongoing failure experience. Thus failed solutions are often functioning to maintain the current problem.

Systems with poorly functioning structures will encounter difficulties meeting members' needs throughout the life-span, including later life. Families that are enmeshed or have poor boundaries around decision-making units (e.g., a marriage) are likely to encounter difficulty adjusting to the normative as well as the non-normative life events. The structures themselves inhibit flexibility needed to adapt well or to communicate clearly about changing needs and preferences.

Even well-functioning families may be challenged by particular events if they lack knowledge about how to meet members' needs or choose a poor strategy for adapting. For example, families with a demented member need a basic understanding of the impact of the disease on the patient and family in order to make appropriate care decisions and to support caregivers adequately. Families who functioned well through previous life events but who lack knowledge of dementia may solve problems ineffectively, and may even become stuck in a failed solution that harms one or more family members. The underlying structure may be functioning well except in one problem area, and thus a very limited psychoeducational intervention may be sufficient to solve the problem.

Assume for the moment that Jillian Jarvis has a vascular dementia that renders her too confused to eat properly and unsteady in gait so she falls often. Jean's decision to place her in a nursing home may be appropriate. John and JoAnn may lack information about the diagnosis or nature of the illness, and are primarily concerned to protect their mother's autonomy. A family meeting in which the cause and nature of the illness is carefully described may be sufficient to engage the three children in shared problem-solving.

Some families bring to later life a long history of poor adaptation with poorly functioning family structures (Florsheim & Herr, 1990). Even an adequate knowledge base regarding dementia care is unlikely to engage the family in a collaborative care-giving experience. If John and JoAnn have long-term unresolved conflicts with Jean that lead them to ally against her on any issue, then a common information base about their mother's needs may be only the first of several steps needed to resolve the family conflict that threatens Jillian's care.

Assessment

What should be assessed? The answer to that question depends on the nature of the problem, of course. There are a few general categories of information a mental health worker would want to know if undertaking a family systems intervention.

Family structure

A graphic depiction of family structure, called a genogram, is a very useful way of organizing efficiently information about several generations of family members (McGoldrick & Gerson, 1985). Figure 6.1 shows an example of Jason Martinez's family.

In addition to depicting the membership of the family according to generational lineage, a genogram can include information about the alliances, bonds, and conflicts in the family. The relationship between Jason and his grandmother is very strong, but his relationship with his mother and father is highly conflicted. The mild conflict between Nancy and Ruth in the past is blossoming into major warfare as they react to Jason's efforts to leave home.

Family development

Another way to describe families is in terms of their stage in the family life cycle. A model of the family life cycle in shown in figure 6.2 (Rodgers & White, 1993). The stages are marked by the entry and exit of members from the nuclear family. Obviously, the stage can only be labeled relative to one particular member. That is, a 50-year-old woman is perhaps in the "launching" stage while her daughter is establishing her family and her mother is in the final stage. Obviously, the life cycle is not a simple linear or even a simple

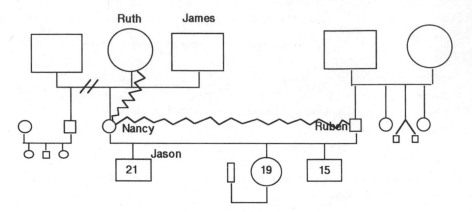

Figure 6.1 Genogram depicting Jason Martinez's family

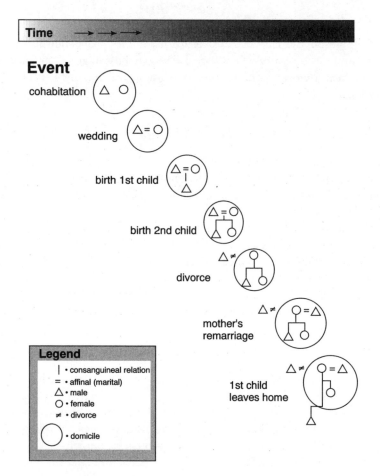

Figure 6.2 Family stages and events
Source: adapted from Rodgers & White, 1993.

circular sequence. Many complications in family development shape the life cycle of a given family. Divorce, chronic illness, the death of a child, and job loss are just a few of the life experiences that might alter the sequencing or meaning of various life stages (Carter & McGoldrick, 1988).

Mental health professionals can use the knowledge of each member's stage to identify ways in which the life tasks of various family members may be interfering with each other. For example, a young adult who is attempting to establish autonomy and independence may resist the desires of her grandmother to knit the family more closely. The family life cycle is a method of identifying the developmental tasks appropriate to each family member that will inevitably affect the family's style of functioning.

Family functioning

Systems approaches want to understand how a family meets members' needs. The structure of the family often becomes apparent by examining closely the patterns of interaction that result as members attempt to meet their needs and accomplish their developmental tasks.

There are several ways to examine family process. Watching family members interact verbally tells a lot about the family's structure and roles. Whose words are heard by everyone? Who expresses emotions? What happens if someone contradicts a family member in a different generation? Who gets the final word? The bonds, alliances, and conflicts described above become evident as one observes family interactions.

Cleveland Shields (1992) observed interactions between family members and a depressed caregiver to an Alzheimer's patient while they discussed a salient issue the family was currently facing. Each small segment of the interaction was given a code for emotion (positive, negative, neutral), and the sequencing of the segments was analyzed. This method of analysis documented a very interesting pattern of interaction. Caregivers who were more depressed than others in the sample were highly likely to respond to family members' negative emotion-laden comments with empathy. In other words, they were taking care of more than just the patient. Caregiver depression was also correlated with another counterintuitive pattern. "Family members of more depressed caregivers respond with more sadness when the caregivers express negative affect, and respond with more anger when the caregivers express positive affect" (Shields, 1992, pp. 25–6). When the most depressed caregivers in the sample are able to generate positive affect, their family members are likely to respond to them with anger! Obviously, the dynamics in these families are far more complex than is often acknowledged when we think of families as sources of support.

Another strategy for learning about family functioning is to identify the sequence of behaviors that family members use to accomplish a task. For example, when a physician calls a caregiver to inform her that the patient's lab tests show some disturbing information, what does that caregiver do? Whom does she call? Does everyone get the same amount of information? Who is involved in decisions? How do family members respond to the caregiver's distress? Which behaviors are experienced as supportive or interfering? Do those match the actor's intention? Herr and Weakland (1979, pp. 103–12) describe a case that illustrates the ways in which behavior that is intended to be supportive may actually reinforce dependency. They describe a mid-life female caring for her father in the home she shares with her husband and two boys. The father has become excessively dependent on the family to do tasks he could do for himself if he would. She has tried several strategies to encourage him to perform activities on his own (e.g., pleading, cajoling, demanding). When the family counselor began to elicit a detailed picture of the sequence of behavior interactions, it became evident that the daughter's behaviors were reinforcing her father's dependent demands. Her threats that she would not serve him were always met with efforts by her father to prove he needed help, to which she responded by "giving in" because it seemed cruel to let him suffer. Only by very carefully eliciting a detailed picture of behavior sequences could the counselor identify this pattern. This analysis is similar to that generated by a behaviorist because her "giving in" behavior is viewed as reinforcement in both models. However, a systems analysis emphasizes the reciprocal patterns of reinforcement rather than viewing the interaction as a linear antecedent-behavior-consequence sequence that relates solely to the father's behavior.

A systems assessment also needs to examine outcomes of family activity: Are members' needs being met and are developmental tasks being accomplished? Families have a myriad of ways of structuring themselves to accomplish the task of supporting members' development. Thus the examination of methods of accomplishing tasks is relevant primarily when some members' needs are not being met. For example, a family may be able to meet the needs of young children but be unable to support the needs of adolescents to launch themselves. Or, in later life, a family may adjust beautifully to the "empty nest" but be unable to adapt to the severe illness of an aging family member whose dependency needs exceed the children's skill or expectations. This functional deficit may become apparent through one member of the family whose behavior is problematic; this person is generally known as "the identified patient" (IP). The IP's abnormal functioning simply signals that the family is unable to meet all members' needs, and thus a thorough assessment of the family would be useful.

Family history

Two aspects of family history may become relevant: how previous generations dealt with aging-related challenges, and how this particular family constellation adapted to previous life transitions. Systems theorists emphasize the importance of intergenerational transmission of family rules, values, interaction patterns, and even anxiety (Boszormenyi-Nagy & Sparks, 1984; Bowen, 1978). A current systems problem may become simpler to solve when compared with the ways in which previous generations managed similar developmental tasks. Given that previous generations were less likely to live until advanced old age, many families are struggling to manage current problems without the benefit of the experience of previous generations. Idealized images may be serving as a proxy for real family experiences with some of the particular challenges and events of old age. On the other hand, families with clear rules for handling aging-related problems may find that those rules do not work well when applied to the needs of a particular aging relative in a particular context.

Although families may experience aging-related challenges to be novel and unfamiliar, in many cases the family's strategies for adapting to previous life events will apply directly to the current difficulties. Families who successfully managed previous family transitions often have resources and strategies for interacting that would be useful to the current dilemma if they are reminded of their previous successes.

Intervention

When working with families, the first task for any professional is to join the family. Professional helpers are obviously not members of the family, so joining the family is in itself an intervention. A common role families create for professional helpers is the "expert consultant." The consultant is presumed to know something about aging and the adaptations required of families, and is expected to support the family as it adapts. Creating this role requires the family to acknowledge formally that there is a problem and to open themselves somewhat to education. The process of joining and assessing the family is often an intervention in itself, so it cannot be readily differentiated from assessment.

Systems models distinguish between interventions that are targeted at "first-order" change and those targeted at "second-order" change (Watzlawick, Weakland, & Fisch, 1974). First-order change is that which modifies behavior patterns without altering substantially the basic structures and functioning patterns of the family. Second-order change alters structures to create a new kind of system. Generally, the principle used by mental health professionals is to begin with interventions targeted at first-order change to see if they are sufficient to solve the problem, and proceed to second-order interventions only if the less intrusive interventions did not work.

Later life families are often dealing with new challenges they simply do not understand. A common first-order intervention is education about the challenge (e.g., an illness, retirement, grief) and about the resources available to assist the family's adaptation and coping. Functionally, education about the problem takes the focus away from the identified patient and onto the problem. Education usually includes not only information about the life event or developmental task, but also about the importance of obtaining support and the resources available in the community for assisting the family.

Second-order change efforts are explicitly targeted at altering the family's structure and familiar ways of functioning. One strategy commonly used is to reorganize the smaller units of the family system that are responsible for particular roles in the family. For example, a family therapist might direct the family to reorganize its decision-making structure if the current structure cannot function well. Or, in a case where a widowed woman and her daughter appear to be engaging in constant conflicts primarily because they do not have any other ways of maintaining appropriate separateness, a therapist might encourage the family to break rules that make it taboo for adult children to tell a parent directly when they do not want to discuss a matter.

Another strategy for accomplishing second-order change is to alter the interaction patterns. Therapists may ask family members to alter where they sit in the therapy room in order to force an immediate restructuring of an alliance. Therapists also may direct the sequencing of an interaction, interrupting familiar and non-productive patterns to allow new interaction patterns to form.

One case that illustrates these principles is that of a 66-year-old woman who brought her 68-year-old husband and 42-year-old daughter to see a family counselor. The therapist immediately recognized a father–daughter alliance against the mother. An obvious enactment of the alliance against the mother was evident in the very way the three members chose their chairs when they walked into the therapist's office: the father and daughter sat next to each other on the couch, leaving the mother the chair across the room next to the therapist. As the family explained to the therapist their reasons for coming, the mother suggested that she was worried about her daughter, who seems to lack initiative. The father interrupted her with, "That's crazy!" and immediately contradicted his wife by naming all of the activities the daughter did this week. The daughter sat silently, leaning against her father as if for support. The father and daughter were allied in their shared view that the daughter's inability to live independently is not a problem. As the assessment reveals, the alliance is interfering with the intimacy of the father and the mother in their marriage (a structure problem) and impeding the daughter from launching into independent adulthood (a developmental problem). Asking the father and mother to move their chairs close to one another and hold hands while discussing their perceptions of their daughter's strengths might force recognition of the marital bond that would be ignored if father and daughter were allowed to enact their alliance. Once the bond is established, the parents' discussion of their concerns about their daughter is much more likely to be productive. The therapist might alter the interaction sequences by creating first a conversation between the mother and the father that the daughter is not allowed to enter, then setting up a conversation between the mother and the daughter that the father is not allowed to enter. If the father's typical role is to run interference for the daughter, then the mother and the daughter will each feel anxious about interacting in a more direct and vulnerable way. This anxiety creates the opportunity for a new pattern of interaction to form, one that is more likely to handle directly the developmental tasks at hand. Therapists must resist a family's efforts to maintain homeostasis by forcing restructuring in order to create second order change (Qualls, 1991).

Other approaches to work with aging families focus more at the level of family values, obligations, and balances in reciprocity (Hargrave & Anderson, 1992). Families pass across generations not only values statements about how it "should" be done (which may or may not be relevant to current social and familial conditions), but also pass along rules and obligations from the lineage (Boszormenyi-Nagy & Sparks, 1984). Family conflict over parent care may be rooted in conflicted values or the sense of being trapped to fulfill obligations. Dialogue to increase awareness of the unspoken forces shaping the family member's interactions with each other is another intervention strategy.

The majority of published research on interventions with aging families has been conducted with one family member, the primary caregiver, for the purpose of assisting him or her to care for another, ill elderly family member (Qualls, 1995a). The majority of interventions focus on first-order interventions such as education, support, and problem-solving about specific illness-generated difficulties (Zarit & Teri, 1991).

One intervention study suggests that the systems approach that targets second-order change may also be useful, even though systems was not the theoretical framework from which the study was derived. Scharlach (1987) involved daughters who served as primary care providers to elderly mothers in one of two intervention conditions. Part of the sample was given information about care-giving and about community resources while encouraging the daughters to focus on meeting their mothers' needs for assistance. The other intervention group involved daughters in modifying unrealistic expectations of responsibility to their aging mothers, and encouraged them to promote self-reliance in their mothers while enhancing their own well-being. Daughters in the second group reported less burden and better relationship quality, while their mothers reported less loneliness than those in the first group (or a control group). Although only the daughters were involved in this intervention, this study could be interpreted as an intervention to teach daughters to set boundaries, thus altering family structure.

Another study shows the benefits of a family intervention that was designed to be flexible enough to include whatever kind of family intervention was helpful. Mittelman and colleagues conducted an intervention study that offered a combination of individual and family counseling to primary caregivers of demented relatives (Mittelman et al., 1993; 1994). When compared with caregivers who received only support-group interventions, the families receiving ongoing counseling reported more involvement from the family network in support of patient and caregiver, increased caregiver satisfaction with the support network, and a reduced rate of institutionalization. The flexibility to include a variety of interventions based on each family's need disallows analysis of which components of the package of intervention strategies were responsible for the positive effect.

Unfortunately, the research base demonstrating the utility of the systems model is meager. However, preliminary results of clinical cases (e.g., Gallagher & Frankel, 1980), clinical analysis (Qualls, 1996; Shields et al., 1995), descriptive research (e.g., Shields, 1992), and outcome research (e.g., Mittelman et al., 1993) are promising. The need for more theoretical and more empirical research is apparent, but the value of using a model for mental health and aging that explicitly incorporates families as a system is also clear.

Summary and Commentary: Choosing Among Models of Mental Disorders in Later Life

In this section we have described several different models of mental health and mental illness. Before we consider the treatment of specific disorders in more detail in the next section, it may be useful to consider a simple question: How do you choose among the various models?

Let's begin to answer this question by reflecting on what we want from a model of mental health or mental illness. Remember, a model is a representation, something like a map that draws our attention to certain aspects of the terrain while allowing us to find our way. Similarly, models cannot fully represent the complexity of an older adult's life situation. Instead, they focus our attention on the most salient elements of the older adult and his or her environment (Reese & Overton, 1970; Pepper, 1942). In doing so, all models provide answers to several basic questions (see table S1). Each model emphasizes certain elements for understanding mental health. By focusing our attention on certain aspects of the individual's functioning, the model explicitly and implicitly asserts that other elements are less important.

Similarly, the model's explanation of what changes in mental disorders and in aging implicitly alerts us to the potential targets of therapeutic intervention. For example, in psychodynamic perspectives, the focus of attention is personality structures. As outlined in chapter 3, structural change is often viewed as a desirable therapeutic goal, but often beyond the capacity of either the therapist or the client.

Models also differ in the *type* of change they predict for the older adult: quantitative (different in degree) or qualitative (different in kind). For example, the behavioral models focus on differences in quantity of behaviors, behavioral excesses, or deficits. In contrast, systems perspectives focus on differences both in quantity and in quality of interactions among the system's components.

Table S1 Choosing among models

Model elements	Psycho-dynamic	Behavioral	Stress and coping	Family systems
• What is studied? • What changes with age or with mental disorder?	• Motivation and personality • Personality structures	• Behavioral interaction • Cognitive and behavior patterns	• Strain, stressor, and interactions • Individual adaptability or stressors or the interaction	• Family system's interactions • Developmental tasks and systems interactions
• What kind of change occurs?	• Qualitative change	• Quantitative change (behaviors) and qualitative change (cognitions)	• Qualitative and quantitative change	• Qualitative and quantitative change
• How is change explained?	• Structure/functional relationships	• Antecedent/consequences chains	• Interaction of the person and the environment	• Interaction among the elements of the system

Finally, the models also differ in how they explain change. This set of assumptions provides the clearest set of suggestions for therapeutic intervention. For example, the behavioral perspectives emphasize the chain of antecedents and consequences that develop and maintain behavior patterns. To alter behavior requires changing this chain by affecting either the antecedents or the consequences of behavior. Similarly, stress theorists assess the interaction of the individual's coping repertoire (including, perhaps, the immune system's stress reactivity) and the stressors that confront him or her.

Applying Models to Individual Life Circumstances

With this understanding of models and their underlying assumptions, let's return to the case that opened this section, that of Mrs Rankin.

Joan Rankin is a 74-year-old woman who lives in her home in a small rural community. Her husband, Jim, died two years ago, following a five-year bout with cancer. Now that she is alone, Joan is tempted to move closer to her children, but cannot quite make up her mind. Her house is paid for, and she is not sure she could buy a comparable house in a city with the proceeds from a sale of this house. She has a modest pension that will be sufficient unless she needs major medical care. Sometimes she worries about not having enough money to carry her through. She chooses to live frugally with an occasional indulgence.

Joan belongs to the local garden club, but is not a particularly active member. She does enjoy working in her own small flower garden during the nice weather seasons. She also attends church almost weekly. Joan has a few close friends, but many of those friendships were strained by the period of Jim's illness. Even two years after his death, she is not sure how to fill her days. Her nights are usually tolerable, although sometimes she lies awake for long periods in the middle of the night. At those times she feels overwhelmingly alone and scared.

Joan is generally healthy, although she has high blood pressure and some difficulties with thyroid and arthritis. She takes Tylenol for the arthritis, propanolol for blood pressure, and synthroid to regulate her thyroid.

Joan's two children live 300 miles away in major cities. Her daughter, Jeannie, is married, has three children (ages 4, 7, and 10), and teaches school. Her son, John, a very successful realtor, is currently engaged to be remarried. He was divorced four years ago from his wife of 18 years, who has custody of their two children, ages 8 and 13. Jeannie and John have never been very close. Nor was John close to his father, although he confided his troubles and joys to his mother privately.

Joan has two younger sisters still living, and two older brothers who died more than five years ago. Her sister Betty lives only two blocks away from Joan, and calls her daily. Sometimes Joan even resents the call because Betty is so perky and enthusiastic about life. Betty insists that Joan get out to social events regardless of how tired or sick Joan is feeling. Betty has always been the cheerful one, encouraging all around her to enjoy life. Recently she has hinted that she might like to move in with Joan to share expenses.

Her other sister Vivian lives with her husband 30 miles away on a farm. They stay busy with farm responsibilities, and with their children and grandchildren. Joan sees them only at family gatherings on holidays. Vivian has always been the quiet, solid one in the family. Joan would like to spend more time with her, but can see that she is too busy with daily responsibilities to socialize.
Her brothers, Elwood and Milt, were in business together in a city 150 miles from Joan's home. They died of heart attacks exactly one year apart. They left their families quite well off financially, and their children and grandchildren have continued their business. Joan only visits with her sisters-in-law or their offspring at the annual family reunion each summer.

How would each model approach Mrs Rankin's life situation?

As outlined in Chapter 3, the psychodynamic perspective assumes that Mrs Rankin's symptoms will resolve if she comes to terms with the normal developmental tasks of later life. Erikson and his colleagues, for example, argue that the primary conflict to be resolved in later life is between ego integrity versus despair (Erikson et al., 1986). Clearly, Mrs Rankin has spent much time and energy in the earlier developmental conflict (generativity vs. self-absorption), providing care for her ailing husband. Within this perspective, much attention would initially focus on her own beliefs and values and the meaning that she attributes to her life, the coherence of the personal narrative that she has developed in thinking about her life. A major goal of treatment within the dynamic perspective might be to provide supportive therapy for Mrs Rankin as she re-evaluates her experience in later life. In doing so, the therapist would begin with an assessment of her capacity for insight, her ability to reflect upon her experiences, and her aptitude for engaging in the therapeutic process.

In contrast, a behaviorally oriented professional would not focus on the underlying structure of Mrs Rankin's personality or the "coherence" of her personal narrative (see Chapter 4). Instead, someone working within the behavioral perspective would focus on assessing specific problem behaviors and the context for the development and continuation of those behaviors. In

Mrs Rankin's case, for example, the focus might fall on her periods of sleeplessness at night. Exactly when and under what conditions does this occur? Conversely, are there conditions under which the sleeplessness does not occur? The therapist might ask Mrs Rankin to keep an activity log or a record of her sleep pattern and context for several days, trying to identify the pattern of antecedents and consequences that affect the sleep disruption. The behavioral treatment would focus on altering the contingencies within Mrs Rankin's context. First, it would be important to identify the desired outcome – in this case, uninterrupted sleep. Next, attention would focus on one of two strategies: expanding the conditions that have led to a full night's sleep in the past, or eliminating the conditions that are associated with the current bouts of sleeplessness. For example, if it were found that Mrs Rankin slept better on the days that she had talked with one of her children, the therapist might enlist the children in a schedule of calls or contact. Similarly, if it were discovered that Mrs Rankin had disrupted sleep on days that Betty called after 4 p.m., the therapist might work with Betty to change the schedule of her contacts. In addition, the therapist might also focus on Mrs Rankin's own thoughts regarding being alone (i.e., her reporting feeling "alone and scared").

A therapist working in the stress and coping framework might try a variety of strategies targeting several key aspects of Mrs Rankin's experience: chronic strains, social resources, Mrs Rankin's own vulnerabilities and resources, and her physical well-being (see chapter 5). For example, the therapist might begin by targeting assessment and treatment for two chronic strains that are currently affecting Mrs Rankin: her concerns about her financial well-being and her coping with her chronic health problems (e.g., arthritis, high blood pressure, and thyroid problems). Another target for assessment and treatment might be Mrs Rankin's social resources. Here, the emphasis might shift to first assessing her current levels of social involvement and then enlisting effective social support for her. A third element of assessment and treatment might emphasize Mrs Rankin's own approach to appraising her situation and the attributions she makes about her current life circumstances. Again, an initial step might be an assessment of her current and previous coping strategies. Treatment would then explore either application of previously successful coping attempts or development of other coping skills. Finally, someone working within the stress and coping framework might focus on improving Mrs Rankin's health practices – perhaps by focusing on a relaxation training or meditation program to decrease her anxiety.

A mental health professional working within a family systems perspective would emphasize other aspects of Mrs Rankin's situation: her family's structure and function (see chapter 6). For example, a therapist working within a system's perspective might start by asking Mrs Rankin to complete a family genogram, including information about the alliances and bonds between and among various members of the family. Similarly, the therapist might be interested in the family stages represented by the various members (e.g., her daughter's children are all under ten; her son's children are also in the school-age years, etc.). This information helps the therapist to be aware of other family members' developmental tasks that may be competing with Mrs Rankin's own challenges. Another focus of assessment would be how this family works: To whom does Mrs Rankin turn in times of crisis? Whom does she call first for everyday help? For major assistance? Treatment within this framework might require both "first-order" and "second-order" change. At the very least, the mental health professional should be clear whether the goal is to change the behavior patterns of the family or to alter the basic structure of the family. Either goal might require the active involvement of several family members in the treatment process.

In summary, each of the therapeutic models offers directions for assessment and treatment. Each has explicit and implicit assumptions about the salient contributors to mental health and mental illness in later life. Each focuses therapeutic attention and effort to specific aspects of Mrs Rankin's life and circumstances.

If all models differ in their basic elements, how do we choose among them?

Reese and Overton (1970) suggested two criteria for selecting among "world hypotheses" (Pepper, 1942) – overarching theoretical frameworks that provide a foundation for specific models – *precision and scope*. Both are useful for assessing each model.

> Precision is the ability to produce an adequate or compelling interpretation of a fact, and the ability to produce only one such interpretation (or at most a few such interpretations). . . . Scope refers to the range of facts that can be interpreted. (Reese & Overton, 1970, p. 122)

To be useful, a model must be both precise and capable of explaining a wide scope of functioning in older adults. This is how we can gauge its success. The four models presented in this section have proven themselves useful from clinical and research perspectives. The challenge for the geriatric practitioner is to assess which perspective will be more helpful in understanding and intervening on behalf of a particular older client.

There are two different approaches that clinicians may follow: the single lens or the kaleidoscope. Some prefer to become an expert within a single framework, knowing its strengths and limitations in depth. (For example, a practitioner may focus on dynamic approaches exclusively.) The clinician comes to learn the precision afforded by the theoretical and practical aspects of the framework in detail. He or she also comes to learn and respect the scope of clinical utility of the framework, respecting that it probably will not be adequate for all clients and all conditions.

Most clinicians, however, report that they are "eclectic," using techniques from a variety of perspectives. In contrast to someone who uses one framework exclusively, these clinicians may emphasize aspects of several different frameworks, as if turning the kaleidoscope to see different facets of the same scene.

In the end, the clinician must ask a differential diagnostic question: Which assessment and treatment approaches for which types of geriatric mental disorders will produce which types of outcomes? Answering this question will force you to detail the precision and scope of your implicit or explicit frameworks.

Part III

Introduction to Mental Disorders

Introduction

Consider the following letter we once received from a client:

Dear Dr Smyer:

I have toyed with the idea of writing you ever since I heard you speak at the Presbyterian Church a couple of years ago. The occasion was one of a series of brown-bag lunches sponsored, I think, by the Area Agency on Aging. You may remember me, since I'm sure you were embarrassed when I substituted one word for another in trying to ask a question about the part inheritance plays in senility. My question made no sense, and you tactfully said, "I don't believe I understand your question," and I repeated it, correctly, saying, "You can see I'm senile already." (I was trying to be funny, but I was not amused.)

The question I asked is one that has haunted me all my adult life (I've just turned 78), and I think I have always known the answer. My father's father, my father, and the three sisters who lived long enough were all senile. I am obviously following in their footsteps, and have discussed the matter with Dr Klein, who became my physician last year. I have told him that I have never taken much medication and have been opposed to "pain-killers," tranquilizers, etc., but that the day may come when I will accept medical help as the lesser of two evils. He assures me that there are new drugs which may help.

My question, Dr Smyer, is this: Since I'm sure there must be ongoing research into the problem of senility, would it be of any value to such research if I volunteered as a test subject? At this point my memory is failing so rapidly, and I suffer such frequent agonies of confusion, that I am at the point of calling on Dr Klein for the help he has promised. But I don't want to do so yet if my experience can be of value to someone else, and particularly to the nine daughters of my sisters, ranging in age from 58 to 70, and to my own daughter, 42, who must be wondering if they too are doomed.

Is there any merit to this proposal? I will be most grateful for any advice you can give me.

Sincerely,

Mrs Rose

(Smyer, 1984)

How would you respond? Immediately, you have to make a clinical judgment about the seriousness of this older woman's concerns. Are her complaints a part of normal aging? Are they part of a pattern of serious mental illness? Your answer implicitly combines information from developmental epidemiology, psychiatric epidemiology, clinical investigations, and the psychology of adult development and aging. If you decide that Mrs Rose has a serious mental illness, what would you do? Your answer reflects your assumptions regarding the cause of the disorder and how effective you can be in altering that cause.

The chapters in this section are designed to describe the patterns of specific mental disorders along with effective methods for assessment and treatment of the disorders. In preparing these chapters we face the same dilemmas as clinicians: How do we know that specific symptoms are part of a picture of pathology? How can we identify specific treatments that are effective with older adults?

A consensus is emerging among researchers and clinicians that our earlier models for describing patterns of disease, causation, and treatment were too simplistic (Pearce, 1996; Susser & Susser, 1996a, 1996b). We would like to reduce the complexity of assessment and treatment to a simple focus on the individual, or perhaps even on one aspect of the individual (e.g., biological functioning). However, an effective understanding of mental illness in later life requires an understanding of the ecology of interactions of several levels of influence, from the molecular to the molar, from genetic predispositions to the social environment, that either protect or exacerbate the individual's vulnerability.

For example, at the request of the US Congress, the Institute of Medicine (IOM) recently developed a research agenda aimed at preventing mental disorders (Mrazek & Haggerty, 1994). The IOM report suggested that we need to consider a new spectrum of mental health interventions for mental disorders. The spectrum includes three major classes of intervention: prevention, treatment, and maintenance (see figure I1).

A central element in the scheme is the concept of risk for a disorder. Formerly, risk might be thought of as solely an individual characteristic, identified by individual indicators (e.g., genetic history, age, sex, SES, etc.).

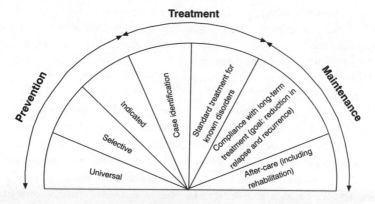

Figure I1 The mental health intervention spectrum for mental disorders
Source: Mrazek & Haggerty, 1994.

However, recent work in epidemiology and clinical investigation suggests that risk for developing a disorder is an interaction of several systems and levels of influence, including aspects of the individual's setting, as well as the individual's own characteristics.

Susser and Susser (1996b) put it this way:

> Systems also relate to one another; they do not exist in isolation. A metaphor may serve to illuminate this ecological perspective. We liken it to Chinese boxes – a conjurer's nest of boxes, each containing a succession of smaller ones. Thus, within localized structures, we envisage successive levels of organization, each of which encompasses the next and simpler level, all with intimate links between them . . .
>
> . . . The outer box might be the overarching physical environment which, in turn, contains societies and populations (the epidemiological terrain), single individuals, and individual physiological systems, tissues and cells, and finally (in biology) molecules. (pp. 675–6)

Gatz and her colleagues (1996) also stressed the interaction of three types of influences on the development and presentation of mental disorders among older adults: the individual's level of vulnerability, which is a product of biological vulnerabilities and psychological factors affecting risk; stress, both environmental and social; and protective factors that can serve as psychological, biological, or social buffers. They argue that the combination of protective and risk factors affects the individual's susceptibility of developing a mental disorder.

To be effective, then, the clinician must understand the context of the individual and the patterns of interaction among several levels of influence. This multilayered ecological perspective will affect how symptoms are labeled, how clinical syndromes are defined, and, ultimately, case identification (see figure I1). It will also affect strategies that are developed for assessment and treatment.

For example, consider Mrs Rose's complaint about memory problems. If we look solely at her individual situation, we may miss important information about the social stresses that may be presenting a challenge for her. Optimally, we would like to place her current functioning in a larger context: Does she have a history of memory problems and complaints? Does she have a family history of such problems? Has she been treated for these difficulties in the past? What is the context of this most recent complaint (e.g., changes in her own functioning, her social context, her physical well-being, etc.)? Have her medications changed recently? Have there been any recent physical illnesses? In short, we would be assessing the three key elements of the scheme proposed by Gatz et al.: individual vulnerability, stresses, and protective factors.

At the same time, we must focus on two types of history: the history of the individual and the history of the disorder. Again, consider Mrs Rose. We want to know much about her personal history and about the history of her memory complaint. Epidemiologists focus on incidence and prevalence rates: patterns of development of new episodes and rates of overall presence of the disorder, regardless of when it began. On the clinical level, we might envision different treatment strategies for two different patterns: some might grow old and get memory problems; others might develop memory problems and grow old (Kahn, 1975). These different life histories and different problem histories would suggest different approaches.

The chapters in these sections take these elements as a starting point: an ecological perspective that acknowledges several layers of interacting influence that produce risk and disorder patterns; individual life history and problem history that affect assessment and treatment; and the necessity for an integrated approach to assessment and treatment that acknowledges individual vulnerability, assesses sources of stress, and builds upon current effective sources of support. The chapters also emphasize effective case identification and treatment. In doing so, they draw from the models of mental health and mental illness described in Section 2. The assessment and treatment approaches outlined in Section 3 embody causal models of each disorder and, therefore, assumptions regarding effective clinical approaches.

7

Cognitive Impairment

Cognitive impairment is a broad term indicating some degree of deterioration in cognitive function that alters a person's ability to perform day-to-day activities. Common causes of cognitive impairment (CI) in later life include delirium, dementia, and depression, although a myriad of other factors can also lead to reduced cognitive functioning. Because of its devastating effect on the autonomy of older adults, CI warrants aggressive assessment and interventions to support the maximum possible level of functioning. Anyone working with older adults must have some familiarity with the causes, consequences, and remedies for CI. This chapter begins by addressing the extent to which cognitive decline is a part of normal aging, then describes the types of impairment that characterize delirium, dementia, and depression. Strategies for assessing cognitive functioning, and for designing interventions to enhance the functioning of cognitively impaired persons, will also be described. Consider the following three cases, which illustrate some of the challenges faced by persons with CI.

Jane Winthrop is an 85-year-old widow who is experiencing increasing difficulty living alone. Her daughter visits every Saturday to write out bills, set up medications for this week in a pillbox, and take her shopping. Jane has trouble figuring out how much of her favorite foods to buy, and typically purchases prepared meals that can be heated in the microwave. Her daughter leaves reminder notes on the microwave about how to work it, and on the entry door to the apartment about what security measures should be taken before bedtime. On the bathroom mirror is a reminder to brush teeth, and on the kitchen table is a reminder to take medications after meals. Jane stays in her apartment most of the time because the hallways and elevator confuse her. Friends in the apartment complex check in on her daily.

Noni Smith's daughter was alarmed when she visited her mother last weekend. Within the space of a week her mother had changed! She had a vacant look in her eyes, was not interested in talking, was dressed in mismatched clothing, and her hair was not combed. The neighbor shared the daughter's concern, indicating she had not seen Noni out walking this week as was her custom. The daughter called Noni's physician, who asked to see her immediately to check whether the new medications he initiated two weeks ago could be causing the problem.

Jim Hunt complains constantly about his poor memory. He is so disturbed by his inability to concentrate and remember things that he has quit two of his favorite hobbies – woodworking and reading about politics. He no longer has the showcase yard of the neighborhood because he only seems able to do the minimum. His family is growing concerned that he may have Alzheimer's disease.

What Jane, Noni, and Jim share in common is a perceived or real loss of abilities to think, remember, solve problems, and handle the affairs of everyday life. Indeed, cognitive impairment (CI) is one of the most feared aspects of aging. Although there are changes in cognitive functioning that are normative with old age, these rarely affect daily functioning. Unfortunately, many people expect cognitive functioning to decline with age, leaving them confused about whether these individuals need to be treated by health-care professionals or simply assisted by family and friends. Even families and professional staff often fail to recognize the extent of cognitive impairment (Mulkerrin et al., 1992). The risks of CI are well documented in both hospitalized and community-dwelling older adults. For example, the risk of hospitalization and a longer length of stay in the hospital are higher in older adults with CI than those with intact cognitive functioning (Binder & Robins, 1990).

What is the range of cognitive functioning that is of interest to mental health providers? Cognition is usually examined within five broad areas: attention, language, memory, visuo-spatial attention, and conceptualization (Albert, 1988). Within each domain are many specific functions. Neuropsychologists organize their analyses of cognitive functioning within a hierarchy that ranges from the simplest functions (e.g., attention) to the most complex (e.g., abstract thinking and problem-solving). This hierarchical organization reflects the foundational role of the simpler functions for all complex cognitive activities that rank higher in the hierarchy. In other words, if basic processes like attention are impaired, all higher order processes will be negatively affected. As a general rule, more complex functions are the most easily disrupted by illness, brain dysfunction, or potentially toxic agents like medications.

Is CI Normal for Older Adults?

The answer to this question is actually a qualified "clearly yes and no." On one hand, tests of cognitive functioning consistently show age-related decrements in many cognitive functions that begin anywhere from the 50s to the 60s. On the other hand, the normative decrements in functioning that are evident in laboratory tests rarely make an impact on daily functioning.

Several factors make it possible for age decrements to be normative but for few effects of those changes to be seen in everyday life. First, laboratory tests push the limits of skills in ways that rarely occur in daily life. The normative cognitive declines are relatively subtle, becoming visible primarily when functioning is pushed to its limits. Second, there is tremendous variability among older adults in the degree of decline experienced in any specific function. Thus, although mean scores may decline, the highest functioning older person may still be functioning well above the average for younger adults. Third, humans are highly adaptive creatures who adjust their behavior to compensate for deficits (Baltes & Baltes, 1990a). Decrements in cognitive impairment may not be evident in daily life because the individual is skilled at compensating for deficits with external aids (e.g., written grocery lists) or drawing upon an intact skill to compensate (e.g., relying on a cognitive map to drive to a friend's house when verbal memory for directions is impaired). In this chapter, CI refers to impairments that affect daily functioning – that is, those that are caused by some serious disease or dysfunction that warrants intervention.

Before discussing clinically significant CI, the types of cognitive deficits that are normative with age will be described. Detailed summaries of findings on normative cognitive changes with age can be found elsewhere (Albert, 1988; Smith, 1996; Sugar & McDowd, 1992). A graph depicting the typical longitudinal picture of cognitive decline with advancing age is presented in figure 7.1, taken from the Seattle Longitudinal Study of Intellectual Abilities (Schaie, 1994). Note that most abilities depicted in this graph remained stable or actually improved throughout middle adulthood. In the 60s and 70s declines in functioning begin to be apparent in some functions, and by the 80s all functions show some degree of deterioration.

Generally, attentional processes are maintained well into advanced old age, as are most language abilities. Language abilities are generally preserved intact until well into the 70s, at which time some deficits are evident in semantic linguistic abilities (e.g., verbal meaning). Performances on complex laboratory tasks (e.g., selective attention) typically show some age-correlated decre-

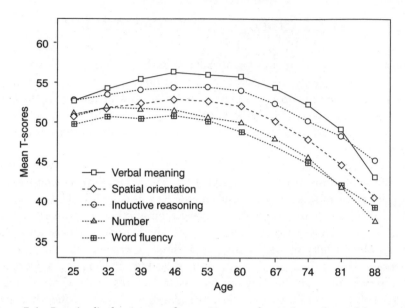

Figure 7.1 Longitudinal estimates of mean T-scores for single markers of the primary mental abilities
Note: From seven-year within-subject data.
Source: Schaie, 1994.

ments, but much more limited deficits than are evident in the complex cognitive functions such as problem-solving or abstract thinking.

Reducing a complex field to a broad summary, we can say that age has a negative effect on memory. Younger adults perform better than adults older than age 50 on most tasks. By age 70, performance within several domains is quite impaired. Of course, the extent of deficit is influenced by the method of assessment and the memory task (e.g., with and without cues, meaningful vs. non-meaningful stimuli, visual and verbal stimuli). Intervention research has demonstrated that some of the deficits seen in long-term memory can be ameliorated by providing additional structure to the memory tasks (e.g., providing cues, instructions in encoding strategies, or use of recognition rather than recall tasks), although memory skill remains lower, on average, for older than younger adults even under enhancement conditions. Memory processes are differentially affected by age. Drawing upon work in a highly complex field, the following generalizations are offered, based on current research (see summaries by Smith, 1996; Sugar and McDowd, 1992). Generally, sensory memory (e.g., immediate visual or auditory trace memory) and primary memory (or very short-term memory of a few moments' duration) are unaffected by age. Learning and retaining information over time (secondary memory) is where the greatest declines with aging are evident.

Abstract reasoning and complex problem-solving abilities also appear to decline by the 60s and 70s (Salthouse, 1991). Tasks such as the Category Test of the Halstead-Reitan, the Block Design subtest on the Wechsler Adult Intelligence Scale-Revised (WAIS-R), and explaining proverbs all elicit lower performances in older adults than in young adults. As is true of most cognitive functions, the method of assessment and the type of task produces variations in the results, although the picture that emerges is essentially consistent.

Knowledge of what is normative within healthy older adults is critical to the formation of appropriate expectations about performance on tests of cognitive functioning in clinical populations. The clinical assessment of CI requires either baseline data on the individual's previous functioning, or normative data on older adults within an appropriate comparison group. The importance of age-appropriate norms will be discussed further in the section on assessment below.

Most instances of CI that become evident to family, friends, and professionals will involve some clinically significant disease or disorder. The most common causes of CI are delirium, dementia, or depression.

Delirium: A Common, Reversible Cause of CI

A delirium is "characterized by a disturbance of consciousness and a change in cognition that develop over a short period of time" (American Psychiatric Association, 1994, p. 123). At times, delirium is referred to as an *acute confusional state* or *reversible dementia*. The case of Noni Smith described above is typical of a case of delirium. The onset is rapid, and the person's behavior is disorganized in ways that are not typical for her.

The cognitive disturbance may be caused by one or more medical conditions, by medications, by substance intoxication or withdrawal, by toxin exposure, or by some combination of factors. The DSM-IV criteria for all deliria, regardless of etiology, are listed in table 7.1. In addition to the criteria which require a disturbance in cognition, persons experiencing delirium are also likely to report a disturbed sleep–wake cycle and unpleasant affect (e.g., fear, depression, anger). Attentional processes are particularly disrupted, leading to impairment in higher level cognitive functions (e.g., memory, problem-solving).

Older adults are especially at risk for delirium because of their increased

Table 7.1   Diagnostic criteria for delirium, regardless of etiology

A.   Disturbance of consciousness (i.e., reduced clarity of awareness of the environment) with reduced ability to focus, sustain, or shift attention

B.   A change in cognition (such as memory deficit, disorientation, language disturbance) or the development of a perceptual disturbance that is not better accounted for by a pre-existing, established, or evolving dementia

C.   The disturbance develops over a short period of time (usually hours to days) and tends to fluctuate during the course of the day.

Source: American Psychiatric Association, 1994.

likelihood of chronic illness and the increased use of medication to manage those illnesses. Delirium states are seen in approximately 25 percent of hospitalized patients at admission, due primarily to infection and congestive heart failure (Rockwood, 1989). Within the community, approximately 0.4 to 1.1 percent of adults over age 55 met diagnostic criteria for delirium (Folstein, Basset, et al., 1991). Common medical causes of delirium include acute illnesses (e.g., urinary tract infections), central nervous system disorders (e.g., stroke), cardiovascular disorders, and metabolic disturbances. Post-operative patients show particularly high rates of delirium, ranging from estimates of 10 to 33 percent for all post-operative patients (Tune, 1991).

Almost any medication, including the most apparently innocuous over-the-counter medications, can cause delirium if the right conditions are present. One reason for vulnerability is that the process by which drugs are distributed, metabolized, and excreted are altered significantly with age (Salzman & Nevis-Olesen, 1992). Changes in several physiological systems contribute to the reduced capacity to metabolize, break down, and excrete drugs from the body. Thus, adverse drug reactions or drug toxicity are significant risk factors for older adults. Older adults are also more vulnerable to medication-induced delirium because of their high rate of medication use. For example, psychotropic drugs are taken by over one-third of older adults in hospitals and as many as 74 percent of nursing-home residents (Salzman & Nevis-Olesen, 1992). The average nursing-home resident is on 9.3 medications (Pollock et al., 1992), at least one of which is likely to be a psychotropic medication (Avorn et al., 1992). The potential for drug interactions is obviously extraordinarily high. Taken together, physiological changes result in altered responsiveness to medications such that even very small doses can produce delirium.

Environmental conditions can also add to the probability of delirium, although deliria are unlikely to result solely from environmental conditions.

Psychosocial factors, sensory deprivation, and sleep deprivation may contribute to the development of delirium when other causal factors (e.g., toxic or metabolic factors) are present (Rabins, 1991).

Dementia: The Most Devastating Cause of CI

Dementias are the class of brain disorders characterized by irreversible declines in cognitive functioning that interfere with social and occupational functioning (American Psychiatric Association, 1994). The most common deficit in dementias is memory decline, although gradual, progressive declines in other cognitive functions are seen also. The criteria that are shared by the dementias are listed in table 7.2. Persons with dementia are usually aware of some degree of deficit (although not always), but they typically underestimate the level of deficit. Family members are often the first to state a concern about daily functioning, as they watch their loved one lose capacity to function at the level they had previously enjoyed. Independence is most threatened by the loss of ability to provide basic self-care functions that are usually measured as activities of daily living (ADLs, including bathing, dressing, eating) and instrumental activities of daily living (IADLs, including management of finances, transportation, telephone use).

Dementias severe enough to impair independent functioning are found in approximately 6 to 8 percent of persons over age 65 (Cummings & Benson, 1992; Canadian Study of Health and Aging Working Group, 1994). Advanced age clearly adds to the probability of dementia, with the risk doubling approximately every five years after age 65 (Jorm et al., 1987; Ritchie et al., 1992), such that about 30 percent of persons over age 85 are diagnosable with dementia (Skoog et al., 1993). Dementias can be produced by 50 or more different causes (Katzman, 1986), although neurodegenerative diseases make up the vast majority.

The two most prevalent dementias are Alzheimer's disease and vascular dementias, which together account for about 90 percent of all dementias (Skoog et al., 1993). The rates of these two disorders differ by region, with some countries reporting higher rates of vascular dementia and other countries reporting higher rates of Alzheimer's disease (Jorm et al., 1987; Skoog et al., 1993).

The cause of Alzheimer's disease (AD) is unknown, although certain specific subtypes of the disease appear to be genetically linked (Youngjohn & Crook, 1996). The pathophysiology of AD includes unusually high rates of neuronal cell loss, along with unusual concentrations of amyloid, and an

Table 7.2 Common diagnostic criteria for dementias

A. The development of multiple cognitive deficits manifested by both
    1) memory impairment (impaired ability to learn new information or to recall previously learned information)
    2) one (or more) of the following cognitive disturbances:
        a) aphasia (language disturbance)
        b) apraxia (impaired ability to carry out motor activities despite intact motor function)
        c) agnosia (failure to recognize or identify objects despite intact sensory function)
        d) disturbance in executive functioning (i.e., planning, organizing, sequencing, abstracting)
B. The cognitive deficits in Criteria A1 and A2 each cause significant impairment in social or occupational functioning and represent a significant decline from a previous level of functioning.

Source: American Psychiatric Association, 1994.

increased prevalence of neuritic plaques and neurofibrillary tangles in the cortex, amygdala, and hippocampus areas of the brain. Decreased levels of acetylcholine, the neurotransmitter involved in learning and memory, as well as other neurotransmitters further compromise brain function.

AD progresses slowly and continuously, leading to declining functional capacities over time but without specific markers of decline. Functional deterioration occurs in approximately the opposite sequence to the gains made early in childhood neurological development. The Global Deterioration Scale (Reisberg et al., 1982) outlines that sequence in a series of seven stages ranging from normal cognitive functioning to severe dementia (see table 7.3).

Vascular dementias are caused by loss of neuronal tissue as a result of occlusions of vessels or small infarctions (i.e., hemorrhages) in the brain, hence the frequently used term multi-infarct dementia. Diagnosis of vascular dementia requires the presence of the cognitive signs of dementia (e.g., memory loss and cognitive decline from previous level of functioning sufficient to interfere with daily functioning), as well as the documented presence of cerebrovascular disease, and some relationship between the dementia and the cerebrovascular disease (American Psychiatric Association, 1994; Roman et al., 1993).

Vascular dementias often present with a stepwise progression of small losses of functioning that result from the small infarcts, although the onset of the dementia may follow a stroke. The prognosis for vascular dementia is

Table 7.3 Global deterioration scale

Stage	Clinical phase	Clinical characteristics
1. No cognitive decline	Normal	• No subjective complains of memory deficit • No memory deficit evident on clinical interview
2. Very mild cognitive decline	Forgetfulness	• Subjective complaints of memory deficit, most frequently in following areas: a) forgetting where one has placed familiar objects and b) forgetting names one formerly knew well • No objective evidence of memory deficit on clinical interview • No objective deficits in employment or social situations • Appropriate concern with respect to symptomatology
3. Mild cognitive decline	Early confusional	• Earliest clear-cut deficits appear, with manifestations in more than one of the following areas: a) patient may get lost when traveling to an unfamiliar location, b) co-workers become aware of patient's relatively poor performance, c) wordfinding and name-finding deficits become evident to intimates, d) patient may read a passage of a book and retain relatively little material, e) patient may demonstrate decreased facility in remembering names on introduction to new people, f) patient may lose or misplace an object of value, and g) concentration deficit may be evident on clinical testing. • Objective evidence of memory deficit is obtained only with an intensive interview conducted by a trained geriatric psychiatrist or neuropsychologist. • Decreased patient performance is apparent in demanding employment and social settings.

Table 7.3 continued

Stage	Clinical phase	Clinical characteristics
		• Denial begins to become manifest in the patient. Mild to moderate anxiety accompanies symptoms.
4. Moderate cognitive decline	Late confusional	• Clear-cut deficit is apparent on careful interview. Deficit manifests in the following areas: a) decreased knowledge of current and recent events, b) difficulty remembering one's personal history, c) concentration deficit elicited on serial subtractions, d) decreased ability to travel, handle finances, and so on.
		• Frequently, no deficit is apparent in the following areas: a) orientation to time and person, b) recognition of familiar person and faces, and c) ability to travel to familiar locations.
		• The patient is unable to perform complex tasks. Denial is the dominant defense mechanism.
		• Flattening of affect and withdrawal from challenging situations occur.
5. Moderately severe cognitive decline	Early dementia	• Patient can no longer survive without some assistance.
		• Patients are unable during interview to recall a major relevant aspect of their current lives (e.g., their addresses or telephone numbers of many years, the names of close members of their families (such as grandchildren), or the names of the high schools or colleges from which they graduated).
		• Frequently, some disorientation to time (date, day of week, season, etc.) or to place is present.
		• An educated person may have difficulty counting back from 40 by 4s or from 20 by 2s. Persons at this stage retain knowledge of many major facts regarding themselves and others.

Table 7.3 continued

Stage	Clinical phase	Clinical characteristics
		They invariably know their own names and generally know their spouse's and children's names.
		• They require no assistance with toileting or eating but may have some difficulty in choosing the proper clothing to wear and may occasionally clothe themselves improperly (e.g., putting shoes on the wrong feet, etc.).
6. Severe cognitive decline	Middle dementia	• They may occasionally forget the name of the spouse on whom they are entirely dependent for survival.
		• They will be largely unaware of all recent events and experiences in their lives.
		• They may retain some knowledge of their past lives but this is very sketchy.
		• They are generally unaware of their surroundings, the year, the season, and so on.
		• They may have difficulty in counting from 10, both backward and, sometimes, forward. They will require some assistance with activities of daily living (e.g., may become incontinent, will require travel assistance but occasionally will display ability to travel to familiar locations).
		• Diurnal rhythms are frequently disturbed.
		• They almost always recall their own names.
		• They frequently continue to be able to distinguish familiar from unfamiliar persons in their own environment.
		• Personality and emotional changes occur; these are quite variable and include a) delusional behavior (e.g., patients may accuse their spouses of

Table 7.3   *continued*

Stage	Clinical phase	Clinical characteristics
		being impostors, may talk to imaginary figures in the environment or to their own reflection in the mirror); b) obsessive symptoms (e.g., person may continually repeat simple cleaning activities); c) anxiety symptoms such as agitation may be present, and even previously non-existent violent behavior may occur; and d) cognitive abulia (e.g., loss of willpower because one cannot carry a thought long enough to determine a purposeful course of action).
7. Very severe cognitive decline	Late dementia	• All verbal abilities are lost. Frequently, there is no speech at all – only grunting. • They are incontinent of urine and require assistance in toileting and feeding. • They lose basic psychomotor skills (e.g., ability to walk). The brain appears to no longer be able to tell the body what to do. • Generalized cortical neurological signs and symptoms are frequently present.

Source: Youngjohn & Crook, 1996.

similar to that of Alzheimer's disease: slow, progressive deterioration in a broad range of cognitive functions. Certainly, dementias can co-present within a patient, such that, for example, vascular dementia and Alzheimer's dementia are both diagnosed.

Subcortical dementias, of which Huntington's disease is considered proto-typical, have a different form of impact on cognitive functioning (Butters et al., 1994). Subcortical dementias, in contrast to the cortical dementias such as Alzheimer's disease, show more specific and limited memory deficits, attentional dysfunction, little or no aphasia, and specific deficits (e.g., Huntington's produces arithmetic deficiencies). Similarities between cortical and subcortical dementias are also notable, however, in the areas of problem-solving deficits, and visuo-perceptual and constructional deficits. The explosion of research in the neurosciences during the past two decades has made it possible to understand the finest of neurological distinctions among these diseases, and often to discriminate among these diseases pre-mortem with the careful application of thorough assessment techniques. Knowledge of the specific diagnosis can be particularly helpful when designing behavior management interventions that need to draw upon the available cognitive abilities to compensate for deficits and behavior problems.

Depression and Cognitive Impairment

Individuals with depression often present either with concerns about their memory and/or with actual deficits in daily cognitive functioning as reported by a family member or other informant. The negative cognitive set associated with depression produces excessively negative self-appraisals in many areas, including cognitive functioning. The case of Jim Hunt, offered at the beginning of the chapter, is a typical presentation of depression. He is very concerned about his own deficits and is withdrawing from activities that bring him pleasure. Obviously, a thorough evaluation is needed to rule out cognitive impairment, but the presentation is also typical of a depressed person.

Depressed adults indeed complain about memory deficits even if no objective memory performance deficit is evident. However, depression is associated with actual cognitive deficits under two circumstances. First, depression can produce cognitive impairment in adults of any age. When the depressed person is elderly, the CI is often referred to as a "dementia syndrome of depression" (LaRue, 1992). By definition, the CI can be attributed to depression only if it remits with successful treatment of the depression. This particular syndrome so sufficiently mimics dementia that it was previously referred to as pseudodementia, a misnomer because the CI is not false. Second, depression and dementia can, and often do, co-exist (Teri, 1996). Approximately 30 percent of demented patients meet the criteria for diagnosis of depression, most often in the early stages of the disease (Teri & Wagner, 1992). Other factors that are often present in older adults also can produce depression and dementia-like symptoms that further complicate matters. For example, disrupted sleep, anxiety, or physical illness can produce concentration deficits or personality changes that are common in either depression or dementia.

Summaries of the research literature on the differential diagnosis of dementia, delirium, and depression indicate there are several key functions that should be examined closely to help differentiate among these disorders (Butters et al., 1994; Kaszniak & Christenson, 1994). A key approach is to examine the types of errors the older client makes. For example, Alzheimer's dementia produces errors that result from not consolidating new information within the memory stores, such that additional assistance with encoding (e.g., teaching strategies) is generally not very useful. Rapid forgetting is a particularly distinct characteristic of dementia. Even mildly demented persons may have no impairment in immediate recall, but they show serious deficits in the ability to recall details from a simple story or design ten minutes after hearing it (Welsh et al., 1991). Furthermore, efforts to recall information are impaired by the tendency for previously learned information to intrude on the more recently learned information. Intrusion errors are evident in almost all Alzheimer's dementias but only in about one-third of other dementias (Fuld et al., 1982). Depression also can be discriminated from dementia with carefully selected examination of specific memory functions (Kaszniak & Christenson, 1994).

Differential diagnosis of depression, dementia, and other sources of cognitive impairment are common challenges to the geriatric mental health provider. Further complications are suggested by recent research which shows that late-onset depression is often a predictor of the onset of dementia within three years (Gatz, Kasl-Godley, & Karel, 1996). Table 7.4 describes some of the ways in which the different disorders can be discriminated. Specific recommendations for discriminating among different dementias, and between dementia and depression, are provided by the contributors to the volume edited by Storandt and VandenBos (1994).

Assessment

In order to discriminate among the various potential causes of mood or cognitive disorders in older adults, multidisciplinary evaluations of medical, pharmacological, neuropsychological, and daily functioning are necessary. Multiple disciplines must be involved in order to gather a picture of the full range of functional abilities and deficits, and to examine all possible causes of deficits. The medical evaluation includes a thorough history and physical, examination of the medical history, and review of current medications. Social workers provide an occupational and social history that also evaluates family

Table 7.4 Differences between dementia, delirium, depression, and normal aging

		Dementia	Delirium	Depression	Normal aging
1)	Current symptoms				
	a) Memory	Reported by others; often patient unaware	Patient often denies problems	Patient usually complains of memory problems	Patient may complain of mild losses
	b) Attention	Often intact	Impaired	Often impaired	Normal
	c) Judgment	Poor; frequent inappropriate behavior	Poor	Variable; patient often perceives impairment	Normal
	d) Insight	Usually absent	Likely impaired; intermittent lucidity possible	Cognitive distortion likely	Normal, consistent with personal history
	e) Sleep	Usually normal; day–night reversals possible	Typically disturbed	Early morning wakening common	Increased likelihood of intermittent wakenings
	f) Hallucinations and delusions	Paranoid accusations sometimes present in early stages; rarely delusions lack depth of analysis	Sometimes vivid hallucinations and well-developed delusions are present	Unusual	Absent
2)	History				
	a) Onset	Variable by etiology but typically insidious	Usually sudden	Variable	Symptoms occur in response to life changes; no specific aging pattern
	b) Duration	Months or years	A few days or weeks	Weeks to years	
	c) Progression	Variable by etiology	Symptoms become	Variable	Minimal change

Table 7.4   continued

		Dementia	Delirium	Depression	Normal aging
			severe within days		over long periods of time
3)	Caregiver report				
	a) Problems in functioning	Mild to extensive impairment	Mild to extensive impairment	Mild to extensive impairment	No, or a few problems
	b) Burden	Mild to severe	Not determined	Mild to severe	If present, related to long-standing relationship problems or physical disability

Source: adapted from Zarit, Orr, & Zarit, 1985, table 3.2.

functioning. Psychologists rate cognitive, emotional, and personality functioning, and neuropsychologists provide an in-depth examination of cognitive and memory functioning. Pharmacy consultants and psychiatrists often contribute to the evaluation of the effects of illnesses and medications on psychological functioning (cognitive as well as mood). Other health professions such as physical therapy, dentistry, or occupational therapy may be involved in the evaluation if problems in posture, range of motion, movement safety, oral health, or functional capacity to fulfill daily tasks are in question.

The medical aspects of the evaluation are particularly critical because reversible causes of CI must be ruled out immediately. Left untreated, reversible causes of CI can produce permanent deficits. The functional components of the examination (e.g., evaluation of ADLs and IADLs) are key to determining the level of independent functioning that is possible and safe. In the case of patients with dementia, evaluation of family functioning is also important. Family caregivers maintain responsibility for patient well-being, and are often stressed.

Neuropsychological examinations often begin with screening tools that evaluate mental status and depression, and proceed to a full evaluation only when needed. Commonly used mental status exams include the Folstein Mini-Mental State Examination (FMMSE; Folstein, Folstein, & McHugh,

Table 7.5 Mini–Mental State Examination (MMSE)

		Score	Points
Orientation			
1. What is the	Year?	___	1
	Season?	___	1
	Date?	___	1
	Day?	___	1
	Month?	___	1
2. Where are we?	State?	___	1
	County?	___	1
	Town or city?	___	1
	Hospital?	___	1
	Floor?	___	1
Registration			
3. Name three objects, taking one second to say each. Then ask the patient all three after you have said them. Give one point for each correct answer. Repeat the answers until the patient learns all three.		___	3
Attention and calculation			
4. Serial sevens. Give one point for each correct answer. Stop after five answers. Alternate: Spell WORLD backwards.		___	5
Recall			
5. Ask for names of three objects learned in question 3. Give one point for each correct answer.		___	3
Language			
6. Point to a pencil and a watch. Have the patient name them as you point.		___	2
7. Have the patient repeat "No ifs, ands, or buts."		___	1
8. Have the patients follow a three-stage command. "Take the paper in your right hand. Fold the paper in half. Put the paper on the floor."		___	3
9. Have the patient read and obey the following: "CLOSE YOUR EYES." (Write it in large letters.)		___	1
10. Have the patient write a sentence of his or her own choice. (The sentence should contain a subject and a verb and should make sense. Ignore spelling errors when scoring.)		___	1
11. Have the patient copy the figure below. (Give one point if all sides and angles are preserved and if the intersecting sides form a quadrangle.)		___	1
		= Total	30

Source: Folstein, Folstein, & McHugh, 1975.

1975) (see table 7.5) and the Mattis Demential Rating Scale (Mattis, 1976). Each screening tool tests functioning in several domains, but with little depth of examination in each area. Any indication of deficit leads to more rigorous examination of cognitive functioning.

A full neuropsychological examination includes tests of specific domains of functioning that can portray a rich picture of the strengths as well as the deficits of a particular patient's functioning. Test data are compared with norms from age-matched older adults living in a similar setting (e.g., community dwelling, nursing home) to determine whether one individual's performance varies from what would be normative for a person of that age in that setting. An example of a neuropsychological battery that is used at a major clinical research center to assess the full range of functions (e.g., attention, memory, problem-solving, language, visuo-spatial abilities, and motor abilities) is listed in table 7.6 (Butters et al., 1994). One illustration of the usefulness of neuropsychological test data is presented in table 7.7, which outlines key findings that differentiate dementia from depression. Note that both disorders produce dysfunctions in many of the same areas being tested, but the pattern of results differs substantially. A clinical interview might very well not be able to discriminate between the two disorders, but test data provide a much richer picture.

A neuropsychological test report provides detailed information on the patient's performance on each test, compared to national norms for healthy older adults, and, if available, persons with various dementias. Test performances are interpreted within the context of the patient's past educational and occupational experiences in order to ensure that any drop in functioning is noted. In highly educated persons, an average score may not appear to be deficient if compared against national norms, but may be well below that person's historical capacity to function. The test report concludes by addressing any specific questions (e.g., capacity to function safely within current living environment or decision-making competency) and summarizing cognitive strengths that can be used to compensate for any deficits.

A thorough evaluation should include assessment of family stress due to the burdens of managing care and the behavior problems that often accompany CI. The Revised Memory and Behavior Problems Checklist (Teri, Truax et al., 1992) is a commonly used tool that identifies significant behavior problems and the degree of distress each problem evokes in the caregiver. Family members should also be evaluated for depression, a distressingly common consequence for caregivers whose sources of pleasure are usually disrupted at the same time that they are dealing with challenging health and behavior problems.

Table 7.6 Neuropsychological test battery used at the University of California, San Diego (La Jolla), Alzheimer's Disease Research Center*

Mental status
- Blessed Information–Memory–Concentration Test
- Mini–Mental Status Examination
- Dementia Rating Scale

Attention
- Digit Span Test (WAIS-R)
- Visual Span Test (Wechsler Memory Scale–Revised (WMS-R))

Memory
- Visual Reproduction Test (WMS)
- California Verbal Learning Test
- Selective Reminding Test
- Logical Memory Subtest (WMS-R)
- Number Information Test

Abstraction/problem-solving
- Modified Wisconsin Card Sorting Test
- Trail Making Test: Parts A and B
- Arithmetic Subtest (WAIS-R)
- Similarities Subtest (WAIS-R)

Language
- Vocabulary Subtest (WAIS-R)
- Boston Naming Test
- Letter and Category Fluency Tests
- American National Adult Reading Test

Constructional/visuospatial
- Block Design Subtest (Wechsler Intelligence Scale for Children–Revised (WISC-R))
- Digit Symbol Substitution Test (WAIS-R)
- Clock Drawing Test
- Clock Setting Test
- Copy-a-Cube Test

Motor
- Grooved Pegboard Test
- Grip Strength Test

★Note: The typical clinical setting would use the most recent version of each test.
Source: Butters, Salmon, & Butters, 1994.

Table 7.7 Summary of neuropsychological test findings in dementia of the Alzheimer's type (DAT) and geriatric depression

	DAT	Geriatric depression
Typical presentation	Disproportionate loss of memory, accompanied by <ul><li>deficits in cognitive flexibility and speeded perceptual–motor integration</li><li>deficits in language production and comprehension, and/or</li><li>visuo-spatial impairments</li></ul>	Depressed mood or pervasive loss of interest, accompanied by <ul><li>mild memory deficit</li><li>mild to moderate visuospatial impairment</li><li>reduced abstraction and cognitive flexibility</li></ul>
Variations in presentation (present in some cases)	Moderate deficits in attention and short-term memory Depression, psychosis, anxiety, or agitation Differential severity of language versus visuo-spatial impairments	Self-critical of performance; may underestimate ability or reject positive comments from the examiner; global as opposed to circumscribed cognitive complaints Complaints of fatigue or physical distress, often accompanied by an objective loss of stamina Complaints of poor concentration, but usually can attend to tasks if encouraged

Most informative tests	Secondary memory measures:
	  Quantitative deficit relative to age and education norms on all such tests
	  Qualitative features present in many cases *Paragraph recall* – intrusions, confabulations; ≥50% decline on delayed recall
	  Associative learning – intrusions; additional decline on delayed recall
	  List learning and recall – impairment in storage as well as retrieval; impaired recognition relative to norms
		List-learning test:
		  Storage, recognition, and rate of forgetting close to normal
		  Mild to moderate impairments in recall
		  Low rate of intrusion errors
		  Benefit from cueing and encoding enhancement
		Intelligence testing:
		  Verbal IQ close to normal levels
		  Digit Span other verbal subtests
		  Mild to moderate impairment on performance

Table 7.7   continued

	DAT	Geriatric depression
	Reproduction of designs – perseveration from one omission of complete figure, gross distortions; Perseveration from one design to the next Semantic memory and language processes: 　Quantitative deficit relative to age and education norms 　Qualitative features present in many cases 　　*Object naming* – marked circumlocution; remote semantic associations; perseverations 　　*Verbal fluency* – perseveration; loss of set 　　*Picture description* – fluent, but many vague terms; word-finding problems	subtests, due primarily to slowing, carelessness, or refusal to complete the task
Findings that raise doubt about the diagnosis	Any of the following in early stages of illness: 　Focal neurological signs and symptoms 　Motor impairments (e.g., gait disturbance, tremor) 　Speech problems 　Severe attention deficits	Depressive symptoms mild or questionable Problems in language comprehension Severe memory deficit
Cautions	Very early DAT cannot be reliably distinguished from normal aging by cognitive tests. Autopsy is required to confirm AD pathology.	Cognitive loss may be linked more closely to global dysfunction than to severity of depression *per se*. Depression often coexists with organic brain disorder. 10–20% of patients have diffuse cognitive problems that are hard to distinguish from DAT or other organic dementias.

Source: La Rue et al., 1992.

Interventions

A thorough assessment can be considered the first and most important intervention for CI. If the cause of the CI is reversible (e.g., delirium or depression), then the evaluation should lead to treatment of the underlying condition, which will partially or completely resolve the problem. When the CI is determined to be caused by a non-reversible etiology, such as a dementia, the focus of intervention turns toward management in order to prevent excess disability and rapid decline. Planning, environmental interventions, behavioral interventions, and education and support for those who will provide care for the impaired person are all useful management strategies. Direct intervention to improve cognitive functioning may be beneficial in certain cases.

Families of demented persons have too often lamented that they were told by their physician something like, "I'm sorry, but your husband has Alzheimer's disease and there's nothing that can be done." The hopelessness and despair produced by such pronouncements of doom are substantial, and truly unnecessary.

Management of progressive, intractable CI focuses on maximizing independent functioning while anticipating the consequences of current and future levels of impairment on the patient and the caregivers. The case of Jane Winthrop, with which the chapter opened, is an example of intensive management to maintain independence in her living environment. Early in a dementing process, families often begin to implement small supportive interventions that allow the person with the disease to maintain independence in his or her own home. For example, a son or daughter may initially "check in" on a mother to make sure she is OK. Later, the adult child may handle complex financial transactions such as taxes, even though the diseased person continues to manage the monthly budget. Later, the checkbook may be handled by an adult child, and eventually even routine grocery shopping may have to be done by a caregiver. In Jane Winthrop's case, the family was using external memory aids so Jane could maintain basic safety in her own home. The implied sequence of increasing care services is illustrated by the continuum of family roles vis-à-vis a demented person that is presented in figure 7.2.

Planning

Ideally, a person with CI has the opportunity when sufficient cognitive abilities remain intact to make important decisions about how legal, financial,

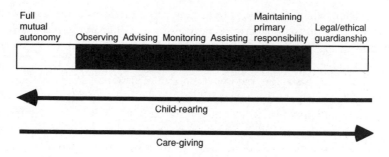

Figure 7.2 Family involvement with members
Source: Qualls, 1997.

housing, and health-care decisions will be made. For example, adults with early stage dementia are encouraged to work with an attorney and family members to determine appropriate financial, legal, and health-care decision-making arrangements for the future when the impairment will disable their decision-making capacity (see chapters 11 and 12).

In recent years several legal tools have been developed to help adults state their intentions for handling their affairs once they are incapacitated. For example, a durable health-care power of attorney identifies and sanctions a legal decision-maker to handle health-care decisions once an individual is incapacitated. A living will identifies the level of medical intervention desired by the individual both when he or she is incapable of stating his or her own needs and when heroic measures might be used to sustain life in the face of death. Housing options, such as life-care communities that guarantee provision of the level of care needed by the older adult who purchased the life-care services ahead of time, allow an individual to select the housing for the future. Advanced planning for finances and other needs ensures that the individual's own desires will be the basis for decisions once capacity to decide is compromised.

When cognitively impaired individuals have not legally stated their wishes for how things should be handled after they are incapacitated, surrogate decision-makers are called upon to make the key decisions. State statutes define who is the surrogate decision-maker of choice for health-care decisions, with a sequence of alternative persons in a specific order. Typically, a spouse is the first person of choice, followed by a parent or an adult child, with specific assignments of priority thereafter. For other decisions (e.g., housing or finances) a similar strategy is typically supported by the legal system even though it may not be defined by statute.

Even a cognitively impaired individual is his or her own legal decision-maker, except when decisions would generate a threat to someone's welfare or the court appoints a guardian. Guardianship is a dramatic step that strips an individual of basic rights and liberties. The decision to appoint a guardian is made by a judge, based upon evidence that relates to the specific state statutes that define the basis for incompetency. No national standard has been established for competency determinations – neither a standard definition of competence and incompetence, nor a standard procedure for determining competency (Sabatino, 1996). Significant variation occurs across the states in standards and practices (Anderer, 1990). In many states, partial or limited guardianships can be granted to cover only domains in which the individual's incapacity is sufficient to warrant an alternative decision-maker (e.g., finances but not housing). However, the vast majority of guardianships are total, and are rarely reversed. Thus guardianship is a serious final step in wresting control of decisions from the patient with CI and giving it to another. Indeed, the determination of competency is a highly complex legal field that rests upon significantly complex psychological and legal constructs (Grisso, 1986; Smyer, Schaie, & Kapp, 1996). An example of one set of guidelines developed for use in the Veterans Affairs medical system will be presented in Chapter 12.

Legal and health professionals consistently encourage adults to plan ahead for the event of their cognitive incapacity so that the wishes of the individual will be available to guide subsequent decisions, regardless of the decision-maker.

Environmental Interventions

Individuals with CI are more vulnerable to the impact of the environment on their capacity to function than are non-impaired individuals (Lawton & Nahemow, 1973). As illustrated in figure 7.3, lower levels of competence limit the range of environments in which the individual can function adequately. Thus the selection of an appropriate environment can profoundly affect, positively or negatively, an individual's capacity for independent functioning. Effective management of cognitively impaired individuals requires the caregivers to identify the level of environmental prosthesis that will support independent functioning maximally, by providing sufficient challenge to require the individual to use available cognitive capacities without generating frustration or excess disability.

Persons with mild CI may be able to live alone in a familiar home or apartment with minimal support. However, substantial CI usually requires at least one move from independent living to a more supportive level of

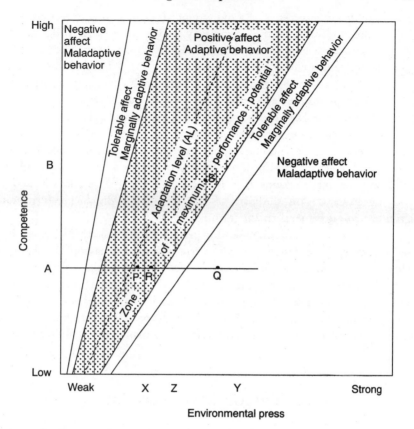

Figure 7.3 Diagrammatic representation of the behavioral and affective outcomes of person–environment transactions

Note: This figure indicates that an individual of high competence will show maximum performance over a larger range of environmental situations that will a less competent person. The range of optimal environments occurs at a higher level of environmental press (A) for the most competent person than it does for the least competent person (B).

Source: Lawton & Nahemow, 1973.

housing. Meals and janitorial, maintenance, and housekeeping services may be sufficient to maintain a state of relative independence. Nursing homes provide the most intensive levels of health-supportive services, including medication dispensing, nutrition monitoring, and skilled nursing services. The high rate of CI in nursing homes noted earlier in this chapter reflects the negative effects of institutional life as well as the increased likelihood of needing the full array of support services once one is cognitively impaired.

The architectural features of a living environment have a profound impact on behavior, especially of the cognitively impaired (Howell, 1980; Lawton, 1979), and are thus appropriate targets for intervention. In their review of the literature on residential factors in programming for older adults, Morse and Wisocki (1991) describe a variety of environmental characteristics that affect the behavior of normal as well as impaired elderly. For example, several studies demonstrate how the arrangement of public and private spaces affects the frequency and value of social interaction to residents of senior housing. Environmental richness (sounds, sights, and tactile stimulation) affects rate of activity and socializing. For demented and depressed individuals with CI, environmental interventions that increase the rate of stimulation without requiring initiation on the part of the impaired individual can produce significant improvements in functioning.

In recent years, facilities devised for persons with Alzheimer's disease have used several creative design features to foster desired behavior. For example, colored blocks inlaid into the surface of a table to look like a placemat have been used to help demented persons identify the territory within which their food is served. Pictures of a resident as a young person as well as a current picture of the aging person may be used instead of a name or number outside the door to enhance the likelihood that the resident can identify his or her own room.

Behavior Management

Cognitive impairment can limit the range of behavior as well as produce problematic behaviors that can benefit from behavior management. Handling behavior problems is one of the most stressful aspects of providing care to a demented person. Behavior management strategies are available to help manage wandering, incontinence, disruptive vocalizations (e.g., screaming), and inappropriate sexual behaviors, as well as to enhance independent self-care behaviors such as grooming, ambulation, and eating (see reviews by Carstensen & Fisher, 1991; Wisocki, 1991). Behavior management is labor intensive, but highly effective. Daily care providers such as family members or certified nurse aids in nursing homes must be trained to implement behavior management protocols in order to achieve successful results (Burgio, 1991; Hussian and Davis, 1985; Pinkston & Linsk, 1984). In contrast to medications that are sometimes used to sedate individuals whose agitation is extremely disruptive to their environment, behavior management programs rarely produce side effects. Ethical concerns about altering the behaviors of persons who are not capable of consenting to treatment warrant careful consideration, however.

The burden of caring for cognitively impaired individuals falls heavily upon family members, who experience the care of individuals with CI as considerably more stressful than that of physically ill relatives (Birkel, 1987). In particular, problem behaviors provoke the most adverse emotional and physical consequences for caregivers (see review by Schulz et al., 1995). The disruptive and odd behavior that often accompany serious CI can significantly interfere with sleep as well as daily routines and social contact. Interventions for families usually focus on education about the disease, problem-solving assistance, encouragement to maintain strong social support, and, when needed, family therapy to resolve serious family dysfunction (Zarit, Orr, & Zarit, 1985).

Interventions to Enhance Cognitive Functioning

Efforts to reverse or slow deterioration in CI include cognitive retraining and pharmacological interventions. Medications to enhance cognitive functioning in Alzheimer's patients have been made available in recent years following evidence of at least limited effectiveness in some patients. Pharmacological effects are produced primarily by increasing the concentration of specific neurotransmitters in the brain. Unfortunately, the medications made available to date have more limited and less consistent effectiveness at altering the progressive cognitive deterioration characteristic of dementias than would be desired. In laboratory settings, older adults have been demonstrated to be capable of benefiting from training to use memory aids, but research has not documented the benefits of that training outside the laboratory setting. Furthermore, the effectiveness of the training for older persons with CI due to organic brain disorders is most equivocal.

Conclusion

Cognitive impairment is one of the most dreaded changes associated with aging because of its profound negative impact on autonomy and the very identity of the person experiencing the disorder. Reversible causes of CI are sufficiently prevalent among older adults to warrant aggressive evaluation of CI. Irreversible causes of CI in older adults are primarily the dementias,

162   *Introduction to Mental Disorders*

which produce devastating, progressive, and long-term effects on cognition. A thorough assessment requires the involvement of multiple disciplines in a coordinated effort to identify a multidimensional picture of the person's physical, psychological, social, and self-care functioning. Based on the assessment, many interventions are possible to assist the impaired person and those caring for him or her.

8

Depression

Jenny Miller's husband of 46 years died three years ago from a sudden heart attack. She keeps thinking she'll get over it and get on with life, but she somehow can't seem to figure out what life is anymore. Her children call her every week, and each one flies out to visit a couple of times each year, but they haven't been able to help her over her grief. Unfortunately, she feels like she has no energy to handle daily routines, let alone try new things. Every day she wakes up about 4 a.m. and is unable to get back to sleep. It is so frustrating for her that she is irritable much of the time, and is sure that other people won't want to be around her anyway. She rarely calls her friends, and complains that most of her "couple" friends obviously don't want to see her now that she is a widow. Although she has enjoyed sewing and needlework all of her life, she hasn't started a project in a couple of years because she just doesn't care that much about it and frankly doesn't believe she has the mental capacity to do it anymore. She is convinced that her memory is failing and complains that she just can't concentrate on anything anymore. Much of her day is spent watching the soap operas and game shows, dozing off occasionally because she is so tired.

Jenny Miller is experiencing what clinicians define as a Major Depressive Disorder (MDD). As described below in more detail, Jenny reports insomnia, fatigue, irritability, social withdrawal, difficulty concentrating, and memory difficulties, and she lacks interest in almost all aspects of her life. She is not particularly sad, nor does she cry excessively, so some people might think she is not depressed. Unfortunately, her experience is what some people imagine is normal for later life, leading the general public and even health professionals to believe that depression is so common among older adults that it is almost expected. Although depression is indeed one of the three most common mental disorders experienced by older adults, it is also the case that fewer older adults than young adults are clinically depressed.

Definition of Depression

The diagnostic and statistical manual, 4th edition (DSMIV; American Psychiatric Association, 1994), classifies depression within the mood disorders because mood disturbance is the most salient characteristic. There are actually several depressive disorders that vary by intensity and duration. Table 8.1 shows the DSM4 classifications for depression with the symptom and duration criteria. The most intense depressions are classified as major depressive disorders,

Table 8.1 DSM4 criteria for diagnosis of depression

Type of depression	*Criteria*
Major depressive disorder	A. Five or more of the following symptoms have been present during the same two-week period and represent a change from previous functioning: at least one of the symptoms is either 1) depressed mood or 2) loss of interest or pleasure. 1) depressed mood most of the day, nearly every day, as indicated by either subjective report (e.g., appears tearful) 2) markedly diminished interest or pleasure in all, or almost all, activities most of the day (as indicated by either subjective account or observation made by others) 3) significant weight loss when not dieting, or weight gain (e.g., a change of more than 5% of body weight in a month), or decrease or increase in appetite nearly every day. 4) insomnia or hypersomnia nearly every day. 5) psychomotor agitation or retardation nearly every day (observable by others, not merely subjective feelings of restlessness or being slowed down) 6) fatigue or loss of energy nearly every day 7) feelings of worthlessness or excessive or inappropriate guilt (which may be delusional) nearly every day (not merely self-reproach or guilt about being sick) 8) diminished ability to think or concentrate, or indecisiveness, nearly every day (either by subjective account or as observed by others)

Table 8.1 continued

Type of depression	Criteria
	9) recurrent thoughts of death (not just fear of dying), recurrent suicidal ideation without a specific plan, or a suicide attempt or a specific plan for committing suicide B. The symptoms cause clinically significant distress or impairment in social, occupational, or other important areas of functioning.

Dysthymic disorder	A. Depressed mood for most of the day, for more days than not, as indicated either by subjective account or observation by others, for at least two years.
	B. Presence, while depressed, of two (or more) of the following:
	  1) poor appetite or overeating
	  2) insomnia or hypersomnia
	  3) low energy or fatigue
	  4) low self-esteem
	  5) poor concentration or difficulty making decisions
	  6) feelings or hopelessness.
	    During the two-year period (one year for children or adolescents) of the disturbance, the person has never been without the symptoms in Criteria A and B for more than two months at a time.

Adjustment disorder	A. The development of emotional or behavioral symptoms with depressive mood in response to an identifiable stressor occurring within three months of the onset of the stressors.
	B. These symptoms or behaviors are clinically significant as evidenced by either of the following:
	  1) marked distress that is in excess of what would be expected from exposure to the stressor
	  2) significant impairment in social or occupational (academic) functioning.

Source: American Psychiatric Association, 1994.

while the most chronic are termed Dysthymia. In addition to the depressive disorders recognized by the DSM4, minor or subsyndromal depression is currently being espoused as a major clinical concern for older adults that may warrant its own diagnostic code.

Epidemiological studies consistently find high rates of depressive symptoms in older adults who do not meet criteria for one of the depressive disorders in the DSM. These minor depressions are receiving increasing attention because of their clinical importance to physical as well as mental health. Blazer and colleagues (1989) analyzed symptom clusters in an effort to identify variant forms of depression. One symptom cluster that emerged from their analysis was found almost exclusively in older adults. The symptoms included depressed mood, psychomotor retardation, difficulty concentrating, and problems performing on the mental status examinations. In addition, these individuals described themselves as having poor health. Although they would not meet criteria for MDD, these older adults were obviously struggling with depression that was associated with physical illness and cognitive impairment. In another study of the symptom patterns of minor depression, Oxman et al. (1990) found that the common symptoms included worry (84 percent), blaming self (79 percent), decreased energy (79 percent), everything an effort (68 percent), irritability (63 percent), disturbed sleep (53 percent), crying (53 percent), and feelings of hopelessness (53 percent). Once again, physical as well as psychological symptoms characterized the minor depression.

Prevalence of Depressions in Older Adults

Recall from the introductory comments to this section that prevalence rates for disorders are reported in a variety of ways. One way of examining population patterns of disorders is in terms of the rates of disorder among a specific population within the past year, referred to as one-year rates. Lifetime rates describe the percentage of a population who have ever experienced the disorder. The prevalence rates reported in this section are drawn from the summary chapters written by Blazer (1994) and Wolfe et al. (1996), who describe the epidemiological literature in considerable detail.

Community-dwelling elderly show very low rates of MDD, with one-year rates of roughly 1 percent for people 65 and older. As shown in figure 8.1, mid-life adults show a much higher rate of MDD than older adults. Dysthymia rates are less than 2 percent for community-dwelling older adults. Prevalence rates for minor or subsyndromal depressions are quite high among older adults (20 to 30 percent). These disorders appear not to

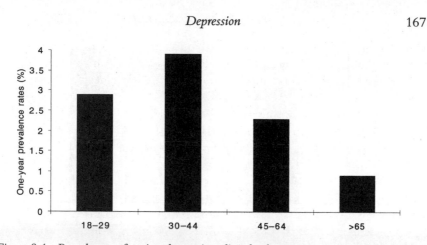

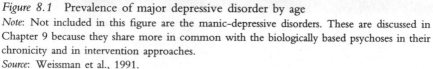

Figure 8.1 Prevalence of major depressive disorder by age
Note: Not included in this figure are the manic-depressive disorders. These are discussed in Chapter 9 because they share more in common with the biologically based psychoses in their chronicity and in intervention approaches.
Source: Weissman et al., 1991.

vary with age, except that the rates are highest among the old-old (75+). Women consistently report more depressive symptoms across the life-span than men.

Viewed from a life-span perspective, the incidence of depression peaks between ages 18 and 44, then declines. However, lifetime prevalence rates of depressive disorders are lower for older adults than for younger adults, despite the fact that their advanced age has afforded many more years in which a disorder could develop. Cohort differences are the likely explanation of this pattern, although differential mortality rates for persons with depressive disorders or differences in recollections of depressive episodes may also be a reason.

The prevalence of depression among older adults varies significantly across settings (see figure 8.2). In sharp contrast to the low prevalence rates for community-dwelling older adults, institutionalized elders show much higher rates of MDD and significant depressive symptoms. Hospitalized older adults also report higher rates of MDD and adjustment disorder with depressed mood than community-dwelling older adults. Note, however, that these rates for hospitalized elderly are still lower for elderly inpatients than for young inpatients. The importance of comorbidity of medical disorders with depression for older adults will be discussed in more detail below. What is particularly noteworthy is the much higher rates of depression among older adults in hospital or nursing-home settings.

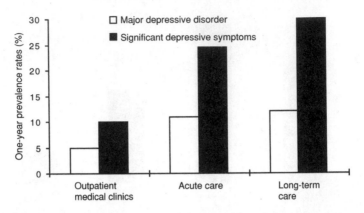

Figure 8.2 Prevalence of depressive disorders in older adults across settings
Source: Blazer, 1994.

Risk Factors for Depression

The cause of depression is not completely clear, although several risk factors for the emergence of depression are well established. In this section, a few of the most thoroughly researched theories of the cause of depression in older persons will be examined.

Psychosocial factors that affect older adults' risk for depression are organized by George (1994) in six categories, which progress from distal to proximal factors (see table 8.2). Demographic variables such as age, gender, and race/ethnicity affect prevalence rates of depression, although the correlation of these variables with depression is often weaker for older than younger adults. Category 2, events and achievements from childhood, such as deprivations (e.g., poverty or parental separation and divorce) and educational attainment, predict depression throughout adulthood. Later events and achievements such as work and marital experiences also predict depression (category 3). For older adults, these characteristics often reflect past life styles more than current experiences, again offering less predictive power. Social integration (category 4) encompasses both individual level characteristics (e.g., social networks) and aggregate level characteristics (e.g., neighborhood disintegration).

The fifth and sixth categories of George's scheme encompass the factors that have been studied most extensively in older adults. Category 5 comprises factors related to chronic stress that render a person vulnerable over time or protected over time. Chronic financial problems, chronic illness, and care-

Table 8.2 Social antecedents of depression

Category	Name	Illustrative indicators
1	Demographic variables	Age, sex, race/ethnicity
2	Early events and achievements	Education, childhood traumas
3	Later events and achievements	Occupation, income, marital status
4	Social integration	Religious affiliation, voluntary organization participation, neighborhood stability
5	Vulnerability and protective factors	Chronic stressors, social support versus isolation
6	Provoking agents and coping efforts	Life events, coping styles and strategies

Source: adapted from George, 1994, p. 132.

giving responsibilities have all been shown to have negative effects upon mental health, and depression in particular. Social support is recognized to have very positive, protective effects against the impact of chronic stress. George (1994) summarizes three types of social support that have been demonstrated to affect mental health: 1) social network (size and structure of network of significant persons); 2) tangible support (e.g., instrumental and emotional services); and 3) perceptions of social support. The individual's perceptions of supportiveness appear to be more powerful buffers of stress than any objective characteristics of the network.

Category 6 covers the factors that are current and salient: life events and coping strategies. Several events are recognized to provoke adaptation in the lives of older adults, including retirement, widowhood, death of friends, and onset of physical illness. Life events show a consistent relationship to depression, although it is a modest one. Clearly, most older adults experience the events of later life without becoming depressed.

One of the life events most widely believed to be responsible for depression in later life is loss and its consequent grief. Perhaps because losses are common in later life, grief is an intuitively compelling predictor. Indeed, the grief process produces emotions, thoughts, and behaviors that are similar to those evoked by depression. Grief, however, typically proceeds forward to resolve the symptoms without the persistent, pervasive effects of depression. The case of Jenny Miller described above illustrates the depression that can result from an unresolved grief process.

It is important to recognize that, while loss is normative in later life, depression is not. Depression is experienced by fewer than 25 percent of widows and widowers in the year following their loss (Zisook & Schuchter, 1991). Furthermore, the majority of those who become depressed following the death of a spouse show no clinically significant depression after one year. However, personally meaningful distress persists for several years that may render the distressed person more vulnerable to other risk factors (Lopata, 1973; Thompson, Gallagher-Thompson et al., 1991).

Coping strategies may be one mediating variable that buffers individuals from the effects of negative life events. Two types of coping appear to be useful: problem-focused or instrumental coping, and emotion-focused or accommodative coping (Lazarus & Folkman, 1987). Persons availing themselves of problem-focused coping tend to try to change the circumstances that produced the impact of the negative event. Emotion-focused coping, on the other hand, directs the person to accommodate to the circumstances by reducing the emotional impact of the stressor. Aldwin (1991) found that older adults' perceptions of control influenced the types of coping mechanisms used, such that situations that were perceived to be under their control elicited use of more instrumental strategies. In addition, age also influenced choice of coping style, with older individuals less likely to report escapist strategies in favor of instrumental action. Furthermore, these variables (perceived controllability and coping strategy) were the mediators of the relationship she found between age and depression.

Personality variables may also place a person at risk for depression. In their investigation of depression as a trait in longitudinal studies of normal aging, Costa and McCrae (1994) reported high levels of stability in the depression trait over a six-year period for adults of all ages. Clinical evidence of comorbidity between personality disorders and depression also suggests an important role for personality as a risk factor for depression. As many as 50 percent of depressed older adults also demonstrate personality disorder (e.g., Thompson, Gallagher, & Czirr, 1988). Whether these disorders are risk factors, are simply comorbid, or are even consequences of depression is unclear, but the risk of a co-existing personality disorder in depressed elderly adults is substantial. Of course, personality traits can also serve as buffers against depression (e.g., optimism).

Physical illness is a major risk factor for depression in older adults. About 30 percent of medical inpatients report high rates of depression symptoms on self-report scales (Rapp et al., 1988). Clinical depression occurs in medically ill patients at approximately 12 times the rate that it appears in community-dwelling older adults (Lichtenberg, 1994). Unfortunately, depression also can complicate healing and rehabilitation because depressed persons are far more likely to report "excess disability," or disability beyond their actual limitations. Excess disability reporting can lead to lack of compliance with re-habilitative efforts that leaves the person vulnerable to reduced functional capacity and further illness. Even more concerning is the tendency of physicians to fail to detect depression (Moore, Silimperi, & Bobula, 1978; Rapp et al., 1988).

Institutionalization is another risk factor for depression. A high rate of nursing-home residents are clinically depressed (6 to 25 percent: Katz & Parmelee, 1994). Over 40 percent of long-term residents show either major or minor depression (Parmelee et al., 1989). Apparently, institutionalization itself places people at risk, in addition to the risks produced by their physical illnesses. The mechanism for this tendency for residents to become depressed is likely a combination of the increased disability due to illness, isolation from personally meaningful relationships, reduced sense of control, and the tendency for staff to support dependent rather than independent behavior.

Theories of Etiology

Each model of mental health and aging generates its own theory of depression. In the following section, each approach to the etiology of depression will be discussed; approaches to assessment and treatment will be considered below.

As described in Chapter 3, the psychodynamic model of depression in older adults describes several mechanisms through which an older adult may become depressed. One central theme revolves around the high rate of losses in later life that challenge the individual's ego functioning (Colarusso & Nemiroff, 1979; Newton et al., 1986). Losses of social roles, friends, family members, spouse, and physical vitality and functioning – all must be grieved. The grief itself is a risk factor for depression, and the fact that the losses are often cumulative in a short period of time yields particular vulnerability to depression. Additional complications of loss may occur if the person experienced a highly significant loss in childhood (e.g., of an attachment figure), which may establish a particular vulnerability for re-experiencing the highly intense grief as it was experienced when a child. Immature defense mechanisms always leave a person vulnerable to complications during significant life transitions because immature defenses offer less flexibility to adapt. Thus individuals with lifelong patterns of immature coping are particularly vulnerable to poor adaptation to the many losses of later life (Vaillant, 1977). Given that a major theme of later life is loss of physical strength and, in some, cognitive abilities, this diminished capacity is also viewed as a risk factor for depression by psychodynamic theorists. Such losses drain the strength of the ego to structure internal and external adaptation, thus leaving the individual vulnerable to feeling out of control, inadequate, and, ultimately, depressed. Finally, psychodynamic theorists describe the importance of integrating later life losses into one's personal narrative in a manner that creates meaning and a coherent life story (Cohler, 1993). Narratives that cannot integrate loss themes in ways that sustain a strong sense of personal meaning can lead to despair and depression.

The behavioral model of depression focuses on the role of behavior and social interaction in the etiology of depression. Lewinsohn & Graf (1973) have demonstrated the contingent relationship between pleasant activities and depression in older, as well as younger, adults. Depressed persons engage in fewer pleasant activities and receive less pleasure from them than do non-depressed persons. Interventions have demonstrated the causal relationships between activities and mood. For example, reducing the frequency of pleasant events in a non-depressed person's life increases their risk of negative mood, while increasing the rate and pleasurableness of pleasant activities also reduces the rate of depression. Thus behaviors and contingent relationships between behavior and reinforcers are viewed as causal agents for mood disorders, as described in more detail in Chapter 4.

Cognitive-behaviorists focus on pervasive effects of depression on thought patterns and vice versa. Several specific distortions are common among depressed persons, including all-or-none reasoning, jumping to conclusions without first checking the evidence, using their emotional state to explain causal sequences, and the use of "should" statements (Thompson, 1996). As has been demonstrated with adults of all ages, specific cognitive distortions create depressed feelings (Beck, Rush et al., 1979). Depression, on the other hand, also maintains cognitively distorted perceptions of the self, the world, and the future.

According to biological models of depression, the disorder is caused either by genetics or chemical deficiencies of particular neurotransmitters. The evidence for genetic influence on depression in older adults is similar to that for younger adults. For example, genetic data from twin studies conducted in Sweden report that approximately 30 percent of the variance in depression among aging twins can be accounted for by genetics (Gatz, Pedersen et al., 1992). The evidence for chemical deficiencies in the brain as a causal factor of depression is based primarily on the observation that altering chemical concentrations using medication alters mood. This finding is as valid for older persons as for younger. However, there is not currently a method of testing concentrations of the neurotransmitters directly, so the search for the mechanisms by which chemical changes might occur is severely hampered.

Table 8.3 Medical conditions commonly associated with depression in the elderly

Coronary artery disease
Hypertension, myocardial infarction, coronary artery bypass surgery, congestive heart failure

Neurologic disorders
Cerebrovascular accidents, Alzheimer's disease, Parkinson's disease, amyotrophic lateral sclerosis, multiple sclerosis, Binswanger's disease

Metabolic disturbances
Diabetes mellitus, hypothyroidism or hyperthyroidism, hypercortisolism, hyperparathyroidism, Addison's disease, auto-immune thyroiditis

Cancer
Pancreatic, breast, lung, colonic, and ovarian carcinoma; lymphoma, and undetected cerebral metastasis

Other conditions
Chronic obstructive pulmonary disease, rheumatoid arthritis, deafness, chronic pain, sexual dysfunction, renal dialysis, chronic constipation

Source: Sunderland, Lawlor, Molchan, & Martinez, 1988.

In older adults, depression is often caused by medical illnesses and medications that alter brain chemistry through various mechanisms, producing depression as a side effect. Table 8.3 provides a list of illnesses that commonly produce depression among older adults.

Assessment

Assessment can serve three major purposes: screening for the presence of a problem, identifying the classification of the problem, and establishing baseline information useful for planning intervention (Futterman et al., 1995). Assessment tools are chosen to meet a specific purpose because each type of tool has its strengths and limitations. Generally, self-report scales are very useful for identifying clinical levels of depression, although they do not provide a diagnosis. Structured interviews are more useful for creating a diagnosis, although they typically take at least two hours to administer. Neither of those strategies is sufficient to serve as a basis for guiding intervention planning or measuring progress toward treatment goals. Treatment planning and evaluation require measurement of the specific domains of functioning targeted by the treatment (e.g., cognition or behavior).

Before describing a select set of tools that can address all three goals of assessment, some general comments regarding the assessment of older adults are needed. First, age-appropriate norms must be used to interpret any assessment scale scores. The norms for older adults are often quite different from those for younger persons. The differences in norms may be based on differences in how cohorts express their distress, the impact of physical illness on the symptom profile of mental disorders, or true differences in the phenomenon of geriatric depression. Second, the medical conditions and medication usage of older adults are particularly likely to affect psychological functioning. Thus, assessment of depression in older adults must include a careful medical and pharmacological evaluation. Third, older adults who abuse substances are particularly unlikely to disclose their substance usage, making substance abuse an important focus of assessment in persons with depressed affect. Refer back to the case of Jenny Miller at the beginning of the chapter. How would you proceed with an evaluation of Jenny? Although there are obvious psychosocial factors we might suspect to be involved in her depression, other factors such as medical illness, pharmacological agents, and substance abuse must be ruled out before proceeding with a psychologically focused intervention for depression.

Self-report measures are used primarily for screening purposes and as a quick indicator of the intensity of clinical symptoms during treatment process. Several short screening instruments that have been used to identify depression in other populations are also useful with older adults. For example, the Center for Epidemiological Studies – Depression (CES-D; Radloff, 1977) scale has been used successfully with older adults on account of its relatively low emphasis on somatic symptoms. The Beck Depression Inventory (Beck, Ward et al., 1961) is another commonly used screening tool. These scales are particularly useful for research that compares young and old because they are not aging-specific. The Geriatric Depression Scale (Yesavage et al., 1983) is one of the most popular instruments designed specifically for use with older adults. As shown in figure 4.1, all of the items of the GDS are appropriate for older adults, in contrast to many of the other scales that contain one or more items that do not apply to older populations. Detailed reviews of the various tools available for assessing depression are provided by Futterman et al. (1995) and Scogin (1994).

Clinical interview is the most common method of assessing depression in everyday practice, typically in unstructured format. However, structured interviews provide increased clinical accuracy by designing questions to elicit details about frequency and intensity of symptoms. Examples of structured interviews that are commonly used for clinical research and training include the Diagnostic Interview Scale (DIS; Robins, Helzer, Croughan, & Ratcliff,

1981) and the Structured Clinical Interview for DSM-III-R (SCID; Spitzer et al., 1990). Each of these has been demonstrated to be useful for older adults.

The focus and strategies of assessment for the purpose of treatment planning is shaped significantly by the theoretical model from which the therapist works. A behavior therapist may focus on assessing the frequency of participation in pleasant and unpleasant events, while a psychodynamic therapist may evaluate in detail the interpersonal relationship style with which the client engages the therapist. Treatment goals such as reducing depressogenic cognitive distortions require specific assessment of the types and frequency of cognitive distortions. Only by documenting the specific, operationalized instances of the distortions can a therapist design an appropriate intervention or measure the impact of the intervention on that specific problem.

Our original point about assessment bears repeating: assessment tools need to be selected to be appropriate for the task at hand. For example, a screening instrument is insufficient to determine a diagnosis, and a clinical interview is insufficient to guide treatment planning. Neither is sufficient to rule out the array of possible causes of Jenny Miller's symptoms. Thus the assessment should begin with a thorough medical evaluation, including a medication review. Once medical causes have been ruled out or addressed, an appropriate assessment strategy might begin with administering a self-report screening instrument such as the Geriatric Depression Scale to determine the intensity and range of symptoms experienced, followed by a clinical interview to identify the appropriate diagnosis. If she is indeed clinically depressed, assessment of her specific problems may be used to form a treatment plan. Further assessment of her grieving process, family and friend relationships, daily activity schedule, cognitive framework, and mental abilities are all needed before treatment can be planned.

Interventions

More research and clinical case studies have focused on interventions with depressed older adults than any other older clinical population. Detailed summaries of clinical outcome studies can be found in the clinical practice guidelines for primary care physicians (Rush et al., 1993) and the report of the NIH Consensus Development Conference (Schneider et al., 1994).

The effectiveness of psychological interventions for clinical levels as well as subclinical levels of depression is quite high (Scogin & McElreath, 1994). Therapy outcome studies find that pharmacotherapy and psychotherapy of various types are approximately equally effective, treating successfully between 50 and 70 percent of older adults with major depressive disorder within 12 to 20 sessions (Rush et al., 1993). The presence of a personality disorder or other complicating factors often reduces the success rate of psychotherapies (Thompson, Gallagher, & Czirr, 1988).

The conceptual and statistical analyses comparing the effectiveness of different therapies (including pharmacotherapy and the range of empirically tested psychotherapies) yields a consistent conclusion: no one therapy is superior to all others, but the therapies are superior to no intervention or placebo. This pattern is comforting to clinicians who typically draw upon a variety of frameworks and techniques to effect change with a wide variety of clients. Of course, the full range of clients who are depressed are not included in research outcome studies. Researchers find it most useful to narrow the possible confounding variables in therapy outcome studies by limiting participation to older adults without other physical and mental health problems. Clinical work in other settings requires more flexibility in working with depression of many varieties combined with various other physical or mental health problems (e.g., arthritis, anxiety, or substance abuse). Thus the therapy outcome studies provide very useful guidance, but the treatment protocols often must be adapted to meet the needs of complex clients.

Cognitive-behavior therapies (CBT) are the most thoroughly tested psychotherapy used with depressed older adults. These attempt to alter the cognitive frameworks of clients to eliminate depressogenic thought patterns (Thompson, 1996) and to change behavior patterns to include a higher rate of pleasant activities (Gallagher, Thompson et al., 1981). The essence of this treatment model is to alter the person's thought patterns and behavior simultaneously by engaging him or her in 12 to 20 structured therapy sessions and substantial homework activity between sessions. Methodologically rigorous outcome studies suggest that this form of therapy shows efficacy rates that are maintained over a two-year period, similar to the success rates of pharmacological treatments and psychodynamic psychotherapy (Teri, Curtis et al., 1994). CBT has been used effectively with depressed caregivers of ill elderly persons and with depressed Alzheimer's patients as well as older adults experiencing Major Depressive Disorder (Teri, Logsdon, Wagner, & Uomoto, 1994). Offered in a group psycho-educational format using nonprofessional as well as professional leaders, or through bibliotherapy, CBT interventions have also been shown to remediate minor depression (Scogin et al., 1990; Thompson, Gallagher, Nies, & Epstein, 1983).

Two forms of psychodynamic therapies have been shown to be effective with depressed older adults. Brief psychodynamic therapy developed by Marmar and Horowitz was tested by Thompson and Gallagher in their clinical trials. Psychodynamic therapies focus on working through grief and loss concerns that generate sufficient anxiety to impede the maturation of functioning. By addressing the anxiety directly, patients are able to proceed with their development toward more mature styles of coping and defense (see Chapter 3 for a more thorough discussion of this model). This form of treatment showed the same success rate as CBT in treating Major Depressive Disorder. Interpersonal therapy (IPT) (Klerman et al., 1984) has also been used effectively with depressed older adults (Sloane et al., 1985). IPT focuses on interpersonal dynamics by addressing four themes considered core to depression: grief, interpersonal disputes, role transitions, and interpersonal deficit. Using a semi-structured, time-limited approach (12 to 20 sessions), IPT involves techniques such as reassurance, clarification of emotional states, improved interpersonal communication, and the testing of performance and perceptions.

Reminiscence therapy (RT) has been recommended for older adults, including depressed older adults (Butler, 1974). As one of the few therapeutic modalities that has arisen from clinical work with older adults, it warrants attention. Building on the theories of Erik Erikson, Butler proposed that conducting a life review is a normal developmental task of later life. The life review requires older adults to integrate the disparate themes of a given life. Persons who do not integrate their lives successfully are vulnerable to despair and depression. Many different forms of reminiscence therapy have been used, although clinical trials have tended to structure the reminiscence around the themes Erikson believed to be salient (e.g., past accomplishments and failures, interpersonal conflicts, meaning). A clinical trial of reminiscence therapy compared with a problem-solving intervention found the RT to be modestly successful in reducing depressive symptoms, but not more successful at treating clinical depression than problem-solving therapy (Arean et al., 1993).

Electroconvulsive therapy (ECT) has been a highly controversial intervention used primarily for severe depressions that have not responded to pharmacotherapy or psychotherapy. The literature on ECT suggests it is a safe form of therapy. Its disproportionate use with older adults may be because it is often used for recalcitrant, recurrent depressions, or when medication is not effective or not tolerated (Sackeim, 1994), or it may reflect ageism in the belief that less dramatic interventions will not work. The effectiveness of ECT has not been compared directly with other therapies in patients of any age, although evidence that it is used effectively with patients for whom other therapies have failed lends credence to the claims of its effectiveness (Rush et al., 1993).

Most older adults seek treatment for depression from their primary care provider rather than from a mental health specialist. Thus it is not surprising that a high percentage of mental health treatment for older adults is pharmacological. The vast majority of medications used to treat depression fall into one of three categories: tricyclic antidepressants, monoamine oxidase (MAO) inhibitors, and serotonin selective reuptake inhibitors (SSRIs). These three classes of drugs work on different aspects of the neurotransmitter structure of the brain. The tricyclic antidepressants work to increase the availability of norepinephrin and serotonin in the brain, and show the same effectiveness in elderly persons that is evident in young adults. Their primary disadvantage is the high probability of side effects that are clinically significant (e.g., weight gain, sedation, cardiovascular effects, postural hypotension, and confusion). The mechanism for MAO inhibitors is unclear. Their usage is complicated by the necessity of dietary and medication restrictions, but they are also effective with older adults. SSRIs increase the availability of serotonin and have the fewest side effects. At this point they represent a first-line medication choice for many older adults (Newhouse, 1996). Medications are chosen according to the following criteria: side effects, prior history of response to medication, history of first-degree relatives' response to medication, concurrent medications and illness that may render one choice more risky than another, likelihood of adherence to the medical regimen, degree of interference with life style, cost, and preference of patient or prescriber (Rush et al., 1993).

Medications should show some positive clinical effects after about 12 weeks (Reynolds, Frank, Perel, Miller et al., 1992). Once treatment has been deemed effective, how long should medication be continued? Currently, research is focusing on the use of maintenance dosages of medications for four to six months following full remission from the index episode in order to prevent recurrence (Reynolds, Frank, Perel, Mazumdar, & Kupfer, 1995). Only a few medication trials have examined the benefits of maintenance therapy, with promising results, especially for older adults (Reynolds, Frank, Kupfer et al., 1996).

With the plethora of useful therapies available for treating depression in older adults, how does one decide which to use and for how long? In the past decade, three groups have worked to identify an appropriate algorithm for treatment decisions. The National Institute of Mental Health sponsored a consensus conference in 1991 that culminated in treatment recommendations. These recommendations emphasized the use of antidepressant medications, with psychosocial therapies as a possible adjunct (Friedhoff, 1994). Drawing heavily on the data and logic used at the previous conference, the Agency for Health Care Policy and Research subsequently published guidelines to assist primary care physicians in identifying, assessing, and treating depression (Rush et al., 1993). These guidelines also recommend medications as the first line of attack, with psychosocial interventions used primarily when medications do not work or cannot be used, or as an adjunct treatment. As might be expected, these guidelines have generated no small amount of controversy. Zeiss and Breckenridge (1997) offer a cogent critique of the logic and analysis by which the guidelines were derived, and suggest that careful analysis of the data would lead to very different recommendations. Specifically, they suggest that a reanalysis of the data would lead to the recommendation to begin with non-pharmacological interventions solely or in conjunction with medication.

The Philadelphia College of Pharmacy and Science also developed algorithms, including guidelines specifically for long-term care (Philadelphia College of Pharmacy and Science, 1995). Figure 8.3 depicts an algorithm for the initial pharmacologic and non-pharmacological treatment of depression in long-term care residents. The algorithm includes guidelines for the sequencing of evaluation, differential diagnosis, and treatment options, and offers advice about handling the variety of responses to therapy that clinicians observe (e.g., partial response, full response, or no response). This figure also contains the suggestion that maintenance therapy be considered for the purpose of preventing relapse, an issue about which we currently know very little.

Before completing a chapter on depression, you need to consider the risk of suicide in older adults. Suicide is a topic that warrants special attention because of the alarmingly high rate of suicides among the elderly population. Approximately one of every five suicides in the USA is committed by a person over age 65, a disproportionate share since the proportion of older adults in the population is only 12.5 percent (National Center for Health Statistics, 1992). In particular, older white males are at risk (45.6 per 100,000 commit suicide; Meehan et al., 1991).

Predictors of suicide include physical illness, social isolation, and stressful life events. Institutionalization may also be a predictor of suicide, although residents of nursing homes tend to use more subtle forms of self-termination that may not be labeled officially as suicide. The majority of older adults who commit suicide were experiencing their first episode of depression without substantial complications, a condition that would be readily treatable. The complicated relationship between depression and physical illness makes it difficult to tell whether the suicide is due solely to the pain of depression in reaction to physical illness. Regardless, physicians and nurses are in a prime position to help with prevention because three-quarters (75 percent) of older adults who committed suicide were in their physicians' offices within a month prior to the suicide (Conwell, 1994). Presumably, many of these suicides could be prevented if health providers were more vigilant for signs

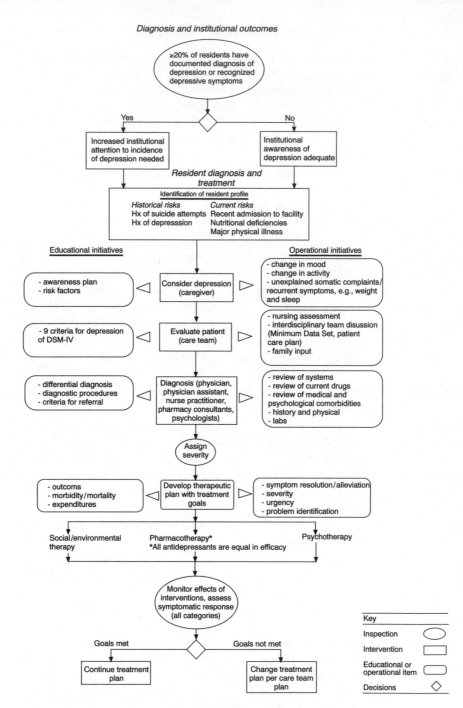

Figure 8.3 Abbreviated overview algorithm: depression in long-term care
Source: Philadelphia College of Pharmacy and Science, 1995.

of depression and more skilled at measuring suicide potential. Obviously, suicidal thought and intent must be assessed in any depressed older adult.

In summary, although depression is a disorder commonly believed to be nearly normative with aging, the rates of clinical depressive disorders in older adults is generally lower than is found in younger adults. However, depression must be taken seriously when it is encountered in older adults, particularly in light of the higher risks of suicide. Methods of assessing and treating older adults are similar to those used with younger adults, with similar rates of effectiveness.

9

Severe Mental Illness in Older Adults: Schizophrenia and other Late-Life Psychoses*

Stephen J. Bartels, MD, MS[1]
Kim T. Mueser, PhD[2]

Introduction

The diagnosis and treatment of severe mental illness has been a major focus of mental health services provided to young adults in community and hospital settings. In contrast, remarkably little is known about the course and treatment of severe mental illness in late life (Light & Lebowitz, 1991). This knowledge gap is especially significant when considering the growing numbers of older adults with late-life psychotic disorders and the substantial costs associated with treatment (Cuffel et al., 1996). Schizophrenia is among the most disabling severe mental disorders, affecting 1 percent of the population and accounting for more beds in psychiatric institutions than any other illness. In this respect schizophrenia has presented a major challenge to the mental health service delivery system and represents the prototypic severe mental disorder requiring long-term mental health care.

Schizophrenia is a severe and persistent mental illness that has a dramatic and debilitating effect on most aspects of life functioning, behavior, and personal experience. Early views of schizophrenia maintained the illness always began in young adulthood and inevitably resulted in a progressive deterioration of function, thinking, and cognition. This perspective was reflected in the name "dementia praecox," first introduced by Kraepelin

* This reseach was supported, in part, by NIMH Division of Aging Grant K07–MH01052.
[1] Associate Professor of Psychiatry and Director of Mental Health and Aging Services Research at the New Hampshire Dartmouth Psychiatric Research Center.
[2] Professor of Psychiatry at Dartmouth Medical School and Senior Research Scientist at the New Hampshire Dartmouth Psychiatric Research Center.

(1971 [1919]) to describe the disorder of schizophrenia. This term implied that people affected by the illness had permanent and progressive mental deterioration beginning at an early age.

Since the original descriptions of dementia praecox, studies of schizophrenia and aging have challenged this unitary view of the illness. Studies of older populations have found that schizophrenia can begin in middle or old age. More importantly, longitudinal research on schizophrenia over the life-span has shown considerable variation in long-term outcome. The majority of patients with schizophrenia experience substantial improvement in symptoms and function as they age; some even undergo full remission. Changes in the treatment system have also affected the course and outcome of the disorder. Although custodial care in institutions was common as an early form of treatment, there is growing use of newer and more effective antipsychotic medications and models of care that emphasize active treatment in the community. For older patients, improvements in mental health care combined with advances in general medical care have resulted in more individuals with schizophrenia surviving into old age than ever before (Moak, 1996). The growing number of elderly persons with severe mental illness will present a major challenge to the health care system and society.

In this chapter we provide an overview on current knowledge about schizophrenia over the life-span, including age of onset, gender differences, and course. We then discuss findings on schizophrenia in late life, illustrated by clinical anecdotes, including specific attention to the disorder of late-onset schizophrenia and other late-life psychoses. Finally, we conclude with a discussion of the implications of research findings for assessment and treatment.

Schizophrenia over the Life-Span: A General Overview

Schizophrenia is a syndrome characterized by disordered perceptions, thinking, and behavior that has a pervasive effect on personal, social, and vocational functioning. For some individuals the earliest signs of the disorder may include problems in pre-morbid (pre-illness) functioning, such as difficulties in social adjustment and interpersonal relationships (Zigler & Glick, 1986). For others there may be no signs of significant psychological problems until the onset of psychosis. The onset of schizophrenia generally develops over a period of months. Early signs typically consist of social withdrawal, depressive symptoms, unusual perceptions or thoughts, and declining interest and spontaneity. For example, a person may fail to show up for work or school and spend long hours in seclusion. Contacts with friends or family may be punctuated by hostile, paranoid, or bizarre comments.

Once schizophrenia has fully developed, there are a variety of symptoms that make up the syndrome, including positive, negative, and affective symptoms. Positive symptoms consist of the primary active symptoms of psychosis, the most common among them being delusions and hallucinations. Examples of other positive symptoms include severe problems in thought processes, such as illogical or poorly related thoughts or illogical and loose associations. Behavioral problems include bizarre behaviors, repetitive or ritualistic behaviors, and posturing. Exacerbations of positive symptoms are the most common signs of acute relapse and may require acute hospitalization. An important goal of the long-term treatment of schizophrenia is to lower patients' vulnerability to relapse. One approach is to use educational sessions to help patients and their families recognize early signs of relapse so that changes can be implemented in treatment to head off the acute psychotic episode (Herz, 1989).

Negative symptoms consist of deficit symptoms or a lack of active or spontaneous behaviors, emotions, or thoughts. Negative symptoms were first used to describe the appearance of neurologically impaired patients who had traumatic brain injuries involving the frontal lobes of the brain (Jackson, 1984). These patients were often passive, spoke few words, and lacked emotional responsiveness. This concept was subsequently applied to a subgroup of patients with schizophrenia who often lacked prominent active positive symptoms of psychosis, but had severe deficits in social, emotional, and cognitive functioning. Common negative symptoms include the "five As": blunted or flat affect (lack of emotional expression), alogia (reduced amount of speech or poverty of content), asociality (social withdrawal), apathy (lack of interest or spontaneity or psychomotor retardation), and attentional impairment (difficulty concentrating or performing sequential tasks). Severe negative symptoms are strongly associated with poor social functioning (Bellack, Morrison et al., 1990) and are relatively stable over time (Lewine, 1990; Mueser, Sayers et al., 1994). Negative symptoms are typically the most resistant to treatment; however, the newer atypical antipsychotic medications, including clozapine, appear in comparison with traditional agents to have a greater impact on these symptoms (Salzman et al., 1995).

In addition to positive and negative symptoms, affective symptoms, such as depression, are common in schizophrenia. Approximately 60 percent of patients with schizophrenia suffer a major depression during the course of their illness, with post-psychotic depression occurring after 25 percent of acute schizophrenic episodes. Depression in schizophrenia is associated with a variety of factors, including medical or substance use disorders (e.g., medication side effects, alcohol and substance abuse, medical disorders), early signs of relapse, and post-psychotic states; states of chronic demoralization often co-occur with major depression. Contrary to early clinical descriptions suggesting better prognosis, depression is associated with poorer outcomes, including increased rate of relapse, longer duration of hospitalization, poorer response to pharmacological treatments, chronicity, and suicide (Bartels & Drake, 1988, 1989). Recent research suggests that individuals with schizophrenia remain at high risk for co-occurring depression in older age (Cohen et al., 1996).

Schizophrenia is a heterogeneous disorder with a wide variety in the type and severity of symptoms across different individuals. However, at some time all patients experience problems initiating and maintaining meaningful interpersonal relationships, fulfilling major roles in society (e.g., education, employment), or engaging in basic self-care or community living skills (e.g., grooming, hygiene, managing finances, etc.). Many people with schizophrenia experience problems obtaining basic needs, including adequate housing and medical care (Drake et al., 1989a; Koranyi, 1979; Koran et al., 1989).

Differences in the Onset, Course, and Outcome of Schizophrenia

The onset of schizophrenia most commonly occurs in late adolescence or early adulthood, between the ages of 16 and 30. However, recent research has determined that the illness can first occur in middle age and, less commonly, in old age. In a review of the literature, Harris and Jeste (1988) found that 23 percent of all patients with schizophrenia have onset of the illness after the age of 40. More recently, Castle and Murray (1993) similarly reported that more than one-quarter (28 percent) of the new cases of schizophrenia in the Camberwell (London) catchment area from 1965 to 1984 occurred after age 44, and 12 percent occurred after age 64. Overall, the annual incidence rate for late-onset schizophrenia was 12.6/100,000, approximately half that for those aged 16 to 25.

Gender differences have been found in age of onset and the outcome of schizophrenia. The mean age of onset in women is approximately five years later than in men (Lewine, 1988). Women with schizophrenia are more likely to marry (Test & Berlin, 1981), are more likely to maintain contact with their children (Test et al., 1990), and, hence, tend to have better social networks compared to men with schizophrenia. Higher levels of social skills have been found in women with schizophrenia (Mueser, Yarnold et al., 1990), perhaps resulting in less social isolation and better function in the community. Male gender, by itself, may represent a risk factor to poorer outcome in schizophrenia (Goldstein, 1988; Seeman, 1986). This increased risk may be due to biological causes, such as structural differences in male and female brains (Lewine et al., 1990), or differences in protective hormonal levels, such as estrogen (Seeman & Lang, 1990). Alternatively, secondary complications of schizophrenia that dramatically affect function and outcome may be less prevalent in women. For example, women with schizophrenia report significantly less substance and alcohol abuse than men (Drake et al., 1989b; Mueser, Yarnold et al., 1990). Substance abuse is associated with a variety of poor outcomes, including increased use of hospitalization and emergency services (Bartels, Teague et al., 1993), aggressive and hostile behaviors (Bartels et al., 1991), and housing instability and homelessness (Drake et al., 1989a; Drake et al., 1991).

Course and outcome

Longitudinal studies have shown that the course of schizophrenia is usually episodic, with some residual impairment between exacerbations. However, there is a trend for gradual improvement and, in some cases, total remission later in life (Ciompi, 1980; Harding et al., 1987a, 1987b). Neuropsychological studies of schizophrenic patients in their third, fourth, fifth, sixth, and seventh decades of life do not suggest progressive dementia or deterioration (Goldberg et al., 1993). Long-term studies of the natural history of schizophrenia suggest that the first ten years of the illness are marked by exacerbations and remissions, but symptoms substantially remit in over half of the individuals with schizophrenia in later life. This improvement is likely a result of many factors. For example, biological changes such as age-related decreases in neurotransmitters may result in symptom reductions. This explanatory model posits that the core symptoms of schizophrenia result from an imbalance in opposing neurotransmitter systems, including a relative excess of dopamine compared to acetylcholine. Hence, psychotic symptoms may remit with age due to a restoration of the balance between dopaminergic and cholinergic neurotransmitter systems resulting from the reduction of dopamine and the relative maintenance of acetylcholine normally occurring with aging. These changes may be modified by age-related shifts in other opposing neurotransmitter systems, including neuroepinephrine, serotonin, and the inhibitory neurotransmitter GABA (Finch & Morgan, 1987).

Other factors that may contribute to improvement with aging for some individuals include the development of skills to manage symptoms better. For example, individuals and their families may acquire illness management skills, including strategies to reduce stress and to improve symptom recognition and medication compliance (Herz, 1989). In addition, individuals may learn over time to avoid the use of alcohol and street drugs that are associated with symptom exacerbation and poorer functioning (Zisook et al., 1992). The prevalence of substance use disorders appears to decrease substantially with age in schizophrenia (Bartels & Liberto, 1995). In general, there is greater optimism for favorable long-term outcomes for many individuals afflicted with schizophrenia, though a sub-group remains that continues to require intensive treatment and long-term mental health care in late life.

The Aging Person with Schizophrenia

Schizophrenia in late life is a heterogeneous disorder with a variety of clinical presentations and outcomes. Two broad groups have been described with overlapping but different clinical characteristics. One group is made up of individuals who had the onset of their disorder as young adults, described by the term "early-onset schizophrenia" (EOS). This group consists of individuals who have endured lifelong schizophrenic illness and have grown old. A second group is composed of older adults who have the onset of their illness in middle or old age, or "late-onset schizophrenia" (LOS). Within these groups there are a variety of age-related factors that appear substantially to affect treatment needs and clinical outcomes. For example, the presence of co-occurring medical illness or cognitive impairment can dramatically affect the functional capacity of the patient and overshadow the treatment needs of the psychiatric disorder.

Other factors that appear to influence functional outcome are related to treatment history among different age groups or cohorts. For example, many of the oldest individuals with EOS developed their disorder before the introduction of antipsychotic medication, at a time when long-term institutionalization was the rule for psychotic disorders. In general, this group of patients lack independent living skills, have poor social skills, and depend on a structured supervised setting to meet their needs. In contrast, a more recent and younger group of aging patients with severe mental illness have spent most of their adult life in community treatment settings following the deinstitutionalization movement of the 1960s. This group is more likely to have social supports in the community, to have used community resources, to have developed community living skills associated with more favorable outcomes, and to have been treated earlier in their illness with newer (and more effective) antipsychotic agents.

At the same time, however, this group is also more likely to have experienced the negative consequences of declining public funds for community mental health services over the last two decades. The initial enthusiasm and commitment of federal and state resources for community mental health centers in the 1960s and 1970s has given way to an eroded and fragmented system of care for severely mentally ill persons (George, 1992). For people with severe mental illness, the last two decades have shown alarming increases in homelessness (Drake et al., 1989a), exposure to crime and victimization (Apfel & Handel, 1996), institutionalization in the criminal justice system (Torrey, 1995), increased exposure to public health epidemics such as HIV infection (Couros & Bakalar, 1996), and high rates of substance use disorder (Drake et al.,1989b; Bartels et al., 1995). In general, these two groups (older individuals with extensive histories of institutional care and younger persons treated in community settings) represent different age and treatment cohorts with substantially different exposures to rehabilitative treatments and opportunities for developing independent living skills, as well as different risk factors for adverse outcomes.

In the following section we will first describe older individuals with lifelong schizophrenia (EOS), illustrating the importance of the factors discussed above in assessment and treatment.

The aging person with early-onset schizophrenia (EOS)

Mr K is a 75-year-old man with a long history of multiple hospitalizations dating back to his early 20s. As a teenager he was somewhat isolated and had few friends. At the age of 19 he became withdrawn and reclusive, quitting his job as a factory worker based on a belief that his foreman had tried to poison him. Thereafter he began to report to his family that voices were telling him that Satan had placed a "spell" on the family. During a gathering over the Christmas holidays he became acutely agitated, screaming at his parents that they were "doomed," and ran out of the house partially clothed. He was picked up by the local police authorities, who brought him to the local hospital. After a brief evaluation he was mandated to the state asylum for the insane, where he was hospitalized for most of the following 30 years. During his hospitalization, in the 1950s, he received a variety of treatments, including multiple electroconvulsive shock treatments (ECT) and treatment with several different types of tranquilizers. In addition to his diagnosis of schizophrenia, he also developed a seizure disorder and was treated with phenobarbital.

In the early 1960s Mr K was placed on a variety of trials of antipsychotic medications and his delusions and hallucinations decreased. However, he remained withdrawn and lacked basic self-care skills. He also developed tardive dyskinesia, causing severe involuntary movements of his face, upper extremities, and fingers. Attempts to reduce his antipsychotic medication to a lower dose were not pursued owing to concerns that he would experience a symptomatic relapse.

At the age of 64 Mr K was transferred to a board and care home, when the long-term care unit at the state hospital was closed. Several months after the transfer he became acutely agitated and depressed, refusing to take his medications. He became acutely paranoid and began to have recurrent seizures. After being hospitalized he was started on different antipsychotic medication with fewer side effects in conjunction with antidepressant medication. His seizure disorder was stabilized on appropriate anticonvulsant medications. He subsequently became less withdrawn and began to take his medications voluntarily once again. He returned to the board and care home, where he continued to need supervision and assistance with basic living and self-care skills.

Over the last several years Mr K has become more forgetful and less able to care for himself. More recently (over the past year) he complained that Satan put a snake in his abdomen, creating intermittent pain and cramping. He lost weight and became increasingly withdrawn and confused. He complained that the snake in his stomach was constantly thirsty, and consumed large amounts of fluids. These complaints were attributed to his long-standing religious delusions, and his antipsychotic medication was increased by his local physician by an order given over the phone. His physical status continued to decline until he eventually stopped eating altogether and was admitted to the hospital acutely dehydrated, weak, and acutely confused. On admission, Mr K was found to have dangerously high blood-glucose levels. With medical treatment, his blood-glucose levels returned to a safe range and his pain and dehydration resolved. He became less confused, yet could not follow the schedule of insulin treatment and glucose testing required by his physician. He was discharged to a nursing home, where he received ongoing nursing care and regulation of his medications.

This case illustrates several key points in the assessment and treatment of the aging person with schizophrenia. First, Mr K has an extremely severe disorder with persistent negative symptoms and limited functional abilities, and he belongs to a generation of patients who were chronically institutionalized. He is representative of the oldest and most severely ill individuals with EOS who first became ill before the development of antipsychotic medication, at a time when treatment generally consisted of long-term institutionalization. Like many, he remained in institutions for most of his adult life, residing first in a state psychiatric hospital, followed by discharge to a board and care home, and then, finally, admission to a nursing home. The years of institutional care have left Mr K with few (if any) social supports outside of the institutional setting, poor social skills, and severe limits in functional abilities. Without adequate independent living skills, he is largely dependent on care-providers for basic needs. Because of these limitations, Mr K initially experienced his transfer to a board and care home as a disorienting and traumatic event, resulting in an acute depression and decompensation.

This case also illustrates the significant interaction of psychiatric illness and medical illness in the older adult with severe mental illness: the psychiatric illness affecting medical symptoms, and the medical disorder affecting psychiatric symptoms. In the first instance, Mr K's psychiatric illness was associated with worsening of his physical health. In a state of depression and agitation following his transfer to a board and care home, he stopped taking medications that were essential to his physical and mental health. His anticonvulsant medications had controlled his seizure disorder for years, yet on stopping these medications he once again suffered from uncontrolled seizures. After resuming his medications in the hospital he recovered. Years later he developed another medical disorder, insulin-dependent diabetes, yet this time this severe condition went undiagnosed. In this instance, his medical condition directly influenced his psychiatric status, causing severe confusion, withdrawal, and physical symptoms that were mistaken for delusions.

Co-occurring medical disorders are a common complication of the aging process and are often undiagnosed and undertreated in patients with severe mental illness. Factors which may contribute to this poor physical health include a high prevalence of health-damaging behaviors such as smoking (Hughes et al., 1986) and substance abuse (Drake et al., 1989b), limited access to good health care because of financial constraints, and a delay in seeking medical treatment as a result of the high pain threshold found in many persons with schizophrenia (Dworkin, 1994). In addition, older persons are more sensitive to the potential neurotoxic effects of antipsychotic medications such as tardive dyskinesia. Antipsychotic-induced tardive dyskinesia is a neurological syndrome of persistent abnormal involuntary movements. The prevalence of tardive dyskinesia for elderly with schizophrenia is 26 to 45 percent (Jeste et al., 1993). The more conservative estimate of 26 percent is nearly six times the rate reported for younger patients (Kane et al., 1988). This neurological disorder caused by traditional antipsychotic medications further complicates the health and physical functioning of the aging person with severe mental illness. In general, the physical health of individuals with schizophrenia in late middle age or early old age may be more typical of the health status of individuals without mental illness who are much older (Mulsant et al., 1993). The high rate of medical comorbidity in persons with schizophrenia underscores the need to include a thorough medical evaluation and ongoing general health-care services as an integrated component of comprehensive psychiatric services to older persons with severe mental illness.

This case also illustrates the development of co-occurring cognitive impairment. In addition to the complication of medical illnesses that often accompanies the aging process, older patients with severe mental illness are also vulnerable to the development of comorbid cognitive impairment. Elderly with EOS and LOS both have global cognitive deficits when compared to normal controls, although these deficits are stable in most patients, and have been described as a static encephalopathy following the initial onset of the disorder (Goldberg et al., 1993; Heaton et al., 1994). However, several studies suggest that a subset of individuals with schizophrenia progress to states of dementia (Lesser et al., 1993; Davidson et al., 1995). For individuals like Mr K, the symptoms of dementia can overshadow the psychosis and become the primary source of functional impairment in late life. At this point a supportive, supervised setting becomes even more of a necessity and nursing-home care may be unavoidable. Comorbid cognitive impairment is one of the most significant differences between elderly with severe mental illness in nursing homes compared to those living in the community. In a study that included 129 elderly with schizophrenia residing in nursing homes and the community, the factors most associated with nursing-home status (after adjusting for age) were more severe cognitive impairment, more severe overall symptom ratings, greater functional impairment, more aggressive behaviors, and having never married. Overall, degree of cognitive impairment may be one of the most important clinical factors associated with level of care and level of function among older persons with schizophrenia (Bartels Mueser, & Miles, in press).

Overall, the case of Mr K illustrates an era of institution-based treatment that is coming to an end. A growing number of aging individuals with severe mental illness have received much of their treatment in the community following deinstitutionalization and have different levels of functional ability and treatment needs.

The following case describes an older person with schizophrenia who has benefited from community support treatment and contemporary medication approaches.

Mrs M is a 62-year-old woman with schizophrenia residing with a companion in a senior housing apartment in the community. She was married at the age of 19 and had her first psychotic episode at age 20. She then underwent a series of psychiatric hospitalizations, at first returning to live with her husband, until her husband eventually became overwhelmed by her recurrent paranoid episodes and pursued a divorce. Thereafter she moved in with her parents and received outpatient treatment at the local community mental health center.

Mrs M continued to have severe paranoid symptoms over the early years of her illness and required episodic hospitalizations. Her parents worked closely with the mental health case managers to develop the needed supports and monitoring of symptoms to keep Mrs M in the community as much as possible. This included notifying treatment providers of the early symptoms of relapse, as well as assuring that Mrs M regularly took the appropriate dose of her antipsychotic medication. During periods of relative remission of symptoms, Mrs M was able to hold down a part-time job and regularly went out for dinner and to cultural events with her parents. Although her psychiatric symptoms were relatively well controlled with her antipsychotic medication (haloperidol), Mrs M had long-standing side effects. These included episodes of muscle stiffness and slowed movement (drug-induced Parkinson's syndrome) and tardive dyskinesia manifest by significant abnormal involuntary movements (twitching and writhing movements) of her face, arms, fingers, and trunk. Attempts to reduce her dose of medication substantially to minimize side effects resulted in psychotic relapse.

When Mrs M turned 55, her father had a stroke and was placed in a nursing home. Shortly thereafter Mrs M's mother had a sudden heart attack and died. Mrs M stopped taking her medication, became acutely psychotic, and was admitted to a psychiatric hospital. On account of her long-standing difficulties with side effects to the haloperidol, Mrs M was started on clozapine. She recompensated and returned to her former level of function. In addition, she no longer had medication-induced Parkinson symptoms and had a decrease in her symptoms of tardive dyskinesia. The discharge planning team recognized her reliance on others for social support and monitoring of medications and symptoms, and recommended that Mrs M be discharged to a senior housing apartment with a roommate, complemented by frequent visits by her case manager from the geriatric mental health outreach team. With active support by the mental health team, Mrs M made this transition without major difficulties and resumed many of her former activities.

This case illustrates several important points. First, Mrs M belongs to a different treatment cohort than Mr K. Most of her treatment occurred in community-based programs with episodic acute hospitalizations. Thus she was able to reside in the community and developed community living skills. Older adults with schizophrenia residing in the community have substantial difficulties in many areas of functioning compared to older people with affective disorders such as major depression (Bartels, Mueser, & Miles, 1997). However, comprehensive support services can overcome many of these problems and facilitate living in the community. Mrs M's treatment included services that sought to minimize institutional dependence (unlike Mr K) and to maximize her ability to live in the least restrictive setting. She was able to develop and maintain social skills and supports. Unfortunately, the severity of her illness resulted in substantial stress to her marriage, resulting in an eventual divorce. Although this was a significant loss, she was able to fall back on the support of her family of origin, moving back to live with her parents.

Secondly, this anecdote illustrates the importance of social supports. One of the major differences between older individuals with severe mental illness residing in the community compared to nursing homes and other institutions is the presence of family members who are able (and willing) to provide assistance with daily activities and needs. Compared to a person without a psychiatric disorder, persons with schizophrenia are less likely to marry, less likely to have children, and less likely to work. In the community, their social networks are often constrained to members of their families of origin and a few friends. In this respect, family supports are especially crucial to community tenure. The family members who provided a stable and supportive environment helped to facilitate Mrs M's ability to remain in the community.

However, this aspect underscores a vulnerability of the patient with severe mental illness who is aging. Many individuals with severe mental illness reside with family members (often parents). The aging, illness, and eventual death of parents who are key supports places these individuals at risk for decompensation and loss of ability to continue to reside in individual placement in the community. The literature on family burden of psychiatric illness is replete with reports of aging parents (usually mothers) caring for their middle-aged children with schizophrenia (e.g., Platt, 1985; MacGregor, 1994; Bulger et al., 1993). Even if parent and child no longer reside together, the parent often plays a critical role in supervising the patient's treatment and life style, as well as in supplementing any other financial resources available to him/her (Salokangas et al., 1991).

When the parent becomes ill or dies, the child, then frequently in his or her forties, is left to cope with the emotional impact of losing a parent and a primary source of social contact and support. At the same time this individual must quickly adjust to a dramatic reduction in financial and social support, which may also coincide with a loss of residence. Even if they feel an emotional bond with their ill relative, siblings are often reluctant to assume the burden previously borne by the parent, contributing to the meager circumstances of many patients' lives. This lack of alternative family caregivers is an important distinguishing feature of aging for many older persons with severe mental illness. Unlike the individual with Alzheimer's disease, who often has involved family members (especially adult children who act as direct caregivers), many individuals with lifelong schizophrenia never had children or have long become alienated from extended family, leaving them without this particular care-provider resource.

This case also illustrates that older persons are especially sensitive to the adverse side effects of medications, and thoughtful attention to choosing the appropriate type and dose of medication can be extremely important. Mrs M had medication-induced Parkinson's syndrome caused by extrapyramidal nervous system side effects (EPS) from haldol. Aging is associated with an increased prevalence of EPS owing to biological changes in neuroreceptor sensitivity and a declining amount of dopamine occurring with age. Clozapine and other newer "atypical" antipsychotic agents (e.g., risperidone, olanzapine, quetiapine, sertindole, and ziprasidone) are associated with little or no EPS. However, some of these newer agents may produce other serious side effects that require especially close monitoring and supervison in the older patient (Marder & Meibach, 1994; Salzman et al., 1995; Wirshing et al., 1997).

Finally, this case illustrates the different characteristics of elderly patients with EOS from different age and treatment cohorts or groups. Many of the oldest patients with EOS have spent most of their lives in institutional settings, as illustrated in the first case example. More recently, a different group of EOS elderly patients has emerged. These individuals are the "young-old" (in their 60s) and are among the first wave of severely mentally ill patients who became ill when states were closing their long-term wards and shifting treatment into the community. This historical cohort of younger patients with schizophrenia includes individuals who have developed inde-pendent living skills and are more likely to continue to live independently in the community in late life.

Late-onset schizophrenia

The diagnosis of late-onset schizophrenia evolved from early descriptions of a disorder called "paraphrenia." Kraepelin (1971 [1919]) used the term paraphrenia to describe a group of patients, frequently older in age, with symptoms similar to "dementia praecox," but with fewer negative and cognitive symptoms. Kay and Roth (1961) later described "late paraphrenia" as a paranoid syndrome occurring in late life that was not accompanied by dementia. Late paraphrenia is characterized by onset after age 45 of a well-organized paranoid delusional system, with or without auditory hallucina-tions, and often occurring with preserved personality. Late paraphrenia is more common among women then men. More recently, psychiatric diagnostic criteria have been revised to reclassify most individuals formally diagnosed with late paraphrenia as schizophrenia. For example, recent revisions allow for a diagnosis of schizophrenia with the first onset of symptoms after age 45 (DSMIV: American Psychiatric Association, 1994).

The following clinical anecdote illustrates many of the characteristics of late-onset schizophrenia in an older patient.

Mrs W is a 63-year-old widowed woman who lives alone in her house. She has two children who live in the next town. During much of her life she worked as a librarian, until she retired at the age of 60. She was seen by many as somewhat odd and eccentric, yet never had any psychiatric hospitalizations or mental health treatment history during her younger years. Her husband died five years earlier from a myocardial infarction. Her own health is quite good, though her hearing has substantially deteriorated. Over the last two years Mrs W has become increasingly concerned for her safety. She initially believed, because of strange noises that she heard in the yard, that there were prowlers or burglars trying to get into her house at night. She made repeated calls to the local police department, who inspected the grounds and found no signs of intruders. Her concerns escalated when she began to believe that a group of men were constantly monitoring her every move with the plan to torture and murder her. She believed that these men regularly entered her bedroom at night and attempted to physically accost her as she slept. She resolved this problem by sitting up most of the night in her living room and falling asleep in her chair – avoiding her bedroom at night.

Attempts to involve mental health professionals in her treatment were unsuccessful. Mrs W insisted that her problems were due to a group of "criminals and rapists" who had targeted her house, and she complained that she only needed better police protection. She refused a psychiatric evaluation or psychiatric medications. By day Mrs W functioned relatively well. She went out for lunch with her daughters on a regular basis and played cards one night a week with a small group of women friends. Her speech and thinking appeared entirely normal, except when discussion turned to issues having to do with crime or her personal safety. Family and friends dealt with the problem by avoiding conversation about these issues altogether.

At the age of 70 Mrs W began to have unexplained episodes of losing consciousness, followed by transient weakness on her right side. Though she was convinced this was due to the group of men who were tying to kill her, an astute mental health case manager insisted on taking Mrs W to her medical physician, who quickly diagnosed transient ischemic attacks (TIAs) and placed her on anticoagulant medication, preventing subsequent attacks. During the hospitalization her physician was able to convince her to attempt a trial of low dose risperidone. In addition, she was evaluated by audiology and was fitted for a hearing aid that substantially improved her hearing. Following discharge, her case manager and a visiting nurse regularly visited her in her home and assured that Mrs W continued to take her medications as prescribed. Within one month she reported no further auditory hallucinations and was significantly less paranoid. Within several months she reported that she no longer believed that she was at risk, as the men had left the neighborhood.

This case example demonstrates several key points about the assessment and treatment of older adults with late-onset schizophrenia (LOS). First, Mrs W had the onset of her psychiatric symptoms in late life (age 63) and in the absence of any significant signs of cognitive impairment or neurological illness. As noted earlier, almost one-quarter (23 percent) of patients with schizophrenia have the onset of their disorder after age 40 (Harris and Jeste, 1988). Consistent with early descriptions of paraphrenia, Mrs W's premorbid personality was generally preserved, so that she maintained many of the appearances of her daily social routine and function. Hence she did not seek or receive treatment for her psychiatric illness until she was medically hospitalized for an unrelated disorder.

Second, this case typifies LOS, since women are overrepresented among those affected by the disorder (Harris and Jeste, 1988). In contrast, most studies of EOS report similar proportions of women to men. Several explanations for this difference have been proposed. One view suggests that EOS and LOS are different forms of schizophrenia with different characteristics, including different rates among men and women. An alternative view suggests that biological factors are responsible for a later onset of schizophrenia in women, resulting in an overrepresentation for LOS of women compared to men. This later hypothesis is supported by findings in studies of EOS showing that the onset in women is approximately five years later than in men (Lewine, 1988). This difference may be even greater among patients with LOS. In a community study which included EOS and LOS, Castle and Murray (1993) found that 16 percent of males had the onset of schizophrenia after age 45, compared to 38 percent of females. Speculation about the difference in age of onset between men and women includes a possible protective effect of estrogens or a precipitating effect of androgens (Castle & Murray, 1993).

Third, this case illustrates the symptoms of LOS, which typically include relatively well-circumscribed, non-bizarre delusions in the absence of a formal disorder in thought processes. Non-bizarre delusions involve situations that may occur in real life, such as being poisoned, afflicted with an incurable disease, stalked, attacked, or deceived by a spouse or lover. In contrast, bizarre delusions involve phenomena that are considered totally implausible within one's culture (American Psychiatric Association, 1994; Yassa & Suranyl-Cadotte, 1993). Mrs W's delusions and hallucinations are relatively clearly defined and involve the psychotic (though theoretically possible) belief that she is in danger of being attacked by a group of criminals who are stalking her. In addition, her thinking processes remain well organized. When she is not focusing on her delusions, her speech and function are almost indistinguishable from those of her friends who do not have a major mental illness. This is in marked contrast to the examples of patients with EOS, where thought disorder and difficulties in basic living skills were prominent. Delusions and hallucinations are common symptoms in late-onset schizophrenia and occur at a rate comparable to those found in young adults with early-onset schizophrenia. Delusions tend to be paranoid and are often systematized (Kay & Roth, 1961; Howard et al., 1993; Almeida et al., 1995a). Auditory hallucinations are substantially more common than visual or somatic hallucinations – similar to young adults with EOS (Almeida et al., 1995a). In contrast to patients with EOS, individuals with LOS are significantly less likely to manifest formal thought disorder, negative symptoms, or inappropriate affect (Kay & Roth, 1961; Pearlson & Rabins, 1988; Pearlson et al., 1989; Howard et al., 1993; Almeida et al., 1995).

The fourth point demonstrated by the case of Mrs W relates to her pre-morbid (pre-illness) level of functioning and subsequent ability to continue to function at a relatively good level during the course of her illness. Compared to those with EOS, individuals with LOS are more likely to show better pre-morbid occupational adjustment (Post, 1966) and higher marriage rates. However, set against normal comparison groups, individuals with LOS are frequently socially isolated and often have schizoid, schizotypal, or paranoid pre-morbid personalities (Kay & Roth, 1961; Harris & Jeste, 1988). Mrs W's reputation for being "odd and eccentric" is consistent with this view of her personality. Nonetheless, her abilities to function independently and engage in some social relationships continued even after the onset of her illness.

Mrs W's case also illustrates the presence of sensory impairment that appears to predate the onset of the disorder. Mrs W has marked sensory (hearing) impairment, a risk factor for LOS. In a review of 27 articles that assess visual and hearing abilities in elderly with late-onset disorders, Prager and Jeste (1993) concluded that sensory deficits were overrepresented. An association between visual impairment and visual hallucinations is suggested by the literature, although a specific relationship between visual impairment and late-onset paranoid psychosis remains controversial. On the other hand, the majority of studies reviewed support a specific association between hearing deficits and late-onset paranoid psychosis. Moderate to severe hearing deficits have been reported in approximately 40 percent of those with late-onset paranoid psychoses (Kay & Roth, 1961; Herbert & Jacobson, 1967). As in Mrs W's case, significant reductions in psychotic symptoms have been reported for some individuals who have late-onset paranoid disorders after fitting with a hearing aid, suggesting that deafness may precipitate or worsen symptoms (Almeida et al., 1993).

Clinically, the strong association between sensory impairments, psychotic symptoms, and LOS suggests that these patients may benefit from systematic instruction in coping strategies for the management of positive symptoms. In recent years, growing evidence has emerged that younger patients with schizophrenia employ a wide range of different strategies for coping with positive symptoms (Carr, 1988; Falloon & Talbot, 1981; Mueser & Gingerich, 1994). Methods for managing positive symptoms typically involve either disattention or relaxation, with coping efficacy strongly related to the number of strategies employed by the patient. One study by Tarrier and his colleagues (1993) indicated that young patients with schizophrenia who were taught coping strategies experienced significant reductions in positive symptoms compared to patients who received training in social problem-solving. This encouraging study suggests that elderly persons with schizophrenia characterized by persistent psychotic symptoms might benefit from receiving similar training in coping skills. However, studies are yet to be conducted on the potential benefit of skills training and other psycho-social rehabilitative interventions for older persons with schizophrenia.

Finally, Mrs W eventually showed significant improvement when treated with a combination of mental health outreach support services and antipsychotic medications. Older adults with LOS have been shown to be as responsive to antipsychotic medications as young patients with schizophrenia when treated with appropriate agents and dosages. For example, response rates of late-onset schizophrenia to antipsychotic medications range from 62 percent (Post, 1966) to 86 percent (Rabins et al., 1984).

Other Severe Mental Disorders Affecting Older Adults

Schizophrenia is one of several severe mental disorders that affect older individuals. A variety of other psychotic disorders can also affect persons in late life, including delusional disorder, psychotic affective disorders such as bipolar disorder, and dementia complicated by psychotic symptoms. These disorders have a dramatic and persistent effect on function and behavior.

Similar to late-onset schizophrenia, delusional disorder is characterized by the presence of prominent non-bizarre delusions. Yet, unlike LOS, hallucinations are absent or rarely occur (Harris & Jeste, 1988). The delusions occurring in delusional disorder tend to be persistent and must occur in the absence of an underlying causative medical disorder. Early descriptions of this disorder remark on significant delusions (usually paranoid in nature) in the absence of a formal disorder of thought. In general, these disorders tend to have limited response to antipsychotic medications (Kay and Roth, 1961; Holden, 1987).

Bipolar disorder is a severe affective (mood) disorder marked by cycles of persistent depressive episodes alternating with periods of mania. During manic episodes, individuals experience euphoric mood, rapid thoughts and speech, marked hyperactivity, poor judgment (including spending sprees and hypersexual or aggressive behavior), and delusions of grandiosity. Patients with manic symptoms make up 5 to 10 percent of all elderly referred for treatment of affective disorders (Shulman & Tohen, 1994). Remarkably little is known about the long-term course of bipolar disorder in older patients. Among two long-term outcome studies following patients over age 60 for six years or more, a 34 to 50 percent mortality rate was found (Dhingra & Rabins, 1991; Shulman & Post, 1980). Among surviving patients, however, functional outcomes were quite favorable, with 72 percent of subjects symptom-free and 80 percent living independently in the community at follow-up (Dhingra & Rabins, 1991).

There appear to be several different clinical sub-groups of older persons with bipolar disorder (Shulman & Post, 1980). For example, one group has long-standing bipolar disorder that has persisted into old age. Another sub-group of individuals is relatively symptom-free until the onset of a major depressive episode first occurring in middle age. After many years of episodic depression (up to 15 years), the individual then has a first episode of mania in late life. Finally, another sub-group has what has been described as "secondary mania." For these individuals, the first appearance of the disorder is a manic psychotic episode occurring in old age. However, this disorder is presumed to be secondary to a medical or neurological disorder. Secondary mania has multiple potential causes, including toxic reactions to medications, metabolic or infectious disorders, and neurological disorders such as stroke or tumor. This disorder is associated with poor prognosis and a relatively high mortality rate (Krauthammer & Klerman, 1978; Shulman & Post, 1980).

Finally, psychotic symptoms can occur secondary to medical causes (formerly organic mental disorders) and are common among older adults with dementia. Approximately 30 percent of individuals with Alzheimer's experience secondary hallucinations or delusions at some time during the course of their disorder. Delusions in Alzheimer's tend to be fragmentary and transient and are often paranoid in nature (Wragg and Jeste, 1989). Similarly, individuals with vascular (multi-infarct) dementia due to stroke and other forms of cerebrovascular disease commonly report episodes of delusions (Cummings, 1985).

Treatment of Schizophrenia in Late Life

Treatment of schizophrenia in late life is best considered within the framework of a bio-psycho-social perspective. This perspective assumes that optimal assessment and treatment addresses the biological, psychological, and social aspects of the person. For the older person with a severe mental illness, this broad spectrum approach is particularly critical. Aging is associated with substantial biological changes that directly affect medication metabolism and side effects. Furthermore, the presence of multiple medical problems and other medical medications must be considered in treatment. The psychological impact of mental illness and the effects of aging must also be carefully weighed in designing a program of treatment. The individual's cognitive abilities must be comprehensively assessed in order to inform the choice of intervention. Finally, social supports and stressors are a major consideration in assessing needed services. One of the most important factors determining whether an older person remains in the community or permanently resides in a nursing home is the presence of social and instrumental supports. In summary, the bio-psycho-social perspective should be the foundation to assure a comprehensive clinical assessment and effective plan of treatment.

Remarkably little is known about effective treatments for the older person with schizophrenia. In the following section we summarize biological and psycho-social approaches to treatment adapted for older persons but largely developed and studied in younger populations.

Biological treatment

The first, and perhaps most critical, step in the biological treatment of the older adult with schizophrenia is to conduct a thorough medical evaluation. Virtually any psychiatric symptom can be caused or exacerbated by an underlying medical illness (Bartels, 1989). Medical disorders are commonly underrecognized and undertreated among individuals with severe mental illness. Even when care-providers are committed to quality health care, it may be especially difficult to provide health services to individuals who are delusional, cognitively impaired, lacking in social or communication skills, uncooperative with assessment, or physically threatening. Furthermore, comorbid medical illness is the rule, not the exception, in older adults. Finally, it is likely that the older individual is on multiple medications for a variety of medical disorders and psychiatric symptoms. Toxicity of combined medication, or failure to take medications as indicated, is a common problem for the older patient.

Once medical causes of psychiatric symptoms have been ruled out or treated, the mainstay of treatment for schizophrenia consists of antipsychotic medications. Many double-blind controlled studies have documented efficacy of antipsychotic medications, which serve two primary purposes in the treatment of schizophrenia. First, they reduce both positive and negative acute symptoms that appear during an exacerbation (Kane & Marder, 1993). Second, the prophylactic administration of antipsychotics after a relapse lowers the probability of subsequent relapses by 30 to 60 percent (Kane, 1989). Research indicates that very low dosages of antipsychotic medication are effective at lowering risk of relapse (Van Putten & Marder, 1986), suggesting that patients' vulnerability to long-term side effects of these medications (e.g., tardive dyskinesia) can be reduced. Furthermore, recent advances in the development of atypical antipsychotic medications (e.g., clozapine, risperidone, olanzapine, quetiapine, sertindole, and ziprasidone) hold promise for improving the functioning of patients who do not respond to the standard antipsychotics (Meltzer, 1990; Marder & Meibach, 1994; Salzman et al., 1995; Wirshing et al., 1997).

Little is known about the pharmacological treatment of elderly with schizophrenia (Jeste et al., 1993). In a review of the few available studies, most report that antipsychotic medications result in a reduction of symptoms and earlier discharge from the hospital (Jeste et al., 1993). However, physiological changes of aging contribute to increased risk of acute adverse side effects to antipsychotic medications in the elderly. Age-related alterations in drug distribution and metabolism may result in higher plasma levels of antipsychotic medications in elderly compared to younger schizophrenic patients. In addition, age-related changes in receptors and neurotransmitters may cause elderly to be more sensitive to the effects of medications. Hence, effective serum levels of medication are achieved with substantially lower doses of antipsychotic medication in elderly patients.

The older person is especially vulnerable to adverse side effects of medications. For example, age and duration of exposure to antipsychotic medications are extensively documented as primary risk factors for the development of tardive dyskinesia (Kane et al., 1992). Among other common side effects of antipsychotic medications are extrapyramidal side effects, including medication-induced Parkinson's syndrome. Patients with this drug-induced syndrome exhibit muscle rigidity, shuffling gait, lack of spontaneous facial expressions, and severe resting tremor of the arms, hands, head, and legs. Other extrapyramidal side effects include severe restlessness or pacing behavior. Older adults may be more vulnerable to all of these side effects on account of their greater sensitivity to lower doses of medication and co-occurring neurological disorders. Hence, ongoing close monitoring of side effects and neurological status is imperative. In addition, use of the new "atypical" antipsychotic agents may be indicated. These agents have little to no extrapyramidal (Parkinsonian) side effects and may be particularly effective in treating both positive and negative symptoms in the older patient (Salzman et al., 1995).

Age is associated with remission of symptoms in more than half of individuals with schizophrenia (Harding et al., 1987a, 1987b), suggesting that some elderly individuals may be spared the risks of continued exposure to antipsychotic medications. Jeste and colleagues (1993) reviewed six double-blind studies of antipsychotic drug withdrawal that included older adults with schizophrenia followed for a mean of six months and found an average relapse rate of 40 percent, compared to a relapse rate of 11 percent for those who continued on medication. The authors concluded that stable, chronic outpatients without a history of antipsychotic discontinuation should be considered for a carefully monitored trial of antipsychotic withdrawal.

Nevertheless, the antipsychotics are not a cure for schizophrenia, and significant residual symptoms usually persist between episodes, resulting in severe impairments in social functioning. For these reasons, antipsychotic medications are a mainstay in all treatment programs for schizophrenia, but there is still a great need for effective psychotherapeutic interventions that affect the pervasive deficits of schizophrenia.

Psycho-social interventions

One way of understanding the role of psycho-social treatment is through the stress–vulnerability model for schizophrenia. This model suggests that the presence and severity of schizophrenic symptoms are the result of the combined influences of biological vulnerability, psychological vulnerability, and environmental stress. Biological vulnerability is believed to be determined early in life by genetic and other biological factors. Environmental stressors include life events (e.g., the death of a significant other), exposure to high levels of negative emotion, and lack of needed structure or support. Psychological vulnerability stems from a lack of coping and living skills needed to deal with the effect of having a mental disorder, as well as the variety of life challenges that occur. (See chapter 5 for a discussion of the stress-vulnerability model.)

The stress-vulnerability model suggests that the outcome of the illness can be improved by reducing either vulnerability or environmental stress, or by enhancing coping skills. Most treatments for schizophrenia share one or more of these goals. For example, biological vulnerability can be lessened by providing antipsychotic medications and decreasing substance abuse. In contrast, psycho-social interventions such as family interventions tend to emphasize reduction of environmental stress (Mueser & Glynn, 1995), whereas individual treatment approaches, such as social skills training (Liberman et al., 1989), tend to focus mainly on improving patients' coping skills.

Reduction of environmental stress has been a major focus of the family intervention research. Family interventions are increasingly important as institutional long-term care becomes less frequent and family members shoulder more of the burden for caring for their mentally ill relatives. Caring for the mentally ill can be a challenging task. A series of studies in the 1970s and 1980s demonstrated that family attitudes assessed at the time of a symptom exacerbation of a schizophrenic person predict relapse during the ensuing nine months (see Kavanagh, 1992, for a recent review). Higher levels of critical comments, hostility, and overinvolvement (high "expressed emotion" or EE) were associated with increased rates of relapse. High EE may play a role in precipitating relapse, although it is also possible that living with a relative with frequent psychotic relapses results in high EE for the family caregiver (Glynn et al., 1990).

A consensus has emerged in the treatment literature establishing that family-based interventions can have a significant, positive impact on many patients with schizophrenia and, frequently, on their relatives as well (Falloon et al., 1982; Hogarty et al., 1986; Leff et al., 1982; Randolph et al., 1994; Xiong et al., 1994). However, it is important to note that these studies have focused largely on younger patients with severe mental illness (generally with older parent care-providers), and implications of this technology for the older patient with mental illness is unknown.

Other family interventions that may have relevance to the older patient with severe mental illness include approaches that have been developed for family care-providers of patients with Alzheimer's and related dementias. For example, interventions that enhance the coping and caring skills of family providers have been shown to delay institutionalization of individuals with Alzheimer's dementia in nursing homes. In a randomized trail, Mittelman and colleagues (1996) studied the effect of a series of family and group sessions designed to improve the skills and supports for family caregivers. The individual with Alzheimer's disease whose family members participated in this intervention remained in the community (on average) for almost one additional year compared to the control group. These demonstrated benefits of an intervention targeting the family caregiver may hold promise for the group of aging individuals with severe mental illness who remain with family members in late life. Thus far, however, similar intervention development and evaluation studies have not been carried out with family caregivers of older adults with severe mental illness.

Social skills training may also have a role in psycho-social treatment of the older adult with schizophrenia. Many patients with schizophrenia require outpatient interventions that can be provided on a group or individual basis, such as social skills training. The fundamental premise of social skills training is that the social impairments of schizophrenia can be decreased through systematically teaching the behavioral components of social skills (Bellack et al., 1984; Bellack & Mueser, 1993; Dobson et al., in press; Hayes, et al., in press). Teaching is conducted through a combination of therapist modeling (i.e., demonstration of the skill), patient behavioral rehearsal (i.e., role playing), positive and corrective feedback, and homework assignments to program generalization of the skill to the natural environment. Targeted social skills span a wide range of adaptive interpersonal and self-care behaviors, including the expression of feelings, conflict resolution skills, and medication management. Overall, the controlled studies on social skills training for schizophrenia provide some support for its efficacy, especially when treatment is provided over the long term (Mueser et al., in press). It is clear that skills training can improve social skills, and there is some evidence supporting its effect on social functioning. The impact of social skills training on the symptoms of schizophrenia is less clear, but it remains an important avenue for improving social functioning (See box 9.1).

Box 9.1   Psychiatric rehabilitation: focus on social skills training

Description: Patients with severe mental illnesses, such as schizophrenia, often experience profound difficulties in their social relationships and ability to interact with other people. Helping these patients improve their skills for dealing with social situations can improve the overall quality of their lives. Social skills can be defined as the specific behaviors (e.g., voice tone, eye contact, verbal content) that are critical for achieving interpersonal goals, such as making friends, purchasing items at a store, or discussing medication issues with a physician. Social skills training is an approach to psychiatric rehabilitation that involves systematically teaching interpersonal skills to enable patients to achieve personal goals and to function effectively in the community or other setting in which they reside.

Logistics: Social skills training can be conducted in an individual, group, or family format, although the group format is most often used. Groups usually include four to eight patients and are led by two leaders. Skills training sessions last between 30 and 75 minutes (depending on the severity of symptoms and cognitive impairments of the patients), with two to four training sessions conducted per week. Groups may run for as brief a time as several weeks to as long as over a year. Social skills groups can be conducted at the hospital or mental health center, or elsewhere in the community, such as a supervised residence. The group is organized so that participants sit in a circle, with the center of the circle reserved for role-playing social skills. Leaders employ visual aids, such as flipcharts, blackboards, and posters, to teach patients skills. The emphasis in the group is on teaching and practicing new skills through frequent role plays and feedback, rather than on fostering "insight." Refreshments are often served during a break or after the group to encourage patients to attend. Homework assignments and community trips are scheduled to program the generalization of social skills taught in the group to patients' natural living environments.

Steps of social skills training: Skills training sessions follow a standard set of steps, including the following:

1. Establish the rationale for the importance of learning the skill (How can it be helpful for patients to learn the skill?).
2. Break the skill down into three or four steps and discuss each step. For example, the skill of "expressing a negative feeling" can be broken down into the following steps: a) look at the person with a serious facial expression, b) tell the person what he or she did that upset you, c) tell the person how it made you feel, d) suggest how the person could prevent this from happening again.
3. The leaders model (demonstrate) the skill in a role play of a realistic situation.
4. Discuss each step of the skill demonstrated in the role play and the overall effectiveness of the leader in that situation.
5. Engage a patient in a role play of the same situation.
6. Elicit positive feedback from group members about specific steps of the skill that were performed well, and provide additional feedback about points not made by group members.
7. Provide corrective feedback about how the skill could be performed better; strive to make feedback as helpful as possible and avoid criticism.

8. Engage the patient in another role play of the same situation, with attention to improving one or two specific steps of the skill.
9. Provide additional positive and corrective feedback, and evaluate whether another role play of the same situation would be useful.
10. After each patient has practiced the skill in at least two role plays, assign homework to practice the skill in real-life situations. Begin the next session by conducting role plays and providing feedback based on patients efforts' to use the skill in personally relevant situations.

Common skills taught in social skills training:

Conversation skills	Dating skills
Assertion skills	Making friends
Conflict resolution	Skills for leisure and recreation
Medication management skills	Skills refusing offers to use alcohol or drugs
Work-related social skills	

Social skills training manuals:

Bellack, A. S., Mueser, K. T., Gingerich, S., & Agresta, J. (1997). *Social skills training for schizophrenia.* New York: Guilford Press.

Liberman, R. P., DeRisi, W. J., & Mueser, K. T. (1989). *Social skills training for psychiatric patients.* Needham Heights, MA: Allyn & Bacon.

Summary

Remarkably, little is known about factors affecting the course or outcome of schizophrenia and other severe mental disorders in late life (Belitsky & McGlashan, 1993). Schizophrenia can occur in late life as part of a lifelong illness (early-onset schizophrenia), or first appear in older age (late-onset schizophrenia). Important factors that may affect the clinical presentation and treatment needs of the older person with schizophrenia (regardless of age of onset) include past history of treatment and cohort effects, comorbid medical illness, comorbid cognitive impairment, and the availability of social supports. Late-onset schizophrenia (LOS) is less common than early-onset schizophrenia (EOS) and is characterized by several distinct differences. Individuals with LOS compared to those with EOS are more likely to be women and to have better pre-morbid functioning, including better occupational history and a greater likelihood of having been married. The clinical presentation of LOS is more likely to include a predominance of positive symptoms, such as paranoid delusions and auditory hallucinations, and less likely to have negative symptoms. Formal thought disorder is rare in LOS but common in EOS.

Among those with EOS who have the onset of their disorder after age 60, there is a greater incidence of hearing loss compared to the general population. Finally, the limited data on treatment suggests that response to antipsychotic medication among individuals with LOS is comparable to those with EOS, but lower doses are indicated and the risk of adverse side effects such as tardive dyskinesia substantially increases with age.

In general, there is a paucity of research on treatments and services for older persons with severe and persistent mental illness, particularly in the area of psycho-social treatment (Light & Lebowitz, 1991). In particular, little attention has focused on the individual with lifelong early-onset schizophrenia who is now in late middle age or old age. Further research is needed to determine the most effective and appropriate pharmacological and psycho-social interventions for the older person with schizophrenia.

10

Other Disorders and Difficulties

Although cognitive impairment and depression are the two mental disorders that have received the most scholarly attention, other disorders are actually more prevalent or can be equally disruptive of daily functioning. This chapter will describe how anxiety, substance abuse, personality disorders, and marital difficulties can be quite troubling to older adults and their families. For each, the epidemiology of the disorder or difficulty will be presented, followed by a description of the problem as experienced by older adults, theories that explain the disorder or problem, and approaches to assessment and treatment.

Anxiety

George still remembers the horror of World War II on a daily basis, although he never talks about it. One by one his buddies "went down" when their ship was sunk. How he survived he'll never quite know, but he prays daily for help living with the memories and the guilt.

Every day Genevieve struggles to make herself do the daily routine. She is so shaky all of the time; if she could just feel safe. The neighborhood is deteriorating, and her fear of what the kids will do to her is growing. She imagines all kinds of torture they could inflict if they decided to, and no one would know. The worst part is the terror she feels when her heart speeds up. She is just sure that this is the final curtain call. If her heart acts up when she is out and about, she gets particularly scared. So recently she has prevailed upon her son and daughter-in-law to bring her groceries and supplies into the house. She rarely leaves now.

Prevalence rates for anxiety disorders have been the source of some controversy, with studies reporting rates as varied as 6 to 33 percent (Blazer, George, & Hughes, 1991; Himmelfarb & Murrell, 1984; Myers et al., 1984). Surprisingly, in many studies the prevalence of the anxiety disorders is much higher than that of other disorders believed to be far more common (e.g., depression). Phobias are the most common, with generalized anxiety disorder next most common, followed by panic, obsessive compulsive disorders, and post-traumatic stress disorder (Sheikh, 1992). As is the case with depression, older adults who do not reach criteria for diagnosis with a clinical disorder continue to report disturbingly high rates of symptoms. Anxiety disorders are somewhat less prevalent in older than in younger adults (Blazer, George, & Hughes, 1991), although researchers state their concerns that older adults may be underreporting their symptoms.

The classification of anxiety disorders within the DSMIV includes several diverse disorders (American Psychiatric Association, 1994). Phobias are characterized by persistent fears of a particular object or situation. Panic disorder is characterized by recurrent episodes of severe anxiety, evidenced by several somatic and cognitive symptoms (e.g., shortness of breath, increased heart rate, sweating, tingling in hands and feet, fear of dying, fear of losing control, or fear of going crazy). The episodes often lack any warning signals, although they may occur in predictable situations (e.g., in an elevator, at a son's house, in a grocery-store line). A common characteristic of the setting in which panic attacks tend to occur is that escape is difficult. As a strategy for coping with the fear of panic, some individuals restrict their activities to safe areas, thus developing agoraphobia over time. Post-traumatic stress disorder can occur following a traumatic event, and is diagnosed when the individual re-experiences the traumatic event in intrusive ways, avoiding certain stimuli related to the event, and encounters a numbing of feeling in response to specific stimuli and increased arousal generally. Obsessive-compulsive disorder is characterized by recurring obsessive thoughts and/or compulsive behaviors performed in response to obsessive thoughts. Common obsessive thought patterns focus on fears of hurting someone, or being contaminated by germs or dirt. Frequent compulsions include hand washing and repetitive checking. Generalized anxiety disorder is the category encompassing a truly generalized experience of anxiety that is excessive or unrealistic, and has persisted over at least a six-month period. All of these anxiety disorders share the requirement that the symptoms are producing clinically significant dis-tress or impairment in social, occupational, or other important aspects of functioning.

In older adults, anxiety syndromes are particularly challenging to differentially diagnose because of the overlapping presentations of anxiety, depression, and physical illness. Symptoms that are quite similar to those of anxiety can be produced by cardiac disease and other illnesses, as well as many common medications (including over-the-counter (OTC) medications). Anxiety can also be a contributing factor to a variety of medical illnesses (e.g., gastrointestinal disorders). Although anxiety and depression can co-exist within an individual, there is also considerable controversy over whether depression and anxiety may actually reflect a single disorder because of the degree of overlap in symptom presentation (Sheikh, 1992). For example, individuals experiencing post-traumatic stress disorder (PTSD), similar to George who is described above, may also experience depression in response to their hopelessness that the PTSD symptoms will ever resolve.

Other mental disorders also show overlap with anxiety symptoms and disorders. For example, dementia (and, in some cases, milder forms of cognitive impairment) produces high rates of anxiety symptoms, particularly restlessness, agitation, and fears (Swearer et al., 1988). Anxiety symptoms in demented persons warrant particular concern since the poor problem-solving skills available to the patients can result in resistant and even assaultive behavior (Fisher & Noll, 1996).

The primary models for conceptualizing anxiety in older adults that have produced distinct approaches to assessment and treatment are biological and cognitive-behavioral. Biological models do not provide a definitive explanation of the causal mechanisms for anxiety, although it has been hypothesized that several neurotransmitters are involved. Certainly, pharmacological agents are the most common way to treat anxiety, perhaps because general physicians are the primary source of treatment (Sunderland, Lawlor, Martinez, & Molchan, 1991). Cognitive-behavioral models focus on thought processes as the mechanisms by which difficult situations produce arousal and subsequently anxiety symptoms (Beck, Emery, & Greenberg, 1985; Beck, Sokal et al., 1992). Specifically, anxiety symptoms are viewed as a natural consequence of irrational thoughts (e.g., My children must approve of me at all times).

Assessment of anxiety can be accomplished through clinical interviews as well as self-report measures. Clinical interviews such as the Structured Clinical Interview for DSMIV Axis I Disorders, Version 2 (SCID-I/P; First et al., 1995) generate specific diagnoses, although in practice most clinicians use a less formal interview format. Self-rating scales such as the State-Trait Anxiety Inventory (Spielberger et al., 1970) or the Beck Anxiety Inventory (Beck, Epstein, Brown, & Steer, 1988) may also be used to gather symptom severity information quickly. Unfortunately, appropriate norms are not available for older adults on most anxiety measures. If the clinical picture of anxiety is quite different in older than in younger adults, which may indeed turn out to be the case, then the development of measures that can accurately identify anxiety diagnoses and measure severity must become a priority.

Much of the current knowledge base is drawn from clinical reports because interventions for anxiety have been poorly studied in controlled research (Niederehe & Schneider, 1998). The pharmacological approach to treatment has been the most frequently used intervention for anxiety. Older adults tend to seek assistance from physicians, who are more likely to prescribe medications than refer for psychotherapeutic intervention. The benzodiazepines are the most commonly prescribed medications, having been prescribed for as many as 50 percent of older adults experiencing anxiety (Markovitz, 1993; Salzman, 1991). Several factors suggest that this class of drugs should be used with caution in older adults, including substantial risk of adverse side effects, difficulties with dosing appropriately for aging bodies that metabolize medications idiosyncratically, and the lack of solid outcome research (Markovitz, 1993). Other medications are also used (e.g., buspirone, beta-blockers, antidepressants), again with little data other than clinical reports to provide evidence of their effectiveness.

A very limited database is also available for psychotherapeutic interventions (Niederehe & Schneider, 1998). Cognitive-behavioral interventions use some form of relaxation training, either for self-management of anxiety symptoms or in combination with graded exposure to images or real situations that generate anxiety (Acierno et al., 1996). For example, interventions designed to treat George's PTSD would include education about PTSD and deliberate exposure to the frightening images of the trauma under safe conditions. Cognitive interventions for anxiety focus on teaching patients how to recognize the dysfunctional cognitions that occur in response to normal physiological processes (e.g., rapid heart rate). The thoughts that generate the distressing physiological and cognitive symptoms are identified and examined more closely for their rational basis. Patients are taught to substitute rational for irrational thoughts. Psychodynamic psychotherapy facilitates insight into the internal conflicts that generate anxiety, especially fear of loss, helplessness, and death in the case of older adults (Verwoerdt, 1981). This form of therapy may also be essentially supportive, with the expectation that the transference relationship will be reassuring. To date, no controlled outcome studies validate the effectiveness of psychodynamic psychotherapy.

A clinical case example that demonstrates the integration of several models of psychotherapy for anxiety is presented by Knight (1992). He describes beginning work with one particular client using relaxation training and assessment of problematic thought patterns, and proceeding to include family systems, psychodynamic, grief, and even a gestalt technique. His integrative approach is probably typical of current psychotherapy practice with older adults.

In summary, anxiety disorders are among the most prevalent of the mental disorders in the older adult population. Very little theoretical work has been done to examine unique causes or consequences of anxiety in later life. Similarly, assessment and treatment of older adults has received little attention by researchers, although clinicians report applying traditional treatment modalities to older clients with success.

Substance Abuse

Lincoln and Lois rarely fought until after his retirement, although their marriage has always been filled with tension. She rarely misses a chance now to let him know just how unhappy she really is with his drinking. He tells her to shut up, that there is no problem, and that she should quit trying to take away one of the peaceful pleasures of his retirement. Lincoln doesn't miss the pressure of work, but he misses the peaceful hours of driving that were a daily occurrence in his job as a traveling salesman. Lois used to think she couldn't wait until Lincoln retired, but now is frustrated every afternoon when she hears the whiskey decanter rattle about 3 o'clock. She knows that by dinner he'll be pretty out of it, and he'll fall asleep by 7 p.m. What kind of retirement is this?

Substance abuse in older adults is focused on a different set of substances than those abused by younger adults, with the exception of alcohol (Atkinson et al., 1992). Compared with younger adults, older adults are far less likely to abuse illegal drugs, and far more likely to misuse or abuse prescription medications and OTC medications. The consequences of this "legal" drug abuse can be as serious as illegal drug use, but has generated far less attention from substance abuse intervention programs.

The substance abuse problem among older adults is a serious one. Alcohol and substance abuse rank third among leading mental disorders in older Americans, accounting for 10 to 12 percent of those who receive services from mental health professionals (Segal, Van Hasselt et al., 1996). Community prevalence rates of alcohol abuse, ranging from 2 to 10 percent, are generally considered to be underestimates because of the tendency of all substance abusers to deny usage (Segal, Van Hasselt et al., 1996). Alcohol abuse prevalence rates in clinical populations, both inpatient and outpatient, are likely to be considerably higher (Liberto et al., 1996).

Abuse of substances intended as medications is another area of serious concern. Older adults are the recipients of 30 percent of all prescribed medications and the consumers of 40 percent of all OTC medications, a percentage far greater than their proportion of the population (12 percent) (HHS Inspector General, 1989). Although it is not necessarily reflective of abuse or misuse patterns, clinicians often describe older patients who use multiple doctors and pharmacies in order to obtain more medication. At minimum, these high rates of usage render older adults vulnerable to a variety of substance-induced symptoms and disorders. In contrast, illicit drug use is very rare, although future usage patterns in older adults may be quite visible as the current cohort of young adults ages.

Two patterns of onset are evident in older adult alcohol abusers: early-onset (young or mid-life adult) lifelong problem drinking, and late-onset alcohol abuse. About one-third to a half of older adult alcohol abusers began drinking problematically late in life. Among the early-onset problem drinkers, aging appears not to lead to resolution of the problem. Indeed, rates of alcohol abuse appear to be relatively stable over the life-span, although current cohorts of older adults have been less intensive users of alcohol than current young adults. In other words, there is a cohort effect, with later born cohorts using significantly more alcohol than earlier born cohorts, but all evidence points to stability over time for each cohort.

Regardless of the time of onset, substance abuse by older adults usually developed as a mechanism for coping. Alcohol use is associated with efforts to enhance socialization, to manage social anxiety, or to avoid problems (Dupree & Schonfeld, 1996). The case of Lincoln and Lois presented above illustrates this pattern. Lincoln increased his rate of drinking following retirement because he lacked sufficiently compelling alternative activities to fill his time and in order to avoid contact with Lois in the evenings. Prescribed and OTC medications are used primarily to cope with pain, although insomnia, family problems, and other mental disorders are also given as reasons for drug usage (Finlayson, 1984).

A key factor in abuse patterns consists of the different physiological responses of aging bodies to chemical substances. As a result of changes in the efficiency with which substances are processed in the body, older adults are more susceptible to adverse drug reactions, drug interactions, and drug toxicity as compared to younger adults. Mental health professionals must be aware of the vulnerability of aging bodies to even the most innocent appearing substances (e.g., aspirin) in altering psychological functioning (for a review of what professionals should know, see Smyer & Downs, 1995).

Assessment of substance abuse is a challenge because clinicians and abusers both tend to deny or fail to recognize the quantity of substance used. Clinicians often fail to inquire about substance use. When a clinician intends to assess substance use and abuse, a clinical interview is the most likely method of assessment. As rapport is established, clients have a greater likelihood of sharing accurate information. Although likely to reflect an underestimate of usage, self-reports of alcohol consumption can be generated from the geriatric version of the Michigan Alcohol Screening Test (G-MAST; Blow et al., 1992) or the CAGE (Mayfield et al., 1974). A richer picture can be generated with a structured behavioral assessment tool, the Gerontology Alcohol Project Drinking Profile (GAP-DP; Dupree et al., 1984).

Another challenge to assessment is the poor match between older adult substance abuse patterns and the DSMIV criteria (American Psychiatric Association, 1994). Mental health professionals who rely on traditional criteria are unlikely to recognize the patterns of substance abuse most problematic among older adults, whose substances are far more likely to be OTC or prescribed medications (Segal, Van Hasselt et al., 1996).

Substance abuse treatments focus on three goals: stabilization and reduction of substance consumption, treatment of co-existing problems, and arrangement of appropriate social interventions (Atkinson et al., 1992). With older adults, education rather than confrontation is usually employed to reduce denial of the abuse pattern. For example, education about the changes in drug metabolism, the interaction of medications, and the importance of obedience to physician instructions can lead to increased compliance. Recent research demonstrates the role of cognitive factors in determining medication compliance (Park et al., 1994). Evidence from laboratory experimentation suggests that altering the presentation of drug usage information can increase understanding and compliance with medication instructions, thus reducing the opportunity for substance misuse.

Education of physicians is an important component of a treatment plan for prescription and OTC abuse. Physicians may not recognize the potential for medication interactions to produce psychological symptoms. They may also be unaware of all of the prescribed medications a patient is using if the patient is obtaining prescriptions from more than one physician. Thus, engaging physician cooperation is critical when attempting to intervene with prescription or OTC misuse.

Treatment of co-existing problems (e.g., pain or social isolation) can reduce the motivation for using substances inappropriately. This strategy is similar to that used with younger adult substance abusers, although the specific problems that need to be addressed may vary with age. In the case of Lincoln, marital therapy and, possibly, treatment of depression would be critical elements of the treatment plan. As long as home life is stressful, and Lincoln lacks a sense of purpose or skill for creating separateness from Lois, he is likely to try to avoid conflict and unpleasant feelings in a familiar way – alcohol.

Finally, training in self-management techniques will generate more effective coping skills, again reducing the urge to use a chemical substance to manage problem situations. For example, Dupree & Schonfeld (1996) present a case of excessive pain medication usage by an older woman. The treatment followed the social learning model, in which the antecedents (situations, thoughts, feelings, and cues) that provoked the substance use behavior, and the short-term and long-term consequences of substance abuse, were first identified. Behavior therapy techniques such as assertion training, self-monitoring, behavior contracting, and reinforcement were used to modify the patient's use of medication.

Treatment outcome studies suggest that older patients respond as well to alcohol interventions as do younger patients (Janik & Dunham, 1983). Interventions that engage older adults in a group treatment context with other older adults appear superior to mixed-age treatment programs (Kashner et al., 1992; Kofoed et al., 1987).

Personality Disorders

Knowledge about personality disorders in older adults, based on research literature, is particularly sparse. Changing definitions of personality disorders across the four editions of the DSM and weak research methodology yield a very limited database from which to draw conclusions. Personality disorder (PD) is defined by the authors of the DSMIV (American Psychiatric Association, 1994) as "an enduring pattern of inner experience and behavior that deviates markedly from the expectations of the individual's culture, is pervasive and inflexible, has an onset in adolescence or early adulthood, is stable over time, and leads to distress or impairment" (p. 629).

The field of personality psychology has struggled with the extent to which personality should be conceptualized as a set of enduring traits versus situationally influenced behaviors, especially patterns of coping with stress (Ruth & Coleman, 1996). Apparently, personality is both stable and adaptable across the life-span. Obviously, models of personality serve as a backdrop for models of disorders. Thus stability in personality traits could be construed as a backdrop for personality disorders, which are also considered stable, with shifting amounts of distress and dysfunction depending on contextual variables, especially stressors.

The epidemiology of personality disorders among the older population is unclear. Changing definitions and conceptualizations of personality disorders, poorly normed assessment devices, and the limited number of research investigations all make prevalence estimates confusing and of limited value. Most studies have been conducted on inpatient units, examining comorbidity of PD with other clinical syndromes. One exception is the community-based Epidemiological Catchment Area (ECA) study, in which Robins et al. (1984) found a prevalence rate of 0.8 percent for PD in those older than 65 years, although this estimate is based on an assessment strategy that is relatively insensitive to most of the personality disorders. PDs are believed to be much more common than is generally recognized by outpatient mental health professionals. For example, among older outpatients with a depression diagnosis, one-third were diagnosed with PDs (Thompson, Gallagher, & Czirr, 1988), most commonly avoidant and dependent PDs. Much higher rates of PD prevalence (e.g., 56 percent) are found in studies of older psychiatric inpatients (e.g., Molinari et al., 1994). A combined inpatient and outpatient sample of depressed older adults yielded a prevalence rate of 63 percent (Molinari & Marmion, 1995).

The question of how personality disorders are affected by aging has been debated but has lacked a research base on which to anchor a definitive answer. Some evidence points to a decline in expression in mid-life of the symptoms associated with the cluster of disorders labeled "dramatic" (including borderline, histrionic, and narcissistic) with an increase in symptoms again in later life (Reich et al., 1988). Others argue that the decline in dramatic PDs relates to a decrease in energy needed to maintain the high energy symptoms.

The stresses of old age are believed to produce personality regressions that mimic personality disorders and to exacerbate the expression of symptoms (Rosowsky & Gurian, 1992; Sadavoy & Fogel, 1992). Loss of control of the environment, characteristic of the increasing dependency that comes with loss of mobility and declining resources, can provoke anxiety that generates PD symptoms. However, the symptom criteria used by the DSM system include life circumstances that may be irrelevant to older adults. For example, difficulties in the work environment and with residential family life may be less relevant because of their lower rate of participation in the workforce and their tendency not to co-reside with family members. Thus the behavioral expressions of personality disorders in older adults may not match the template typically used to identify PDs in younger adults.

Assessment of PDs is challenging. Screening instruments are not readily available to help identify quickly the personality disorders. Structured clinical interviews rely heavily on the DSM classification system, and are thus vulnerable to underdiagnosis for reasons just discussed. However, clinicians using informal interviews identify many fewer PDs than are captured by the structured interviews. Structured self-report instruments (e.g., the Minnesota Multiphasic Personality Inventory (MMPI) or the Millon Clinical Multiaxial Inventory (MCMI)) must be interpreted cautiously (Segal, Hersen et al., in press). Older adult samples, including both non-psychiatric and psychiatric populations, show substantial elevations on several scales of the MMPI, making it difficult to interpret the scores (Taylor et al., 1989). Obviously, specific norms for older adults must be used to determine clinical cutoff points. Unfortunately, older adults' norms are not available for the MMPI-II. Very little research has been conducted on reliability or validity of the various versions of the MCMI for older adults.

Persons with PD seek treatment primarily when their familiar methods of meeting their own needs can no longer be enacted or are distressing someone else, who then demands that treatment occur. Thus older adults whose dependency needs have increased will often distress the caregivers who have forced contact with them, and against whom the acting-out behavior is targeted (Rosowsky & Gurian, 1992).

Working within a psychodynamic model, Sadavoy (1987; Sadavoy & Fogel, 1992) identified four goals of treatment: 1) containing and limiting pathological behavior; 2) establishing a working alliance between patient, staff, and family; 3) developing a cohesive team approach to the patient; and 4) reducing the patient's reliance on primitive pathological behavior by decreasing inner tension levels, altering interpersonal stresses, and, infrequently, changing or modifying defense mechanisms. As is evident, the goal of treatment is directed more at management of the disorder than at full remission.

Marital Conflicts

Conflict and difficulties within the intimate domain of marital and family relationships can be very distressing to older adults. The distress may provoke the emergence of psychiatric symptoms (e.g., anxiety or depression) or declines in daily functioning. Just as marriage and family relationships can provide support for optimal mental well-being, so they can undermine mental health. In this section, the events and tasks that challenge marital and family functioning in the latest stages of life will be described, and strategies for assessing difficulties and designing effective interventions will be presented.

Despite the higher probability of widowhood with advancing age, 75 percent of non-institutionalized men over age 65 are married, compared with only 41 percent of non-institutionalized women in the same age group (Taeuber, 1993). Although not as prevalent among this group as among young adults, marriage is one of the intimate relationships that is of vital importance to older adults (Carstensen, 1991).

Changes in physical health, retirement, and disruptions in the lives of adult children can all challenge the familiar patterns of marital functioning (Qualls, 1995b). These life events spawn changes in the contexts, meaning, and practices of marriage that are experienced by the couple as developmental challenges or tasks (Cole, 1986). For example, Lincoln's retirement eliminated his structure for creating separateness: business trips. Unless he renegotiates another method of securing separateness, he and Lois will both continue to feel intruded upon and annoyed. In their case, alcohol use is a method they employ to maintain separateness without fighting, but it is a self-destructive method. Table 10.1 shows the effects of these three categories

Table 10.1 Impact of events of later life on marital processes

Events	Marital processes					
	Time structure	Roles	Communication	Power balance	Nurturance	Relationships with children
Retirement	*End of work-structured separateness *Increase in togetherness at home	*Dedifferentiation (decreased uniqueness, increased overlap) *Potential to decrease gender typing	*Need strategies to negotiate separateness and role transition *More shared experience decreases need for oral reporting	*Role transition provokes shift in power balance *Power from previous domain may be altered *Potential of egalitarianism increased in traditional couples	*Increased opportunity for small daily expressions	*Opportunity for increased contact and more directly involved roles *Visits with children often occur on distance turf
Onset of impairment from chronic illness	*Usually increased portion of time devoted to basic care *Health	*Ill spouse experiences role loss *Well spouse experiences role gain	*Anger expressions are more threatening or complicated *Impairment may constrain	*Source of power for ill spouse decreases *Well spouse's increase in	*Ill spouse's opportunity to nurture may be constrained *Well spouse's care-giving	*Children may be more "inside" the marriage than previously (boundary

constrains activity options	ill spouse's capacity to communicate (e.g., stroke, cognitive impairment, decreased initiation)	responsibility brings increased power	role creates imbalance in time spent nurturing	issues salient) *Children's role in supporting primary caregiver or ill parent may threaten spouse
Disruptions in children's lives	*Increased time spent experiencing and expressing concern as co-parents *Potential for increase in responsibility and decrease in leisure time	*Ambiguity in parenting roles increases *May provoke increase in financial, child-care, or other support responsibilities	*Need for problem-solving communications may increase *Negotiating support within appropriate boundaries challenges communication patterns	*Boundary around marital dyad may be stretched *Can triangulate the marriage	*Nurturance often needs to be redirected outside marriage again (increased strain on marital satisfaction)	*Complex roles *Opportunity for reciprocity salient as aging *Parents again are giving

Source: Qualls, 1995b.

of events on key areas of marital functioning: time structure, roles, communication, power balance, nurturance, and relationships with children. Obviously, the last phase of life brings challenges to even long-term relationships.

An important distinction should be made between distressed marriages that have a long history of conflict and those for whom distress is a recent phenomenon. Long-term conflicted marriages are those that settled into entrenched but stable patterns of conflict. The patterns that maintained the long-term conflict are difficult to treat successfully. However, later life events can unsettle the stability enough to create crises which can be addressed. Long-term satisfied marriages are likely to have been increasingly satisfactory as the years progressed (Anderson, Russell, & Schumm, 1983). Conflicts seen in the later years are a direct indicator of difficulty adapting to the developmental tasks of later life. Research studies focusing on changes in marital satisfaction across the life-span suggest that, with increasing age, married couples report higher levels of marital satisfaction (Levenson et al., 1994). Recent conflict within a long-term satisfied marriage may occur if the couple lack understanding of how to adapt to changes in their life circumstances or change in their individual functioning (e.g., due to disability).

Regardless of marital satisfaction history, a key question for someone looking to help a conflicted couple is why they have currently sought therapy (Herr & Weakland, 1979). Indeed, some event or change in the structure or functioning of their marriage must have occurred in order to trigger help-seeking efforts. The goal of intervention may be merely to restore equilibrium and a tolerable level of distance and/or conflict. In higher functioning couples interventions may reap benefits beyond just immediate coping, by promoting deeper intimacy within the marriage (Wolinsky, 1990).

A special problem for aging couples can occur within the sexual aspects of their relationship. Physiological aging alters the sexual response cycle, primarily by slowing the responses. In addition, illnesses that increase in prevalence with age (e.g., cardiovascular disease, diabetes, and arthritis) can also adversely affect sexual functioning. Unfortunately, many older couples believe that loss of sexual functioning is normal and expectable with age, and fail to seek assistance because of their negative expectations.

Data from an andrology clinic within the Palo Alto VA Medical Center show that a combination of medical and psycho-social factors contributed to sexual dysfunction in over 80 percent of a sample of 324 older male veterans seeking assistance with sexual functioning (Zeiss et al., 1992). Assessment, therefore, encompassed medical and pharmacological evaluation, a thorough appraisal of beliefs and expectations about sexuality and aging, and relationship factors. Advocating an approach of implementing the least intrusive intervention necessary, the staff of the andrology clinic organize their interventions according to the PLISSIT model (Annon, 1975). This anacronym spells out the first letters of the four stages in the model: Permission, Limited Information, Specific Suggestion, and Intensive Therapy. Almost half of the patients are offered the first three levels of intervention, and the vast majority accept this. Intensive therapy usually requires the partner's involvement, and is more frequently refused. For patients who accepted the full range of treatment available and recommended, the success rate was very high (95 percent). Obviously, effective treatment for geriatric sexual dysfunctions is available. However, these researchers identified two challenges to providing the range and scope of services that would be useful to older adults. First, the public and professionals must come to believe that aging sexuality is valued and meaningful, so the assessment and intervention tools that are available will be used. Second, the higher rates of success when partners are involved suggest that strategies for increasing the likelihood of partner involvement need to be developed. Intervention programs such as the one described here lay the foundation for changing beliefs about what is possible, as well as investigating ways to improve treatment effectiveness.

Family Problems

Viola has had serious health problems since mid-life. Currently, heart and lung disease severely limit her physical capacities. She becomes short of breath after only a few steps, despite the help of oxygen to which she is tethered 24 hours a day. As long as Dad was alive, the children were buffered fairly well from the constancy of her needs. Since his death the extent of her dependency has become clearer. Viola can do very little basic household maintenance for herself. Fixing lunch exhausts her, and vacuuming is beyond her capability. On her limited income she cannot hire household assistance. She is terrified of falling and of losing capacity to breathe. She has demanded that the children install emergency bells in every room, just in case she gets sick or someone tries to break in. The children are spread across the country, but each weekend one of them visits. Before his death, the children promised their father that they would not place Viola in a nursing home. But the demands of caring are wearing them all out.

Problems in later life families often focus on dependency needs of aging parents or their adult children. Families are trying to figure out how to assist adult members who would prefer to be autonomous and whose disabilities usually limit some but not all autonomous functioning. Often the amount of assistance required is somewhat ambiguous, generating multiple interpretations of what should be done. For many families the current generation of older adults is living longer, with more chronic illnesses than in any previous generation. Thus there is no model available in their own family for how to adapt to the current aging-related transitions within the family.

Researchers in the past two decades have documented the intensive involvement of older adults with their family members (Shanas, 1979). The myth that families in Western civilizations now abandon their elderly has been effectively debunked by the repeated documentation of high rates of contact between adult children and aging parents and high rates of assistance (Bengtson et al., 1996). Furthermore, patterns of assistance in families are multi-directional: aging parents and their adult children are engaged in reciprocal giving and receiving of both instrumental (practical assistance with tasks or finances) and emotional support. Thus the image of aging parents abandoned by their adult children at the time when they are dependent on them is a false image on several counts.

Despite the fact that most older adults are independent, giving as much as they receive, the transition that is probably most disruptive to families in this phase of life relates to increasing dependency. As one person's needs for assistance become greater, other family members take on more of the care-giving function. Rarely does one become a caregiver or care receiver over-night. As depicted in figure 10.1, the transition is a process that can be conceptualized as a career that "requires an orderly restructuring of respon-sibilities and activities that take place across time" (Aneshensel et al., 1995). Viola, who was described at the beginning of this section, is typical of the dilemmas and commitments faced by families of ill older adults.

The restructuring inherent to care-giving alters the family system, often in dramatic ways. When one or more members take on an increased role of monitoring the well-being of another, the caregivers are then limited in time and resources available for other relationships (e.g., siblings or children). Viola's children must balance the needs of their mother with other commit-ments in their lives (e.g., jobs, children, friends, and community responsibili-ties). The meaning of the relationship between caregiver and care receiver also changes, as the balance of mutuality is altered. Whereas Viola may have been limited in the domains of relationship she could experience with her children in the past, she is even further limited now. The role of care receiver is most salient for her now, likely overshadowing other dimensions of their relationship. The more anxious and concerned the children become about their decisions regarding her care, the more care-giving will dominate the relationship.

Caregivers of frail older persons report high rates of stress from their role strain and role loss that result in negative consequences for their mental and

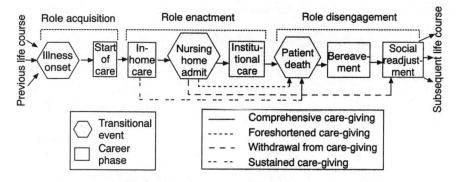

Figure 10.1 Progression of care-giving careers
Source: Aneshensel et al., 1995.

physical health (Schulz et al., 1995; Wright et al., 1993). The deleterious effects of care giving vary over time as the demands of the care-giving career impact daily functioning (Aneshensel et al., 1995). As shown in figure 10.2, the impact of care-giving responsibilities is mediated by cognitive appraisals of the situation and resource availability as well as by objective demands of the care recipients' needs (Gatz, Bengtson, & Blum, 1990).

Assessment of caregiver distress often includes measures of psychiatric symptoms, physical health difficulties, and patient-related burden (Zarit, Orr, & Zarit, 1985). In addition, assessment should examine characteristics of the relationship between caregiver and care receiver and some exploration of the presence of support or conflict within the larger extended family network. Assessment of family functioning that extends beyond the care-giving role may focus on the structure and functioning of the family and on family history as it relates to current patterns of stressful interaction (see chapter 6).

Interventions for care-giving families typically consist of education, support, specific suggestions for managing care, and, on rare occasions, intensive family therapy (Zarit, Orr, & Zarit, 1985). Although the evidence for the effectiveness of caregiver support groups in reducing distress is equivocal at best, the family participants report benefiting from such groups (see review by Zarit & Teri, 1991). The benefits are not evident on measures of mental health and well-being, however. One intervention that included support group participation as well as individual and family counseling reduced the deterioration in the caregiver's mental and physical functioning that is typically seen over time, and also decreased the number of nursing-home admissions (Mittelman, Ferris, Steinberg et al., 1993). Building on their model of the care-giving career, Aneshensel et al. (1995) recommend matching inter-

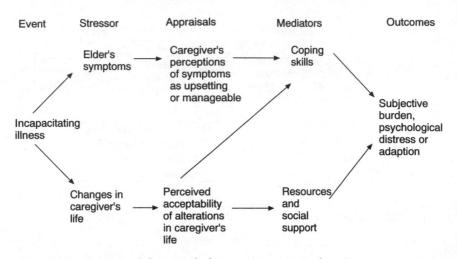

Figure 10.2 Conceptual framework for caregiver stress and coping
Source: Gatz, Bengtson, & Blum, 1990.

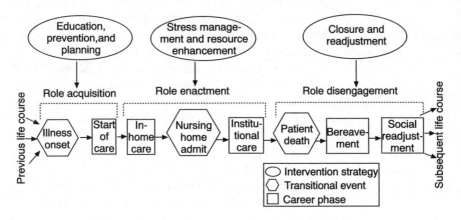

Figure 10.3 Intervention strategies across the care–giving career
Source: Aneshensel et al., 1995.

vention strategies with the needs of the particular stage in the care–giving
career. For example, during the *role induction* stage, caregivers need information and assistance identifying the varied parts of their role and building skill
in the role. Later, during the *role enactment* stage, problem-solving and
assistance-garnering support for the long haul are likely to be more appropriate (see figure 10.3).

Conclusion

Although less thoroughly studied, the disorders and difficulties described in this chapter obviously also challenge some later life families. It may be that anxiety, substance abuse, personality disorders, and marital and family problems are each more prevalent than other difficulties more commonly associated with aging (e.g., depression). Much more research is needed to determine the prevalence and nature of these difficulties with older adults. As with disorders discussed in other chapters, the comorbidity of mental disorders with physical illness raises questions about whether the disorder presents itself in similar ways and can be determined reliably using traditional assessment devices. Research on the reliability and validity of assessment tools is needed, with the possibility existing that new tools will be needed to identify problems accurately in older populations. In the areas of marital and family functioning, the medical model is probably not the most useful way to conceptualize problems or strategies for addressing those problems. The intersection of individual development and disorders with family structures and functioning provokes changes that require significant adaptation. Conceptualizations of normal family development in later life, along with models of adaptation that define positive results as well as negative outcomes, are needed to begin to map the dimensions of marital and family difficulties. For all of the disorders and difficulties described in this chapter, systematic research on interventions is weak or non-existent. Clinical reports of interventions that apply traditional models of psychotherapy or psycho-educational interventions to these problems show promise, but lack validating data.

Part IV

Contexts of Practice

Introduction

Geriatric practice occurs in a complex context of governmental regulation, insurance industry incentives and barriers, and the ethical and practice expectations of various mental health professions. The chapters in this section are designed to alert you to the impact of these contexts on the process of responding to mental illness in later life.

Willie Sutton, the famous bank robber, was asked why he robbed banks. He replied: "That's where the money is." In a similar way, we focus in Chapter 11 on the major receiving site for mentally ill elderly in the United States: nursing homes. That's where the mentally ill elderly are. These settings were originally designed to provide physical health care, primarily for older adults. Over the last thirty years, however, they have replaced state mental hospitals as a primary source of mental health care for older adults.

Thus, if you're concerned about working with mentally ill elderly, a primary place to ply your trade is in nursing homes. However, to be effective in working in nursing homes requires that you understand something about the residents you will encounter there, the other staff members who have direct contact with and responsibility for the residents, and the incentives and disincentives for mental health services in the setting. We discuss each of these elements in Chapter 11.

Chapter 12 takes a broader focus on the wider contexts of geriatric practice. Here we try to share information about the practical aspects of working with older adults – those aspects of professional life that are often implicit as you begin to work in the field. For example, each geriatric mental health practitioner is not a totally free agent. He or she must pursue a practice career within several intersecting contexts: the profession's self-definition of expertise and training needed for working with older adults; how to cooperate with other professions to assure the best possible outcome for your older client or patient; societal definitions of what is worth paying for through social insurance plans such as Medicare and Medicaid; and the impact of larger social policy developments on the types of issues that become salient for geriatric mental health care.

Bronfenbrenner (1979) argued that individual development is affected by several interacting systems: the microsystem (the most immediate physical and social environment); the mesosystem (the proximal institutional environment, such as a nursing home or hospice setting), and the exosystem (the larger social policy and social movement contexts). In many ways, geriatric practice is also affected by these three levels. The two chapters in this section outline the impact of these levels on the development and provision of geriatric mental health services.

11

Institutional Contexts for Mental Health Services

Introduction

You have just received a referral from the physician at a nursing home where you consult: "Please have psychologist see Mr Johnson for sexual acting out." Your initial discussion with the day-shift nursing supervisor provides the following details.

Ralph Johnson is a 77-year-old retired mailman who has resided in the intermediate care section of the nursing home for 15 months. He was admitted from home because his wife was unable to care for him after he suffered a series of two cardiovascular accidents over an 11-month period. Mrs Johnson visits one to two times per week, always with her daughter, Elaine, because she does not drive.

Mr Johnson's strokes have left him with residual right-sided weakness and somewhat slurred speech. The supervisor states that he is confused at times. Other medical problems include high blood pressure, for which he takes capaten 50mg., and diabetes, which had been well controlled by diet until recently, when he began eating less and losing weight. He has now been put on insulin. He also suffers from some arthritis and carries a diagnosis of "chronic anxiety," for which he takes xanax.

Mr Johnson is able to move around with a walker, but he has been walking less and less over the past several months. The supervisor remembers that he was initially fairly active in the home's recreational activities program, and assumes that he still attends programs regularly. He sleeps well, and enjoys watching television in his room and chatting with his one cognitively-intact roommate.

When asked about the physician's referral, the supervisor provided very little direct information: "I really have no idea about that. We've never had any trouble with him. The nurses on second shift got the doctor to write that order."
(Spayd, 1993)

This referral reflects the complexity of mental health consultation and service provision in nursing homes: issues of comorbidity, continuity of staff effort across shifts, interdisciplinary collaboration, and effective assessment, communication, and treatment approaches. These issues will be the focus of this chapter.

We will begin with a simple question: Is there a nursing home in your future? We hope to convince you that these settings may be personally and professionally salient for you. Next, we will briefly consider the changing role of nursing homes in our society – settings that have become major treatment sites for mentally ill elderly (Smyer, 1989). We will then consider the current array of nursing-home residents, staff, and mental health services: Who lives and works in nursing homes and how is this relevant for mental health service providers (Smyer, Cohn, & Brannon, 1988)? The effects of public policy decisions on nursing homes and mental health service provision will also be outlined (e.g., Smyer, 1989). Finally, the specific assessment and treatment strategies that are useful in nursing homes will be discussed (Spayd & Smyer, 1996).

Is There a Nursing Home in your Future?

A senior colleague recently asked, "Why even bother with nursing homes? After all, only 5 percent of the elderly are in nursing homes at any one point in time." And that's true: in the USA there are only about 1.6 million people in some 17,000 nursing homes in any one point in time (Krauss et al., 1997). But, as in other areas, the cross-sectional view is simplistically deceptive. It hides the lifetime risk for nursing-home use and it overlooks the interlacing of lives that assure that we are interdependent across life. Nursing-home care is not just individual care, but also care for family members (Freedman et al., 1994). So, one reason to be concerned about nursing-home care is the very real personal risk that *you* will be a consumer of nursing-home services at some point.

For example, Kemper & Murtaugh (1991) used data from the National Long-Term Care Survey to simulate the risks of nursing-home care for a cohort, a group of people, all of whom turned 65 in 1990. Kemper and Murtaugh focused on a different question: What is the lifetime risk for using a nursing home? They pointed out that almost a third of the men and just over half of the women who turned 65 in 1990 could be expected to spend some time in a nursing home before death – substantially higher rates of use than the 5 percent cross-sectional view.

Family risks are also substantial, beyond the individual risks. As Kemper and Murtaugh (1991) reported, for couples with both members turning 65 in 1990, about seven out of ten can expect that at least one member will spend some time in a nursing home. Seven out of ten couples will be consumers of nursing-home care.

Of course, families are not limited to spouses. Children are also likely to encounter nursing-home care issues. Again, in a simulated family with four parents turning 65 in 1990 (parents *and in-laws*), nine out of ten children who had four parents who turned 65 in 1990 could expect to have at least one parent enter a nursing home (Kemper & Murtaugh, 1991). Nine out of ten. In short, nursing-home care is very relevant for families, and nursing-home care is a family issue in our aging society. So, when we ask the question "Is there a nursing home in *your* future?" the answer may very well be yes, depending upon your age and generational position in your family.

That's one reason to worry about nursing homes. Another, of course, is that nursing homes are a growth industry. With the aging of our society, we can anticipate more than a 60 percent increase in the nursing-home population over the next 25 years. The oldest old, those aged 85 and above, will form an increasingly larger percentage of the nursing-home population (Wiener et al., 1994).

Nursing homes also cost a lot of money. For example, in 1993 almost $55 billion was spent for nursing-home care (see table 11.1). Of that, $22 billion came from the Medicaid program – not the Medicare program, which is the health insurance program for older adults, but the Medicaid program, which is the social insurance policy and health insurance policy for indigent members of our society. Note also that $28 billion of the nursing-home bill was paid for by older adults and their family members out of pocket. Nursing-home care is the largest out-of-pocket health-care expense for older adults and their families in our society. Finally, table 11.1 depicts their costs are

Table 11.1 Total expenditures for nursing-home and home care, by source of payment, selected periods ($billion at 1993 levels)

Payment source	1993	2008	2018	Percent increase 1993 to 2018
Nursing homes				
Medicaid	22.4	35.4	49.0	119
Medicare	4.3	7.6	10.0	133
Patients' cash income	17.0	28.3	42.6	151
Patients' assets	11.0	17.2	26.6	142

Source: Wiener et al., 1994.

expected to grow substantially in the 25 years from 1993 to 2018, as the
baby-boomers enter later life.

Thus, from personal and civic viewpoints, nursing homes will likely affect
you. However, several other elements make nursing homes important professional settings for clinicians working with the elderly.

The Nursing-Home Community

It is useful to think of nursing homes as communities, with several
interlocking roles and types of influences (Smyer, Cohn, & Brannon, 1988).
As in all communities, nursing homes are affected by outside forces (e.g.,
federal and state policies; local labor markets) and by the characteristics of the
community members and the structure of the community itself. Three aspects
are particularly important for mental health treatment: the residents, the staff,
and the fit between resident needs and staff skills.

The residents

How do you describe almost two million elderly, conveying both their
diversity and their common problems? Biography is as important as biology
when dealing with older adults in very late life, especially when faced with
severe impairment (Cohen, 1993). The following case description, by the
New York Times columnist Russell Baker (1982), illustrates the interweaving
of biography and biology:

> At the age of 80, my mother had her last bad fall, and after that her mind
> wandered free through time. Some days she went to weddings and funerals that
> had taken place half a century earlier. On others she presided over the family
> dinners cooked on Sunday afternoons for children who were now gray with age.
> Through all this, she lay in bed but moved across time, traveling among the
> dead decades with a speed and ease beyond the gift of physical science. "Where's
> Russell?" she asked one day, when I came to visit at the nursing home. "I'm
> Russell," I said. She gazed at this improbably overgrown figure out of an
> inconceivable future and promptly dismissed it. "Russell's only this big," she
> said, holding her hand palm down two feet from the floor. That day, she was
> a young country wife with chickens in the back yard and a view of hazy blue
> Virginia mountains behind the apple orchard, and I was a stranger, old enough
> to be her father. (p. 1)

Baker's compelling description quickly reminds us of the combination of
problems that nursing-home residents often face: combinations of mental *and*

physical disability. For example, Strahan and Burns (1991) summarized information from the 1985 National Nursing Home Survey. They pointed out that *65 percent* of nursing-home residents have at least one mental disorder.

Nursing-home residents have a variety of mental disorders. The most common form is dementia of any type, including Alzheimer's disease, followed by schizophrenia and other psychoses, depressive disorders, and anxiety disorders. Remember that, of those nursing-home residents with mental disorders, 72 percent have a dementia of some kind, including Alzheimer's disease (see figure 11.1).

Another estimate of rates of mental disorders comes from the National Medical Expenditure Survey (NMES) (Lair & Lefkowitz, 1990). This also reported that the majority of residents have a mental disorder, with, again, dementia playing a prominent role. Thus one way to think about nursing-home residents is that they are *mentally ill* older adults, and nursing homes are important potential settings for mental health services – a theme to which we will return later.

Another perspective emerges from the changing role of nursing homes in our society, particularly since the era of deinstitutionalization – an emptying of the state mental hospitals as a public policy priority (Gatz & Smyer, 1992; Shadish et al., 1989; Smyer, 1989). Kiesler and his colleagues have argued

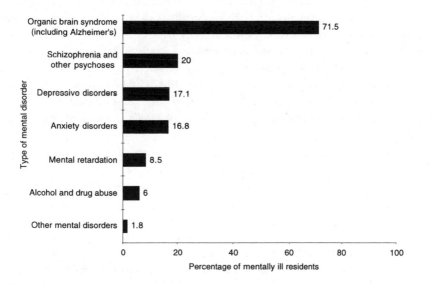

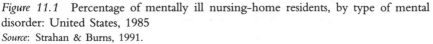

Figure 11.1 Percentage of mentally ill nursing-home residents, by type of mental disorder: United States, 1985
Source: Strahan & Burns, 1991.

Table 11.2   Change in resident populations in institutional settings, 1977–87

Health-care organization	1977	1987	Percentage change, 1977–87
State and county mental hospitals	165,990	103,463	−37.7
Private psychiatric hospitals	12,980	26,587	+104.8
Non-federal general hospitals	22,992	35,170	+53.0
VA medical centers	30,408	20,422	−32.8
Nursing homes	228,100	474,490	+108.0

Source: Shea, 1994.

that the process of deinstitutionalization has been accompanied by expansion in *both* outpatient and inpatient services (Kiesler, 1991; Kiesler & Sibulkin, 1987; Kiesler & Simpkins, 1991). The highest rate of growth has been in the private sector, especially among private psychiatric hospitals and units in general hospitals. Shea (1994) recently summarized the changes in inpatient service provision between 1977 and 1987. His data are consistent with the overall assessment of the growing role of private sector settings and nursing homes (see table 11.2).

In the aftermath of deinstitutionalization, nursing homes play a prominent role in mental health care for older adults. As Russell Baker's mother reminds us, nursing-home residents are both physically and mentally ill. For example, in the 1985 National Nursing Home Survey data a majority of nursing-home residents needed help with self-care activities, such as bathing, dressing, etc. – a common proxy for physical disability (Cohen et al., 1993). A similar pattern was reflected in data from the 1987 NMES survey (Lair and Lefkowitz, 1990). However, nursing homes are not designed for treating *mental* health problems; they are staffed for *physically* ill residents (see figure 11.2).

Most nursing-home residents struggle with issues of comorbidity – combinations of more than one mental or physical challenge. For example, Strahan and Burns (1991) reported from the National Nursing Home Survey that, on the average, dependencies in self-care capacity for nursing-home residents are steeper in later life for those residents who have a mental disorder. Those with a mental disorder show increasing rates of activities of daily living (ADL) self-care limitations, at the increasing ages, while those without the presence of mental disorder show a relatively stable pattern of ADL impairment across the upper ages. (This pattern might reflect the progress of dementia, the most frequent mental disorder in the setting.)

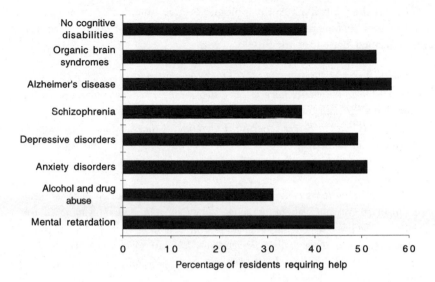

Figure 11.2 Percentage of nursing-home residents 65 years of age and over who had selected cognitive disabilities and required help of another person for five to seven activities of daily living: United States, 1985

Note: Data based on personal interviews of the nursing-home staff most knowledgeable about the residents sampled.

Source: National Center for Health Statistics: data from the National Nursing Home Survey.

The more recent 1996 Medical Expenditure Panel Survey (MEPS) also found that over 80 percent of nursing-home residents needed help with three or more activities of daily living, while nearly half had some form of dementia (Krauss et al., 1997). Thus patterns of a combination of physical and mental illness are very common, not just for Russell Baker's mother, but for nursing-home residents at large.

The staff

Who takes care of these physically and mentally ill residents? Who are the staff? Data from the 1977 National Nursing Home Survey (1985) reflect the general patterns of care. For either full-time or part-time care, nursing assistants or nurses aides are the predominant caregivers, providing 72 percent of the full-time and 57 percent of the part-time workforce. They are, on average, high-school graduates, working for minimum wage. These are the people with the most contact with residents (Brannon & Smyer, 1990, 1994). They are also potentially important therapeutic allies for geriatric mental health professionals working in nursing homes.

What is their job like? Anthropologist Renée Shield, in her observational study *Uneasy Endings*, depicts life in an American nursing home. One nurses' aide described her work for Shield (1988):

> *I give baths. I do TRPs – which is temp, respiration, and pulse. I take blood pressures. I do weights. I have to serve two meals. Foot care, hand care; make sure that their nails are cleaned and trimmed . . .*
>
> *. . . My job can be very stressful, frustrating at times. I find it especially so when we are understaffed. When there are three nurses in the wing, three nursing assistants, it's really beautiful. Because you have the extra time to spend with them.*
>
> *. . . A lot of times when I go in to make their bed or just go in to say hello to them, they want you to sit down. They want to talk to you for a few minutes. So when we are fully staffed, you are able to do that. But when you're understaffed, the work load is tremendous. It's just tremendous. When I go home, I feel good in my heart, but my body physically is just exhausted. (p. 223)*

A major challenge for nursing homes is staff turnover. Some homes report annual turnover rates as high as 100 percent, requiring substantial investments of time and money in staff training. The high turnover rates cannot be explained only by the nature of the work itself. For example, Brannon and her colleagues (Brannon et al., 1990) surveyed 489 nursing assistants and LPNs in 21 nursing homes to assess their perceptions of their jobs. Compared to other workers (e.g., female workers, high-school graduates, those in small organizations, those who are hourly workers), the nursing assistants reported that their jobs were average on many dimensions. However, they stated that their jobs were above average on one important dimension: task significance, or the impact of their work on people.

Brannon and her colleagues also asked the nursing assistants how satisfied they were with various aspects of their job (e.g., supervision, pay, co-workers, job security). They were above average in their satisfaction with their co-workers. However, they were below average in their view of their pay.

Brannon and Smyer (1990) summarized the impact of the nursing assistants' perception of pay on the industry's turnover problem:

> Aides reportedly change jobs for pay increases as small as 25- to 50-cents per hour (Institute of Medicine, 1989). Many nursing homes find that their staff-retention efforts are not competitive with employment opportunities in the fast food industry. (p. 64)

Moreover, Brannon and Smyer (1990) described the projected needs in nursing-home staff. They noted that, by the year 2000, nursing homes might need as many as 1 million nursing assistants, 339,000 licensed practical nurses and vocational nurses, and 838,000 registered nurses. In summary, there will be great growth in staffing and increased competition for long-term care staff members.

The fit between residents and staff

Nurses' aides provide the majority of direct contact with nursing-home residents. This brings up the third element of the community mix: the fit between the residents' needs and the staff services that are available.

Given the complex mixture of mental and physical health needs of residents, it is important to assess the complexity of services provided in nursing homes. A recent analysis of the 1987 NMES data evaluated patterns of mental health service use and provision (Smyer, Shea, & Streit, 1994). The results are mixed. Approximately 60 percent of nursing homes reported providing counseling or mental health services, most often through a contract with an outside provider. Psychiatrists are the professionals most often listed as the providers of mental health services, followed by psychiatric social workers, psychologists, and other mental health professionals (Smyer, Shea, & Streit, 1994).

However, Burns and her colleagues reported an analysis of the National Nursing Home Survey data that suggests that optimism is not called for (Burns et al., 1993). Of those two-thirds of residents with a mental disorder, only 4.5 percent received any mental health treatment in a one-month period – 4.5 percent (Burns et al., 1993). Half of that service was provided by a general practitioner (e.g., a primary care physician), most of whom have little or no specialty training in geriatric mental health issues.

A similar pattern of inadequate service provision is reflected in the NMES data (Smyer, Shea, & Streit, 1994). Of those residents with a mental disorder, almost 80 percent are in a facility that reported having mental health services available. However, despite being in a facility with such services, fewer than 20 percent of residents with a mental disorder actually received mental health services *sometime in the last year*, using a very liberal definition of "service received."

In short, whether the view is on a monthly basis (Burns et al., 1993) or an annual basis (Smyer, Shea, & Streit, 1994), it is clear that there is inadequate professional provision of mental health services in nursing homes: the fit between residents' needs and staff skills is not good. We see a very high need for mental health interventions and a very low rate of professional service provision. Lichtenberg (1994) points out that nursing assistants could perform a variety of roles that affect the mental well-being of nursing-home residents (e.g., behavior management, family outreach, helping with special activities). Thus far, however, such efforts have not been included in the traditional nursing assistants' role.

The Nursing Home Reform Act of 1987

The "fit" between residents' needs and staff members' skills in your local nursing home is affected by the national policy context of Medicare and Medicaid regulations and congressional actions focused on nursing homes. For example, most of the depictions of service use patterns in this chapter come from national data sets gathered in 1985 and 1987, the most recent data available. Yet they were gathered before the implementation of the most important piece of legislation affecting nursing homes in the last decade or more: the Nursing Home Reform Act of 1987 (Smyer, 1989).

The Nursing Home Reform Act was an attempt by Congress to improve the quality of care in nursing homes, primarily through regulatory reform, in contrast to President Reagan's deregulation emphasis. The act had three major components: pre-admission screening; improving residents' rights; and increasing the training of nurses' aides.

Pre-admission screening

The purpose of the pre-admission screening was simple: screen out people who are *only* mentally ill, that is, those who need mental health care but not nursing-home care. The idea is straightforward: anyone who seeks nursing-home admission – whether private pay or federal pay – must be screened. Each state has the responsibility for setting up a screening and assessment process. Many psychologists have been involved in performing pre-admission screening and annual resident review (PASARR) assessments.

Several research groups have simulated the OBRA 87 regulations on national data sets to assess the likely impact of such screening procedures (e.g., Freiman et al., 1990). Lair and Smyer (1994) used the NMES survey data to gauge the effect of the pre-admission criteria.

The Nursing Home Reform Act's impact depends upon the definition of two major elements: dementia and mental illness. The OBRA regulations specifically exclude any resident with a dementia from any further screening. In other words, if you have a dementia, you can go directly to the nursing home – despite the fact that the dementias are the most prevalent mental disorder among nursing-home residents. The Alzheimer's Association was very effective in lobbying Congress and assuring that dementia was viewed as a physical illness and not a mental illness, despite the behavioral correlates of dementia and the behavioral problems that often accompany them (e.g., Light & Lebowitz, 1991). Similarly, the regulations are somewhat open to narrow or broader interpretation regarding mental illness. What is a mental illness?

In simulating the effects of the Nursing Home Reform Act, Lair and Smyer (1994) asked three basic questions. First, does the person's status reflect a need for nursing services? Only 11 percent of those seeking admission in 1987 did not have a clear need for nursing services. In other words, 89 percent had a need for nursing services and therefore would not be screened any further because they needed nursing-home care. Second, does the person have a dementia, as reflected by either a primary or secondary diagnosis of organic brain syndrome? If so, no further screening is needed. Thirdly, does the person have a mental illness – either by a narrow definition, for example, psychosis only; or a broader definition. If so, that person would need to be screened. Using these criteria, we estimate that somewhere between 2 and 5 percent of older adults seeking nursing-home admissions will be excluded under the reform act's regulations. Thus we do not expect the pattern of resident comorbidity – the mixture of physical and mental disorders – to change as a result of the act's screening process.

The Nursing Home Reform Act has not significantly altered the general nursing-home admissions profile. Instead, three general groups remain candidates for mental health treatment: the physically ill but cognitively capable; the mentally ill but cognitively capable; and the demented (Lichtenberg, 1994).

Residents' rights

The residents' rights portion of the act was also important, since it focused attention on the right to be free from unnecessary physical or chemical restraints – drugging, overdrugging, overmedication – the right to self-determination, and the right to active mental health treatment. Recent work suggests that concern regarding chemical restraints is warranted (e.g., Beardsley et al., 1989; Beers et al., 1988; Buck, 1988; Burns & Kamerow, 1988; Ray et al., 1980). For example, Spore and her colleagues reported on antipsychotic use for a sample of 419 nursing-home residents (Spore et al., 1992). Approximately 50 percent of these residents had a mental illness diagnosis, with 42 percent having a diagnosis of dementia, consistent with national patterns. When comparing antipsychotic users and non-users, there are significant group differences in diagnosis. However, 22 percent of those receiving antipsychotics had *no* mental illness diagnosis, and 42 percent of those not receiving antipsychotics had a mental illness diagnosis. Thus the regulatory concern regarding inappropriate use of medications as chemical restraints is clearly warranted. If nursing homes decrease inappropriate use of chemical and physical restraints, we might expect increased attention to alternative treatment approaches. Mental health clinicians should be involved in developing alternative, psycho-social approaches for mental health treatment (Smyer, 1989).

Preliminary work on residents' abilities to be involved in health-care decision-making, the self-determination part of the residents' rights component, suggests that this is another area that requires attention. For example, Goodwin, Smyer, and Lair (1995) analyzed data from the NMES data set and found that more than 50 percent of nursing-home residents could be deemed incompetent under a model statute that focuses on the resident's functional ability as a criterion for assessing decision-making capacity. In short, there is much work to be done in assessing the most effective ways to implement the residents' rights intent of the Nursing Home Reform Act with the very impaired residents of nursing homes.

A third element of the resident's rights portion focused on the resident's right to active mental health treatment. The act requires nursing homes to provide basic mental health services for all residents and to give active mental health treatment to residents who are admitted with a serious mental illness. Shea and his colleagues (1993) estimated that the cost of mandated services may range from $480 million to more than $1.3 billion annually, depending upon the types of services provided and the definitions used to identify those in need of services. Again, mental health clinicians should be actively involved in the development and implementation of treatment plans for mentally ill residents – a theme to which we will return later.

Staff training

So what about the third element of the Nursing Home Reform Act – training of nurses' aides? Although we were optimistic that the initial regulations and requirements might include a strong emphasis on mental health treatment issues, much of the orientation training now required for nursing assistants focuses on health and safety issues (fire codes, the proper way to lift patients, etc.), with mental health issues becoming a commonly ancillary topic, treated only in supplementary training (Smyer, Brannon, & Cohn, 1992).

Lichtenberg (1994) summarized the training efforts that have targeted nursing assistants as mental health caregivers. He noted that training programs have included both skills (e.g., counseling strategies, behavioral modification) and knowledge areas (e.g., psychopharmacology, neuropsychology) (see table 11.3). No single training program includes all of these elements.

What's a Clinician to Do?

The conceptualization of nursing homes as communities provides a context for specific roles and activities that clinicians can play. Focusing on the various community members (staff, consultants, residents, family members) alerts us to the complexity of mental health intervention in an institutional setting.

It is essential that mental health professionals understand the historical and contemporary roles of these settings, since they shape the expectations and resources that clinicians can call upon in working with mentally ill nursing-home residents (Smyer, 1989). For example, the Nursing Home Reform Act of 1987 significantly changed the regulatory requirements on nursing homes. It affects both staff training and residents' rights in the setting. Geriatric mental health professionals can use their expertise in three major activities in nursing homes: assessment (both individual and organizational), treatment, and consultation.

Assessment

Consider again the case of Mr Johnson which started this chapter. As a nursing home mental health specialist, one of your first tasks may be to assess both the individual nursing-home resident and the organizational context in which he or she is functioning. In Mr Johnson's case, the referral is for "sexual acting out." A series of questions follow from this simple description: What is meant by this term in this context? What is the pattern of "sexual acting out" (e.g., are there differences across times of day, places within the home, etc.)? Whose problem is this? The referral indicates that the "nurses on second shift got the doctor to write." What will success look like in this case? Will a behavior be eliminated, reduced in frequency, or allowed to occur only in certain contexts? Will a shift in Mr Johnson's pattern of activity (e.g., from the day room to his own semi-private room) be success?

To answer these questions requires the clinician to understand how the setting works, how the staff's and residents' patterns of functioning are interwoven and interdependent (Baltes & Reisenzein, 1986). For example, what are the staffing patterns of this nursing home? Nursing homes typically adopt one of two patterns: stable assignment of residents to a nursing assistant

Table 11.3 Areas of training for mental health workers involved in long-term care

---

Counseling
a) Empathy
b) Warmth
c) Genuineness
d) Active listening

Major mental illness
a) Schizophrenia/delusional disorder
b) Bipolar disorder
c) Major depression

Alzheimer's and other dementias
a) Cognitive effects
b) Behavioral problems
c) Caregiver burden and depression

Psychopharmacology
a) Common antipsychotic medications
b) Common antidepressant medications
c) Common anti-anxiety medications

Behavioral modification
a) Positive reinforcement/punishment
b) Differential reinforcement of other behavior (DRO)
c) Time out
d) Shaping
e) Chaining

Neuropsychology
a) Basic organization of cortex
b) Use of tests
c) Procedures and practice for standardized administration

Grief
a) Phases: shock, searching, suffering, healing
b) Stages: denial, anger, bargaining, depression, acceptance

Case conferences
a) Organizing case material
b) Presenting case material

Source: Lichtenberg, 1994, p. 89.

or rotating assignment of residents to caregivers. Care-giving job design can affect staff functioning (Brannon et al., 1994) and residents' psycho-social functioning (Teresi et al., 1993). Similarly, the supervisory leadership of the charge nurses (LPNs and RNs) can affect staff performance (Brannon et al., 1994). Thus understanding the job design and leadership structure within the organization and their potential impact on residents and staff is important.

Although these themes are important, they are often overlooked in traditional mental health consultation in nursing homes for two reasons: clinical training and reimbursement patterns. Many mental health specialists are trained to focus on the individual resident, without considering the impact of the setting and the organizational structure on resident functioning. Similarly, most reimbursement schemes (e.g., Medicaid) focus on service provision to an individual client or resident, *not* organizational consultation and staff development.

However, organizational assessment provides the context for assessing the individual. Clinicians may find several challenges to effective individual assessment in nursing homes (Williams & Shadish, 1991): the patients are disabled and disoriented, making traditional assessment approaches difficult; few assessment devices have been normed and developed for use in the nursing home; and few psychologists have experience with assessing this group of older adults.

Despite the difficulties, however, there is consensus regarding the essential areas for geriatric assessment in nursing homes (Gatz, Smyer et al., 1991; Williams & Shadish, 1991). Four areas are important for general assessment, in addition to a general physical work-up to rule out medical disorders that may be complicating factors: cognitive functioning; psychological functioning; self-care capacity; and behavioral observations.

A starting point for cognitive assessment is a standardized mental status questionnaire. There are several brief, screening instruments that have been developed for use with impaired older adults, including the brief Mental Status Questionnaire (Pfeiffer, 1975), the Mini Mental Status Exam (MMSE) (Cockrell & Folstein, 1988; Folstein et al., 1975), and the Mattis Dementia Rating Scale (Coblentz et al., 1973; Mattis, 1976). The MMSE, for example, includes items that tap orientation, registration of information, attention and calculation, recall, and both expressive and receptive language. Lichtenberg (1994) summarized the tests that make up a comprehensive neuropsychological battery for assessing dementia. A sample of the instruments and areas tapped is presented in table 11.4.

There are several standardized measures of psychological functioning with norms available for older adults (Overall & Rhoades, 1988); unfortunately, comparable norms for nursing-home residents are usually not available

Table 11.4 Examples of a neuropsychological battery to assess dementia

Instruments	Areas assessed
General intellectual/cognitive functioning	
Weschsler Adult Intelligence Scale-Revised (WAIS-R)	General measure of intelligence; full-scale verbal and performance IQ scores; subtest scores (see below)
Dementia Rating Scale (DRS)	Basic measure of cognitive functioning (e.g., attention, memory, visuomotor, abstract reasoning)
Attention	
Digit Span (WAIS-R)	Immediate auditory attention
Visual Attention Subtest (DRS)	Visual scanning
Trails A	Simple visual motor tracking
Language	
Aphasia Screening Test	Covers basic language areas: naming, reading, repetition, comprehension, expression
Boston Naming Test	More difficult test of confrontational naming
Vocabulary (WAIS-R)	Word knowledge
Memory	
Recall and Recognition Subtests (DRS)	Recall for sentences, recognition for designs and words
Logical Memory Subtest (Wechsler Memory Scale-Revised)	Immediate and delayed recall for verbal contextual information
Visual Reproduction Subtest (Wechsler Memory Scale-Revised)	Immediate and delayed recall for visuo-spatial material
Fuld Object Memory Exam	Verbal learning and memory, recognition and delayed recall; over five trials, learning ten items that were handled and named
Rey Auditory Verbal Learning Test	Learning 15 unrelated words over five trials; short delay and recognition tasks
Visuo-spatial	
Picture Completion (WAIS-R)	Recognizing missing details

Table 11.4   continued

Instruments	Areas assessed
Picture Arrangement (WAIS-R)	Non-verbal test of social judgment and organization
Digit Symbol (WAIS-R)	Visual-motor copying
Abstract reasoning	
Similarities (WAIS-R)	Verbal abstract reasoning
Block Design (WAIS-R)	Visuo-spatial abstract reasoning
Affect	
Geriatric Depression Scale	Screening measure of depression
Alcohol abuse	
CAGE Questionnaire	Screening test for alcohol abuse

Source: adapted from Lichtenberg, 1994.

(Williams & Shadish, 1991). Two different approaches have been suggested here: self-report measures that assess a number of domains and measures that assess single disorders. Commonly used comprehensive measures are the 53-item Brief Symptom Inventory (Derogatis & Spencer, 1982), developed from the Hopkins Symptoms Check List (Derogatis, 1977), and the Brief Psychiatric Rating Scale (Overall & Gorham, 1962, 1988; Overall & Beller, 1984).

There are also several scales available for assessing geriatric depression (Gallagher, 1986; Thompson, Futterman, & Gallagher, 1988) and for the other disorders that have been highlighted in earlier chapters. In most cases, however, norms are lacking for institutionalized older adults. Therefore the clinician must adapt the measures, using them more as indicators of functioning rather than seeking specific cutoffs that indicate presence or absence of psychopathology. In addition to the usual diagnostic difficulties that geriatric patients present, nursing-home residents have the added challenge of frail physical conditions that must also be considered as part of the diagnostic work-up (Cohen, 1985, 1992).

A third area of assessment is the resident's self-care capacity. Activities of daily living (ADL) and Instrumental activities of daily living (IADL), commonly known as functional health, are the two most frequently assessed areas of self-care capacity (Lawton, 1988). ADL activities include items such as bathing, dressing, toileting, walking, and transferring from the bed to a chair or wheelchair. IADL activities include items such as using the telephone, balancing a checkbook, shopping, and using public transportation. These areas are useful for nursing-home assessment for three reasons: they are important basic activities for daily life; mentally ill residents are commonly impaired in these domains (Lair & Lefkowitz, 1990); and these activities serve as proxies for underlying cognitive and social abilities (Kemp & Mitchell, 1992).

A fourth assessment area is behavioral observation. Behavioral observation can be undertaken on an individual basis, not using psychometrically based tools (e.g., Edinberg, 1985; Hussian, 1986). However, by using an organized rating scheme the psychologist can accomplish two goals: capitalize upon the key informants or observers in the setting (the nursing staff) and provide a standardized means of comparing current and future functioning across time and across situations (e.g., time of day, staff arrangements, roommate assignments). Several rating systems have been used in nursing-home settings, such as the Nurses Observation Scale for Inpatient Evaluation (NOSIE) (Honigfeld & Klett, 1965), the Multidimensional Observation Scale for Elderly Subjects (MOSES) (Helmes, 1988; Helmes et al., 1987; Pruchno et al., 1988), and the Revised Memory and Behavior Problem Checklist (Teri, Truax et al., 1992).

A critical issue in behavioral analysis is establishing uniformity in describing the behavior, its antecedents (or causes), and its consequences (Cohn, Smyer, & Horgas, 1994). For example, Cohn and her colleagues developed a behavioral curriculum for nursing assistants. They focused on the "ABCs" of behavior change: *A*ctions, *B*ecauses, and *C*onsequences (see table 11.5).

One goal of the training was to establish a common set of observation strategies to improve communication about specific problems. For example, if faced with the referral for Mr Johnson's "sexual acting out," Cohn and her colleagues would use their scheme to be more specific: about the action (e.g., what, where, etc.); the potential causes (e.g., the context of the behavior); and the consequences of the behavior (e.g., what reaction does the "sexual acting out" get, does it differ at different times of day, with differing staff members, etc.?).

Treatment

In earlier chapters we identified major treatment approaches for major categories of psychopathology (e.g., anxiety, depression, cognitive impairment). These approaches also form the context for treatment of nursing-home residents (Spayd & Smyer, 1996). In addition, Spayd and Smyer (1996)

Table 11.5 The ABCs of behavior change

Observation of steps

A) Describe the actions
    What is the resident doing?
    Where is this happening?
    How long has this been going on?
    How strong is this? More or less than usual?
    For whom is this a problem?

B) Describe becauses
    What else is going on around the resident?
    What might be happening inside?
    Who else is there?
    What are they doing?
    What has changed?

C) Describe the consequences
    How does the resident respond?
    What does the resident do next?
    What do others do next?
    Talk observations over with co-workers?

Change steps

A) Set behavioral goals
    What do we want the resident to do?
    Is this a single step?
    Is it specific?
    It is realistic?

B) New becauses
    What old Becauses can be eliminated or
    changed?
    What new triggers or cues can be used for the
    desired behavior?

C) New consequences
    What unhelpful reinforcers can be eliminated?
    What new reinforcers will encourage new
    behavior?
    Talk these possibilities over with co-workers.

Source: adapted from Cohn, Smyer, & Horgas, 1994.

outline five procedural steps for selecting an appropriate and effective intervention for a mentally ill nursing-home resident:

1   identify the problem in behavioral terms
2   determine realistic and mutually agreeable goals for intervention
3   identify all available mental health resources
4   assess the available interventions in light of the individual resident's problem and characteristics
5   consider the potential problems with available treatments and the possibility of not intervening.

Spayd and Smyer (1996) begin with the particular elements of the problem. By focusing on specific behaviors, they urge us to avoid global complaints from staff, such as the referral problem for Mr Johnson: "sexual acting out." In following up on this referral, a first step would be to become clearer about what specific activities were involved, under what conditions (e.g., time of day, particular persons present, etc.).

The second step – determining *mutually* agreeable goals – requires assessing whose problem needs to be addressed. In Mr Johnson's case, the nursing director suggests that the problem occurs only on second shift. Thus one of the key elements in setting the goals will be to identify those who must be involved in developing the agreement: the resident, the relevant staff, other residents and family members (as appropriate), and the psychologist. Involving all of those with a stake in the problem can be very complicated in nursing homes. For example, residents may have shifting moments of lucidity as a function of their underlying physical and mental disorders (Smyer, Schaie, & Kapp, 1996). At the same time, different staff members may have different views, depending upon the other demands they face. For example, is Mr Johnson's behavior more disruptive to the second shift staff members because of the other demands that occur around bed-time for the residents?

Finally, reaching mutually agreeable goals means negotiating a solution across staff levels, times of day, and, at times, conflicting perspectives. For the clinician, this often represents the intersection of individual and organizational practice.

The third step – identifying all available mental health resources – reminds us that the treatment plan may include other members of the nursing-home community (e.g., residents, staff, family members, visitors) as well as outside expertise. In charting available mental health resources, of course, payment will be an important issue: Who will pay? Most federal and private insurance schemes focus only on individual treatment, with no funding for staff training or consultation. Finally, an assessment of the resident's own capacities as resources is also essential (e.g., Does the resident have sufficient cognitive capacity to be actively engaged in the therapeutic process?).

Given an appreciation of both the appropriate goals and resources available for this resident's problem situation, an essential next step is to assess the possible interventions. In this step the clinician serves as the scientist-practitioner, assessing what is known from the literature and gauging what is feasible within the constraints of the individual resident and their context and the professional and paraprofessional resources of the setting. Common approaches to intervention include medication, behavior management, psychotherapy (individual and group), and referral for increased use of activities, social visits, or other existing services.

The final step is a variation on the first rule of medical intervention: First do no harm. With a clear understanding of the problem, the resources and potential interventions available, we will be able to consider the limitations of treatment as well as the benefits. Brink (1979) highlighted Segal's *principle of minimal interference*, with a goal of disturbing established patterns of living as little as possible. Others (e.g., Burnside, 1980; Sundberg et al., 1983) have noted that any intervention requires some interference with the resident's life. Thus we should consider the full range of options – including the option of not intervening – before we undertake treatment. All of the specific treatment approaches described in earlier chapters for the major mental disorders of older adults can be adapted for use in nursing homes. These strategies typically focus on the individual resident. Other approaches focus on broader intervention through consultation. The following case illustrates the complexity of working with a demented nursing-home resident (Lichtenberg, 1994).

Ms C was the youngest of three children. She was a star pupil and her father, a postmaster, encouraged her schooling. After graduating from high school she entered a teaching college and earned a certificate to teach history and Latin. She was to remain a schoolteacher for 43 years. In her twenties Ms C refused a marriage proposition so that she could care for her aging parents; in addition, her elder brother was mentally ill and required care at home. Her sister had a history of severe depression that ultimately led to suicide when she was in her sixties. Her brother and father died shortly thereafter. Ms C continued to care for her mother until the mother died in her nineties. In the same year, while in her sixties, she retired from teaching.

Ms C spent the next 20 years living alone on the family farm, and, according to her nieces, she gradually became stubborn and eccentric. Early in her seventies she had fallen and broken her hip. Later she experienced a depressive episode. She suffered a gradual onset of Alzheimer's disease beginning in her late seventies. Early cognitive declines included claiming to her niece that things were stolen. This occurred repeatedly, despite the fact that the niece always found the lost objects in Ms C's house. Finally, when some of her cows died and she failed to have them removed, Ms C was brought to long-term care.

Ms C's medical condition caused significant cognitive fluctuation. She had thorough neuropsychological assessments in September 1988 and January 1989, as well as screening assessments in August 1988 and December 1988. The results of these will be presented alongside of Ms C's fluctuating medical condition. Upon admission (August 1988), Ms C was noted to have poor hearing and an acute confusional state. Wrist restraints and medication were used to subdue her. A neurology assessment found her to be uncooperative and inattentive. One week later, however, it was discovered that she had experienced a myocardial infarction.

Ms C continued to suffer from medical complications, including a temperature of 102, urinary tract infections, fecal impactions, and chronic constipation. Her level of alertness varied throughout the month; it was later discovered that she had suffered another myocardial infarction.

The first thorough neuropsychological assessment came at about that same time. Ms C was disoriented as to time and place. Deficiencies were noted in attention, verbal abstract reasoning, and memory. Verbal skills were determined to be less efficient than visuo-spatial ones.

Ms C's medical condition stabilized between her first and second neuropsychological assessment. A three-and-a-quarter-pound weight gain was noted, leaving her underweight by seven pounds. She began gait training and was regularly using her walker. She refused to consider a hearing aid, however. On the second evaluation, performance on well-learned information was above average, but social judgment and abstract reasoning were below expectation and represented a decline. Verbal recall was above average, but some mild naming difficulties were present. Visuo-spatial abilities were severely impaired, as was non-verbal memory. It was concluded that verbal abilities were clearly a strength relative to visuo-spatial abilities. On the long-term care unit, it was recommended that verbal instructions be used and that recreational activities be directed toward reading and conversation.

Ms C's history revealed a high-functioning woman who was used to being self-sufficient and socially isolated. She has a progressing dementia that interfered with her ability to provide for her own care and, due to her declines in the past year, made her an unsuitable candidate for returning home. Neuropsychological reassessments following medical improvement revealed a woman with greater cognitive skills than were exhibited on the first assessment, especially in areas of verbal functioning. Her ability to integrate facts and provide good judgments, however, was faulty. Ms C's chief need was to adjust to her decline by grieving her loss of autonomy and health, yet her neuropsychological deficits interfered with her ability to do this.

One of the saddest aspects of providing psychological treatment to dementia patients is their experience of grief. Dementia patients clearly have intense grief, and they can be helped by supportive intervention, but only momentarily. Due to their cognitive limitations they do not remember – nor can they integrate – their grieving episodes so that they can form some type of healing process. They often remain stuck in grief. The grief symptoms in the demented appear to be the same as those in normal elderly, but often any progress in successful grief is a very slow process. Ms C provided an example of some progress in her grieving. She was seen by the therapist twice a week, for 15 to 30 minutes each session.

Early on, she believed that she could live alone and that her neighbors would help her. This was clearly an experience of denial. Two months later she told the staff that she came into a lot of money and could now pay someone to take complete care of her at home. This reflected a form of bargaining. Although attempts were made to increase her pleasant events, she refused any such offerings. Later she stated that if she could not return home she would die. Soon thereafter depressive symptoms such as fearfulness and a new somber attitude were noted. Slowly, she began to enjoy reminiscing and reciting well-learned poetry. She was clearly healing some from her grief. Her talk about returning home subsided significantly. At this point a number of pleasant events were added to her day: drawing, reading, reminiscing, and cooking. Her depression resolved, and she became very close to the staff.

Ms C's case highlights important components of psychotherapy with demented patients. First, traditional supportive therapy can help to build trust and prepare the patient for a behavioral approach. Ms C was unable to increase her pleasurable activities until she trusted, and felt understood by, the therapist. By first allowing her to work through her feelings, she was later able to delight in the opportunities presented in long-term care.

(Lichtenberg, 1994, pp. 163–5)

Consultation

It is important that mental health clinicians "leverage" their expertise: there simply are not enough specialists available, and there is not enough funding available, to assure that clinicians can provide one-to-one mental health interventions in nursing homes. Therefore an appropriate use of talent is to serve as a consultant to the setting, seeking to engage key members of the nursing-home community as elements of the mental health treatment team (Cohn & Smyer, 1988).

There are several steps in the consultation process: 1) preparation; 2) relationship development; 3) problem assessment; 4) formulation and delivery of interventions; and 5) follow-up (Caplan, 1970). For clinicians, starting a nursing-home consultation practice requires background knowledge and experience – learning the territory of nursing homes and mental health reimbursement, and developing relationships with administrators, directors of nursing, and other key referral sources.

As with individual treatment, the consultation process is informed by the theoretical perspective of the consultant. We have found two frameworks particularly useful in nursing homes: behavioral approaches (Baltes & Reisenzein, 1986; Vernberg & Reppucci, 1986) and organizational development techniques (Keys, 1986). Behavioral approaches, for example, focus on the learning processes that lead to both adaptive and maladaptive behaviors, especially the influence of all nursing-home community members on residents' behavior. Organizational development approaches, in contrast, are focused on the working of the institutional setting itself.

Brannon et al. (1994) recently summarized the interaction of these perspectives. Their work illustrates a potential role for mental health clinicians: development and implementation of staff training approaches focused on mental health treatment in order eventually to affect the well-being of mentally ill residents. Brannon and her colleagues (Brannon & Smyer, 1994; Smyer, Brannon, & Cohn, 1992) have documented that nurses' aides can improve their knowledge of behavioral approaches to mental illness among nursing-home residents. They also found, however, that this training was not "transferred" from the classroom to the floor where the nursing assistants work (Smyer, Brannon, & Cohn, 1992). Two organizational aspects had particularly striking effects on the impact of the training – the supervisory leadership that the nursing assistants experienced; and the design of the nursing assistants' role (e.g., stable vs. rotating assignment of residents to nursing assistants) (see box 11.1). In short, Brannon and her colleagues (1994) found that both behavioral and organizational frameworks are helpful, and linked, in understanding the impact of consultation approaches in nursing homes. Their work suggests that consultation and training will be most effective in settings that have experienced supervisors who are supportive of the training and a staff system that lends stability to the staffing pattern.

Mental health consultants in nursing homes must clarify several elements in the consultation (Cohn & Smyer, 1988): Who is the consumer or client (e.g., residents, staff members, family members)? When does the consultation occur in the cycle of the problem process (e.g., before a problem occurs or in the midst of a crisis)? At what level does the consultation occur (e.g., at the

Box 11.1 The Penn State Nursing Home Intervention Project

The Penn State Nursing Home Intervention Project was a short-term longitudinal study to assess the single and combined effects of two interventions –
job redesign and skills training – on nursing assistants' skills and motivation
(Smyer & Walls, 1994; Smyer, Brannon, & Cohn, 1992). The skills training
increased the nursing assistants' knowledge of behavioral treatment strategies
and their application to residents' disorientation, agitation, and depression.
However, the nursing assistants' motivation was not affected. in addition, the
interventions had no impact on the nursing assistants' work with residents, as
reflected in supervisors' ratings.

Based on these findings, we suggest that improvement of residents' well-
being will be affected by an interaction of nursing assistants' skills, knowledge,
and beliefs, supervisors' actions and beliefs, and the organization of the nurses'
work (e.g., stable vs. rotating assignments). The following figure summarizes
these elements.

A model of the care-giving environment

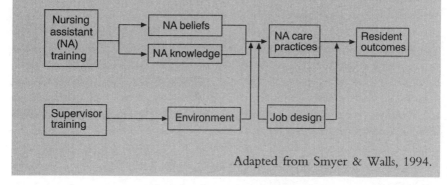

Adapted from Smyer & Walls, 1994.

resident level or at the administrative level)? What is the route of expected
intervention (e.g., directly with the resident or indirectly through working
with other staff members)? Perhaps most importantly, what is the goal for the
consultative intervention (e.g., treatment of a specific resident; development
of a policy)?

Although the conceptual base for mental health consultation in nursing
homes is on hand (Cohn & Smyer, 1988), much work remains to make this
type of mental health service available. One major barrier to more consultation is the absence of clear funding streams for consultation: Who will pay for
staff consultation and training? Our mental health delivery system is based
upon an individual, one-to-one model of service provision and reimburse-

ment. It remains for clinicians to develop and implement innovative and effective consultation processes for this setting.

Summary

Nursing homes present a challenge for older residents and their caregivers: how to cope effectively with a combination of physical and mental health problems. Unfortunately, the staffing and reimbursement patterns are not designed to provide services for the array of residents' physical and mental disorders. The challenge, therefore, is how to leverage geriatric mental health expertise in assessment, treatment, and consultation.

12

The Contexts and Pragmatics of Practice

The time: 1.50 p.m. The place: Your office. You get a phone call and the following conversation ensues:

Hello, Dr? I'm glad I reached you. This is Dr B. I've only got ten minutes between clients and I need some advice. I'm going to start consulting at a nursing home tomorrow, and I haven't worked with the elderly. You've done a lot of work with older adults. What do I need to know?

How would you answer? What would be helpful to you and to the potential consultant?

This conversation actually took place a couple of years ago, at a time when mental health consultation companies discovered geriatric mental health issues in general and nursing homes in particular. Our advice to the would-be consultant (and to students who want to work successfully with mentally ill elderly) is that effective practice is a function of three contexts: the profession's definition of practice competence; the opportunities and constraints of funding sources, especially managed care; and other social and policy initiatives that affect mental health issues for older adults. This chapter is designed to introduce each of these elements and to help you assess the impact of each on the daily pragmatic choices that shape how mental health services are provided for older adults. At the same time, the chapter provides a summary of several key areas covered earlier in the book (e.g., geriatric assessment and intervention).

The Profession's Definition of Practice Competence, or What Does a Geriatric Mental Health Practitioner Do?

The four core mental health disciplines (psychiatry, psychology, social work, and nursing) have sought to define the expertise necessary for working effectively with older adults. We will often use psychology as an example, since it's the profession with which we are most familiar. However, each profession has faced similar challenges.

Lebowitz (1993) suggested that there have been three distinct phases of interest in mental health and aging: an early period when it was a "career buster"; a second period, beginning in the early 1970s, when aging was equated with Alzheimer's disease; and the more recent phase of "mainstreaming" interests in aging, linking aging issues to larger societal concerns regarding the impact of mental and physical health care. This assessment also fits geriatric mental health service provision.

Geriatric mental health has emerged from a "cottage industry" marked by early clinical and case vignettes (e.g., Rechtschaffen, 1959) to a systematic inquiry into which approaches are most effective for which types of disorders (Smyer, Zarit, & Qualls, 1990; Zarit & Knight, 1996). Currently, geriatric practice is in a transition to becoming "mainstreamed" and swept along in the debate regarding the defining characteristics of the core mental health professions – both within each profession and within the larger society. It is this transitional status that has caused some concerns regarding who can be called a geriatric mental health specialist and what is implied regarding expertise with older adults.

In psychology, the debate has focused on what type of training should be required for working with older adults (Knight et al., 1995). A consensus has emerged that there should be three different levels of training in adult development and aging for practicing psychologists: general exposure, generalist training with additional experience, and specialists with identifiable expertise. A working group from the American Psychological Association has suggested elements that should be included within each level (see table 12.1). The proposed levels of training are designed to complement the basic training in psychological methods that each student would receive in clinical, counseling, or other applied areas of psychology.

The psychiatric profession has also developed a series of training and credentialing expectations linked to a certificate of added qualification in geriatric psychiatry. Under procedures developed and monitored by the American Board of Psychiatry and Neurology, a physician must first become board certified in psychiatry. Board certification is gauged by the candidate's successful completion of a written and an oral examination. Typically, the process requires approximately two years after completing residency training. The certificate of added qualification in geriatric psychiatry necessitates an additional 12 months of training at an approved institution, after which the candidate must successfully complete an additional examination. Only then can the physician claim added qualification in geriatric psychiatry.

Table 12.1   Proposed training in aging-related knowledge and skills

---

Training in aging-related knowledge and skills should occur at three levels:

Level 1: **General exposure to aging.** All practice-oriented psychologists should have some course work relating to the aging process and older adulthood as part of their clinical training. Given the likelihood that most practicing psychologists will deal with patients and associated family members of diverse ages, a rounded education should include training with a life span-developmental perspective that includes knowledge of a range of age groups, including the elderly.

Level 2: **Generalist training in clinical geropsychology.** Psychologists whose clinical practice involves some work with older clients should receive sufficient training to achieve a generalist's or journeyman level of competence in clinical geropsychology. This level of preparation generally corresponds to the concept of a proficiency practice area, and certification might be a suitable credentialing procedure for psychologists who have acquired the requisite elements of competence.

Level 3: **Specialist training in clinical geropsychology.** Psychologists who will function as full specialists in clinical geropsychology should receive extensive training, typically in concentrated programs where they acquire a breadth and depth of expertise in the field. Others will typically refer special problems in aging to these practitioners for diagnosis and treatment. Such specialists, for whom clinical geropsychology is the prime or exclusive professional focus, will represent a minority of those practicing within the field. The specialist level of training is appropriate for academics, teachers in the field, and specialized clinical geropsychological researchers as well as practitioners. This level is generally compatible with the notion that clinical geropsychology represents a specialty within psychology. For the practitioner, an appropriate credentialing method might be an American Board of Professional Psychology-style diplomate.

Source: Niederehe & Teri, 1996.

Thus a simple answer to the question "*What do I need to know?*" is:"It depends on whether or not you're advertising yourself as a generalist or a specialist within your profession."

If you want to be a specialist, the consensus is that you need both to know the theory underlying our understanding of mental health and mental illness in later life and to develop skills in several domains: assessment of older

adults; psychological intervention with older adults; the challenges of modifying assessment and intervention approaches for use in specific settings; how
to work effectively with other disciplines; and how to cope with the ethical
issues that often accompany older adults' mental health problems (Niederehe
& Teri, 1996).

Geriatric assessment

In thinking about geriatric assessment, it may be useful to take a reporter's
perspective. Ask yourself several questions about geriatric assessment: What?
Why? How? Who?

A National Institute of Health consensus conference (NIH Consensus
Statement, 1988) offered one definition of what geriatric assessment is:

> . . . *a multidisciplinary evaluation in which the multiple problems of older
> persons are uncovered, described, and explained, if possible, and in which the
> resources and strengths of the person are catalogued, the need for services assessed,
> and a coordinated care plan developed. (p. 342)*

This definition contains several important aspects. First, it immediately draws
our attention to the collaborative aspects of geriatric assessment; geriatric
assessment is inherently a team effort that requires the resources of several
professions. Second, the phases of description, explanation, and intervention
are integrally linked to our assessment process. We assess potential causes
of underlying distress while ruling out competing hypotheses about the
source of the distress. Third, comprehensive assessment focuses on a balanced
view of the individual, capturing both strengths and weaknesses. Finally,
optimally, the assessment results should be linked to the intervention and
service steps.

Why do we undertake geriatric assessment? Zarit, Eiler, & Hassinger
(1985) suggested four purposes: 1) to determine a diagnosis; 2) to assess broad
patterns of behavior, thoughts, and emotions in order to capture adequately
current functioning; 3) to evaluate specific variables that can assist in care
planning (e.g., family resources, physical environment, etc.); and 4) to
measure critical variables for evaluating the outcomes of intervention. Thus
geriatric assessment is not solely to arrive at an accurate diagnosis. Equally
important, comprehensive assessment should provide a complete picture of
the older adult in context. In addition it should provide a benchmark for
comparison at a later time: we should be able to describe the individual's
pattern of stability or change in contrast to his or her functioning at the time
of assessment.

How can we accomplish these ambitious goals for geriatric assessment? Knight (1986) outlined several characteristics of an optimal assessment approach. He urged that we use measurements or approaches that have:

1 age-specific norms
2 proven reliability and validity with older adults
3 a suitability for being repeated
4 a capability of distinguishing among and between various disorders (e.g., depression and dementia)
5 a capacity to reflect our basic understanding of normal aging and pathology
6 a brief and non-threatening format.

Knight's wish-list is not always honored in the everyday world of geriatric assessment. Many of our measures lack specific age norms, particularly for the oldest old group (85+). Other approaches lack proven reliability and validity for use with older adults. For example, clinical interviews form the foundation of many assessment approaches. However, there is little information available about the reliability and validity of clinical interviews with the elderly (e.g., Edelstein & Semenchuk, 1996).

Similarly, we are often confronted with the dilemma of self-report: Can we trust the older adult or their family members to be accurate informants on the individual's functioning? For example, Willis (1996) reported on the gap between self-report and actual performance among community-dwelling older adults when they were asked to describe their own self-care capacity (e.g., taking medications, using the telephone, handling personal finances, etc.) (see figure 12.1). In almost every area, older adults overreported their ability to carry out these important self-care tasks. This has important implications for assessment: When in doubt, observe the actual task, don't just ask, "can you do it?"

Two important approaches to geriatric assessment are screening instruments and comprehensive assessment batteries. Screening instruments are used to provide an initial review of the individual's functioning. If the patient has trouble with the relatively simple aspects of a brief screening instrument, then further assessment information is called for. For example, the Mini-Mental State Examination (MMSE) (Folstein et al., 1975; Cockrell & Folstein, 1988) is an 11-item test that provides a brief assessment of several cognitive capacities, including orientation to time and place, attention, recall, and receptive and expressive language functioning.

In contrast, the Older Americans Resources and Services (OARS) questionnaire was developed to provide a comprehensive assessment that would

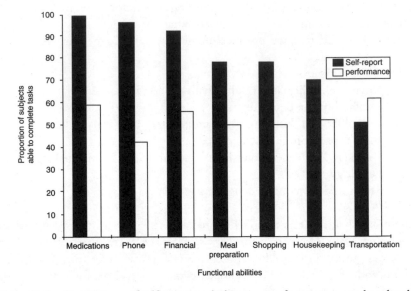

Figure 12.1 Comparison of self-report and objective performance on tasks related to seven functional ability domains
Source: adapted from Willis, 1996.

be useful in gauging the service needs of individuals and in evaluating the impact of programs of intervention (Fillenbaum & Smyer, 1981). It focuses on several aspects of the older adult and their environment: social resources; economic resources; physical health; mental health; self-care ability; service availability and use; and physical environment. It takes more than an hour to complete the OARS with an older adult. In addition, at several points the interview requires an informant to provide confirmation of the older adult's self-report.

Of course, screening tests and comprehensive questionnaires are only two of the many approaches available (e.g., neuro-imaging tests, etc.). The effective geriatric assessment uses the full range of approaches required to provide a comprehensive, valid picture of the older adult's functioning.

To accomplish such an assessment often requires a team approach. Who should be on the team depends upon the purpose of the assessment. For example, if the assessment is to rule out a brain tumor, neuropsychological testing and neuro-imaging approaches may be called for, requiring the active collaboration of a psychologist and a neurologist. If, on the other hand, cognitive capacity is not in question and the issue is the appropriate level of housing support, a physician's evaluation of medical

Table 12.2 Mental health intervention, by timing and level

Level Timing	Individual	Family	Community
Prevention	Classes in skills to manage moods	Cooperative Extension Service, Family After 40 Series	NIMH Depression Awareness Project
Treatment	Psychotherapy Pharmacotherapy	Family therapy	Outreach programs in senior housing
Maintenance	After-care programs	Family support group	Alzheimer support group

functioning and a social worker's evaluation of resources and ADL needs might be more appropriate.

Oftentimes, there are many different people involved in the assessment: family members, professionals, paraprofessionals, and agency members. To be effective, there must be an assessment coordinator among the various professionals and stakeholders in the process. Who plays this role may vary by the setting and the funding source that provide the context for the assessment.

Geriatric intervention

Geriatric mental health interventions vary along two key dimensions: level of intervention and timing of intervention (Smyer & Gatz, 1986). The level may vary from individually oriented treatment (e.g., pharmacotherapy, psychotherapy, or some combination) (Schneider, 1995) to community-based interventions. Similarly, the timing of intervention may vary from prevention to maintenance (Mrazek & Haggerty, 1994) (see table 12.2).

Mental health professionals are involved in developing, implementing, and evaluating interventions across the spectra of timing and level. For example, Thompson and his colleagues (1983) developed group approaches for educating older adults in steps to prevent mild or moderate depression. Similarly, Rashcko (1985) trained employees in a variety of industries that have contact with older adults (e.g., postal service, banks, utility companies) to identify older adults who may be at risk for mental or physical illness.

In this book we have emphasized individual interventions that focus on diagnosis and treatment. These are the most traditional approaches to mental health problems in later life. They also form the foundation necessary for developing either preventive or maintenance programs for mental health in later life.

Thus there is another way of answering our caller's question "*What do I need to know?*" One of the first things you need to know is your own profession's emphases on the basic dimensions of assessment and intervention.

Modifying your approach for a specific setting

The majority of mentally ill elderly receive treatment outside of traditional mental health settings, if they receive treatment at all. In addition, many older adults encounter mental health issues in the context of other challenges that they may be facing (e.g., coping with chronic physical illness; reacting to the necessity of moving to a new home; learning to live alone as a widow after decades of married life, etc.). Thus geriatric mental health professionals may provide services in a range of contexts, from working with older adults living in their own homes, to consulting with residents of a senior-citizen apartment complex, to working with residents in a continuing-care retirement community, to providing services to residents in an assisted living building, to consulting in a nursing home or in a hospice setting. In addition to these varied residential settings, geriatric mental health professionals may find themselves working in a range of treatment settings (e.g., a hospital's social services department; the information and referral division of the local area agency on aging; the adult protective services section of a county social services agency). Each setting represents a different set of challenges for the clinician – challenges of consultation and collaboration with other disciplines, challenges of reimbursement, challenges of different patterns of comorbidity of physical and mental disorders, and challenges of different points of leverage (e.g., individual psychotherapy, staff training, or psychoeducational program development) (see box 12.1).

In chapter 11 we discussed one setting, nursing homes, in much more detail. Here, however, we want to consider the emerging self-definition of standards of care being developed by psychologists who focus on nursing-home care. Consider, for example, the proposed Standards of Care developed by the network of Psychologists in Long Term Care (see table 12.3a) (PLTC, 1997). These standards were developed with several audiences in mind: psychologists who might consider working in nursing homes; nursing-home administrators and staff who need help in choosing an appropriate mental health practitioner; family members who are seeking help for an older resident. (A slightly revised version of the standards can be found in Lichtenberg et al., 1998).

12.1   The mental health challenges of public housing

Public housing as a mental health treatment setting? It may be more appropriate than you think. Approximately 600,000 older adults live in public housing that accommodates low-income elderly. A recent study (Rabins, et al., 1996) suggests that the rates of mental illness are substantial among this group of older adults: a 58 percent lifetime prevalence of psychiatric disorders; a one-month prevalence of 28 percent. The most common current disorders were cognitive disorders (11 percent), mood disorders (8 percent), psychotic disorders (5 percent), and substance abuse or dependence (4 percent).

Rabins and his colleagues point out that public housing may differentially attract older adults who are at risk following deinstitutionalization. Lacking social and economic resources, these older adults may turn to settings that give priority to those without resources. Unfortunately, public housing sites rarely provide adequate mental health outreach and treatment. One potential approach might focus on staff training to enable public housing staff who have daily contact with the residents to identify older adults who are at risk and in need of additional mental health consultation.

Several aspects of the standards are important: first, there is a clear statement of who is qualified to provide services (an attempt by the profession to set expectations and standards); second, the major activities of assessment and treatment are clearly highlighted – these are the domains of expertise you can expect from a geropsychologist in nursing homes; third, the links to potential funding sources are clear (a topic we consider in a later section); and, finally, the importance of effective collaborations with other disciplines is highlighted.

These elements – qualifications, activities, funding patterns, interdisciplinary interdependence – are all aspects of another answer to Dr B's simple question *"What do I need to know?"* The answer will vary depending upon the setting. Whatever the setting, however, the mental health practitioner needs to know a range of assessment and intervention skills, current reimbursement policies, and how to work effectively with other disciplines.

Interdisciplinary Collaboration: What Can You Expect from Others and What Can They Expect from You?

Think about the following case example:

Table 12.3a Standards for psychological services in long-term care facilities

I. **Providers**
    A. Psychologists are graduates of a doctoral program in psychology and are licensed in their state of practice.
    B. There are three categories of psychologists who practice in long-term care:
        1) psychologists who are trained, experienced, and competent in geropsychology service provision★
        2) psychologists who have formal training in geropsychology but are not yet experienced and are supervised by an experienced and competent geropsychologist (Category 1 above)★
        3) psychologists who are actively obtaining continuing education in geropsychology and are supervised by an experienced and competent geropsychologist (Category 1 above)★

    ★*Note*: For further discussion of these issues, see the draft report of the APA Interdivisional Task Force on Qualifications for Practice in Clinical and Applied Geropsychology, 1996, Section II (Clinical Geropsychology) of Division 12 (Clinical Psychology) and
    Division 20 (Adult Development and Aging), American Psychological Association. Category 1 includes psychologists who have either a generalist or a specialist level of training in clinical geropsychology, as these levels are defined in the draft report.

II. **Referral for psychological services**
    A. Residents in long-term care facilities who are appropriate for psychological services exhibit behavioral, cognitive, or emotional disturbance. Examples of behaviors that may trigger referral include cognitive decline, excessive crying, withdrawal from social contact or other signs of depression, personality changes (e.g., excessively demanding behavior), aggressive or combative behavior, inappropriate sexual behavior, or psychotic behavior. Psychologists encourage the referral source to be as specific as possible about the presenting problem. Standing or "prn" orders for psychological services are discouraged.
    B. In addition to direct assessment and treatment of patients referred for psychological services, psychologists may also provide staff consultation and advisement, staff training and education, family consultation and advisement, design and implementation of preventive screening and other institutional programs, environmental assessment, behavioral analysis and design of behavioral management programs, and other services.
    Psychologists are aware that many of these latter services may not be third-party reimbursable.

Table 12.3a   continued

III. Assessment

A. In order to provide cost-effective and quality treatment, psychologists assess the cognitive, emotional and behavioral functioning of their patients. Assessment procedures may include:

1) assessment of mental status through clinical interviews, mental status questionnaires, and information obtained from family, staff, or other informants

2) psychological testing, including assessments of personality, emotional functioning, and psychopathology, using measures or instruments consistent with current standard professional practice★

3) neurobehavioral testing, which serves to determine cognitive strengths and weaknesses, memory capacities, and specific neuropsychological impairments. Such testing may include assessments of attentional, language, memory, visuo-spatial, and abstract reasoning skills. Testing time may be brief. Reasons for neurobehavioral testing may include: resolving diagnostic ambiguities (e.g., whether dementia or depression or both are present), assessing sudden cognitive declines or changes (e.g., whether delirium is present), profiling cognitive strengths and weaknesses (e.g., for treatment planning), determining the level of care needed for a patient, planning a program of rehabilitation, and determining competency

4) functional assessments, which address a range of behaviors relevant to overall daily functioning, including self-care skills and everyday living skills. Functional assessments often augment personality, mental status, and neurobehavioral assessments

5) behavioral observation and analysis, which includes the systematic observation and recording of behavior and stimulus-response and response-reinforcement contingencies, in order to design behavioral interventions to increase the frequency of positive behaviors and decrease the frequency of negative behaviors.

★*Note*: See, for example, the Geropsychology Assessment Resource Guide, 1996 revision. National Technical Information Service, US Department of Commerce, 5285 Port Royal Road, Springfield, VA 22161. Request publication #PB96-144365.

B. Psychologists are aware of their responsibility, as an integral part of an interdisciplinary team, to work together with their medical and pharmaceutical colleagues to develop and implement an integrated plan of service delivery. Psychologists encourage appropriate medical and physical examinations, including laboratory tests and radiological studies, to rule out reversible cause of functional impairment, such as medically treatable illnesses.

Table 12.3a   continued

IV. Treatment

A. Treatment plan:
   1) Each patient has an individual treatment plan which is based on the specific findings of a psychological assessment and which addresses the referral question.
   2) The treatment plan includes a diagnosis and specific therapeutic modalities to achieve short-term and long-term goals.
   3) When treatment frequency deviates from standard practice it is justified in the treatment plan.
   4) Changes in clinical status are reflected by changes in the treatment plan.

B. Treatment process:
   1) Treatments are chosen which best address each patient's diagnosis and presenting symptoms.
   2) Treatment modalities may include, separately or in conjunction, individual psychotherapy, behavior therapy and behavior modification, group psychotherapy, and family psychotherapy.
   3) Treatments are empirically informed and reflect current standards of geropsychological practice.
   4) Psychologists are aware that most third-party reimbursement requires the full duration of treatment sessions to be spent in face-to-face contact with the patient and/or the patient's family, and that other important and necessary treatment-related time, such as consultation with staff, may not be third-party reimbursable.
   5) Psychologists are aware of their responsibility to spend adequate time in face-to-face treatment with each patient and to consult and coordinate with the interdisciplinary team, and do not attempt to treat an excessive and inordinate number of patients in a single day.
   6) Treatment continues when emotional, cognitive, or behavioral progress toward a goal can be demonstrated. When no such progress can be demonstrated, but the patient appears to benefit from a social visit, appropriate recommendations for friendly visitors, activities, etc., are made.
   7) When treatment is ended, termination is conducted in an orderly manner; the patient is prepared and given appropriate notice, and issues involving termination are addressed.

C. Outcomes:
   1) Patient progress toward stated goals is regularly monitored and documented to determine if treatment is effective, and whether it should be continued, modified, or terminated. Such monitoring is done at least every three months.

Table 12.3a continued

    2) Treatment outcomes can be measured in multiple domains, including affective, cognitive, or behavioral domains.

    3) Positive treatment outcomes can include stabilization of mental and behavioral disorder where decline would be expected in the absence of treatment. However, when treatment for such a patient is long term, attempts are made to decrease the frequency of service. If the patient responds with a worsening of symptoms then treatment can be reinitiated.

D. Documentation:

    1) Psychologists provide timely and clear documentation of each patient's diagnosis, treatment plan, progress, and outcome in accordance with current ethical and legal standards.

Source: PLTC, 1997.

You get a call from a nursing home. Alyce's daughter wants to fill out a living will for her mother. She is very clear that she wants "no heroic measures" taken to extend her mother's life. The question is simple: Who should be able to decide on the content of the living will – Alyce or her daughter?

You agree to meet with the daughter, with the staff, and with the medical director. In addition, you ask for permission to talk with Alyce's lawyer, to verify that she did not have a living will already in place.

In some ways this is an easy example. You are being called upon for an assessment, a traditional part of the geriatric mental health expertise. On the other hand, to assess Alyce's capacity for decision-making effectively you must consult with nurses, nurses' aides, physicians, nursing-home administrators, and lawyers. To do so, you must appreciate both the skills and expertise that each discipline brings to this task. You must also appreciate what their expectations are of you as a mental health professional.

Each profession approaches the tasks of assessment and intervention with distinct assumptions about the logic of assessment, the appropriate focus of professional efforts, the locus of responsibility, and the pace of action in gerontological intervention (Qualls & Czirr, 1988). There is a continuum of problem definition underlying the logic of assessment for different professions. Some professions, for example medicine, focus on ruling out problems. The goal is systematically to eliminate hypotheses until a single problem and solution are identified. Other professions (e.g., psychology, social work) emphasize "ruling in" problems, encompassing a comprehensive view of the problem, factors contributing to it, and interacting elements that may affect the outcome of assessment and intervention.

The different professions also emphasize different types of intervention. For example, physicians may focus on acute care, physical symptoms, and physiological treatments. Other professions (e.g., nursing, social work, psychology) might emphasize a functional view, assessing the social and daily consequences of impairment and including these elements in a definition of success or failure for intervention.

Assumptions regarding the responsibility for change also differentiate the professions. For example, when faced with a mental health problem, the traditionally trained physician may view his or her role as the medical expert who analyzes the problem and provides direct orders for the patient to follow. Other professionals might see their role as a collaborative consultant, working with the patient to help develop and implement treatment options.

Finally, the professions may differ in their expectations regarding the pace of change. In some settings (e.g., emergency rooms, acute care hospitals, etc.) immediate action is essential. In other settings (e.g., continuing care retirement communities) there may be a premium on taking a longer view, setting expectations for gradual change and improvement at a pace that the older adult can tolerate.

In collaborating on Alyce's case, you may strive for agreement on three aspects of interdisciplinary or multidisciplinary collaboration: the focus of the group's attention; expectations regarding team decision-making; and beliefs about interdisciplinary interdependence (Qualls & Czirr, 1988).

Discussion of living wills could focus on several sources of information and on several levels of analysis. For example, in considering Alyce's case, the team might concentrate on Alyce's condition, her capacity for decision-making, her personal preferences and values. On the other hand they might use Alyce's situation as a chance to review the institution's stance on living wills, do-not-resuscitate orders, and the responsibility for assuring that these policies are carried out. As you begin the consultation around Alyce's situation, it will be important to clarify for yourself and for all other participants what is the most appropriate focus for the discussion: Alyce's case, institutional policy, or some combination of the two.

Similarly, as you begin meeting with the various members of the care team, it is important to clarify the setting's expectations about decision-making. Is this a setting in which there is a single source for treatment decisions? If so, who is that person and what role will you play in informing that decision-maker? Or is this a setting that operates on a consensus model, requiring agreement among all team members before proceeding? If so, who assures that all of the relevant people are consulted? Again, what would your role be in the consensus development process?

Finally, it is important to clarify each participant's assumption regarding interdisciplinary interdependence. For example, does Alyce's lawyer assume that any decisions regarding living wills are up to her alone, with no need for consultation with geriatric mental health specialists? Do the medical director and nursing staff assume that they will make the end-of-life decisions, without consultation with Alyce's lawyer or minister? Is this institution affiliated with a religious organization that defines the underlying values and explicit choices regarding end-of-life treatment? Is there an institutional ethics board, with its own mandate regarding how these decisions must be made? These assumptions shape the type of contribution you can make to solving Alyce's daughter's question.

Thus another way emerges in which to answer "*What do I need to know?*": you need to know the opportunities, expectations, and limits of interdisciplinary collaboration in the setting.

Ethical issues

Another aspect of geriatric practice is a concern for a range of ethical issues. As an illustration, consider the standards for working in nursing homes of the network of Psychologists in Long Term Care (see table 12.3b). Note that the ethical issues highlighted here are a function of the institutional setting itself. While confidentiality and privacy concerns are constants across many service settings, the particular challenges to confidentiality and privacy vary in significant ways in the institution. Take the example of Alyce's ability to exercise

Table 12.3b Standards for psychological services in long-term care facilities, continued

---

V. Ethical issues★
    A. Informed consent:
        1) Informed consent decisions are based on the legal competency of the patient to make informed decisions regarding health care, knowledge of the long-term care setting, the cognitive ability of the patient, the availability of family members, and the acuity of the psychological condition needing treatment.
            a) For competent persons without significant cognitive impairment, before psychological services are rendered, the psychologist provides to the patient a clear statement of the condition warranting psychological services, what services are to be rendered, and the possible consequences of accepting or refusing services.

Table 12.3b   continued

b) For patients declared legally incompetent, the psychologist provides to the guardian a clear statement of the condition warranting psychological services, what services are to be rendered, and the possible consequences of accepting or refusing services. Although informed consent must be given by the guardian, the psychologist also attempts to help the patient understand the rationale for treatment (within the limits of the patient's cognitive abilities).

c) For patients with significant cognitive impairment who are deemed to be without the capacity to understand the rationale for treatment but who have not been declared legally incompetent, the psychologist identifies the responsible party and provides the rationale for treatment to the designated legally responsible party. The psychologist also attempts to help the patient understand the rationale for treatment.

d) Consent for services is not required if the patient is considered dangerous to self or others (as defined by applicable state law).

2) Psychologists who are part of a staff institutional team, privileged by the institution to provide services, and covered by a general institutional consent do not need to get a separate informed consent before implementing treatment. Consulting psychologists who are not part of the staff institutional treatment team must get a separate informed consent as above before services are provided.

B. Confidentiality:

1) Patients in long-term care facilities have the same right to confidentiality regarding psychological services as all other patients, and information about this right to confidentiality as well as its limits is offered to the patient, guardian, or responsible party as part of the informed consent process prior to service delivery.

2) Psychologists are aware of limits to confidentiality and make every effort to reconcile these limits with the rights of their patients.

a) Although competent patients, guardians, or responsible parties have rights concerning what information is given to the staff in a long-term care facility, these rights do not extend to information which is deemed critical to protecting the resident from harming self or others.

b) Confidentiality standards must be consistent with the reporting/charting regulations within which the facility must operate. If a conflict arises, the psychologist strives to work with the facility to achieve maximum consistency.

Table 12.3b   continued

c) Confidentiality standards should allow for the demands of the psychologist's role as an active member of an institutional treatment team who shares pertinent information with other health professionals.

C. Privacy:

1) Psychologists try to ensure that psychological services are provided in the most private manner possible.

2) Psychologists often need to be creative in meeting the privacy standard. Some long-term care facilities offer a private consulting room for psychologists to provide services but many do not. When no consulting room is available or the patient is bedridden, services may be provided at bedside. If the patient is in a non-private room, the psychologist may request that the roommate leave until the session is over and then close the door. If the roommate is also bedridden or refuses to leave the room, the session may be conducted (with the roommate's consent) by drawing the curtain around the bed to provide some privacy. Nursing staff are notified so that they know where the patient can be found and so that they do not interrupt the session.

3) Psychologists are aware of facility/state/federal regulations regarding treatment privacy.

4) Patients are consulted regarding their comfort with privacy arrangements prior to a treatment session, and every effort is made to accommodate their wishes.

D. Conflict of interest:

1) Psychologists self-refer only if a need for psychological services is identified and members of the interdisciplinary treatment team are made aware of the need for services.

2) Psychologists are aware that at times the interests of the facility and the patient may not coincide, and make every effort to resolve the conflict in the best interests of the patient.

3) Psychologists try to assure the patients receive proper continuity of care. If psychological services are interrupted due to payment issues, institutional barriers, or other non-clinical reasons, the psychologist follows accepted professional standards regarding proper therapeutic closure and transfer of care via referral.

4) Psychologists are aware of the rules and regulations governing third-party reimbursement and follow them when billing for reimbursable services, but patient-care decisions are guided by the best interests of the patient and are not dominated by reimbursement considerations. When reimbursement regulations are felt to be in need of revision, psychologists attempt to secure appropriate changes from state and federal agencies and private insurers.

Table 12.3b   continued

E. Advocacy:
    1) Psychologists advocate for the appropriate use of mental health
        services to reduce excess disability and improve quality of life.
    2) When mental health services are not being used or are being used
        inappropriately, psychologists strive to educate other care providers
        to improve the delivery of care consistent with a bio-psycho-social
        approach to the assessment and treatment of older adults.

    Note: In addition to the standards presented here, psychologists follow the
    APA Ethics Code (American Psychological Association, 1992). *Ethical prin-
    ciples of psychologists and code of conduct*. Washington, DC: Author; also
    published in *American Psychologist*, 47, 1597–1611.

Source: PTLC, 1997.

a living will. Who is your client in this consultation: Alyce, her daughter, the
nursing home? Will your answer affect your view of the confidentiality of the
information you receive from Alyce?

Another ethical issue is perhaps the most basic one of all: every mental
health profession requires that its members practice within the limits of their
expertise. Thus, for psychologists, the American Psychological Association's
code of ethics clearly states that psychologists must not practice outside their
areas of expertise. If psychologists want to expand their areas of expertise,
they could hire a supervisor to help develop additional experience (Qualls,
1998). Thus another answer to Dr B's phone call from the beginning of this
chapter is a simple one: "*What do you need to know?*" You need to know your
own profession's code of ethics and that you are ethically bound to practice
within your scope of expertise.

Funding: Who Will Pay the Bills?

The costs of mental health care clearly warrant discussion. For example, in
1990 approximately $54 billion was spent on mental health and substance
abuse treatment in the United States (Frank et al., 1994), roughly 10 percent
of all personal health expenditures (Arons et al., 1994). The largest portion
(79 percent) was spent on mental health services. Rice et al. (1992) have
assessed costs by age and gender. They found that in 1985 $17.3 billion of
core costs (direct costs plus indirect morbidity and mortality costs) were for
persons aged 65 and older, with more than two-thirds attributable to costs for

women over the age of 65. Therefore those concerned with mental health care for older adults inevitably will be affected by themes of health-care cost containment.

Many mental health professionals work in settings or systems that include geriatric mental health expertise on their staff as an element of first-rate quality of care (e.g., the Veterans Administration system; Jewish Homes for the Aged; senior-citizen housing complexes; some nursing homes). Most mental health professionals, however, find themselves working within two major systems: a fee-for-service market and a managed-care market. The fee-for-service approach allows unrestricted access to providers and little, if any, monitoring of the appropriateness of the treatment or its effectiveness. In contrast, managed-care approaches focus on limiting both access and the intensity of service use.

The term "managed care" encompasses a variety of approaches that have one underlying element in common: a single organization is responsible for both the payment and the delivery of care (Kane & Friedman, 1996). Mental health care for older adults is increasingly affected by managed-care approaches for health care in general. Thus managed-care approaches affect the types of services provided (by including or excluding certain procedures), the length of service provision (by placing a cap on the total number of service sessions that can be used in a specified time), and who can be a service provider for older adults (by limiting service providers to certified members of the managed-care panel of providers).

Most mental health practitioners' main contact with mental health care funding comes at a local level. Here we will use the United States' experience, but the general lessons apply to other developed countries as well. In the United Kingdom, for example, the 1990 National Health Service and Community Care Act aimed at changing the provision and financing of health and social care, including mental health care (Kavanagh & Knapp, 1995).

For most practitioners there are three major players in managed mental health care: Medicare, the government program for health care for older adults; Medicaid, the government program for health care for indigent citizens; and private insurers. Edmunds and her colleagues (1997) have summarized the differences between the public and private sectors in mental health care (see table 12.4).

Most practitioners must work within both sectors. In addition, most older adults have a combination of public and private coverage. For example, more than 60 percent of older adults have private insurance to supplement Medicare coverage (Chollet, 1989) through "Medigap" policies, private insurance plans that fill in the gaps left by Medicare coverage, or through insurance provided by a former employer.

Table 12.4 Comparision of public and private sectors of care in mental health

Characteristics	Public-sector mental health care	Private-sector mental health care
Population served	Mostly uninsured, emphasis on the seriously mentally ill	Those with coverage
Funding of care	State general funds, Medicaid and Medicare revenues, local and other funds	Insurance premiums
Locus of treatment responsibility	Local authority (e.g., county government), community mental health center	Insurance plan and/or provider
Predominant services	Case management, medications, housing support, rehabilitation, crisis intervention, and hospitalization	Outpatient therapy, medications, and hospitalization

Source: Edmunds et al., 1997, p. 138.

Table 12.5 Medicare vs. Medicaid

Medicare	Medicaid
Federal health insurance for the elderly and disabled	Federal/state shared funding for medical services to the indigent
Anyone eligible for social security is entitled to Medicare	Welfare-based eligibility
Uniform federal criteria nationwide	Federal criterion of "medical necessity" asdefined by the states
Administered by the federal government (DHHS/HCFA)	Administered by the states
	Coverage of mental health "optional"

The basic elements of the Medicare and Medicaid programs are outlined in table 12.5. The programs differ in terms of target groups, eligibility criteria, uniformity of program elements, and administrative features. The legislative elements may differ across the programs, but both Medicare and Medicaid share a division among three levels of responsibility: legislative, regulatory, and implementation (see table 12.6).

Table 12.6   Medicare: an example of levels of policy and process

---

Legislative level
Congress:
- passes statutes of general applicability
- e.g., psychologists may be reimbursed as independent practitioners.

Regulatory level
US Department of Health and Human Services Health Care Financing Administration (HCFA):
- implements statutes according to congressional intent through regulation and instructions
- e.g., how reimbursed, payment level methodology.

Implementation level
Local Medicare carriers: (Blue Cross, Aetna, etc.)
- act as HCFA's fiscal agents in processing claims and paying practitioners
- set payment rates pursuant to HCFA criteria
- set implementation criteria for processing claims (e.g., define what documents medical necessity).

Most practitioners become acquainted with federal or private insurers at the implementation level. The local insurance carriers determine who can provide services, which service will be covered, and the basic fee structure for those services.

Increasingly, the Medicaid and Medicare programs are relying upon managed-care approaches for provision of care. For example, between 1991 and 1995 there was a 217 percent increase in the percentage of Medicaid enrollees and a 60 percent increase in the percentage of Medicare enrollees covered by managed care. Recent estimates suggest an even more important role for managed care in the coming years (see figure 12.2).

A recent summary of the current situation seems apt for both the United States and the United Kingdom: "Managed mental health care: can't live with it and can't live without it" (Eisdorfer, 1995). Carl Eisdorfer, who is both a clinical psychologist and a psychiatrist, provided an insightful summary of the impact, thus far, of managed care on mental health services for older adults:

> *The focus of managed care has been on managing acute medical care with secondary concerns about mental health care and long-term care. What is troublesome about this is not the continued and unjustified discriminatory*

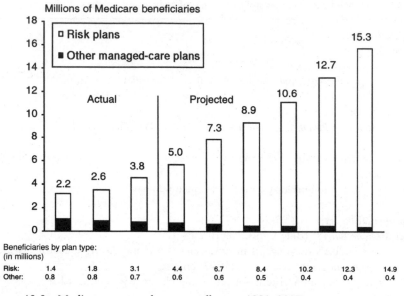

Figure 12.2   Medicare managed–care enrollment, 1991–2007
Source: Kaiser Medicare Policy Project, 1997, p. 63.

reimbursement for mental health services and the lack of reimbursement for long-
term care. It is the limited success in educating policy makers about how to create
a system of integrated care and the lack of incentives to integrate mental health
care into primary and chronic care. This has negative implications for all age
groups but it places older persons at perhaps the highest risk for inadequate care.
. . . Some programs have controlled access to outpatient care, driving patients
to more costly inpatient care as untreated problems become more severe. These
inpatient care costs have been controlled by hospital admissions and length of
stay limits. Outpatient care costs have also been controlled by requiring utiliza-
tion review of services, by efforts to employ the least costly providers (shifting
from psychiatrist to psychologist to social worker), by limiting psychotherapy to
shorter or crisis-focused treatment, and recently by using case managers who refer
to clinical textbooks designed to make more efficient use of diagnostic and
treatment protocols. (Eisdorfer, 1995, pp. 5–6)

As Eisdorfer implies, regulatory and implementation decisions affect how
geriatric clinicians can work, the roles and responsibilities they can undertake,
and the fees and funding that they can count on.

Thus another answer to Dr B's simple question *"What do I need to know?"*

You must be knowledgeable about current legislative and regulatory developments and how they are being implemented by your local carrier.

Social Policy Initiatives that Affect Geriatric Mental Health Care: The Example of Decision-Making Capacity

Geriatric mental health clinicians are also affected by social policy initiatives that focus attention on the well-being and functioning of older adults. Consider, again, the case of Alyce's daughter, who wants to establish and implement a living will. Her request represents an intersection of public policy and individual functioning: the area of decision-making capacity (Smyer, 1993). For example, in the United States, the theme of patients' rights to involvement in health-care decision-making is a major focus of the portions of the Patient Self-Determination Act that were implemented in December 1991 (American Bar Association, 1991). Under this act, institutions that receive Medicare or Medicaid funding must provide written information to each resident or patient regarding the "right to accept or refuse medical or surgical treatment and [the] right to formulate advanced directives."

Similarly, as pointed out in chapter 11, the Nursing Home Reform Act of 1987 was an attempt to improve the quality of nursing-home care through regulatory reform. It also included several residents' rights provisions, among them the right to choose a personal physician, to be informed in advance about care, to participate in care planning, to self-administer drugs, and to refuse treatment. While initial implementation of the Nursing Home Reform Act was marked by judicial and regulatory discussion about the limits of residents' rights, the intent is clear: to the fullest extent possible, nursing-home residents are to be involved in health-care decision-making.

The developments reflect a larger trend in legal issues that has transformed the underlying assumptions equating advanced age with incompetence (Anderer, 1990; Smyer, 1993). Recent statutes have replaced an age-based definition of incompetence with three key components: 1) the presence of disorders or disabilities; 2) decision-making/communicating impairment; and 3) functional impairment. Sabatino (1996) has noted that similar criteria are incorporated in the new Uniform Health Care Decisions Act, emphasizing the person's capacity to make decisions.

As the American Bar Association has outlined (American Bar Association,

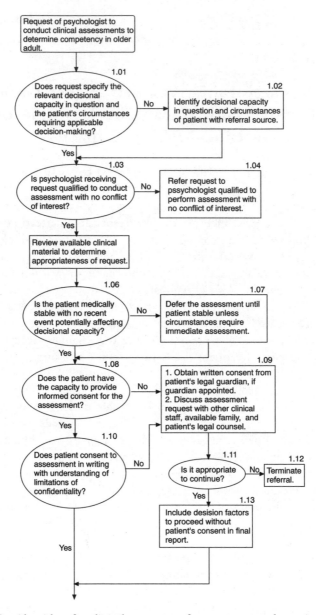

Figure 12.3 Algorithm for clinical assessment for competency determination of the older adult: a practice guideline for psychologists

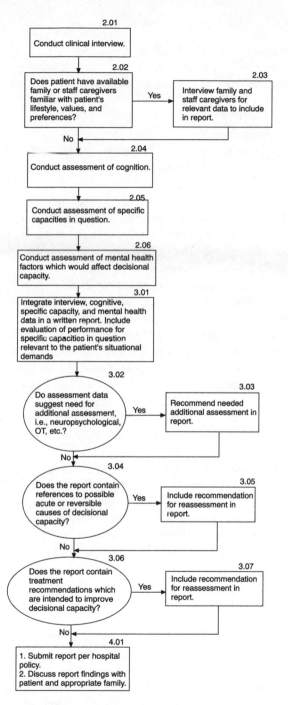

Figure 12.3 continued
Source: Department of Veterans Affairs, 1997.

1991), decision-making capacity requires three elements: 1) possession
of a set of values and goals; 2) the ability to communicate and to
understand information; and 3) the ability to reason and deliberate about
one's choices.

*Following up the request from Alyce's daughter, you arrange to meet with Alyce
at the nursing home the next day. You are preparing your assessment kit to take
to the nursing home. What will you take?*

Assessment of older adults' changing abilities is a key element in the legal and
clinical process (Sabatino, 1996). Unfortunately, a recent summary still seems
apt: "Present procedures to assess decisional capacity are seriously flawed"
(Hofland & David, 1990, p. 92). Because of our understanding of aging and
mental disorders and assessment approaches, this is an area in which geriatric
mental health practitioners can have an important impact.

What are your responsibilities to Alyce? Who will give consent if you're
not sure that she's competent? The complexity of these issues is reflected in
a proposed algorithm for clinical assessment of decision-making capacity,
developed for psychologists who work in the Veterans Administration system
(Department of Veterans Affairs, 1997) (see figure 12.3). Note that the
algorithm starts with clarifying questions: Do we understand the decision-
making issue involved? Are you qualified to undertake this assessment without a conflict of interest? The algorithm then focuses attention on the
physical and mental health status of the older adult, the comorbidities we
have discussed earlier.

In addition, our attention is drawn to the underlying capacity for informed consent. Several investigators have suggested that decision-making
capacity can be assessed at three levels: a) awareness and assent; b) understanding of alternatives and choice; and c) appreciation of consequences and
rationality (Drane, 1984; Grisso, 1994; Appelbaum et al., 1987). Only after
these steps does the fuller assessment begin. In that process, the traditional
domains of geriatric assessment are in focus.

Throughout, however, the clinician interacts with several key participants:
the patient; the patient's family members; staff members; other health care
providers; and, if necessary, lawyers.

In summary, the domain of decision-making capacity in older adults
reflects several general elements that are important for geriatric clinicians:
first, being aware that many target problems lie at the intersection of individual functioning and public policy contexts; second, building a collaboration that draws upon both research and clinical expertise; and, third,
developing screening assessments that will allow us better to define the

conditions under which we need advanced, specialized assessment procedures.

Conclusion

In this chapter we have emphasized that several elements affect geriatric mental health practice. Each profession's self-definition and self-expectation set a standard for credentials, quality of care, and expected ranges of activities in assessment and intervention. In addition, funding schemes affect the roles that clinicians can play, the clients they can see, the services they can provide, and the fees they can charge. Finally, social policy initiatives (e.g., the recent emphasis on patients' rights to be involved in decision-making) affect geriatric practice both directly and indirectly. In summary, a short answer to Dr B's question *"What do I need to know?"*: Lots.

Epilogue

... to make an end is to make a beginning.
The end is where we start from.
T. S. Eliot, *Four Quartets*, "Little Gidding"

In this book we have tried to provide a framework for assessing effective mental health treatments for older adults. In doing so, we have provided a snapshot of theoretical and practice concepts at the end of the twentieth century. Effective geriatric intervention will continue to evolve as a function of three elements: the changing characteristics of cohorts of elderly in the future; developments in the basic understanding of the processes that affect geriatric mental health; and alterations in the public policy contexts that affect the provision of mental health services for older adults.

Today's elderly represent a unique intersection of individual and historical time. There are some indications that tomorrow's elderly may arrive in later life with different patterns of mental health and illness. For example, some have suggested that today's younger and middle-aged adults have higher rates of depression than the current elderly did at a comparable point in their lives (e.g., Zarate & Tohen, 1996). In addition, the elderly of the future may arrive in later life with increased experience with and increased expectations regarding mental health treatment: they may rely more upon mental health services, thereby demanding greater access and efficacy from the mental health system. Finally, tomorrow's elderly will arrive in later life with a different set of experiences of historical and personal life stresses. Together, these patterns may alter the rates and presentation of mental disorders in the future.

While the elderly of the future will change, so will our understanding of three areas that shape the development and implementation of mental health services for older adults: gerontology; mental illness; and effective mental health treatment. Study of the basic processes of aging continue to uncover a more differentiated view of the processes and prospects of normal aging (e.g., Task Force on Aging Research, 1995). At the same time, inquiry regarding the precursors of mental illness in later life remains an important part of the scientific agenda (e.g., Smyer, 1995b). These investigations of the processes of aging and mental illness will be accompanied by continued scrutiny of the most effective treatment approaches for older adults and their families. Increasingly, these will involve interdisciplinary collaboration. In short, the knowledge base for effective practice will continue to evolve.

Changes in the elderly themselves and in our understanding of the processes of aging will force changes in the public policies that affect geriatric mental health practice. For example, current debates regarding the fiscal health of Medicare, Medicaid, and social security will shape the scope and costs of mental health services for older adults in the future, as well as access to those services. For example, we may see a shift from an age-based set of policies to an arrangement that focuses on need or insuring against the contingencies of later life (Hudson, 1993). We may also see an increase in funding for interdisciplinary collaboration to serve older adults more effectively.

The congressionally mandated Task Force on Aging Research summarized the prospects:

> *Science is currently engaged in the search for answers to questions about aging – in body and mind, in family and work, in politics and society. These answers would transform our lives and our lifestyles. They would add years, health, abilities, accomplishments, relationships, and meaning to life and aging. From biology to behavioral science, we stand at the threshold of discovery. (Task Force on Aging Research, 1995, p. iii)*

Whatever the emerging policy consensus, the provision of geriatric mental health services will be a function of that policy context, along with the characteristics of the elderly of the future and the evolving understanding of aging and mental health. This book provides a good foundation for treatment today and the unfolding of treatment options in the future.

References

Acierno, R., Hersen, M., & Van Hasselt, V. B. (1996). Anxiety-based disorders. In M. Hersen & V. B. Van Hasselt (eds), *Psychological treatment of older adults* (pp. 149–80). New York: Plenum.

Advisory Panel on Alzheimer's Disease (1993). *Fourth report of the Advisory Panel on Alzheimer's Disease, 1992* (NIH Publication no. 93-3520). Washington, DC: US Government Printing Office.

Albert, M. (1988). Assessment of cognitive dysfunction. In M. S. Albert & M. B. Moss (eds), *Geriatric neuropsychology* (pp. 57–81). New York: Guilford Press.

Aldwin, C., Folkman, S., Coyne, J., Schaefer, C., & Lazarus, R. S. (1980). The ways of coping scale: a process approach. Paper presented at the annual meeting of the American Psychological Association, Montreal, Quebec, Canada.

Aldwin, C. M. (1991). Does age affect the stress and coping process? Implications of age differences in perceived control. *Journals of Gerontology*, 46 (4), 174–80.

Aldwin, C. M. (1994). *Stress, coping, and development: an integrative perspective.* New York: Guilford Press.

Almeida, O. P., Förstl, H., Howard, R., & David, A. S. (1993). Unilateral auditory hallucinations. *British Journal of Psychiatry*, 162, 262–4.

Almeida, O. P., Howard, R. J., Levy, R., & David, A. (1995). Psychotic states arising in late life (late paraphrenia): the role of risk factors. *British Journal of Psychiatry*, 166, 215–28.

American Bar Association (ABA) (1991). *Patient Self-Determination Act: state law guide.* Washington, DC: ABA Commission on Legal Problems of the Elderly.

American Psychiatric Association (1994). *DSMIV: diagnostic and statistical manual of mental disorders*, 4th edn. Washington, DC: American Psychiatric Association.

Anderer, S. (1990). *Determining competency in guardianship proceedings.* Washington, DC: American Bar Association.

Andersen, B. L., Kiecolt-Glaser, J. K., & Glaser, R. (1994). A biobehavioral model of cancer stress and disease course. *American Psychologist*, 49 (5), 389–404.

Anderson, S. A., Russell, C. S., & Schumm, W. A. (1983). Perceived marital quality and family life-cycle categories: a further analysis. *Journal of Marriage and the Family*, 45, 127–39.

Aneshensel, C. S., Pearlin, L. I., Mullan, J. T., Zarit, S. H., & Whitlatch, C. J. (1995). *Profiles in caregiving: the unexpected career.* San Diego: Academic Press.

Annon, J. F. (1975). *The behavioral treatment of sexual problems*. Honolulu: Enabling Systems.

Antonucci, T. C., & Akiyama, H. (1995). Convoys of social relations: family and friendships within the lifespan context. In R. Blieszner & V. H. Bedford (eds), *Handbook on aging and the family* (pp. 355–71). Westport, CT: Greenwood Press.

Apfel, R., & Handel, M. (1996). Women with long-term mental illness: a different voice. In S. M. Soreff (ed.), *Handbook for the treatment of the seriously mentally ill* (pp. 325–49). Seattle: Hogrefe & Huber.

Applebaum, P. S., Lidz, C. W., & Meisel, A. (1987). *Informed consent: legal theory and clinical practice*. New York: Oxford University Press.

Arean, P. A., Perri, M. G., Nezu, A. M., Schein, R. L., Christopher, F., & Joseph, T. X. (1993). Comparative effectiveness of social problem-solving therapy and reminiscence therapy as treatments for depression in older adults. *Journal of Consulting and Clinical Psychology*, 61, 1003–10.

Arons, B. S., Frank, R. G., Goldman, H. H., McGuire, T. G., & Stephens, S. (1994). Mental health and substance abuse coverage. *Health Affairs*, 13 (1), 192–205.

Atkinson, R. M., Ganzini, L., & Bernstein, M. J. (1992). Alcohol and substance-use disorders in the elderly. In J. E. Birren, R. B. Sloane, & G. D. Cohen (eds), *Handbook of mental health and aging*, 2nd edn (pp. 515–55). San Diego: Academic Press.

Avorn, J., Soumerai, S. B., Everitt, D. E., & Ross, D. D. (1992). A randomized trial of a program to reduce the use of psychoactive drugs in nursing homes. *New England Journal of Medicine*, 327, 168–73.

Baker, R. (1982). *Growing up*. New York: New American Library.

Baltes, M. (1988). The etiology and maintenance of dependency in the elderly: three phases of operant research. *Behavior Therapy*, 19, 301–20.

Baltes, M. M., & Barton, E. M. (1979). Behavioral analysis of aging: a review of the operant model and research. *International Journal of Behavioral Development*, 2 (3), 297–320.

Baltes, M. M., & Reisenzein, R. (1986). The social world in long term care institutions: psychological control toward dependency? In M. M. Baltes & P. B. Baltes (eds), *The psychology of control and aging* (pp. 315–43). Hillsdale, NJ: Lawrence Erlbaum.

Baltes, P. B., & Baltes, M. M. (1990a). Selective optimization with compensation. In P. B. Baltes & M. M. Baltes (eds), *Successful aging: perspectives from the behavioral sciences* (pp. 1–34). New York: Cambridge University Press.

Baltes, P. B., & Baltes, M. M. (1990b). *Successful aging: perspectives from the behavioral sciences*. New York: Cambridge University Press.

Baltes, P. B., Reese, H. W., & Lipsitt, L. P. (1980). Life-span developmental psychology. *Annual Review of Psychology*, 31, 65–110.

Bandura, A. (1977). Self-efficacy: toward a unifying theory of behavioral change. *Psychological Review*, 84, 191–215.

Banner, C. (1992). Recent insights into the biology of Alzheimer's disease. *Generations*, 16 (4), 31–4.

Bartels, S. J. (1989). Organic mental disorder: when to suspect medical illness as a cause of psychiatric symptoms. In J. M. Ellison (ed.), *Psychopharmacology: a primer for the psychotherapist.* Chicago: Year Book Medical Publishers.

Bartels, S. J., & Drake, R. E. (1988). Depressive symptoms in schizophrenia: comprehensive differential diagnosis. *Comprehensive Psychiatry*, 29, 467–83.

Bartels, S. J., & Drake, R. E. (1989). Depression in schizophrenia: current guidelines to treatment. *Psychiatric Quarterly*, 60, 333–45.

Bartels, S. J., Drake, R. E., Wallach, M. A., & Freeman, D. H. (1991). Characteristic hostility in schizophrenic outpatients. *Schizophrenia Bulletin*, 17, 163–71.

Bartels, S. J., & Liberto, J. (1995). Dual diagnosis in the elderly. In A. F. Lehman & L. Dixon (eds), *Substance disorders among persons with chronic mental illness* (pp. 139–57). New York: Harwood Academic.

Bartels, S. J., Mueser, K. T., & Miles, K. M. (1997). Functional impairments in elderly patients with schizophrenia and major affective disorder living in the community: social skills, living skills, and behavior problems. *Behavior Therapy*, 28, 43–63.

Bartels, S. J., Mueser, K. T., & Miles, K. M. (in press). A comparative study of elderly with schizophrenia and bipolar disorder in nursing homes and the community. *Schizophrenia Research.*

Bartels, S. J., Teague, G. B., Drake, R. E., Clark, R. E., Bush, P., & Noordsy, D. L. (1993). Service utilization and costs associated with substance abuse among rural schizophrenic patients. *Journal of Nervous and Mental Disease*, 181, 227–32.

Beardsley, R. S., Larson, D. B., Burns, B. J., Thompson, J. W., & Kamerow, D. B. (1989). Prescribing of psychotropics in elderly nursing home patients. *Journal of the American Geriatrics Society*, 37, 327–30.

Beck, A. T., Emery, G., & Greenberg, R. L. (1985). *Anxiety disorders and phobias: a cognitive perspective.* New York: Basic Books.

Beck, A. T., Epstein, N., Brown, G., & Steer, R. (1988). An inventory for measuring clinical anxiety: psychometric properties. *Journal of Consulting and Clinical Psychology*, 56, 893–7.

Beck, A. T., Rush, A. J., Shaw, B. F., & Emery, G. (1979). *Cognitive therapy of depression.* New York: Guilford Press.

Beck, A. T., Sokal, L., Clark, D. A., Berchick, R., & Wright, F. (1992). A crossover study of focused cognitive therapy for panic disorder. *American Journal of Psychiatry*, 149, 778–83.

Beck, A. T., Ward, C. H., Mendelson, M., Mock, J., & Erbaugh, J. (1961). An inventory for measuring depression. *Archives of General Psychiatry*, 4, 561–71.

Becker, E. (1973). *The denial of death.* New York: Macmillan.

Bedford, V. H. (1995). Siblings in middle and later adulthood. In R. Blieszner & V. H. Bedford (eds), *Handbook on aging and the family* (pp. 201–22). Westport, CT: Greenwood Press.

Beers, M., Avorn, J., Soumerai, S., Everitt, D., Sherman, D., & Salem, S. (1988). Psychoactive medication use in intermediate-care facility residents. *Journal of the American Medical Association*, 260, 3016–20.

Belitsky, R., & McGlashan, T. H. (1993). The manifestations of schizophrenia in late life: a dearth of data. *Schizophrenia Bulletin*, 19, 683–9.

Bellack, A. S., Morrison, R. L., Wixted, J. T., & Mueser, K. T. (1990). An analysis of social competence in schizophrenia. *British Journal of Psychiatry*, 156, 809–18.

Bellack, A. S., & Mueser, K. T. (1993). Psychosocial treatment of schizophrenia. *Schizophrenia Bulletin*, 19, 317–36.

Bellack, A. S., Turner, S. M., Hersen, M., & Luber, R. F. (1984). An examination of the efficacy of social skills training for chronic schizophrenic patients. *Hospital and Community Psychiatry*, 35, 1023–8.

Belle, D. (1990). Poverty and women's mental health. *American Psychologist*, 45 (3), 385–9.

Bengtson, V. L., & Kuypers, J. A. (1984). The family support cycle: psychosocial issues in the aging family. In J. M. A. Munnichs, P. Mussen, E. Olbrich, & P. G. Coleman (eds), *Life-span and change in a gerontological perspective* (pp. 257–73). Orlando, FL: Academic Press.

Bengtson, V. L., Rosenthal, C., & Burton, L. (1996). Paradoxes of families and aging. In R. H. Binstock & L. K. George (eds), *Handbook of aging and the social sciences*, 4th edn (pp. 253–82). San Diego: Academic Press.

Berezin, M. A. (1972). Psychodynamic considerations of aging and the aged: an overview. *American Journal of Psychiatry*, 128, 1483–91.

Binder, E. F., & Robins, L. N. (1990). Cognitive impairment and length of hospital stay in older persons. *Journal of the American Geriatric Society*, 38, 759–76.

Birkel, R. C. (1987). Toward a social ecology of the home-care household. *Psychology and Aging*, 2, 294–301.

Birren, J. E., & Renner, V. J. (1980). Concepts and issues of mental health and aging. In J. E. Birren & R. B. Sloane (eds), *Handbook of mental health and aging* (pp. 3–33). Englewood Cliffs, NJ: Prentice-Hall.

Blazer, D. G. (1993). *Depression in late life*, 2nd edn. St Louis: Mosby.

Blazer, D. G. (1994). Epidemiology of late-life depression. In L. S. Schneider, C. F. Reynolds, B. D. Lebowitz, and A. J. Friedhoff (eds), *Diagnosis and treatment of depression in late life* (pp. 9–19). Washington, DC: American Psychiatric Press.

Blazer, D., George, L. K., & Hughes, D. (1991). The epidemiology of anxiety disorders: an age comparison. In C. Salzman & B. D. Lebowitz (eds), *Anxiety in the elderly: treatment and research* (pp. 17–30). New York: Springer.

Blazer, D. G., Woodbury, M., Hughes, D. C., George, L.K., & Manton, K. G. (1989). A statistical analysis of the classification of depression in a mixed community and clinical sample. *Journal of Affective Disorders*, 16, 11–20.

Blow, F. C., Brower, J. K., Sculenberg, J. E., Demo-Dananberg, L. M., Young, K. J., & Beresford, T. P. (1992). The Michigan alcoholism screening test: geriatric version (MAST-G): a new elderly-specific screening instrument. *Alcoholism*, 16, 372.

Bootzin, R. R., Epstein, D., Engle-Friedman, M., & Salvio, M. A. (1996). Sleep disturbances. In L. L. Carstensen, B. Edelstein, & L. Dornbrand (eds), *Practical handbook of clinical gerontology* (pp. 398–420). Thousand Oaks, CA: Sage.

Boszormenyi-Nagy, I., & Sparks, G. M. (1984). *Invisible loyalties*. New York: Brunner/Mazel.

Bowen, M. (1978). *Family therapy in clinical practice*. New York: J. Aronson.

Bowlby, J. (1969). *Attachment and loss*, vol. 1: *Attachment*. New York: Basic Books.

Bowlby, J. (1980). *Attachment and loss*, vol. 3. New York: Basic Books.

Brannon, D., Cohn, M. D., & Smyer, M. A. (1990). Caregiving as work: how nurses' aides rate it. *Journal of Long-Term Care Administration*, 18 (1), 10–14.

Brannon, D., & Smyer, M. A. (1990). Who will provide long-term care in the future? *Generations*, 14 (2), 64–7.

Brannon, D., & Smyer, M. (1994). Good work and good care in nursing homes. *Generations*, 17, 34–8.

Brannon, D., Smyer, M. A., Cohn, M. D., Downs, M. G., & Rovine, M. J. (1994). Transfer of training effects in nursing homes: staff outcomes. Unpublished manuscript, Pennsylvania State University.

Brink, T. L. (1979). *Geriatric psychotherapy*. New York: Human Sciences Press.

Bronfenbrenner, U. (1979). *The ecology of human development: experiments by nature and design*. Cambridge, MA: Harvard University Press.

Buck, J. A. (1988). Psychotropic drug practice in nursing homes. *Journal of the American Geriatrics Society*, 36, 409–18.

Bulger, M. W., Wandersman, A., & Goldman, C. R. (1993). Burdens and gratifications of caregiving: appraisal of parental care of adults with schizophrenia. *American Journal of Orthopsychiatry*, 63, 255–65.

Burgio, L. D. (1991). Behavioral staff training and management in geriatric long-term care facilities. In P. A. Wisocki (ed.), *Handbook of clinical behavior therapy with the elderly client* (pp. 423–38). New York: Plenum.

Burgio, L. (1996). Interventions for the behavioral complications of Alzheimer's disease: behavioral approaches. *International Psychogeriatrics*, 8, 45–52.

Burgio, L. D., & Locher, J. L. (1996). Urinary incontinence. In L. L. Carstensen, B. Edelstein, & L. Dornbrand (eds), *Practical handbook of clinical gerontology* (pp. 349–73). Thousand Oaks, CA: Sage.

Burgio, L. D., & Sinnott, J. (1989). Behavioral treatments and pharmacotherapy: acceptability ratings for elderly individuals. *Journals of Gerontology*, 44, P3–P8.

Burns, B. J., & Kamerow, D. B. (1988). Psychotropic drug prescriptions for nursing home residents. *Journal of Family Practice*, 26, 155–60.

Burns, B., & Taube, C. A. (1990). Mental health services in general medical care and nursing homes. In B. S. Fogel, A. Furino, & G. Gottlieb (eds), *Protecting minds at risk* (pp. 63–84). Washington, DC: American Psychiatric Association.

Burns, B. J., Wagner, R., Taube, J. E., Magaziner, J., Purmutt, T., & Landerman, L. R. (1993). Mental health service use by the elderly in nursing homes. *American Journal of Public Health*, 83 (3), 331–7.

Burns, D. D., & Nolen-Hoeksema, S. (1991). Coping styles, homework compliance, and the effectiveness of cognitive-behavioral therapy. *Journal of Consulting and Clinical Psychology*, 59 (2), 305–11.

Burns, D. D., Shaw, B. F., & Crocker, W. (1987). Thinking styles and coping strategies of depressed women: an empirical investigation. *Behavioral Research and Therapy*, 25, 223–5.

Burnside, I. M. (1980). Symptomatic behaviors in the elderly. In J. E. Birren & R. B. Sloane (eds), *Handbook of mental health and aging* (pp. 719–44). Englewood Cliffs, NJ: Prentice-Hall.

Busse, E. W., & Pfeiffer, E. (1969). *Behavior and adaption in late life.* Boston: Little, Brown.

Butler, R. (1974). Successful aging and the role of life review. *Journal of the American Geriatric Society*, 22, 529–35.

Butler, R. N., Lewis, M., & Sunderland, T. (1991). *Aging and mental health: positive psychosocial and biomedical approaches*, 4th edn. New York: Merrill.

Butler, S. F., & Strupp, H. H. (1991). Psychodynamic psychotherapy. In M. Hersen, A. E. Kazdin, & A. S. Bellack (eds), *The clinical psychology handbook*, 2nd edn (pp. 519–33). New York: Pergamon Press.

Butters, M. A., Salmon, D. P., & Butters, N. (1994). Neuropsychological assessment of dementia. In M. Storandt & G. R. VandenBos (eds), *Neuropsychological assessment of dementia and depression in older adults: a clinician's guide* (pp. 33–59). Washington, DC: American Psychological Association.

Canadian Study of Health and Aging Working Group (1994). Canadian study of health and aging: study methods and prevalence of dementia. *Canadian Medical Association Journal*, 150, 899–912.

Caplan, G. (1970). *The theory and practice of mental health consultation.* New York: Basic Books.

Carr, V. (1988). Patients' techniques for coping with schizophrenia: an exploratory study. *British Journal of Medical Psychology*, 61, 339–52.

Carson, R. C., & Butcher, J. N. (1992). *Abnormal psychology and modern life*, 9th edn. New York: Harper Collins.

Carstensen, L. L. (1991). Selectivity theory: social activity in life-span context. In K. W. Schaie (ed.), *Annual review of gerontology and geriatrics* (pp. 195–217). New York: Springer.

Carstensen, L., & Fisher, J. E. (1991). Problems of the elderly in nursing homes. In P. Wisocki (ed.), *Handbook of clinical behavior therapy with the elderly client* (pp. 337–62). New York: Plenum.

Carter, E., & McGoldrick, M. (1988). *The changing family life cycle: a framework for family therapy*, 2nd edn. New York: Gardner Press.

Cassel, C. K., Rudberg, M. A., & Olshansky, S. J. (1992). The price of success: health care in an aging society. *Health Affairs*, 11 (2), 87–99.

Castle, D. J., & Murray, R. M. (1993). The epidemiology of late-onset schizophrenia. *Schizophrenia Bulletin*, 19, 691–700.

Chollet, D. (1989). Retiree health insurance benefits: trends and issues. In *Retiree health benefits: what is the promise?* Washington, DC: Employee Benefit Research Institute.

Ciompi, L. (1980). The natural history of schizophrenia in the long term. *British Journal of Psychiatry*, 136, 413–20.

Coblentz, J. M., Mattis, S., Zingesser, L. H., Hasoff, S. S., Wisniewski, H. M., & Katzman, R. (1973). Presenile dementia: clinical aspects and evaluation of cerebrospinal fluid dynamics. *Archives of Neurology,* 29, 299–308.

Cockrell, J. R., & Folstein, M. F. (1988). Mini-mental state examination (MMSE). *Psychopharmacology Bulletin,* 24 (4), 689–92.

Cohen, C. I., Talavera, N., Hartung, R. (1996). Depression among aging persons with schizophrenia who live in the community. *Psychiatric Services,* 47, 601–7.

Cohen, G. D. (1985). Toward an interface of mental and physical health phenomena in geriatrics: clinical findings and questions. In C. M. Gaitz & T. Samorajski (eds), *Aging 2000: our health care destiny: biomedical issues,* vol. 1 (pp. 283–99). New York: Springer.

Cohen, G. D. (1990). Psychopathology and mental health in the mature and elderly adult. In J. E. Birren & K. W. Schaie (eds), *Handbook of the psychology of aging,* 3rd edn (pp. 359–71). San Diego: Academic Press.

Cohen, G. D. (1992). The future of mental health and aging. In J. E. Birren, R. B. Sloane, & G. D. Cohen (eds), *Handbook of mental health and aging,* 2nd edn. (pp. 893–914). San Diego: Academic Press.

Cohen, G. D. (1993). Comprehensive assessment: capturing strengths, not just weaknesses. In M. A. Smyer (ed.), *Mental health and aging: progress and prospects* (pp. 93–100). New York: Springer.

Cohen, R. A., Van Nostrand, J. F., & Furner, S. E. (eds) (1993). Chartbook on health data on older Americans: United States (1991). National Center for Health Statistics. *Vital and Health Statistics,* 3 (29).

Cohen, S., Kamarck, T., & Mermelstein, R. (1983). A global measure of perceived stress. *Journal of Health and Social Behavior,* 24, 385–96.

Cohen, S., & Williamson, G. (1988). Perceived stress in a probability sample of the United States. In S. Spacapan & S. Oskamp (eds), *The social psychology of health* (pp. 31–67). Newbury Park, CA: Sage.

Cohen-Mansfield, J., Werner, P., Culpepper, W. J., Wolfson, M. A., & Bickel, E. (1996). In L. L. Carstensen, B. Edelstein, & L. Dornbrand (eds), *Practical handbook of clinical gerontology* (pp. 374–97). Thousand Oaks, CA: Sage.

Cohler, B. J. (1993). Aging, morale, and meaning: the nexus of narrative. In T. R. Cole, W. A. Achenbaum, P. L. Jakobi, & R. Kastenbaum (eds), *Voices and visions of aging: toward a critical gerontology* (pp. 107–33). New York: Springer.

Cohler, B. J., & Grunebaum, H. U. (1981). *Mothers, grandmothers and daughters: personality and childcare in three generation families.* New York: Wiley.

Cohn, M. D., & Smyer, M. A. (1988). Mental health consultation: process, professions, and models. In M. A. Smyer, M. D. Cohn, & D. Brannon (eds), *Mental health consultation in nursing homes* (pp. 46–63). New York: New York University Press.

Cohn, M. D., Smyer, M. A., & Horgas, A. L. (1994). *The ABCs of behavior change: skills for working with behavior problems in nursing homes.* State College, PA: Venture.

Colarusso, C. A., & Nemiroff, R. A. (1979). Some observations and hypotheses about the psychoanalytic theory of adult development. *International Journal of Psycho-Analysis*, 60, 59–71.

Cole, C. L. (1986). Developmental tasks affecting the marital relationship in later life. *American Behavioral Scientist*, 29, 389–403.

Coles, R. (1967). *Children of crisis*, vol. I: *A study of courage and fear*. Boston: Little, Brown.

Conwell, Y. (1994). Suicide in elderly patients. In L. S. Schneider, C. F. Reynolds, B. D. Lebowitz, & A. J. Friedhoff (eds), *Diagnosis and treatment of depression in late life: results of the NIH consensus development conference* (pp. 397–419). Washington, DC: American Psychiatric Press.

Cook, J. (1988). Who mothers the chronically mentally ill? *Family Relations*, 37, 42–9.

Costa, P. T., Jr, & McCrae, R. R. (1985). *The NEO personality inventory manual*. Odessa, FL: Psychological Assessment Resources.

Costa, P. T., Jr, & McCrae, R. R. (1988). Personality in adulthood: a six-year longitudinal study of self-reports and spouse ratings on the NEO personality inventory. *Journal of Personality and Social Psychology*, 54, 853–63.

Costa, P. T., Jr, & McCrae, R. R. (1992a). Trait psychology comes of age. In T. B. Sonderegger (ed.), *Nebraska symposium on motivation: psychology and aging* (pp. 169–204). Lincoln, NE: University of Nebraska Press.

Costa, P. T., Jr, & McCrae, R. R. (1992b). *Revised NEO personality inventory (NEO-PI-R) and NEO five factor inventory (NEO-FFI) professional manual*. Odessa, FL: Psychological Assessment Resources.

Costa, P. T., & McCrae, R. R. (1994). Depression as an enduring disposition. In L. S. Schneider, C. F. Reynolds, B. D. Lebowitz, and A. J. Friedhoff (eds), *Diagnosis and treatment of depression in late life* (pp. 155–67). Washington, DC: American Psychiatric Press.

Costa, P. T., Jr, Metter, E. J., & McCrae, R. R. (1994). Personality stability and its contribution to successful aging. *Journal of Geriatric Psychiatry*, 27 (1), 41–59.

Couros, F. & Bakalar, N. (eds) (1996). *Aids and people with severe mental illness: a handbook for mental health professionals*. New Haven, CT: Yale University Press.

Coyne, J. C., & Downey, G. (1991). Social factors and psychopathology: stress, social support, and coping processes. *Annual Review of Psychology*, 42, 401–25.

Coyne, J., & Smith, D. A. F. (1991). Couples coping with a myocardial infarction: a contextual perspective on wives' distress. *Journal of Personality and Social Psychology*, 61, 404–12.

Cuffel B. J., Jeste D. V., Halpain, M., Pratt, C., Tarke, H., & Patterson, T. L. (1996). Treatment costs and use of community mental health services for schizophrenia by age cohorts. *American Journal of Psychiatry*, 153, 870–6.

Cummings, J. (1985). Organic delusions: phenomenology, anatomical correlations and review. *British Journal of Psychiatry*, 145, 184–97.

Cummings, J. L., & Benson, D. F. (1992). *Dementia: a clinical approach*, 2nd edn. Boston: Butterworth-Heinemann.

Davidson, M., Harvey, P. D., Powchick, P., Parrella, M., White, L., Knobler, H. Y., Losonczy, M. F., Keefe, R. S., Katz, S., & Frecska, E. (1995). Severity of symptoms in chronically institutionalized geriatric schizophrenic patients. *American Journal of Psychiatry*, 152, 197–207.

Davison, G. C., & Neale, J. M. (1994). *Abnormal psychology*, 6th edn. New York: Wiley.

DeLongis, A., Folkman, S., & Lazarus, R. S. (1988). The impact of daily stress on health and mood: psychology and social resources as mediators. *Journal of Personality and Social Psychology*, 54, 486–95.

Department of Veterans Affairs (1997). *Clinical assessment for competency determination of the older adult: a practice guideline for psychologists*. Milwaukee: National Center for Cost Containment, Department of Veterans Affairs.

Derogatis, L. R. (1977). *Scl-90 administration, scoring, & procedures manual-I*. Baltimore: Johns Hopkins University School of Medicine, Clinical Psychometrics Research Unit.

Derogatis, L. R., & Spencer, P. M. (1982). *The brief symptom inventory (BSI) administration, scoring, & procedures manual-I*. Baltimore: Johns Hopkins University School of Medicine, Clinical Psychometrics Research Unit.

Dhingra, U., & Rabins, P. V. (1991). Mania in the elderly: a 5–7 year follow-up. *Journal of the American Geriatrics Society*, 39, 581–3.

Diehl, M., Coyle, N., & Labouvie-Vief, G. (1996). Age and sex differences in strategies of coping and defense across the life-span. *Psychology and Aging*, 42, 127–39.

Dobson, D. J. G., McDougall, G., Busheikin, J., & Aldous, J. (in press). Social skills training and symptomatology in schizophrenia. *Psychiatric Services*.

Dohrenwend, B. S., Krasnoff, L., Askenasy, A. R., & Dohrenwend, B. P. (1978). Exemplification of a method for scoring life events: the PERI life events scale. *Journal of Health and Social Behavior*, 19, 205–29.

Drake, R. E., Osher, F. C., & Wallach, M. A. (1989b). Alcohol use and abuse in schizophrenia: a prospective community study. *Journal of Nervous and Mental Disease*, 177, 408–14.

Drake, R. E., Osher, F. C., & Wallach, M. A. (1991). Homelessness in dual diagnosis patients. *American Psychologist*, 46, 1149–58.

Drake, R. E., Wallach, M. A., & Hoffman, J. S. (1989a). Housing instability and homelessness among aftercare patients of an urban state hospital. *Hospital and Community Psychiatry*, 40, 46–51.

Drane, J. F. (1984). Competency to give consent: a model for making clinical assessments. *Journal of the American Medical Association*, 252, 925–7.

Dupree, L. W., Broskowski, H., & Schonfeld, L. (1984). The gerontology alcohol project: a behavioral treatment program for elderly alcohol abusers. *The Gerontologist*, 24, 510–16.

Dupree, L. W., & Schonfeld, L. (1996). Substance abuse. In M. Hersen & V. B. Van Hasselt (eds), *Psychological treatment of older adults* (pp. 281–97). New York: Plenum.

Dworkin, R. H. (1994). Pain insensitivity in schizophrenia: a neglected phenomenon and some implications. *Schizophrenia Bulletin*, 20, 235–48.

Edelstein, B. A., & Semenchuk, E. M. (1996). Interviewing older adults. In L. L. Carstensen, B. A. Edelstein, & L. Dornbrand (eds), *The practical handbook of clinical gerontology* (pp. 153–73). Thousand Oaks, CA: Sage.

Edinberg, M. A. (1985). *Mental health practice with the elderly*. Englewood Cliffs, NJ: Prentice-Hall.

Edmunds, M., Frank, R., Hogan, M., McCarty, D., Robinson-Beale, R., & Weisner, C. (eds) (1997). *Managing managed care: quality improvement in behavioral health*. Washington, DC: National Academy Press.

Eisdorfer, C. (1995). Managed mental health care: can't live with it and can't live without it. *Journal of Mental Health and Aging*, 1 (1), 5–6.

Elder, G. H., Jr (1974). *Children of the great depression: social change and life experiences*. Chicago: University of Chicago Press.

Erikson, E. H. (1963). *Childhood and society*, 2nd edn. New York: W. W. Norton.

Erikson, E. H., Erikson, J. M., & Kivnik, H. Q. (1986). *Vital involvement in old age: the experience of old age in our time*. New York: W. W. Norton.

Exner, J. E. (1974). *The Rorschach: a comprehensive system*, vol. 1. New York: Wiley.

Exner, J. E. (1978). *The Rorschach: a comprehensive system*, vol. 2. New York: Wiley-Interscience.

Falloon, I., Boyd, J., McGill, C., Razani, J., Moss, H., & Gilderman, A. (1982). Family management in the prevention of exacerbations of schizophrenia. *New England Journal of Medicine*, 306, 1437–40.

Falloon, I., & Talbot, R. E. (1981). Persistent auditory hallucinations: coping mechanisms and implications for management. *Psychological Medicine*, 11, 329–39.

Fillenbaum, G., & Smyer, M. (1981). The development, validity, and reliability of the OARS multidimensional functional assessment questionnaire. *Journal of Gerontology*, 36, 428–34.

Finch, C. E., & Morgan, D. (1987). Aging and schizophrenia: a hypothesis relating to asynchrony in neural aging processes to the manifestations of schizophrenia and other neurologic diseases with age. In N. E. Miller & G. Cohen (eds), *Schizophrenia and Aging* (pp. 97–108). New York: Guilford Press.

Finlayson, R. E. (1984). Prescription drug abuse in older persons. In R. M. Atkinson (ed.), *Alcohol and drug abuse in old age* (pp. 61–70). Washington, DC: American Psychiatric Press.

First, M. B., Spitzer, R. L., Gibbon, M., & Williams, J. B. W. (1995). *Structured clinical interview for DSM-IV Axis I disorders: patient edition (SCID-I/P, Version 2.0)*. New York: Biometrics Research Department, New York State Psychiatric Institute.

Fisher, J. E., & Noll, J. P. (1996). Anxiety disorders. In L L. Carstensen, B. A. Edelstein, & L. Dornbrand (eds), *The practical handbook of clinical gerontology* (pp. 304–23). Thousand Oaks, CA: Sage.

Florsheim, M. J., & Herr, J. J. (1990). Family counseling with elders. *Generations*, 14 (1), 40–2.

Folkman, S., & Lazarus, R. S. (1980). An analysis of coping in a middle-aged community sample. *Journal of Health and Social Behavior*, 21, 219–39.

Folkman, S., Lazarus, R. S., Dunkel-Schetter, C., Delongis, A., & Gruen, R. (1986). The dynamics of a stressful encounter: cognitive appraisal, coping, and encounter outcomes. *Journal of personality and social psychology*, 50, 992–1003.

Folkman, S., Lazarus, R. S., Gruen, R., & DeLongis, A. (1986). Appraisal, coping, health status, and psychological symptoms. *Journal of Personality and Social Psychology*, 50, 571–9.

Folkman, S., Lazarus, R. S., Pimley, S., & Novacek, J. (1987). Age differences in stress and coping processes. *Psychology and Aging*, 2 (2), 171–84.

Folstein, M. F., Bassett, S. S., Romanoski, A. J., & Nestadt, G. (1991). The epidemiology of delirium in the community: the eastern Baltimore mental health survey. *International Psychogeriatrics*, 3, 169–76.

Folstein, M. F., Folstein, S. E., & McHugh, P. R. (1975). 'Mini mental state': a practical method for grading the cognitive state of patients for the clinician. *Journal of Psychiatric Research*, 12, 189–98.

Frank, R. G., McGuire, T. G., Regier, D. A., Manderschied, R., & Woodward, A. (1994). Paying for mental health and substance abuse care. *Health Affairs*, 13 (1), 337–42.

Freedman, V. A., Berkman, L. F., Rapp, S. R., & Ostfeld, A. M. (1994). Family networks: predictors of nursing home entry. *American Journal of Public Health*, 84 (5), 843–5.

Freiman, M. P., Arons, B. S., Goldman, H. H., & Burns, B. J. (1990). Nursing home reform and the mentally ill. *Health Affairs*, 9 (4), 47–60.

Freud, A. (1937). *The ego and the mechanisms of defense*. London: Hogarth Press.

Freud, S. (1933). The dissection of the psychical personality. New introductory lectures on psycho-analysis. In J. Strachey (ed.) (1964), *The standard edition of the complete psychological works of Sigmund Freud*, vol. 22. London: Hogarth Press.

Freud, S. (1940). An outline of psychoanalysis. In J. Strachey (ed.) (1964). *The standard edition of the complete psychological works of Sigmund Freud*, vol. 23. London: Hogarth Press.

Friedhoff, A. (1994). Consensus development conference statement: diagnosis and treatment of depression in late life. In L. S. Schneider, C. F. Reynolds, B. D. Lebowitz, & A. J. Friendhoff (eds), *Diagnosis and treatment of depression in late life* (pp. 493–511). Washington, DC: American Psychiatric Press.

Fuld, P., Katzman, R., Davies, P., & Terry, R. D. (1982). Intrusions as a sign of Alzheimer dementia: chemical and pathological verification. *Annals of Neurology*, 11, 155–9.

Futterman, A., Thompson, L. W., Gallagher-Thompson, D., & Ferris, R. (1995). Depression in later life: epidemiology, assessment, etiology and treatment. In E. Beckham & R. Leber (eds), *Handbook of depression*, 2nd edn (pp. 494–525). New York: Guilford Press.

Gallagher, D. (1986). Assessment of depression by interview methods and psychiatric rating scales. In L. W. Poon (ed.), *Handbook for clinical memory assessment of older adults* (pp. 202–12). Washington, DC: American Psychological Association.

Gallagher, D., & Frankel, A. S. (1980). Depression in older adult(s): a moderate structuralist viewpoint. *Psychotherapy: Theory, Research and Practice,* 17 (1), 101–4.

Gallagher, D. E., & Thompson, L. W. (1983). Effectiveness of psycho-therapy for both endogenous and non-endogenous depression in older adults. *Journal of Gerontology,* 18, 707–12.

Gallagher, D., Thompson, L. W., Baffa, G., Piatt, C., Ringering, L., & Stone, V. (1981). *Depression in the elderly: a behavioral treatment manual.* Los Angeles: University of Southern California Press.

Gallagher-Thompson, D., Hanley-Peterson, P., & Thompson, L. W. (1990). Maintenance of gains versus relapse following brief psychotherapy for depression. *Journal of Consulting and Clinical Psychology,* 58, 371–4.

Gallagher-Thompson, D., & Thompson, L. W. (1996). Applying cognitive-behavioral therapy to the psychological problems of later life. In S. H. Zarit & B. G. Knight (eds), *A guide to psychotherapy and aging* (pp. 61–82). Washington, DC: American Psychological Association.

Gatz, M. (1992). Stress, control, and psychological interventions. In M. L. Wykle, E. Kahana, & J. Kowal (eds), *Stress and health among the elderly* (pp. 209–22). New York: Springer.

Gatz, M., Bengtson, V. L., & Blum, M. J. (1990). Caregiving families. In J. E. Birren & K. W. Schaie (eds), *Handbook of psychology and aging,* 3rd edn (pp. 404–26). San Diego: Academic.

Gatz, M., Kasl-Godley, J. E., & Karel, M. J. (1996). Aging and mental disorders. In J. E. Birren & K. W. Schaie (eds), *Handbook of the psychology of aging,* 4th edn. (pp. 365–82). San Diego: Academic Press.

Gatz, M., Lowe, B., Berg, S., Mortimer, J., & Pedersen, N. (1994). Dementia: not just a search for the gene. *The Gerontologist,* 34 (2), 251–5.

Gatz, M., Pedersen, N. L., Plomin, R., & Nesselroade, J. R. (1992). Importance of shared genes and shared environments for symptoms of depression in older adults. *Journal of Abnormal Psychology,* 101, 701–8.

Gatz, M., & Smyer, M. A. (1992). The mental health system and older adults in the 1990s. *American Psychologist,* 47 (6), 741–51.

Gatz, M., Smyer, M. A., Garfein, A. J., & Seward, M. (1991). Essentials of assessment in long-term care settings. In M. S. Harper (ed.), *Management and care of the elderly: psychosocial perspectives* (pp. 293–309). Newbury Park, CA: Sage.

George, L. K. (1992). Community and home care for mentally ill adults. In J. E. Birren, R. B. Sloane, G. D. Cohen, N. R. Hooyman, B. D. Lebowitz, M. H. Wykle, & D. E. Deutschman (eds), *Handbook of mental health and aging,* 2nd edn (pp. 793–813). San Diego: Academic Press.

George, L. K. (1994). Social factors and depression in late life. In L. S. Schneider, C. F. Reynolds, B. D. Lebowitz, and A. J. Friedhoff (eds), *Diagnosis and treatment of depression in late life* (pp. 131–53). Washington, DC: American Psychiatric Press.

Gilford, R., & Bengtson, V. (1979). Measuring marital satisfaction in three generations: positive and negative dimensions. *Journal of Marriage and the Family*, 41, 387–98.

Gleser, G. C., & Ihilevich, D. (1969). An objective instrument for measuring defense mechanisms. *Journal of Consulting and Clinical Psychology*, 33, 51–60.

Glynn, S., Randolph, E., Eth, S., Paz, G., Shaner, A., & Strachan, A. (1990). Patient psychopathology and expressed emotion in schizophrenia. *British Journal of Psychiatry*, 157, 877–80.

Goffman, E. (1961). *Asylums*. Garden City, NY: Anchor Books.

Goldberg, T. E., Hyde, T. M., Kleinman, J. E., & Weinberger, D. R. (1993). Course of schizophrenia: neuropsychological evidence for a static encephalopathy. *Schizophrenia Bulletin*, 19, 797–804.

Goldstein, J. M. (1988). Gender differences in the course of schizophrenia. *American Journal of Psychiatry*, 145, 684–9.

Goodwin, P., Smyer, M. A., & Lair, T. I. (1995). Decision-making incapacity among nursing home residents: results from the 1987 NMES survey. *Behavioral Sciences and the Law*, 13, 405–14.

Gough, H. G. (1987). *California psychological inventory: administrator's guide*. Palo Alto, CA: Consulting Psychologists Press.

Gould, R. L. (1978). *Transformations: growth and change in adult life*. New York: Simon & Schuster.

Greenberg, J., Pyszczynski, T., Solomon, S., Simon, L., & Breus, M. (1994). Role of consciousness and accessibility of death-related thoughts in mortality salience effects. *Journal of Personality and Social Psychology*, 67, 627–37.

Grisso, T. (1986). *Evaluating competencies: forensic assessments and instruments*. New York: Plenum.

Grisso, T. (1994). Clinical assessments for legal competence of older adults. In M. Storandt & G. R. VandenBos (eds), *Neuropsychological assessment of dementia and depression in older adults: a clinician's guide* (pp. 119–39). Washington, DC: American Psychological Association.

Groth-Marnat, G. (1984). *Handbook of psychological assessment*. New York: Van Nostrand Reinhold.

Grotjahn, M. (1955). Analytic psychotherapy with the elderly. *Psychoanalytic Review*, 42, 419–27.

Grundmann, M. (1996). Historical context of father absence: some consequences for the family formation of German men. *International Journal of Behavioral Development*, 19 (2), 415–31.

Gutmann, D. L. (1986). Oedipus and the aging male: a comparative perspective. Special issue: toward a new psychology of men: psychoanalytic and social perspectives. *Psychoanalytic Review*, 73 (4), 541–52.

Gutmann, D. L. (1987). *Reclaimed powers: toward a new psychology of men and women in later life*. New York: Basic Books.

Gutmann, D. L. (1992). Toward a dynamic geropsychology. In J. W. Barron, M. N.

Eagle, & D. L. Wolitzky (eds), *Interface of psychoanalysis and psychology* (pp. 284–96). Washington, DC: American Psychological Association.

Hagestad, G. O. (1986). The aging society as a context for family life. *Daedalus*, 115, 119–39.

Hagestad, G. O. (1988). Demographic change and the life course: some emerging trends in the family realm. *Family Relations*, 37, 405–10.

Harding, C. M., Brooks, G. W., Ashikaga, T., Strauss, J. S., & Breier, A. (1987a). The Vermont longitudinal study of persons with severe mental illness, I: Methodology, study sample, and overall status 32 years later. *American Journal of Psychiatry*, 144, 718–26.

Harding, C. M., Brooks, G. W., Ashikaga, T., Strauss, J. S., & Breier, A. (1987b). The Vermont longitudinal study of persons with severe mental illness, II: Long-term outcome of subjects who retrospectively met DSM-III criteria for schizophrenia. *American Journal of Psychiatry*, 144, 727–35.

Hargrave, T. D., & Anderson, W. T. (1992). *Finishing well: aging and reparation in the intergenerational family*. New York: Brunner/Mazel.

Harris, M., & Jeste, D. (1988). Late-onset schizophrenia: an overview. *Schizophrenia Bulletin*, 14, 39–55.

Hartman, A. (1997). Aging holocaust survivors and PTSD. *Dimensions*, 4 (3), 3–5.

Hawkins, A. M., Burgio, L. D., Langford, A., & Engel, B. T. (1992). The effects of verbal and written supervisory feedback on staff compliance with assigned prompted voiding in a nursing home. *Journal of Organizational Behavior Management*, 13, 137–50.

Hayes, R. L., Halford, W. K., & Varghese, F. T. (in press). Social skills training with chronic schizophrenic patients: effects on community functioning. *Behavior Therapy*.

Hayslip, B., & Lowman, R. D. (1986). The clinical use of projective techniques with the aged: a critical review and synthesis. *Clinical Gerontologist*, 5, 63–93.

Heaton, R., Paulsen, J. S., McAdams, L. A., Kuck, J., Zisook, S., Braff, D., Harris, M. J., & Jeste, D. V. (1994). Neuropsychological deficits in schizophrenics: relationship to age, chronicity, and dementia. *Archives of General Psychiatry*, 51, 469–76.

Helmes, E. (1988). Multidimensional observation scale for elderly subjects (MOSES), *Psychopharmacology Bulletin*, 24 (4), 733–45.

Helmes, E., Csapo, K. G., & Short, J. A. (1987). Standardization and validation of the multidimensional observation scale for elderly subjects (MOSES). *Journal of Gerontology*, 42, 395–405.

Herbert, M., & Jacobson, S. (1967). Late paraphrenia. *British Journal of Psychiatry*, 113, 461–9.

Herbert, T. B., & Cohen, S. (1993a). Stress and immunity in humans: a meta-analytic review. *Psychosomatic Medicine*, 55, 364–79.

Herbert, T. B., & Cohen, S. (1993b). Depression and immunity: a meta-analytic review. *Psychological Bulletin*, 113 (3), 472–86.

Herr, J. J., & Weakland, J. H. (1979). *Counseling elders and their families.* New York: Springer.

Hersen, M., & Barlow, D. (1976). *Single case experimental designs: strategies for studying behavior change.* New York: Pergamon Press.

Herz, M. I. (1989). Prodromal symptoms and prevention of relapse in schizophrenia. *Journal of Clinical Psychiatry*, 46, 22–5.

HHS Inspector General, US Department of Health and Human Services (1989). *Expenses incurred by Medicare beneficiaries of prescription drugs.* Washington, DC: US Department of Health and Human Services.

Himmelfarb, S., & Murrell, S. A. (1984). The prevalence and correlates of anxiety symptoms in older adults. *Journal of Psychology*, 116, 159–67.

Hofland B. F., & David, D. (1990). Autonomy and long-term-care practice: conclusions and next steps. *Generations*, 14 (suppl.), 91–4.

Hogarty, G. E., Anderson, C. M., Reiss, D. J., Kornblith, S. J., Greenwald D. P., Javna, C. D., & Madonia, M. J. (1986). Family psychoeducation, social skills training, and maintenance chemotherapy in the aftercare treatment of schizophrenia, I: One-year effects of a controlled study on relapse and expressed emotion. *Archives of General Psychiatry*, 43, 633–42.

Holden, N. L. (1987). Late paraphrenia or the paraphrenias? A descriptive study with a 10 year follow-up. *British Journal of Psychiatry*, 150, 635–9.

Holmes, T., & Rahe, R. (1967). The social readjustment rating scale. *Journal of Psychosomatic Research*, 11, 213–18.

Honigfeld, G., & Klett, C. J. (1965). Nurses' observation scale for inpatient evaluation: a new scale for measuring improvement in chronic schizophrenia. *Journal of Clinical Psychology*, 21, 65–71.

Horgas, A. L., Wahl, H. W., & Baltes, M. M. (1996). Dependency in later life. In L. L. Carstensen, B. A. Edelstein, & L. Dornbrand (eds), *The practical handbook of clinical gerontology* (pp. 54–75). Thousand Oaks, CA: Sage.

Horney, K. A. (1945). *Our inner conflicts.* New York: W. W. Norton.

House, J. S., Kessler, R. C., Herzog, A. R., Mero, R. P., Kinney, A. M., & Breslow, M. J. (1992). Social stratification, age, and health. In K. W. Schaie, D. Blazer, & J. House (eds), *Aging, health behaviors, and health outcomes* (pp. 1–37). Hillsdale, NJ: Lawrence Erlbaum Associates.

Howard, R., Castle, D., Wessely, S., & Murray, R. (1993). A comparative study of 470 cases of early- and late-onset schizophrenia. *British Journal of Psychiatry*, 163, 352–7.

Howell, S. C. (1980). *Designing for aging.* Cambridge, MA: MIT Press.

Hudson, R. B. (1993). Social contingencies: the aged and public policy. *Milbank Memorial Quarterly*, 73, 253–77.

Hughes, J. R., Hatsukami, D. K., Mitchell, J. E., & Dahlgren, L. A. (1986). Prevalence of smoking among psychiatric outpatients. *American Journal of Psychiatry*, 143, 993–7.

Hussian, R. A. (1986). Severe behavioral problems. In L. Teri & P. M. Lewinsohn (eds), *Geropsychological assessment and treatment* (pp. 121–44). New York: Springer.

Hussian, R., & Davis, R. (1985). *Responsive care.* Champaign, IL: Research Press.

Ihilevich, D., & Gleser, G. C. (1986). *Defense mechanisms: their classification, correlates, and measurement with the defense mechanism inventory.* Owosso, MI: DMI Associates.

Jackson J. H. (1984). Remarks on the evolution and dissolution of the nervous system. *Journal of Mental Science,* 33, 25–48.

Jahoda, M. (1958). *Current concepts of positive mental health.* New York: Basic Books.

Janik, S. W., & Dunham, R. G. (1983). A nationwide examination of the need for specific alcoholism treatment programs for the elderly. *Journal of Studies on Alcohol,* 44, 307–17.

Jensen, G. A., & Morrisey, M. A. (1992). Employer-sponsored postretirement health benefits: not your mother's Medigap plan. *The Gerontologist,* 32 (5), 693–703.

Jeste, D. V., Lacro, J. P., Gilbert, P. L., Kline, J., & Kline, N. (1993). Treatment of late-life schizophrenia with neuroleptics. *Schizophrenia Bulletin,* 19, 817–30.

Johnson, C. J., & Johnson, F. A. (1992). Psychological distress among inner-city American elderly: structural, developmental, and situational contexts. *Journal of Cross-Cultural Gerontology,* 7 (3), 221–36.

Jorm, A. F., Korten, A. E., & Henderson, A. S. (1987). The prevalence of dementia: a quantitative integration of the literature. *Acta Psychiatrica Scandinavica,* 76, 465–79.

Joseph, J. (1991). Warning. In S. Martz (ed.), *When I am an old woman I shall wear purple.* Watsonville, CA: Papier-Mache Press.

Jung, C. G. (1933). *Modern man in search of a soul.* New York: Harcourt, Brace.

Kahana, E. (1982). A congruence model of person–environment interaction. In M. P. Lawton, P. G. Windley, & T. O. Byerts (eds), *Aging and the environment: directions and perspectives* (pp. 97–121). New York: Springer.

Kahn, R. L. (1975). The mental health system and the future aged. *The Gerontologist,* 15 (2), 24–31.

Kahn, R. L. (1977). Perspectives in the evaluation of psychological mental health problems for the aged. In W. D. Gentry (ed.), *Geropsychology: a model of training and clinical service* (pp. 9–19). Cambridge, MA: Ballinger.

Kaiser Medicare Policy Project (1997). *Medicare managed care enrollment, Medicare chart book: historical data from the Health Care Financing Administration, Office of Managed Care, 1995. Projections from the Congressional Budget Office, 1997.* Menlo Park, CA: Henry J. Kaiser Family Foundation.

Kane, J., Jeste, D., Barnes, T., Casey, D., Cole, J., Davis, J., Gualtieri, C., Schooler, N., Sprague, R., & Wettstein, R. (1992). *Tardive dyskinesia: a task force report of the American Psychiatric Association.* Washington, DC: American Psychiatric Association.

Kane, J., Woerner, M., & Lieberman, J. (1988). Tardive dyskinesia: prevalence, incidence, and risk factors. *Journal of Clinical Psychopharmacology,* 8, 52–6.

Kane, J. M. (1989). Innovations in the psychopharmacologic treatment of schizophrenia. In A. S. Bellack (ed.), *A clinical guide for the treatment of schizophrenia* (pp. 43–75). New York: Plenum.

Kane, J. M., & Marder, S. R. (1993). Psychopharmacologic treatment of schizophrenia. *Schizophrenia Bulletin*, 19, 287–302.

Kane, R. L., & Friedman, B. (1996). Health care and services. In J. Birren (ed.), *Encyclopedia of gerontology: age, aging, and the aged*, vol. I (pp. 635–41). New York: Academic Press.

Kashner, T. M., Rodell, D. E., Ogden, S. R., Guggenheim, F. G., & Karson, C. N. (1992). Outcomes and costs of two VA inpatient treatment programs for older alcoholic patients. *Hospital and Community Psychiatry*, 43, 958–89.

Kaszniak, A. W., & Christenson, G. D. (1994). Differential diagnosis of dementia and depression. In M. Storandt & G. R. VandenBos (eds), *Neuropsychological assessment of dementia and depression in older adults: a clinician's guide* (pp. 87–117). Washington, DC: American Psychological Association.

Katz, I. R., & Parmelee, P. A. (1994). Depression in elderly patients in residential care settings. In L. S. Schneider, C. F. Reynolds, B. D. Lebowitz, & A. J. Friedhoff (eds), *Diagnosis and treatment of depression in late life*. Washington, DC: American Psychiatric Press.

Katzman, R. (1986). Alzheimer's disease. *New England Journal of Medicine*, 314, 964–73.

Kavanagh, D. J. (1992). Recent developments in expressed emotion and schizophrenia. *British Journal of Psychiatry*, 160, 601–20.

Kavanagh, S., & Knapp, M. (1995). Market rationales, rationing, and rationality: mental health care reform in the United Kingdom. *Health Affairs*, 14 (3), 260–8.

Kay, D., & Roth, M. (1961). Environmental and hereditary factors in the schizophrenias of old age ("late paraphrenia") and their bearing on the general problem of causation in schizophrenia. *Journal of Mental Science*, 107, 649–86.

Kazdin, A. (1975). *Behavior modification in applied settings*. Homewood, IL: Dorsey Press.

Kemp, B. J., & Mitchell, J. M. (1992). Functional impairment in geriatric mental health. In J. E. Birren, R. B. Sloane, & G. D. Cohen (eds), *Handbook of mental health and aging*, 2nd edn (pp. 671–97). San Diego: Academic Press.

Kemper, P., & Murtaugh, C. M. (1991). Lifetime use of nursing home care. *New England Journal of Medicine*, 324 (9), 595–600.

Keys, C. B. (1986). Organization development: an approach to mental health consultation. In F. V. Mannino, E. J. Trickett, M. F. Shore, M. G. Kidder, & G. Levin (eds), *Handbook of mental health consultation* (Publication No. (ADM) 86–1446) (pp. 81–112). Washington, DC: Department of Health & Human Services.

Kiecolt-Glaser, J. K., Dura, J. R., Speicher, C. E., Trask, J., & Glaser, R. (1991). Spousal caregivers of dementia victims: longitudinal changes in immunity and health. *Psychosomatic Medicine*, 53, 345–62.

Kiecolt-Glaser, J. K., & Glaser, R. (1992). Psychoneuroimmunology: can psychological interventions modulate immunity? *Journal of Consulting and Clinical Psychology*, 60 (4), 569–75.

Kiesler, C. A. (1991). Changes in general hospital psychiatric care, 1980–1985. *American Psychologist*, 46, 416–21.

Kiesler, C. A., & Sibulkin, A. E. (1987). *Medical hospitalization: myths and facts about a national crisis*. Newbury Park, CA: Sage.

Kiesler, C. A., & Simpkins, C. (1991). The de facto national system of psychiatric inpatient care. *American Psychologist*, 46, 579–84.

King, P. H. (1980). The life cycle as indicated by the transference in the psychoanalysis of the middle-aged and the elderly. *International Journal of Psychoanalysis*, 61, 153–60.

Kinsella, K. (1995). Aging and the family: present and future demographic issues. In R. Blieszner & V. H. Bedford (eds), *Handbook on aging and the family* (pp. 32–56). Westport, CT: Greenwood Press.

Kivnick, H. Q. (1985). Grandparenthood and mental health. In V. L. Bengtson & J. F. Robertson (eds), *Grandparenthood* (pp. 211–24). Beverly Hills, CA: Sage.

Kivnick, H. Q. (1993). Everyday mental health: a guide to assessing life strengths. In M. A. Smyer (ed.), *Mental health and aging* (pp. 19–36). New York: Springer.

Klerman, G. L., Weissman, M. M., Rounsaville, B. J., & Chevron, E. (1984). *Interpersonal psychotherapy of depression*. New York: Basic Books.

Knight, B. (1986). *Psychotherapy with older adults*. Newbury Park, CA: Sage.

Knight, B. G. (1992). *Older adults in psychotherapy: case histories*. Newbury Park, CA: Sage.

Knight, B. (1993). Psychotherapy as applied gerontology: a contextual, cohort-based maturity-specific challenge model. In M. A. Smyer (ed.), *Mental health and aging* (pp. 125–34). New York: Springer.

Knight, B. (1996). *Psychotherapy with older adults*, 2nd edn. Thousand Oaks, CA: Sage.

Knight, B. G., & Qualls, S. H. (1995). The older client in developmental context: life course and family systems perspectives. *Clinical Psychologist*, 48 (2), 11–17.

Knight, B. G., Teri, L., Wohlford, P., & Santos, J. (eds) (1995). *Mental health services for older adults: implications for training and practice in geropsychology*. Washington, DC: American Psychological Association.

Koenig, H. G., George, L. K., & Siegler, I. C. (1988). The use of religion and other emotion-regulating coping strategies among older adults. *The Gerontologist*, 28 (3), 303–10.

Kofoed, L. L., Tolson, R. L., Atkinson, R. M., Toth, R. L., & Turner, J. A. (1987). Treatment compliance of older alcoholics: an elder-specific approach is superior to "mainstreaming." *Journal of Studies on Alcohol*, 48, 47–51.

Kohut, H. (1977). *The restoration of the self*. New York: International Universities Press.

Koran, L. M., Sox, H. C., Marton, K. I., Moltzen, S., Sox, C. H., Kraemer, H. C., Imai, K., Kelsey, T. G., Rose, T. G., Jr, & Levin, L. C. (1989). Medical evaluation of psychiatric patients. *Archives of General Psychiatry*, 46, 733–40.

Koranyi, E. K. (1979). Morbidity and rate of undiagnosed physical illnesses in a psychiatric clinic population. *Archives of General Psychiatry*, 36, 414–19.

Kraepelin, E. (1971). *Dementia praecox and paraphrenia*, trans. R. M. Barclay. Huntington, NY: Rovert E. Kreiger [original pubd 1919].

Krause, N. (1991). Stress and isolation from close ties in later life. *Journal of Gerontology: Social Sciences*, 46, S183–S194.

Krause, N. (1995a). Stress and well-being in later life: using research findings to inform intervention design. In L. A. Bond, S. J. Cutler, & A. Grams (eds), *Promoting successful and productive aging* (pp. 203–19). Thousand Oaks, CA: Sage.

Krause, N. (1995b). Stress, alcohol use, and depressive symptoms in later life. *The Gerontologist*, 35 (3), 296–307.

Krauss, N. A., Freiman, M. P., Rhoades, J. A., Altman, B. M., Brown, E., Jr, & Potter, D. E. B. (1997). Characteristics of nursing home facilities and residents. *Medical Expenditure Panel Survey*, July (2), 1–3.

Krauthammer, C., & Klerman, G. L. (1978). Secondary mania: manic syndromes associated with antecedent physical illness or drugs. *Archives of General Psychiatry*, 35, 1333–9.

Lair, T., & Lefkowitz, D. (1990). Mental health and functional status of residents of nursing and personal care homes. In *National Medical Expenditure Survey Research Findings*, 7 (DHHS Publication no. PHS90-3470). Rockville, MD: Public Health Service, Agency for Health Care Policy and Research.

Lair, T. J., & Smyer, M. A. (1994). The impact of OBRA 1987 preadmission screening: a simulation from the National Medical Expenditure Survey. Unpublished manuscript.

LaRue, A. (1992). *Aging and neuropsychological assessment*. New York: Plenum.

LaRue, A., Yang, J., & Osato, S. (1992). Neuropsychological assessment. *Handbook of mental health and aging* (pp. 643–70). San Diego: Academic Press.

Lawton, M. P. (1979). Therapeutic environments for the aged. In D. Canter & S. Canter (eds), *Designing for therapeutic environments* (pp. 233–76). New York: Wiley.

Lawton, M. P. (1980). *Environment and aging*. Monterey, CA: Brooks/Cole.

Lawton, M. P. (1982). Competence, environmental press, and the adaptation of older people. In M. P. Lawton, P. G. Windley, & T. O. Byerts (eds), *Aging and the environment: theoretical approaches* (pp. 33–59). New York: Springer.

Lawton, M. P. (1988). Scales to measure competence in everyday activities. *Psychopharmacology Bulletin*, 24 (4), 609–14.

Lawton, M. P., & Nahemow, L. (1973). Ecology and the aging process. In C. Eisdorfer & M. P. Lawton (eds), *The psychology of adult development and aging* (pp. 619–74). Washington, DC: American Psychological Association.

Lazarus, R. S. (1990). Theory-based stress measurement. *Psychological Inquiry*, 1, 3–13.

Lazarus, R. S., & Folkman, S. (1984). *Stress, appraisal, and coping*. New York: Springer.

Lazarus, R. S., & Folkman, S. (1987). Coping and adaptation. In W. Doyle Gentry (ed.), *Handbook of behavioral medicine* (pp. 282–325). New York: Guilford Press.

Lebowitz, B. D. (1993). Mental health and aging: federal perspectives. In M. A.

Smyer (ed.), *Mental health and aging: progress and prospects* (pp. 135–42). New York: Springer.

Lebowitz, B. D., & Niederehe, G. (1992). Concepts and issues in mental health and aging. In J. E. Birren, R. B. Sloane, & G. D. Cohen (eds), *Handbook of mental health and aging*, 2nd edn (pp. 3–26). San Diego: Academic Press.

Leff, J., Kuipers, L., Berkowitz, R., Eberlein-Vries, R., & Sturgeon, D. (1982). A controlled trial of social intervention in the families of schizophrenic patients. *British Journal of Psychiatry*, 141, 121–34.

Lesser, I., Miller, B., Swartz, R., Boone, K., Mehringer, C., & Mena, I. (1993). Brain imaging in late-life schizophrenia and related psychoses. *Schizophrenia Bulletin*, 19, 773–82.

Levenson, R. W., Carstensen, L. L., & Gottman, J. M. (1993). Long-term marriage: age, gender, and satisfaction. *Psychology and Aging*, 8, 301–13.

Levinson, D. J., Darrow, C. N., & Klein, E. B. (1978). *The seasons of a man's life*. New York: Alfred A. Knopf.

Lewin, K. (1935). *A dynamic theory of personality: selected papers of Kurt Lewin*. New York: McGraw Hill.

Lewine, R. J. (1988). Gender in schizophrenia. In H. A. Nasrallah (ed.), *Handbook of schizophrenia*, vol. 3 (pp. 379–97). Amsterdam: Elsevier.

Lewine, R. J. (1990). A discriminant validity study of negative symptoms with a special focus on depression and antipsychotic medication. *American Journal of Psychiatry*, 147, 1463–6.

Lewine, R. J., Gulley, L. R., Risch, S. C., Jewart, R., & Houpt, J. L. (1990). Sexual dimorphism, brain morphology, and schizophrenia. *Schizophrenia Bulletin*, 16, 195–203.

Lewinsohn, P. M., & Graf, M. (1973). Pleasant activities and depression. *Journal of Consulting and Clinical Psychology*, 41, 261–8.

Lewinsohn, P. M., Munoz, R. F., Youngren, M. A., & Zeiss, A. M. (1986). *Control your depression*, rev. edn. New York: Prentice Hall.

Liberman, R. P., DeRisi, W. D., & Mueser, K. T. (1989). *Social skills training for psychiatric patients*. Needham Heights, MA: Allyn & Bacon.

Liberto, J. G., Oslin, D. W., & Ruskin, P. E. (1996). In L. L. Carstensen, B. A. Edelstein, & L. Dornbrand (eds), *The practical handbook of clinical gerontology* (pp. 324–48). Thousand Oaks, CA: Sage.

Lichtenberg, P. A. (1994). *A guide to psychological practice in geriatric long-term care*. New York: Haworth Press.

Lichtenberg, P. A., Smith, M., Frazer, D., Molinari, V., Rosowsky, E., Crose, R., Stillwell, N., Kramer, N., Hartman-Stein, P., Qualls, S., Salamon, M., Duffy, M., Parr, J., & Gallagher-Thompson, D. (1998). Standards for psychological services in long-term care facilities. *The Gerontologist*, 38, 122–7.

Light, E., & Lebowitz, B. D. (eds) (1990). *Alzheimer's disease: treatment and family stress*. New York: Hemisphere.

Light, E., & Lebowitz, B. D. (eds) (1991). *The elderly with chronic mental illness*. New York: Springer.

306 References

Lopata, H. Z. (1973). *Widowhood in an American city*. Cambridge, MA: Schenkman.

Mace, N. L., & Rabins, P. V. (1981). *The 36 hour day*. Baltimore: Johns Hopkins University Press.

MacGregor, P. (1994). Grief: the unrecognized parental response to mental illness in a child. *Social Work*, 39, 160–6.

Mahoney, M. J. (1974). *Cognition and behavior modification*. Cambridge, MA: Ballinger.

Malmgren, R. (1994). Epidemiology of aging. In C. E. Coffey & J. L. Cummings (eds), *Textbook of geriatric neuropsychiatry* (pp. 17–34). Washington, DC: American Psychiatric Press.

Manne, S. L., & Zautra, A. J. (1990). Couples coping with chronic illness: women with rheumatoid arthritis and their healthy husbands. *Journal of Behavioral Medicine*, 13, 327–42.

Manton, K. G., Corder, L. S., & Stallard, E. (1993). Estimates of change in chronic disability and institutional incidence and prevalence rates in the US elderly population from the 1982, 1984, and 1989 National Long Term Care Survey *Journal of Gerontology: Social Sciences*, 48 (4), S153–S166.

Marder, S. R. & Meibach, R. (1994). Risperidone in the treatment of schizophrenia. *American Journal of Psychiatry*, 151, 825–35.

Markovitz, P. J. (1993). Treatment of anxiety in the elderly. *Journal of Clinical Psychiatry*, 54 (suppl.), 64–8.

Marsiske, M., Lang, F. R., Baltes, P. B., & Baltes, M. M. (1995). Selective optimization with compensation: life-span perspectives on successful human development. In R. A. Dixon & L. Backman (eds), *Compensating for psychological deficits and declines: managing losses and promoting gains* (pp. 35–79). Mahwah, NJ: Erlbaum.

Martin, P., & Smyer, M. A. (1990). The experience of micro- and macroevents: a life span analysis. *Research on Aging*, 12 (3), 294–310.

Mattis, S. (1976). Mental status examination for organic mental syndrome in the elderly patient. In L. Bellak & T. B. Karasu (eds), *Geriatric psychiatry* (pp. 79–121). New York: Grune & Stratton.

Mayfield, D., McLeod, G., & Hall, P. (1974). The CAGE questionnaire: validation of a new alcoholism screening instrument. *American Journal of Psychiatry*, 131, 1121–3.

McCrae, R. R. (1989). Age differences and changes in the use of coping mechanisms. *Journal of Gerontology: Psychological Sciences*, 44 (6), P161–P169.

McCrae, R. R., & Costa, P. T., Jr (1990). *Personality in adulthood*. New York: Guilford Press.

McGoldrick, M., & Gerson, R. (1985). *Genograms in family assessment*. New York: W. W. Norton.

McKhann, G., Drachman, D., Folstein, M., Katzman, R., Price, D., & Stadlan, E. M. (1984). Clinical diagnosis of Alzheimer's disease: report of the NINCDS-ADRDA work group under the auspices of Department of Health and Human Services task force on Alzheimer's disease. *Neurology*, 34, 939–44.

Meehan, P. J., Saltzman, L. E., & Sattin, R. W. (1991). Suicides among older United States residents: epidemiologic characteristics and trends. *American Journal of Public Health*, 81, 1198–200.

Meltzer, H. Y. (1990). Clozapine: mechanism of action in relation to its clinical advantages. In A. Kales, C. N. Stefanis, & J. Talbott (eds), *Recent advances in schizophrenia* (pp. 237–56). New York: Springer.

Minuchin, S. (1974). *Families and family therapy*. Cambridge, MA: Harvard University Press.

Mittelman, M. S., Ferris, S. H., Shulman, E., Steinberg, G., & Levin, B. (1996). A family intervention to delay nursing home placement of patients with Alzheimer's disease: a randomized controlled study. *Journal of the American Medical Association*, 276, 1725–31.

Mittelman, M. S., Ferris, S. H., Shulman, E., Steinberg, G., Mackell, J., & Ambinder, A. (1994). Efficacy of multicomponent individualized treatment to improve the well-being of Alzheimer's caregivers. In E. Light, G. Niederehe, & B. D. Lebowitz (eds), *Stress effects on family caregivers of Alzheimer's patients* (pp. 156–84). New York: Springer.

Mittelman, M., Ferris, S. H., Steinberg, G., Shulman, E., Mackell, J., Ambinder, A., & Cohen, J. (1993). An intervention that delays institutionalization of Alzheimer's disease patients: treatment of spouse-caregivers. *The Gerontologist*, 33, 730–40.

Moak, G. S. (1996). When the seriously mentally ill patient grows old. In S. M. Sorreff (ed.), *Handbook for the treatment of the seriously mentally ill* (pp. 279–94). Seattle: Hogrefe & Huber.

Molinari, V., Ames, A., & Essa, M. (1994). Prevalence of personality disorders in two geropsychiatric inpatient units. *Journal of Geriatric Psychiatry and Neurology*, 7, 209–15.

Molinari, V., & Marmion, J. (1995). Relationship between affective disorders and Axis II diagnoses in geropsychiatric patients. *Journal of Geriatric Psychiatry and Neurology*, 8, 61–4.

Moore, J. T., Silimperi, D. R., & Bobula, J. A. (1978). Recognition of depression by family medicine residents: the impact of screening. *Journal of Family Practice*, 7, 509–13.

Morse, C., & Wisocki, P. (1991). Residential factors in programming for elderly. In P. A. Wisocki (ed.), *Handbook of clinical behavior therapy with the elderly client* (pp. 97–120). New York: Plenum.

Mrazek, P. J., & Haggerty, R. J. (eds) (1994). *Reducing risks for mental disorders: frontiers for preventive intervention research*. Washington, DC: National Academy Press.

Mueser, K. T., & Gingerich, S. (1994). *Coping with schizophrenia: a guide for families*. Oakland, CA: New Harbinger.

Mueser, K. T., & Glynn, S. M. (1995). *Behavioral family therapy for psychiatric disorders*. Needham Heights, MA: Allyn & Bacon.

Mueser, K. T., Sayers, S. L., Schooler, N. R., Mance, R. M., & Haas, G. L. (1994). A multi-site investigation of the reliability of the scale for the assessment of negative symptoms. *American Journal of Psychiatry*, 151, 1453–62.

Mueser, K. T., Wallace, C. J., & Liberman, R. P. (in press). New developments in social skills training. *Behaviour Change*.

308 References

Mueser, K. T., Yarnold, P. R., Levinson, D. F., Singh, H., Bellack, A. S., Kee, K., Morrison, R. L., & Yadalam, K. G. (1990). Prevalence of substance abuse in schizophrenia: demographic and clinical correlates. *Schizophrenia Bulletin*, 16, 31–56.

Mulkerrin, E., Nicklason, F., Sykes, D., & Dewar, R. (1992). Recognition of cognitive impairment in elderly patients being discharged from hospital. *Clinical Gerontologist*, 12, 3–25.

Mulsant, B. H., Stergiou, A., Keshavan, M. S., Sweet, R. A., Rifai, A. H., Pasternak, R., & Zubenko, G. S. (1993). Schizophrenia in late life: elderly patients admitted to an acute care psychiatric hospital. *Schizophrenia Bulletin*, 19, 709–21.

Murphy, E., Lindesay, J., & Grundy, E. (1986). 60 years of suicide in England and Wales. *Archives of General Psychiatry*, 43, 969–76.

Myers, J. K., Weissman, M. M., Tischler, G. L., Holzer, C. E., Leaf, P. J., Orvaschel, H., Anthony, J. C., Boyd, J. H., Burke, J. D., Kramer, M., & Stolzman, R. (1984). Six month prevalence of psychiatric disorders in three communities: 1980–1982. *Archives of General Psychiatry*, 41, 959–67.

National Center for Health Statistics (1992). Advance report of final mortality statistics, 1989. *NCHS Monthly Vital Statistics Report*, 40 (8, suppl. 2).

National Nursing Home Survey (1985). Vital and health statistics (DHHS Publication No. PHS 89-1758). *National Health Survey Series 13*, no. 97.

Nemiroff, R. A., & Colarusso, C. A. (1990). Frontiers of adult development in theory and practice. In R. A. Nemiroff & C. A. Colarusso (eds), *New dimensions in adult development* (pp. 97–124). New York: Basic Books.

Neugarten, B. L. (1979). Time, age and the life cycle. *American Journal of Psychiatry*, 136, 887–95.

Newhouse, P. A. (1996). Use of serotonin selective reuptake inhibitors in geriatric depression. *Journal of Clinical Psychiatry*, 57 (suppl. 5), 12–22.

Newton, N., Brauer, D., Gutmann, D. L., & Grunes, J. (1986). Psychodynamic therapy with the aged: a review. *Clinical Gerontologist*, 5, 205–29.

Niederehe, G., & Schneider, L. S. (1998). Treatment of depression and anxiety in the aged. In P. E. Nathan & J. M. Gorman (eds), *Treatments that work*. New York: Oxford University Press.

Niederehe, G., & Teri, L. (1996). Draft report of the APA interdivisional task force on qualifications for practice in clinical and applied geropsychology. Unpublished manuscript, American Psychological Association, Division 12, Section II, and Division 20.

NIH Consensus Panel on Assessment & NIH Consensus Panel on Depression in Late Life (1992). Diagnosis and treatment of depression in late life. *Journal of the American Medical Association*, 268 (8), 1018–24.

NIH Consensus Statement: Geriatric assessment methods for clinical decision-making (1988). *Journal of the American Geriatrics Society*, 36, 342–7.

Overall, J. E., & Beller, S. A. (1984). The brief psychiatric rating scale (BPRS) in geropsychiatric research, I: Factor structure on an inpatient unit. *Journal of Gerontology*, 39, 187–93.

Overall, J. E., & Gorham, D. R. (1962). The brief psychiatric rating scale. *Psychological Reports*, 10, 799–812.

Overall, J. E., & Gorham, D. R. (1988). Introduction: The brief psychiatric rating scale (BPRS): recent developments in ascertainment and scaling. *Psychopharmacology Bulletin*, 24, 97–9.

Overall, J. E., & Rhoades, H. M. (1988). Clinician-rated scales for multidimensional assessment of psychopathology in the elderly. *Psychopharmacology Bulletin*, 24, 587–94.

Oxman, T. E., Barret, J. E., Barret, J., & Gerber, T. (1990). Symptomatology of late-life minor depression among primary care patients. *Psychosomatics*, 31, 174–80.

Pargament, K. I., Van Haitsma, K. S., & Ensing, D. S. (1995). Religion and coping. In M. A. Kimble, S. H. McFadden, J. W. Ellor, & J. J. Seeber (eds), *Aging spirituality and religion: a handbook* (pp. 47–67). Minneapolis: Fortress Press.

Park, D. C., Willis, S. L., Morrow, D., Diehl, M., & Gaines, C. L. (1994). Cognitive function and medication usage in older adults. *Journal of Applied Gerontology*, 13, 39–57.

Parmelee, P. A., Katz, I. R., & Lawton, M. P. (1989). Depression among institutionalized aged: assessment and prevalence estimation. *Journal of Gerontology*, 44, M22–M29.

Parsons, T. (1949). The social structure of the family. In R. Anshen (ed.), *The family: its function and destiny* (pp. 173–201). New York: Harper & Row.

Pearce, N. (1996). Traditional epidemiology, modern epidemiology, and public health. *American Journal of Public Health*, 86 (5), 678–83.

Pearlin, L. I., & Skaff, M. M. (1995). Stressors and adaptation in late life. Paper presented at the White House mini-conference on Emerging Issues in Mental Health and Aging, Washington, DC.

Pearlson, G. D, Kreger, L., Rabins, P. V., Chase, G. A., Cohen, B., Wirth, J. B., Schlaepfer, T. B., & Tune, L. E. (1989). A chart review study of late onset and early-onset schizophrenia. *American Journal of Psychiatry*, 146, 1568–74.

Pearlson, G. D., & Rabins, P. V. (1988). The late onset psychoses: possible risk factors. *Psychiatric Clinics of North America, Psychosis and Depression in the Elderly*, 11, 15–33.

Pepper, S. C. (1942). *World hypotheses*. Berkeley, CA: University of California Press.

Pfeiffer, E. (1975). A short portable mental status questionnaire for the assessment of organic brain deficit in elderly patients. *Journal of the American Geriatrics Society*, 23, 433–41.

Philadelphia College of Pharmacy and Science (1995). Tailoring the AHCPR clinical practice guidelines on depression in primary care for use in long-term care facilities. Unpublished manuscript.

Philibert, M. (1979). Philosophical approach to gerontology. In J. Hendricks & C. Davis Hendricks (eds), *Dimensions of aging* (pp. 379–94). Cambridge, MA: Winthrop.

Pinkston, E. M., & Linsk, N. L. (1984). *Care of the elderly: a family approach*. New York: Pergamon Press.

Platt, S. (1985). Measuring the burden of psychiatric illness on the family: an evaluation of some rating scales. *Psychological Medicine*, 15, 383–93.

PLTC (1997). Standards for psychological services in long term care facilities. *Psychologists in Long Term Care Newsletter,* 11 (1).

Pollock, B. G., Perel, J. M., Altieri, L. P., & Kirshner, M. (1992). Debrisoquine hydroxylation phenotyping in geriatric psychopharmacology. *Psychopharmacology Bulletin*, 28, 163–7.

Post, F. (1966). *Persistent persecutory states of the elderly.* London: Pergamon Press.

Prager, S., & Jeste, D. V. (1993). Sensory impairment in late-life schizophrenia. *Schizophrenia Bulletin*, 19, 755–72.

Pruchno, R. A., Blow, F. C., & Smyer, M. A. (1984). Life events and interdependent lives: implications for research and intervention. *Human Development*, 27, 31–41.

Pruchno, R. A., Kleban, M. H., & Resch, N. L. (1988). Psychometric assessment of the multidimensional observation scale for elderly subjects (MOSES). *Journal of Gerontology: Psychological Sciences*, 43, P164–P169.

Qualls, S. H. (1991). Resistance of older families to therapeutic intervention. *Clinical Gerontologist*, 11, 59–68.

Qualls, S. H. (1995a). Clinical interventions with later life families. In R. Blieszner & V. H. Bedford (eds), *Handbook on aging and the family* (pp. 474–87). Westport, CT: Greenwood Press.

Qualls, S. H. (1995b). Marital therapy with later life couples. *Journal of Geriatric Psychiatry*, 28, 139–63.

Qualls, S. H. (1996). Family therapy with aging families. In B. Knight & S. H. Zarit (eds), *Psychotherapy and aging* (pp. 121–37). Washington, DC: American Psychological Association.

Qualls, S. H. (1997). Transitions in autonomy: the essential caregiving challenge. *Family Relations*, 46, 41–5.

Qualls, S. H. (1998). Training in geropsychology: preparing to meet the demand. *Professional Psychology: Research and Practice*, 29, 23–8.

Qualls, S. H., & Czirr, R. (1988). Geriatric health teams: classifying models of professional and team functioning. *The Gerontologist*, 28, 372–6.

Rabins, P. V. (1991). Psychosocial and management aspects of delirium. *International Psychogeriatrics*, 3, 319–24.

Rabins, P. V. (1992). Prevention of mental disorder in the elderly: current perspectives and future prospects. *Journal of the American Geriatrics Society*, 40, 727–33.

Rabins, P. V., Black, B., German P., Roca, R., McGuire, M., Brant, L., & Cook, J. (1996). The prevalence of psychiatric disorders in elderly residents of public housing. *Journal of Gerontology: Medical Sciences*, 51A, M319–M324.

Rabins, P. V., Pauker, S., & Thomas, J. (1984). Can schizophrenia begin after age 44? *Comprehensive Psychiatry*, 25, 290–3.

Radloff, L. (1977). The CES-D scale: a self-report depression scale for research in the general population. *Applied Psychological Measurement*, 1, 385–401.

Randolph, E. T., Eth, S., Glynn, S. M., Paz, G. G., Leong, G. B., Shaner, A. L.,

Strachan, A., Van Vort, W., Escobar, J. I., & Liberman, R. P. (1994). Behavioural family management in schizophrenia: outcome of a clinic-based intervention. *British Journal of Psychiatry*, 164, 501–6.

Rapp, S. R., Parisi, S. A., & Walsh, D. A. (1988). Psychological dysfunction and physical health among elderly medical inpatients. *Journal of Consulting and Clinical Psychology*, 56, 851–5.

Rashcko, R. (1985). Systems integration at the program level: aging and mental health. *The Gerontologist*, 25, 460–3.

Ray, W. A., Federspiel, C. F., & Schaffner, W. (1980). A study of antipsychotic drug use in nursing homes: epidemiologic evidence suggesting misuse. *American Journal of Public Health*, 70, 485–91.

Rechtschaffen, A. (1959). Psychotherapy with geriatric patients: a review of the literature. *Journal of Gerontology*, 14, 73–84.

Reese, H. W., & Overton, W. F. (1970). Models of development and theories of development. In L. R. Goulet & P. B. Baltes (eds), *Life-span developmental psychology* (pp. 116–49). New York: Academic Press.

Regan, C. A., Lorig, K., & Thoresen, C. E. (1988). Arthritis appraisal and ways of coping: scale development. *Arthritis Care and Research*, 1, 139–50.

Regier, D. A., Boyd, J. H., Burke, J. D., & Rae, D. S. (1988). One-month prevalence of mental disorders in the United States. *Archive of General Psychiatry*, 45, 977–86.

Reich, J., Nduaguba, M., & Yates, W. (1988). Age and sex distribution of DSM-III personality cluster traits in a community population. *Comprehensive Psychiatry*, 29, 298–303.

Reich, J. W., & Zautra, A. J. (1989). A perceived control intervention for at-risk older adults. *Psychology and Aging*, 4, 415–24.

Reich, J. W., & Zautra, A. J. (1990). Dispositional control beliefs and the consequences of a control-enhancing intervention. *Journal of Gerontology: Psychological Sciences*, 45, P46–P51.

Reisberg, B., Ferris, S. H., de Leon, M. J., & Crook, T. (1982). The global deterioration scale for assessment of primary degenerative dementia. *American Journal of Psychiatry*, 139, 1136–9.

Reynolds, C. F., Frank, E., Kupfer, D. J., Thase, M. E., Perel, J. M., Mazumdar, S., & Houck, P. R. (1996). Treatment outcome in recurrent major depression: a post hoc comparison of elderly ("young old") and midlife patients. *American Journal of Psychiatry*, 153, 1288–92.

Reynolds, C. F., Frank, E., Perel, J. M., Mazumdar, S., & Kupfer, D. J. (1995). Maintenance therapies for late-life recurrent major depression: research and review circa 1995. *International psychogeriatrics*, 7 (suppl.), 27–39.

Reynolds, C. F., Frank, E., Perel, J. M., Miller, M. D., Cornes, C., Rifai, A. H., Pollock, B. G., Mazumdar, S., George, C. J., Houck, P. R., & Kupfer, D. J. (1992). Combined pharmacotherapy and psychotherapy in the acute and continuation treatment of elderly patients with recurrent major depression: a preliminary report. *American Journal of Psychiatry*, 149, 1687–92.

Rice, D. P., Kelman, S., & Miller, L. S. (1992). The economic burden of mental illness. *Hospital and Community Psychiatry*, 43 (12), 1227–32.

Rice, T., & Thomas, K. (1992). Evaluating the new Medigap standardization regulations. *Health Affairs*, 11 (1), 194–207.

Ritchie, K., Kildea, D., & Robine, J. M. (1992). The relationship between age and the prevalence of senile dementia: a meta-analysis of recent data. *International Journal of Epidemiology*, 21, 763–9.

Robertson, J. F. (1995). Grandparenting in an era of rapid change. In R. Blieszner & V. H. Bedford (eds), *Handbook on aging and the family* (pp. 243–60). Westport, CT: Greenwood Press.

Robins, L. N., Helzer, J. C., Weissman, M. M., Owaschel, H., Bruenberg, E., Burke, J. O., & Regier, D. A. (1984). Lifetime prevalence of specific psychiatric disorders in three sites. *Archives of General Psychiatry*, 41, 949–58.

Robins, L. N., Helzer, J. E., Croughan, J., & Ratcliff, K. S. (1981). National Institute of Mental Health diagnostic interview schedule: its history, characteristics, and validity. *Archives of General Psychiatry*, 38, 381–9.

Rockwood, K. (1989). Acute confusion in elderly medical patients. *Journal of the American Geriatrics Society*, 37, 150–4.

Rodgers, R. H., & White, J. W. (1993). Family development theory. In P. G. Boss, W. J. Doherty, R. LaRossa, W. R. Schumm, & S. K. Steinmetz (eds), *Sourcebook of family theories and methods* (pp. 225–54). New York: Plenum.

Roman, G. C., Tatemichi, T. K., Erkinjuntti, T., Cummings, J. L., Masdeu, J. C., & Garcia, J. H. (1993). Vascular dementia: diagnostic criteria for research studies. Report of the NINDS-AIREN International Workshop. *Neurology*, 43, 250–60.

Rosenstein, M. J., Milazzo-Sayre, L. J., & Manderscheid, R. W. (1990). Characteristics of persons using specialty inpatient, outpatient, and partial care programs in 1986. In R. W. Manderscheid & M. A. Sonnenschein (eds), *Mental health, United States, 1990* (pp. 139–72). Washington, DC: US Government Printing Office.

Rosowsky, E., & Gurian, B. (1992). Impact of borderline personality disorder in late life on systems of care. *Hospital and Community Psychiatry*, 43, 386–9.

Rowe, J., & Kahn, R. (1987). Human aging: usual and successful. *Science*, 237, 143–9.

Rush, A. J., Golden, W. E., Hall, G. W., Herrera, M., Houston, A., Kathol, R. G., Katon, W., Matchett, C. L., Petty, F., Schulberg, H. C., Smith, G. R., & Stuart, G. W. (1993). *Depression in primary care*, vol. 2: *Treatment of major depression. Clinical practice guideline, no. 5*. Rockville, MD: US Department of Health and Human Services, Public Health Service, Agency for Health Care Policy and Research. AHCPR Publication no. 93-0551.

Ruth, J. E., & Coleman, P. (1996). Personality and aging: coping and management of the self in later life. In J. E. Birren & K. W. Schaie (eds), *Handbook of the psychology of aging*, 4th edn (pp. 308–22). New York: Academic Press.

Ryff, C. (1982). Successful aging: a developmental approach. *The Gerontologist*, 22, 209–14.

Sabatino, C. (1996). Competency: refining our legal fictions. In M. A. Smyer, K. W. Schaie, & M. B. Kapp (eds), *Older adults' decision-making and the law*. New York: Springer.

Sackeim, H. A. (1994). Use of electroconvulsive therapy in late-life depression. In L. S. Schneider, C. F. Reynolds, B. D. Lebowitz, & A. J. Friedhoff (eds), *Diagnosis and treatment of depression in late life* (pp. 259–73). Washington, DC: American Psychiatric Press.

Sadavoy, J. (1987). Character disorders in the elderly: an overview. In J. Sadavoy & M. Leszcz (eds), *Treating the elderly with psychotherapy: the scope for change in later life* (pp. 175–229). Madison, CT: International Universities Press.

Sadavoy, J., & Fogel, B. (1992). Personality disorders in old age. In J. E. Birren, R. B. Sloane, & G. D. Cohen (eds), *Handbook of mental health and aging*, 2nd edn (pp. 433–62). San Diego: Academic Press.

Salokangas, R. K. R., Palo-Oja, T., & Ojanen, M. (1991). The need for social support among out-patients suffering from functional psychosis. *Psychological Medicine*, 21, 209–17.

Salthouse, T. A. (1991). Cognitive competence and expertise in aging. In J. E. Birren & K. W. Schaie (eds), *Handbook of the psychology of aging*, 3rd edn (pp. 310–46). San Diego: Academic Press.

Salzman, C. (1991). Pharmacological treatment of the anxious elderly patient. In C. Salzman & B. D. Lebowitz (eds), *Anxiety in the elderly: treatment and research* (pp. 149–73). New York: Springer.

Salzman, C., & Nevis-Olesen, J. (1992). Psychopharmacologic treatment. In J. E. Birren, R. B. Sloane, & G. D. Cohen (eds), *Handbook of mental health and aging*, 2nd edn (pp. 721–62). San Diego: Academic Press.

Salzman, C., Vaccaro, B., & Lief, J. (1995). Clozapine in older patients with psychosis and behavioral disruption. *American Journal of Geriatric Psychiatry*, 3, 26–33.

Schaie, K. W. (1994). The course of adult intellectual development. *American Psychologist*, 49, 304–13.

Schaie, K. W. (1995). Training materials in geropsychology: developmental issues. In B. G. Knight, L. Teri, P. Wohlford, & J. Santos (eds), *Mental health services for older adults: implications for training and practice in geropsychology* (pp. 33–9). Washington, DC: American Psychological Association.

Schaie, K. W. (1996). Intellectual development in adulthood. In J. E. Birren & K. W. Schaie (eds), *Handbook of the psychology of aging*, 4th edn (pp. 266–86). San Diego: Academic Press.

Schaie, K. W., & Willis, S. L. (1991). *Adult development and aging*, 3rd edn. New York: Harper Collins.

Scharlach, A. E. (1987). Relieving feelings of strain among women with elderly mothers. *Psychology and Aging*, 2, 9–13.

Schneider, L. S. (1995). Efficacy of clinical treatment for mental disorders among older persons. In M. Gatz (Ed.), *Emerging issues in mental health and aging* (pp. 19–71). Washington, DC: American Psychological Association.

Schneider, L. S., Reynolds, C. F., Lebowitz, B. D., & Friedhoff, A. J. (eds) (1994).

Diagnosis and treatment of depression in late life. Washington, DC: American Psychiatric Press.

Schulz, R., O'Brien, A. T., Bookwala, J., & Fleissner, K. (1995). Psychiatric and physical morbidity effects of dementia caregiving: prevalence, correlates, and causes. *The Gerontologist*, 35, 771–91.

Scogin, F. R. (1994). Assessment of depression in older adults: a guide for practitioners. In M. Storandt & G. R. VandenBos (eds), *Neuropsychological assessment of dementia and depression in older adults: a clinician's guide* (pp. 61–80). Washington, DC: American Psychological Association.

Scogin, F. R., Jamison, C, & Davis, N. (1990). Two-year follow-up of bibliotherapy for depression in older adults. *Journal of Consulting and Clinical Psychology*, 58, 665–7.

Scogin, F. R., & McElreath, L. (1994). Efficacy of psychosocial treatments for geriatric depression. *Journal of Consulting and Clinical Psychology*, 62, 69–74.

Seeman, M. V. (1986). Current outcome in schizophrenia: women vs. men. *Acta Psychiatrica Scandinavica*, 73, 609–17.

Seeman, M. V., & Lang, M. (1990). The role of estrogens in schizophrenia gender differences. *Schizophrenia Bulletin*, 16, 185–94.

Segal, D. L., Hersen, M., Van Hasselt, V. B., Silberman, C. S., & Roth, L. (in press). Diagnosis and assessment of personality disorders in older adults: a critical review. *Journal of Personality Disorders*.

Segal, D. L., Van Hasselt, V. B., Hersen, M., & King, C. (1996). Treatment of substance abuse in older adults. In J. R. Cautela & W. Ishaq (eds), *Contemporary issues in behavior therapy: improving the human condition*. New York: Plenum.

Shadish, W. R., Lurigio, A. J., & Lewis, D. A. (1989). After deinstitutionalization: the present and future of mental health long-term care policy. *Journal of Social Issues*, 45, 1–16.

Shanas, E. (1979). Social myth as hypothesis: the case of the family relations of old people. *The Gerontologist*, 19, 3–9.

Shanas, E. (1980). Older people and their families: the new pioneers. *Journal of Marriage and the Family*, 42, 9–15.

Shaver, P., & Hazan C. (1988). A biased overview of the study of love. *Journal of Social and Personal Relationships*, 5 (4), 473–501.

Shea, D. G. (1994). Nursing homes and the costs of mental disorders. Unpublished manuscript, Pennsylvania State University, College of Health & Human Development.

Shea, D. G., Smyer, M. A., & Streit, A. (1993). Mental health services for nursing home residents: what will it cost? *Journal of Mental Health Administration*, 20 (3), 223–35.

Sheikh, J. I. (1992). Anxiety and its disorders in old age. In J. E. Birren, R. B. Sloane, & G. D. Cohen (eds), *Handbook of mental health and aging*, 2nd edn (pp. 409–32). New York: Academic Press.

Shield, R. R. (1988). *Uneasy endings: daily life in an american nursing home*. Ithaca, NY: Cornell University Press.

Shields, C. G. (1992). Family interaction and caregivers of Alzheimer's disease patients: correlates of depression. *Family Process*, 31, 19–33.

Shields, C. G., King, D. A., & Wynne, L. C. (1995). Interventions with later life families. In R. H. Mikesell, D. Lusterman, & S. H. McDaniel (eds), *Integrating family therapy: handbook of family psychology and systems theory* (pp. 141–58). Washington, DC: American Psychological Association.

Short, P. F., & Leon, J. (1990). *Use of home and community services by persons ages 65 and older with functional difficulties*. DHHS Publication no. PHS90-3466, National Medical Expenditure Survey Research Findings 5. Rockville, MD: Public Health Service, Agency for Health Care Policy and Research.

Shulman, K., & Post, F. (1980). Bipolar affective disorder in old age. *British Journal of Psychiatry*, 136, 26–32.

Shulman, K. I., & Tohen, M. (1994). Unipolar mania reconsidered: evidence from an elderly cohort. *British Journal of Psychiatry*, 164, 547–9.

Skinner, B. F. (1953). *Science and human behavior*. New York: Free Press.

Skoog, I., Nilsson, L., Palmertz, B., Andreasson, L., & Svanborg, A. (1993). A population-based study of dementia in 85-year-olds. *New England Journal of Medicine*, 328 (3), 153–8.

Sloane, R. B., Staples, F. R., & Schneider, L. S. (1985). Interpersonal therapy versus nortriptyline for depression in the elderly. In G. D. Burrows, T. R. Norman, & L. Dennerstein (eds), *Clinical and pharmacological studies in psychiatric disorders* (pp. 344–6). London: John Libbey.

Smith, A. D. (1996). Memory. In J. E. Birren & K. W. Schaie (eds), *Handbook of the psychology of aging*, 4th edn (pp. 236–50). San Diego: Academic Press.

Smyer, M. A. (1984). Life transitions and aging: implications for counseling older adults. *Counseling Psychologist*, 12 (2), 17–28.

Smyer, M. A. (1989). Nursing homes as a setting for psychological practice: public policy perspectives. *American Psychologist*, 44 (10), 1307–14.

Smyer, M. A. (ed.) (1993). *Mental health & aging*. New York: Springer.

Smyer, M. A. (1995a). Formal support in later life: lessons for prevention. In L. A. Bond, S. J. Cutler, & A. Grams (eds), *Promoting successful and productive aging* (pp. 186–202). Thousand Oaks, CA: Sage.

Smyer, M. A. (1995b). Mental disorders. In Task Force on Aging Research, *The threshold of discovery: future directions for research on aging* (pp. 103–24). Washington, DC: US Department of Health and Human Services.

Smyer, M. A., Brannon, D., & Cohn, M. D. (1992). Improving nursing home care through training and job redesign. *The Gerontologist*, 33 (3), 327–33.

Smyer, M. A., Cohn, M. D., & Brannon, D. (eds) (1988). *Mental health consultation in nursing homes*. New York: New York University Press.

Smyer, M. A., & Downs, M. G. (1995). Psychopharmacology: an essential element in educating clinical psychologists for working with older adults. In B. G. Knight, L. Teri, P. Wohlford, & J. Santos (eds), *Mental health services for older adults: implications for training and practice in geropsychology* (pp. 73–83). Washington, DC: American Psychological Association.

Smyer, M. A., & Gatz, M. (1986). Intervention research approaches. *Research on Aging*, 8, 536–58.

Smyer, M. A., Schaie, K. W., & Kapp, M. B. (1996). *Older adults' decision-making and the law*. New York: Springer.

Smyer, M. A., & Shea, D. G. (1996). Mental health among the elderly. In L. A. Vitt & J. Siegenthaler (eds), *Encyclopedia of financial gerontology* (pp. 365–71). Westport, CT: Greenwood Press.

Smyer, M. A., Shea, D., & Streit, A. (1994). The provision and use of mental health services in nursing homes: results from the national medical expenditure survey. *American Journal of Public Health*, 84 (2), 284–7.

Smyer, M. A., & Walls, C. T. (1994). Design and evaluation of interventions in nursing homes. In C. B. Fisher & R. M. Lerner (eds), *Applied developmental psychology*. Cambridge, MA: McGraw-Hill.

Smyer, M. A., Zarit, S. H., & Qualls, S. H. (1990). Psychological intervention with the aging individual. In J. E. Birren & K. W. Schaie (eds), *Handbook of the psychology of aging*, 3rd edn (pp. 375–403). San Diego: Academic Press.

Spayd, C. S. (1993). Psychological consultation in the nursing home: group brain-storming case example. Unpublished workshop material.

Spayd, C. S., & Smyer, M. A. (1996). Psychological interventions in nursing homes. In S. H. Zarit & B. G. Knight (eds), *A guide to psychotherapy and aging: effective clinical interventions in a life-stage context* (pp. 241–68). Washington, DC: American Psychological Association.

Spielberger, C., Gorsuch, R., & Lushene, R. (1970). *STAI manual for the state-trait anxiety inventory*. Palo Alto, CA: Consulting Psychologists Press.

Spitzer, R. L., Williams, J. B. W., Gibbon, M., & First, M. B. (1990). *Structured clinical interview for DSM-III-R (SCID)*. Washington, DC: American Psychiatric Press.

Spore, D. L., Horgas, A. L., Smyer, M. A., & Marks, L. N. (1992). The relationship of antipsychotic drug use, resident behavior, and diagnoses among nursing home residents. *Journal of Aging and Health*, 4 (4), 514–35.

Starr, B. D., Weiner, M. B., & Rabetz, M. (1979). *The projective assessment of aging method (PAAM)*. New York: Springer.

Stewart, A. L., Greenfield, S., Hays, R. D., Wells, K., Rogers, W. H., Berry, S. D., McGlynn, E. A., & Ware, J. E. (1989). Functional status and well-being of patients with chronic conditions: results from the medical outcomes study. *Journal of the American Medical Association*, 262 (7), 907–13.

Stone, A. A., & Porter, L. S. (1995). Psychological coping: its importance for treating medical problems. *Mind/Body Medicine*, 1 (1), 46–53.

Storandt, M., & VandenBos, G. R. (eds) (1994). *Neuropsychological assessment of dementia and depression in older adults: a clinician's guide* (pp. 33–59). Washington, DC: American Psychological Association.

Strahan, G. W., & Burns, B. J. (1991). Mental illness in nursing homes: United States, 1985. *Vital Health Statistics Series 13*, no. 105. Data from the National Health Survey; no. 97 DHHS publication; no. (PHS) 89-1758.

Sugar, J. A., & McDowd, J. M. (1992). Memory, learning, and attention. In J. E. Birren, R. B. Sloane, & G. D. Cohen (eds), *Handbook of mental health and aging*, 2nd edn (pp. 307–37). San Diego: Academic Press.

Sullivan, H. S. (1953). *The interpersonal theory of psychiatry*. New York: W.W. Norton.

Sundberg, N. D., Taplin, J. R., & Tyler, L. E. (1983). *Introduction to clinical psychology: perspectives, issues, and contributions to human service*. Englewood Cliffs, NJ: Prentice-Hall.

Sunderland, T., Lawlor, B. A., Martinez, R. A., & Molchan, S. E. (1991). Anxiety in the elderly: neurobiological and clincial interface. In C. Salzman & B. D. Lebowitz (eds), *Anxiety in the elderly: treatment and research* (pp. 105–21). New York: Springer.

Sunderland, T., Lawlor, B. A., Molchan, S. E., & Martinez, R. A. (1988). Depressive syndromes in the elderly: special concerns. *Psychopharmacology Bulletin*, 24, 567–76.

Susser, M. B., & Susser, E. (1996a). Choosing a future for epidemiology, I: Eras and paradigms. *American Journal of Public Health*, 86 (5), 668–73.

Susser, M. B., & Susser, E. (1996b). Choosing a future for epidemiology, II: From black box to Chinese boxes and eco-epidemiology. *American Journal of Public Health*, 86 (5), 674–7.

Swearer, J. M., Drachman, D. A., O'Donnell, B. F., & Mitchell, A. L. (1988). Troublesome and disruptive behaviors in dementia: relationships to diagnosis and disease severity. *Journal of the American Geriatrics Society*, 36, 784–90.

Taeuber, C. M. (1993). *Sixty-five plus in America*. Washington, DC: US Department of Commerce, Economics, and Statistics Administration, Bureau of the Census.

Tarrier, N., Beckett, R., Harwood, S., Baker, A., Yusupoff, L., & Ugarteburu, I. (1993). A trial of two cognitive behavioral methods of treating drug-resistant residual psychotic symptoms in schizophrenic patients, I: Outcome. *British Journal of Psychiatry*, 162, 524–32.

Task Force on Aging Research (1995). *The threshold of discovery: future directions for research on aging*. Washington, DC: US Department of Health and Human Services.

Taylor, J. R., Strassberg, D. S., & Turner, C. W. (1989). Utility of the MMPI in a geriatric population. *Journal of Personality Assessment*, 53, 655–76.

Teresi, J., Holmes, D., Benenson, E., Monaco, C., Barrett, V., Ramirez, M., & Koren, M. J. (1993). A primary care nursing model in long-term care facilities: evaluation of impact on affect, behavior, and socialization. *The Gerontologist*, 33 (5), 667–74.

Teri, L. (1996). Depression in Alzheimer's disease. In M. Hersen & V. B. Van Hasselt (eds), *Psychological treatment of older adults: an introductory text* (pp. 209–22). New York: Plenum.

Teri, L. Curtis, J., Gallagher-Thompson, D., & Thompson, L. W. (1994). Cognitive-behavior therapy with depressed older adults. In L. S. Schneider, C. F. Reynolds, B. D. Lebowitz, & A. J. Friedhoff (eds), *Diagnosis and treatment of depression in late life* (pp. 279–91). Washington, DC: American Psychiatric Press.

Teri, L., & Lewinsohn, P. M. (1982). Modification of the pleasant and unpleasant event schedules for use with the elderly. *Journal of Consulting and Clinical Psychology*, 50, 444–5.

Teri, L., Logsdon, R. G., Uomoto, J., & McCurry, S. M. (1997). Behavioral treatment of depression in dementia patients: a controlled clinical trial. *Journals of Gerontology*, 52B, P159–P166.

Teri, L., Logsdon, R., Wagner, A., & Uomoto, J. (1994). The caregiver role in behavioral treatment of depression in dementia patients. In E. Ligtht, G. Niederehe, & B. D. Lebowitz (eds), *Stress effects on family caregivers of Alzheimer's patients* (pp. 185–204). New York: Springer.

Teri, L., Truax, P., Logsdon, R., Uomoto, J., Zarit, S., & Vitaliano, P. P. (1992). Assessment of behavioral problems in dementia: the revised memory and behavior problems checklist. *Psychology and Aging*, 7 (4), 622–31.

Teri, L., & Wagner, A. (1992). Alzheimer's disease and depression. *Journal of Consulting and Clinical Psychology*, 3, 379–91.

Test, M. A., & Berlin, S. B. (1981). Issues of special concern to chronically mentally ill women. *Professional Psychology*, 12, 136–45.

Test, M. A., Burke, S. S., & Wallisch, L. S. (1990). Gender differences of young adults with schizophrenic disorders in community care. *Schizophrenia Bulletin*, 16, 331–44.

Thompson, L. W. (1996). Cognitive-behavioral therapy and treatment for late-life depression. *Journal of Clinical Psychiatry*, 57, 29–37.

Thompson, L. W., Futterman, A., & Gallagher, D. (1988). Assessment of late-life depression. *Psychopharmacology Bulletin*, 24 (4), 577–86.

Thompson, L. W., Gallagher, D., & Breckenridge, J. S. (1987). Comparative effectiveness of psychotherapies for depressed elders. *Journal of Consulting and Clinical Psychology*, 55, 385–90.

Thompson, L. W., Gallagher, D., & Czirr, R. (1988). Personality disorder and outcome in the treatment of late-life depression. *Journal of Geriatric Psychiatry*, 21, 133–46.

Thompson, L. W., Gallagher, D., Nies, G., & Epstein, D. (1983). Evaluation of the effectiveness of professionals and nonprofessionals as instructors of "coping with depression" classes for elders. *The Gerontologist*, 23, 390–6.

Thompson, L. W., Gallagher-Thompson, D., Futterman, A., Gilewski, M., & Peterson, J. (1991). The effects of late-life spousal bereavement over a 30 month interval. *Psychology and Aging*, 6, 434–41.

Torrey, E. F. (1995). Editorial: Jails and prisons: America's new mental hospitals. *American Journal of Public Health*, 85, 1611–13.

Troll, L. E., & Bengtson, V. L. (1993). The oldest-old in families: an intergenerational perspective. In L. Burton (ed.), *Families and aging* (pp. 79–89). Amityville, NY: Baywood Press.

Tune, L. E. (1991). Postoperative delirium. *International Psychogeriatrics*, 3, 325–32.

US Department of Commerce (1994). Americans with disabilities. *Statistical brief, January* (Publication no. SB/94-1). Washington, DC: US Government Printing Office.

US Department of Commerce (1995). Sixty-five plus in the United States. *Statistical brief* (SB/95-8). Washington, DC: US Government Printing Office.

US Senate Special Committee on Aging (1987–8). *Aging America: trends and projections.* Washington, DC: US Department of Health & Human Services.

Vaillant, G. E. (1977). *Adaptation to life.* Boston: Little, Brown.

Vaillant, G. E. (1993). *The wisdom of the ego.* Cambridge, MA: Harvard University Press.

Vaillant, G. E., & Vaillant, C. O. (1990). Natural history of male psychological health, XII: A 45-year study of predictors of successful aging at age 65. *American Journal of Psychiatry,* 147, 31–7.

Van Putten, T., & Marder, S. R. (1986). Low-dose treatment strategies. *Journal of Clinical Psychiatry,* 47 (suppl. 5), 12–6.

Vernberg, E. M., & Reppucci, N. D. (1986). Behavioral consultation. In F. V. Mannino, E. J. Trickett, M. F. Shore, M. G. Kidder, & G. Levin (eds), *Handbook of mental health consultation,* Publication no. (ADM) 86-1446 (pp. 49–80). Washington, DC: Department of Health & Human Services.

Verwoerdt, A. (1981). *Clinical geropsychiatry,* 2nd edn. Baltimore: Williams & Wilkins.

Vitaliano, P., Russo, J., Carr, J., Maiuro, R., & Becker, J. (1985). The ways of coping checklist: revision and psychometric properties. *Multivariate Behavioral Research,* 20, 3–26.

Watzlawick, P., Beavin, J. H., & Jackson, D. D. (1967). *Pragmatics of human communication. a study of interactional patterns, pathologies, and paradoxes.* New York: W. W. Norton.

Watzlawick, P., Weakland, J. H., & Fisch, R. (1974). *Change.* New York: W. W. Norton.

Weisse, C. S. (1992). Depression and immunocompetence: a review of the literature. *Psychological Bulletin,* 111 (3), 475–89.

Weissman, M. M., Bruce, M. L., Leaf, P. J., Florio, L. P., & Holzer, C. E. (1991). Affective disorders. In L. N. Robins & D. A. Regier (eds), *Psychiatric disorders in America* (pp. 53–80). New York: Free Press.

Welsh, K., Butters, N., Hughes, J., Mohs, R., & Heyman, A. (1991). Detection of abnormal memory decline in mild cases of Alzheimer's disease using CERAD neuropsychological measures. *Archives of Neurology,* 48, 278–81.

Whitchurch, G. G., & Constantine, L. L. (1993). Systems theory. In P. G. Boss, W. J. Doherty, R. LaRossa, W. R. Schumm, & S. K. Steinmetz (eds), *Sourcebook of family theories and methods* (pp. 325–55). New York: Plenum.

Wiener, J. M., Illston, L. H., & Hanley, R. J. (1994). *Sharing the burden: strategies for public and private long-term care insurance.* Washington, DC: Brookings Institution.

Williams, J. M., & Shadish, W. R. (1991). Practical psychological assessment in nursing homes by nursing personnel. In M. S. Harper (ed.), *Management and care of the elderly: psychosocial perspectives* (pp. 310–19). Newbury Park, CA: Sage.

Willis, S. L. (1996). Assessing everyday competence in the cognitively challenged elderly. In M. Smyer, K. W. Schaie, & M. B. Kapp (eds), *Older adults' decision-making and the law* (pp. 87–127). New York: Springer.

Wirshing, D. A., Wirshing, W. C., Marder, S. R., Saunders, C. S., Rossotto, E. H., & Erhart, S. M. (1997). Atypical antipsychotics: a practical review. *Medscape Psychiatry*, 2 (10) [electronic journal].

Wisocki, P. A. (1991). Behavioral gerontology. In P. A. Wisocki (ed.), *Handbook of clinical behavior therapy with the elderly client* (pp. 3–51). New York: Plenum.

Wolfe, R., Morrow, J., & Fredrickson, B. L. (1996). Mood disorders in older adults. In L. L. Carstensen, B. A. Edelstein, & L. Dronbrand (eds), *The practical handbook of clinical gerontology* (pp. 274–303). Thousand Oaks, CA: Sage.

Wolinsky, M A. (1990). *A heart of wisdom: marital counseling with older and elderly couples.* New York: Brunner/Mazel.

Wragg, R., & Jeste, D. V. (1989). An overview of depression and psychosis in Alzheimer's disease. *American Journal of Psychiatry*, 146, 577–87.

Wright, L. K., Clipp, E. C., & George, L. K. (1993). Health consequences of caregiver stress. *Medicine, Exercise, Nutrition, & Health*, 2, 181–95.

Xiong, W., Phillips, M. R., Hu, X., Ruiwen, W., Dai, Q., Kleinman, J., & Kleinman, A. (1994). Family-based intervention for schizophrenic patients in China: a randomised controlled trial. *British Journal of Psychiatry*, 165, 239–47.

Yassa, R., & Suranyl-Cadotte, B. (1993). Clinical characteristics of late-onset schizophrenia and delusional disorder. *Schizophrenia Bulletin*, 19, 701–7.

Yesavage, J. A., Brink, T. L., Rose, T. L., Lum, O., Huang, V., Adey, M., & Leirer, V. O. (1983). Development and validation of a geriatric depression screening scale: a preliminary report. *Journal of Psychiatric Research*, 17, 37–49.

Youngjohn, J. R., & Crook, T. H. (1996). Dementia. In L. L. Carstensen, B. A. Edelstein, & L. Dornbrand (eds), *The practical handbook of clinical gerontology* (pp. 239–54). Thousand Oaks, CA: Sage.

Zarate, C. A., & Tohen, M. (1996). Epidemiology of mood disorders throughout the life cycle. In K. I. Shulman, M. Tohen, & S. P. Kutcher (eds), *Mood disorders across the life span* (pp. 17–33). New York: Wiley-Liss.

Zarit, S. H., Eiler, J., & Hassinger, M. (1985). Clinical assessment. In J. E. Birren & K. W. Schaie (eds), *Handbook of the psychology of aging*, 2nd edn (pp. 725–54). New York: Van Nostrand Reinhold.

Zarit, S. H., & Knight, B. G. (eds) (1996). *A guide to psychotherapy and aging: effective clinical interventions in a life-stage context.* Washington, DC: American Psychological Association.

Zarit, S. H., Orr, N. K., & Zarit, J. M. (1985). *The hidden victims of Alzheimer's disease: families under stress.* New York: New York University Press.

Zarit, S. H., & Teri, L. (1991). Interventions and services for family caregivers. *Annual Review of Gerontology and Geriatrics*, 11, 287–310.

Zautra, A. J., Reich, J. W., & Newsom, J. T. (1995). Autonomy and sense of control among older adults: an examination of their effects on mental health. In L. A.

Bond, S. J. Cutler, & A. Grams (eds), *Promoting successful and productive aging* (pp. 153–70). Thousand Oaks, CA: Sage.

Zeiss, A. M., & Breckenridge, J. S. (1997). Treatment of late life depression: a response to the NIH consensus conference. *Behavior Therapy*, 28, 3–21.

Zeiss, A. M., & Steffen, A. (1996). Behavioral and cognitive-behavioral treatments: an overview of social learning. In S. H. Zarit & B. G. Knight (eds), *A guide to psychotherapy and aging* (pp. 35–59). Washington, DC: American Psychological Association.

Zeiss, A. M., Zeiss, R. A., & Dornbrand, L. (1992). Working with geriatric couples on sexual problems and concerns. Paper presented at the Gerontological Society of America, Washington, DC.

Zigler, E., & Glick, M. (1986). *A developmental approach to adult psychopathology*. New York: Wiley.

Zisook, S., Heaton, R., Moranville, J., Kuck, J., Jernigan, T., & Braff, D. (1992). Past substance abuse and clinical course of schizophrenia. *American Journal of Psychiatry*, 149, 552–3.

Zisook, S., & Shuchter, S. R. (1991). Depression through the first year after the death of a spouse. *American Journal of Psychiatry*, 148, 1346–52.

Zubin, J., & Spring, B. (1977). Vulnerability: a new view of schizophrenia. *Journal of Abnormal Psychology*, 86 (2), 103–26.

Author Index

Subject Index

abstract reasoning, 139, 252
accommodative coping, 170
Activities of Daily Living (ADL), 5, 141, 236, 237, 247
acute confusional state, 139, 252
adaptation, 54, 68, 70, 85, 90, 91, 92, 97, 100, 113, 117–18, 169, 171–2, 225
adult development, 45–6, 50–1, 132, 258
age-appropriate norms, 139, 174, 210, 250
age changes, 18, 23–4
age differences, 18, 23–4
age-graded, 19, 87
Agency for Health Care Policy and Research (AHCPR), 178
alcohol, 113, 185–7, 212–15, 217
alcohol abuse, early-onset/late-onset, 212–13
algorithms, 178–9, 282
alliances, 111, 113, 115, 126
Alzheimer's, 4, 160–1, 193, 199–200, 211, 251, 258
  biological basis, 10
  cause, 141, 142
  depression, 147, 149, 150, 176
  diagnosis, 142–5, 148–51, 241, 246
  prevalence, 10, 19, 235, 237
  progression/prognosis, 142–5, 156–7
  social impact, 10, 107, 115, 136, 203
  subtypes, 10, 141, 142, 146
  see also cognitive impairment; nursing home, residents; vascular dementias
American Bar Association (ABA), 279

androgynous, 50
antecedents, 66–7, 69–70, 116, 123, 125, 214, 248
antipsychotic, 183–4, 187–90, 192, 194, 198–203, 207, 241–2
  effects of, 190, 201, 202
  schizophrenia, 183, 184, 187, 189, 198, 201, 207
anxiety, 7, 44, 57, 60–3, 66–7, 76, 78, 117, 125, 176–7, 213, 225, 231, 248
  affective disorders, 67, 211, 235
  causes, 41, 45, 50, 53, 62, 86, 177, 210, 211, 216–17
  defense mechanisms, 42, 60, 177
  impact, 42, 55, 119, 147
  prevalence, 208, 209
anxiety disorders, 208–9, 235
assessment, 64–6, 76–8, 94, 96, 101–2, 113, 116–17, 119, 123, 125–7, 183, 201, 208, 213, 215–16, 220–5, 232, 252, 254, 256–61, 263, 264–5, 269, 270, 282–3
  anxiety, 210, 211
  batteries, 173, 174, 175, 260, 261, 262
  behavioral, 66, 71, 72, 73
  cognitive impairment, 135, 138, 139, 147, 152, 156
  depression, 171, 174, 175
  individual assessment, 11, 78, 124, 132, 134, 162, 260
  nursing homes, 236, 240, 243, 245, 247, 248, 250
  psychodynamic, 57, 58, 64
  schizophrenia, 188, 189, 196, 200